GREENWICH VILLAGE

GREENWICH VILLAGE

CULTURE
AND
COUNTERCULTURE

EDITED BY

Rick Beard

AND

Leslie Cohen Berlowitz

PUBLISHED FOR

THE MUSEUM OF THE CITY OF NEW YORK

BY RUTGERS UNIVERSITY PRESS

NEW BRUNSWICK, NEW JERSEY

Library of Congress Cataloging-in-Publication Data

Greenwich Village : culture and counterculture / edited by Rick Beard
   and Leslie Cohen Berlowitz.
     p. cm.
   Includes bibliographical references and index.
   ISBN 0-8135-1946-2
   1. Greenwich Village (New York, N.Y.)—Civilization.   2. New York
(N.Y.)—Civilization. I. Beard, Rick. II. Berlowitz, Leslie Cohen.
III. Museum of the City of New York.
F128.68.G8G74   1993
974.7′1—dc20   92-30445
                                             CIP

      British Cataloging-in-Publication information available

Frontispiece: Bettmann Archives

CONTENTS

· · · ·

CONTENTS

CONTENTS

FOREWORD

When I speak of Greenwich Village I have no geographical
conception in view. The term Greenwich Village is to me
a spiritual zone of mind. . . . The city which hasn't a
Greenwich Village is to be pitied. It has no life, no illusion,
no art.

—HIPPOLYTE HAVEL, "The Spirit of Greenwich Village,"
1915

Over the years Greenwich Village
has symbolized for many Americans the very idea of intellectual daring, of
freedom of thought and expression, and of radical creativity. At the same
time Greenwich Village is a very concrete place with a wonderful history; it
has been and remains a vital part of New York City, providing a sanctuary
from the humdrum everyday, a haven for thought, an opportunity for education, entertainment, and enlightenment. The following anthology explores the Village, the idea and the place, and the people who created both.

In 1826 the heart of the Village—a potter's field and execution ground—
was transformed into a parade ground and renamed Washington Square to
honor the hero of the American Revolution. Within a few years the north
side of the Square became the home of New York's upper class, while the
neighborhood to the south was by century's end the destination for thousands of Old World immigrants. Early in the twentieth century a new wave
of artists, writers, and political activists began to transform Village life with
a renewed commitment to cultural exploration and radical change. Several
members of this generation went so far in 1917 as to declare the "independence" of the Village from the rest of the United States as a "new territory
of the mind and soul."

The failure of this tongue-in-cheek insurrection notwithstanding, Greenwich Village was then and continues to be a powerful magnet for America's
most creative minds. Since that time a procession of writers, artists, and
activists has enriched and redefined what it means to be "a Villager."
Writers, poets, and critics as different in tone and temperament as Willa
Cather, Theodore Dreiser, Edmund Wilson, Edna St. Vincent Millay,

Allen Ginsberg, and James Baldwin; painters with sensibilities as varied as those of John Sloan, George Luks, Charles Demuth, Robert Motherwell, and Jackson Pollack; and musicians and composers as different as Edgar Varèse, Thelonious Monk, and Charlie Parker have all drawn sustenance from the spirit and the place that is Greenwich Village. It endures as a cultural crossroads filled with a widely varying, many-textured intellectual and artistic life.

It was a strong commitment to Greenwich Village as a home neighborhood for New York University and as a topic of primary interest for the Museum of the City of New York that led these two institutions to recognize and explore the neighborhood's history. We felt that it was time to express something of what we owe—indeed, what the country and world owe—to the Village as a source of cultural knowledge and insight. In 1990 the Museum mounted the exhibition "Within Bohemia's Borders: Greenwich Village, 1830–1930"; at the same time the Humanities Council at New York University and the Museum collaborated in presenting a series of public lectures and programs on Village history and culture to accompany the exhibition. These essays, many of which were presented as lectures, provide a retrospective on Greenwich Village.

The Museum and the University are grateful to the editors, Rick Beard and Leslie Cohen Berlowitz, and the authors of the following essays for their work in capturing the history and spirit of Greenwich Village. This anthology deepens our knowledge of the Village. It also invites us to appreciate the role the Village has played in forming America's "spiritual zone of mind."

ROBERT R. MACDONALD
Director
Museum of the City of New York

L. JAY OLIVA
President
New York University

ACKNOWLEDGMENTS

The editors wish to acknowledge the generous support of the National Endowment for the Humanities, which provided support for the earlier volume, *Around the Square*, as well as for many of the newly commissioned essays that are published here for the first time. The New York Council for the Humanities provided early and vital support for the initial series of eleven lectures, five of which are included in this volume.

The collaboration between the Museum of the City of New York and New York University's Humanities Council began at the suggestion of Professor Thomas Bender, whose suggestion that the Museum's plans for a modest lecture series on Greenwich Village might interest staff at the Humanities Council set in motion a working relationship that continues to enrich both parties and further the understanding of New York City's past.

At the Museum Elizabeth Smith and Randy West were responsible for gathering the visual materials and the necessary permissions to publish, a time-consuming chore they executed with skill and good humor. Marylee V. Kiarsis, Manager of Information Systems and Training at Shearman & Sterling, facilitated the translation of the manuscript into a consistent computer language and format. Jan Seidler Ramirez, Assistant Director for Collections and Curator of Paintings and Sculpture, provided the intellectual spark that fired the Museum's decision to explore Greenwich Village's history. She organized the exhibition "Within Bohemia's Borders: Greenwich Village, 1830–1930," wrote the accompanying script from which this volume's photoessays are extracted, and contributed an essay. This project would not have happened without her.

At New York University we are indebted to the faculty members who serve on the Humanities Council and especially to Brooks McNamara, Professor of Performance Studies, who provided support throughout the lecture series and the development of the book. Lynda Smith, Barbara Vlahides, and Linda Hughes, staff members at the Humanities Council, provided invaluable liaison and helped assemble manuscripts from members of the New York University community. We are also grateful to Robert Noto and

ACKNOWLEDGMENTS

William Leach for their wise counsel and contributions. Mindy Cantor generously supported the reissue of several of the essays that appeared in *Around the Square*, the volume she earlier edited.

This volume would not have been possible without the encouragement and support of Dr. L. Jay Oliva, President of New York University, and Robert Macdonald, Director of the Museum of the City of New York, who recognized the promise of this project and helped and encouraged us to follow it through to its completion.

INTRODUCTION

This collection of essays explores the history of one of the world's most noted centers of difference—New York's Greenwich Village. For better than 150 years, the Village has been a magnet for creativity, a locus for men and women at odds with the larger society. The neighborhood's tangled web of streets has provided an almost continuous haven for those seeking to effect change—artistic, literary, political—as well as those pursuing more personal visions, serious or frivolous.

Those exploring the margins of American society and culture, however, have comprised but a small portion of the people who have called the Village home. Others include the Dutch and English farmers who first settled the area, the free blacks who congregated in the Village beginning around the time of the American Revolution, the members of New York's first families whose homes lined the northern border of Washington Square, the Irish, Italian, and Jewish immigrants who found shelter south of the Square, and the myriad tradesmen and -women who undergirded the Village economy. Today the Village continues to be New York's most vibrant and tolerant district, a place that is home to a colorful mélange of college students, artists, writers, and thousands simply seeking an urban alternative.

Greenwich Village: Culture and Counterculture focuses on the history of the Village from the seventeenth century into our own time. It treats the Village as an urban microcosm, exploring its architecture and art, its cultural aspirations and achievements, its political life, and the people and groups who have laid claim to it. This collection of essays, one of the most extensive and far-ranging assessments of Greenwich Village yet to appear in print, evolved from a series of public lectures cosponsored by the Museum of the City of New York and New York University's Humanities Council in 1990–1991 and presented in conjunction with the exhibition "Within Bohemia's Borders: Greenwich Village, 1830–1930." This volume consists of commissioned essays, essays based on the lecture series, and several revised pieces that previously appeared in *Around the Square, 1830–1890: Essays on Life, Letters, and Architecture in Greenwich Village*, edited by Mindy

Cantor in 1982 (those by Thomas Bender, Sarah Bradford Landau, Mindy Cantor, Bayrd Still, Carol Ruth Berkin, Josephine Gattuso Hendin, Daniel J. Walkowitz, Paul R. Baker, and Denis Donoghue). We have been extremely fortunate in being able to integrate these materials into one complete volume.

We have divided the collection into five parts, each of which begins with a photographic essay with extended captions. Each of these pictorial essays provides visual documentation of a particular aspect of the Village's history and expands on the themes developed in the accompanying essays. "'A Maze of Crooked Streets': Village Landscapes" explores the physical and social changes the neighborhood underwent. The history of Christopher Street reveals a process of social evolution that characterized the experience of the Village as a whole. The role urban archaeology plays in uncovering the neighborhood's past is examined in a report on the findings from the Greenwich Mews dig. Other essays provide revealing glimpses into the architectural shapes and structures, from Washington Arch to Judson Memorial Church, that helped to give the Village its special style and character.

The six essays that comprise "'Bourgeoisie and Bohemians': Village Peoples" explore the community of free black men and women who first settled in Greenwich Village during the 1700s; the rich merchants—and their wives, families, and servants—who dominated the north side of Washington Square; the working-class Italians who enlivened the Square's south side; the homosexual men and lesbian women who found freedom and well-being in the Village; and "the Beats"—Allen Ginsberg, Gregory Corso, and Jack Kerouac among them—who fled middle-class uniformity in the 1950s for refuge in the Village.

"'Radical Agendas': Village Politics" features an essay exploring the stonecutters' riot of 1834, one of the earliest manifestations of radical political activity in the Village, as well as essays limning the lasting impact of such well-known Village habitués as Emma Goldman, Randolph Bourne, Mabel Dodge, Max Eastman, Floyd Dell, Mike Gold, Crystal Eastman, and Eleanor Roosevelt.

The fourth section of the book, "'A Spiritual Zone of the Mind': Village Culture," pays special attention to the many brilliant artists, actors, writers, and playwrights who lived and worked in the Village. Henry James, Mark Twain, Willa Cather, John Reed and his colleagues at *The Masses*, Edmund Wilson, and Edna St. Vincent Millay are among the literary luminaries featured. The world of the theater is explored with a look at George Cram Cook, Susan Glaspell, Eugene O'Neill, and their colleagues in such companies as the Washington Square Players and the Provincetown Players. The artistic ferment of the post–World War II Village is captured in an investigation of the circle of abstract expressionists who came to be known as the New York School.

Greenwich Village: Culture and Counterculture closes with "'Greenwich Thrillage': Village Commerce," a look at the growth and spread of the tourist business throughout the district. Essays on the district's varied, always entertaining nightlife and on the explosion of commercial development in the second decade of the twentieth century provide a deeper understanding of the manner in which the Village became a point of destination for those seeking "forbidden entertainments."

Greenwich Village: Culture and Counterculture is a portrait of a crucial American place that takes into account the good and the bad, the wonderful experiments and inventions as well as the mundane, and the conflicts and costs. It is a complex picture—at once informative, critical, and uplifting.

"A MAZE OF CROOKED STREETS"
VILLAGE LANDSCAPES

A District of Difference

Called "Sapponckanican" by the Indians who hunted and fished there, the locale later known as Greenwich Village stood more than two miles north of Nieuw Amsterdam, the seventeenth-century trading post that occupied the southern tip of Manhattan. Originally a marshy terrain improved into farmland by Dutch and English settlers, the Village survived the Revolution as a pastoral suburb still remote from the Battery. This isolation eroded in the face of a series of virulent fever outbreaks that led epidemic evacuees to flee northward from the city core, swelling the Village's population fourfold between 1825 and 1840. In response residential construction accelerated, and rows of neat dwellings soon lined its labyrinthine roadways.

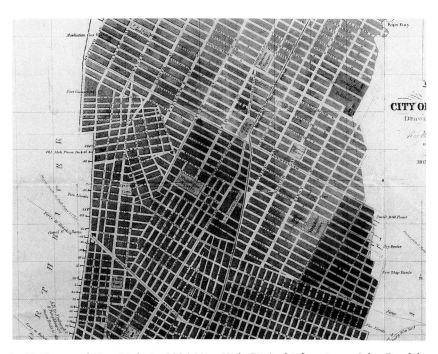

1. **1846 map of New York** In 1806 New York City's chief engineer, John Randel, laid out an orderly street system that would anticipate Manhattan's northward expansion. When his rigidly symmetrical plan—avenues were to flow north-south and numbered streets to run river to river—was adopted eleven years later, residents successfully pressured the Common Council to incorporate only those portions of the Village east of present-day Sixth Avenue. The Village's discordant street pattern is clearly visible. (*Museum of the City of New York*)

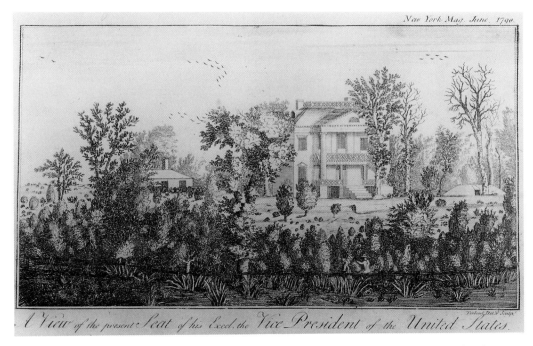

A View of the present Seat of his Excel. the Vice-President of the United States.

2. Richmond Hill House Built in 1767, this country retreat served variously as temporary headquarters for George Washington, a vice presidential residence for John Adams, home to Aaron Burr at the time of his duel with Alexander Hamilton, and lodgings for Gov. DeWitt Clinton. The house was moved to a nearby site in the early 1820s, serving successively as a tavern, a pleasure resort, and a series of theaters prior to its demolition in 1849. *(Museum of the City of New York)*

3. Newgate State Prison Opened in 1797 as one of the earliest reform prisons in the United States, the Newgate had separate quarters for women, bathing facilities, and training workshops. The prison's presence at the foot of Christopher Street spurred the construction of the Greenwich Hotel and the establishment of regular stage service between the hotel and Federal Hall, keeping the West Village in constant contact with the city to the south. Frequent revolts and prison breaks forced the closing of the facility in 1827. *(Museum of the City of New York)*

"The Bank" in Greenwich Village

4. The Bank of New York in Greenwich Village In 1798 a summer fever prompted the Bank of New York to relocate its offices temporarily from Wall Street to Greenwich Village, where it purchased land and erected an emergency facility for its personnel. The investment proved farsighted, as major epidemics again quarantined the densely populated city core in 1799, 1803, 1805, and 1821. The road where this satellite office stood acquired the name *Bank Street*, reflecting the outposting of other financial institutions to this Village address. *(The Bank of New York Company)*

5. The last of Greenwich Village The rapid development of Greenwich Village after 1850 ended its reign as a pastoral resort, prompting artists of the period to record the vestiges of this halcyon era before they completely disappeared. In this 1869 pen-and-ink sketch Eliza Greatorex pictured the Warren–Van Nest homestead, which had been built in 1726 on a plot of land bounded by Bleecker, Fourth, Charles, and Perry streets. The mansion was razed after the death of Abraham Van Nest in 1864 to make way for a row of new brownstones. *(Museum of the City of New York)*

The Evolution of Bleecker Street

"No street in the Metropolis has changed more than Bleecker," observed a New Yorker after the Civil War. "The grand mansions stand conspicuously in the thoroughfare, with a semblance of departed greatness, and an acknowledgement of surrendered splendor." Over the latter part of the nineteenth century, much of the older housing stock along Bleecker and elsewhere in the Village grew derelict. Some row houses were subdivided into multiple-family dwellings to accommodate the press of immigrant newcomers, and shabbier structures were selectively demolished to make room for high-density tenements. Simultaneously the street gained wide disreputability for the bawdyhouses, sweatshops, and "long haired, queerly dressed" drifters who had invaded it. A final indignity was delivered by the extension of Sixth Avenue, which severed one half of Bleecker Street from the other.

6. Mr. and Mrs. Charles A. Carter at home on Bleecker Street When the ambitious young hospital administrator Charles Carter brought his bride to 123 Bleecker Street in the mid-nineteenth century, it was still a proud roadway whose fashionable dwellings epitomized the cosmopolitan taste of the city's mercantile elite. By 1900 a flophouse for the "poor and homeless" stood near the site of the once-stylish Carter abode. *(Museum of the City of New York)*

7. Rookeries on Bleecker Street While artists perceived these ramshackle "rookeries" as picturesque, and developers viewed them as potential building lots, social reformers such as Jacob Riis, who took this photograph in the late 1880s, blamed them for the rising incidence of crime, disease, and poverty. *(Museum of the City of New York)*

8. Thompson and Bleecker streets The arrival of different immigrant groups on the squalid blocks of the south Village by the late nineteenth century proved an intriguing transition for artists of the period. George Luks's 1905 interpretation of this ethnic hubbub diverged markedly from the images of serene town houses and smartly attired citizens that had characterized the area's earlier pictorial treatment. *(Private collection: James Palmer; courtesy Babcock Galleries, New York City)*

9. Bleecker Street, Saturday night In 1918 John Sloan recorded this old dormered structure on the corner of Bleecker Street, which reveals the scar of partial amputation suffered when the extension of Seventh Avenue South below Eleventh Street slashed a path through Greenwich Village, leveling homes, churches, and businesses in the process. *(Collection IBM Corporation, Armonk, N.Y.)*

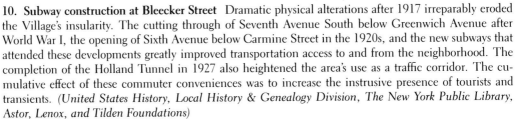

10. Subway construction at Bleecker Street Dramatic physical alterations after 1917 irreparably eroded the Village's insularity. The cutting through of Seventh Avenue South below Greenwich Avenue after World War I, the opening of Sixth Avenue below Carmine Street in the 1920s, and the new subways that attended these developments greatly improved transportation access to and from the neighborhood. The completion of the Holland Tunnel in 1927 also heightened the area's use as a traffic corridor. The cumulative effect of these commuter conveniences was to increase the instrusive presence of tourists and transients. *(United States History, Local History & Genealogy Division, The New York Public Library, Astor, Lenox, and Tilden Foundations)*

The Arch Triumphant

The Washington Arch that exists today replaced a temporary structure built in 1889 to commemorate the centennial of George Washington's inauguration. Designed by Stanford White and made of plaster and wooden lathing, this original portal, which straddled Fifth Avenue slightly to the north of its present location, proved so popular that a private subscription was raised for a marble replacement, also by White. Erected between 1890 and 1892, the marble arch reflected the patriotic pride of the Greenwich Village gentry who piloted the campaign for its permanent construction. As the new century unfolded, however, the monument came to symbolize the division between the patrician holdouts on the north and the bohemian newcomers and immigrants to the south, or, as the Village writer Djuna Barnes observed, "satin and motorcars on this side, squalor and pushcarts on that."

11. **Temporary Washington Arch in 1889** (*Museum of the City of New York*)

12. Washington Arch under construction in 1892 *(Courtesy of The New-York Historical Society, N.Y.C.)*

13. Washington Square Park about 1900 Originally a marshland, the eight-acre parcel was purchased by the city in the 1780s for use as a potter's field and as a site for a public gallows. In 1826 it was named to honor George Washington and rehabilitated as a parade ground, a use that proved impractical when the heavy artillery sometimes caved into the graves below. By the mid-1850s the Square had been reconfigured as an airy commons, complete with a fountain and intersecting pedestrian paths. *(Museum of the City of New York)*

14. Washington Arch and Number One Fifth Avenue under construction The prevalence of sandy subsoil south of Fourteenth Street stalled the construction of high-rise buildings in Greenwich Village before 1926. The following year, however, the northern horizon of Washington Square was filled by the rising silhouette of Number One Fifth Avenue, a twenty-seven-floor luxury apartment hotel, the first of a fleet of modern apartment buildings that soon appeared on the borders north and west of the Square. *(Museum of the City of New York)*

Village Backstreets and Landmarks

As the Village entered the present century, it retained the intimacy of a small town nestled in the heart of Manhattan. Its labyrinth of secluded courtyards, odd lanes, and low, dormered houses crumbling into disrepair led to frequent comparisons with such artistic enclaves of Paris as Montmartre, Montparnasse, and the Latin Quarter. Like them, the Village had a picturesque configuration of older buildings and convoluted alleys, a lively café society, and an array of demimonde entertainments along its marginal streets. It also boasted a wealth of cheap lodgings in the timeworn residences vacated by Victorian society. Intimate, inexpensive, and attractively quaint, the Village was an ideal refuge for artists, writers, actors, and social radicals of all varieties. As Max Eastman explained in 1914: "I want to be very close to that exciting current of life and business that flows north and south on the main avenues. . . . But I don't want to live right in it, because I can't stand the strain. And so I seek out the little low-roofed cove . . . where only an occasional backwater eddy of the mainstream reaches me."

15. Minetta Lane Artists (like Glenn C. Coleman, here) were fascinated by the narrow, moody complex known as the Minettas (Lane, Street, Place, and Court). Lined with old-fashioned dwellings, the area was by the turn of the century a notorious slum. As a young reporter Stephen Crane described Minetta Lane as "a small and becobbled valley between hills of dingy brick" swarming with "desperadoes," where sin shone "like a new headlight." Despite their menacing character, the Minettas whetted the interest of realtors, who in the 1910s began to invest in these run-down properties and to promote rentals by comparing their quaint configuration to the byways of Paris. *(Museum of the City of New York)*

16. **Minetta Court** *(Museum of the City of New York)*

17. **Renovation on Minetta Street during the twenties** During the 1920s Vincent Pepe was in the forefront of amassing tumbledown tenements and row houses. Dubbed the "Croesus of Village landlords" by more than one detractor, he and his company specialized in upgrading depressed blocks of housing by carving multiple flats out of them and advertising these units as combining Latin Quarter character with all the modern amenities of midtown living. His efforts were said to have triggered the gentrification campaign that resulted in a 140 percent inflation in local rents between 1920 and 1930. *(Museum of the City of New York)*

18. **Grove Court** *(Museum of the City of New York)*

19. **Sixth Avenue and the Old Jefferson Market Jail** The Jefferson Market opened in 1833 as one of four public markets in Greenwich Village. Soon thereafter its central location led city officials to construct a tall watchtower with a fire bell. Public assembly rooms and a local police pound followed, and a new courthouse and adjoining jail were added in 1876. *(Museum of the City of New York)*

Within the drawing:
"The Old Grapevine"
windows on font too narrow
time 2.30 p.m. Jan 23 —
The old vinyard cor. 9th st and 6th av. ny. 1911

20. The Old Grapevine Located at Sixth Avenue and West Eleventh Street, this historic roadhouse dated from 1838. Appropriated by early Village bohemians as an informal social club, it also supplied local actors and artists with fast-breaking news, thereby giving rise to the colloquialism "hearing it on the grapevine" as a term describing one's source of information. *(Courtesy of The New-York Historical Society, N.Y.C.)*

21. Brevoort Hotel Opened in 1854, the Brevoort Hotel at the corner of Fifth Avenue and Eighth Street was an architectural amalgam of three row houses. Initially the berth of choice for visiting gourmets, cultural highbrows, and titled aristocracy, the hotel acquired a pronounced Parisian flavor after French-born Raymond Orteig bought it in 1902. Dinners to celebrate the sale of a book, play, or painting were reserved for the Brevoort Café, as were the breakfast parties that traditionally followed all-night Village balls. The cubicled dining room also served as a leisurely meeting place for a number of organizations that indulged bohemian interests. The Brevoort was razed in 1954. *(Museum of the City of New York)*

22. The Martin The "Old Martin" stood a few blocks away from the Brevoort on University Place. French food, wines, and atmosphere were the trademarks of the original establishment, opened in 1883. The hotel's Left Bank personality continued to cling when Raymond Orteig assumed management in 1902, rechristening it the Lafayette. Patrons were encouraged to linger over coffee and cordials in a manner reminiscent of French cafés, and the bar featured foreign newspapers, comfortable divans, and gaming boards. The hotel closed in 1949. *(Museum of the City of New York)*

23. Sheridan Square Named for Civil War general Philip Henry Sheridan, the intersection of Seventh Avenue and West Fourth Street entered the twentieth century as a relatively tranquil Village crossroads. The extension of the IRT subway beneath it in 1917–1918, and the rush of traffic that followed, quickly transformed the area into a smaller variant of Times Square. *(Museum of the City of New York)*

24. Aerial view of Washington Square and environs Although Lower Manhattan by 1910 boasted more than 550 buildings of ten stories or higher, the skyscraper form virtually bypassed the Village, leading French architect Le Corbusier to disparage Greenwich Village as "an urban no man's land made up of miserable low buildings—poor streets of dirty brick." By 1930 progress had irreversibly intruded into this valley. *(United States History, Local History & Genealogy Division, The New York Public Library, Astor, Lenox, and Tilden Foundations)*

WASHINGTON SQUARE IN THE GROWING CITY

Thomas Bender

When the new City Hall was completed in 1811, its east, west, and south facades were finished with impressive and expensive white marble. The northern one, the back of the building, was faced with cheaper brownstone. Assuming that a perspective on the City Hall from the north was unlikely for many years to come, a group of city fathers had decided to save the taxpayers' money. The decision seemed reasonable at the time, but events rapidly overtook their assumption. In no time at all the city extended north into the area of Washington Square and far beyond. Another group of men, however—the commissioners who in 1811 laid out the city in its now familiar grid pattern—had envisioned a city that would cover the whole of Manhattan Island. By extending their grid north, block after block, to 155th Street, the commissioners invited ridicule. Yet they had better grasped the transformation and expansion of New York that would follow the War of 1812. The plan of the commissioners described New York in its modern form.

The 1811 plan and the spatial reorganization it implied were part of a larger reorganization of the social life of the city. These changes created modern New York, and much of their cultural meaning can be illuminated by reflecting on the relation of the history of Washington Square to the

• • • •
27

growth of the larger city of New York between 1830 and 1890. The useful-
ness of Washington Square's history in this connection does not derive from
its representative character. The development around the Square is not a
microcosm of developments in the city at large. Though it is representative
of the first stage of the creation of the modern city—the development of
distinctively residential districts—it does not participate in most of the innovative tendencies that shaped the city after about 1850. In the second half
of the century, rather, the Square's development provides an older perspective from which to view the newer ways of growth in New York.

Washington Square was born in death. During the cholera epidemic of
1798, in which 1,310 New Yorkers died, the city established an out-of-town
burial ground on the present site of the park. Over the next three decades it
was a potter's field where the indigent were buried. It was also the burial
place for those who met their end on the hangman's tree at the northwest
corner of the present park.

Greenwich Village, a sleepy country town, lay to the west of this ground.
It was the location of the state's first prison (at the foot of Christopher Street),
some farms, and summer retreats for the city's elite, particularly when epidemics hit the city. The severe yellow fever epidemic of 1822 caused a
rather large influx of city people, and after the epidemic subsided significant
numbers stayed. By 1825 the editor of the *New York Commercial Advertiser*
could remark that "Greenwich is now no longer a country village. Such has
been the growth of our city that the building of one block more will completely connect the two places." Two years later the city government decided
to convert the burial ground into a parade ground and to open Fifth Avenue
to development. The official opening of the Square took place on July 4,
1828, with a great public barbecue for which two roasted oxen and two
hundred hams were prepared.

During the late 1820s and 1830s, residential construction began in the
neighborhood of the Square. What James Fenimore Cooper called "second-
rate genteel houses" went up in the 1820s in the area now designated
the Charlton–King–Van Dam Historic District, while elegant upper-class
homes were built on Bleecker Street, especially the block known as LeRoy
Place between Mercer and Greene streets, and east of Broadway on Bond
and Great Jones streets and Lafayette Place. All this new building represented a revolution in urban life. The development of residential neighborhoods around the Square was the first instance in the city of the modern
pattern of life that separates work and residence. It was in the region
of Washington Square that an exclusively residential housing market for
middle- and upper-class commuters was created. This event marked not
only a new spatial order in the city, but a new social order as well. The
reorganization of urban space was ultimately bound up with the formation
of the modern class system.

· · · ·

25. Lafayette Place at Great Jones Street about 1866 *(Courtesy of The New-York Historical Society, N.Y.C.)*

What happened at Washington Square was generated by changes downtown. By the 1820s the growth of downtown business had overrun residential streets. The volume of commercial activity along the East River grew rapidly, particularly with the opening of the Erie Canal, and commerce spilled from Pearl onto Wall Street. There had long been a few commercial buildings, mostly banking and insurance companies, on the street, but there was nothing about the scale, outward appearance, or even the level of traffic they generated that sharply distinguished these businesses from residences. By the end of the 1820s, however, the general onslaught of commerce had made the street unsuitable for residence. Wall Street became the first fashionable residential street to fall before commerce. As early as 1819 John Pintard, secretary of the Mutual Insurance Company at 52 Wall Street, complained about the changes on the street. The company had provided him with an apartment above the office, and, as the character of the street changed, his rent-free residence became less and less attractive. In a letter to his daughter, he described the discomforts that caused middle-class New Yorkers to seek purely residential neighborhoods. "Our abode," he wrote, "is not very favourable to make domestics contented, being attended with many inconveniences in consequence of the office which supports me." After bemoaning the cost of obtaining a house elsewhere and hoping that perhaps next year prices might fall, he concluded: "Let us live in hope of better accommodations for Mama and Sister, who are nearly prisoners during the hours of business in Wall Street."

Gulian Verplanck, who grew up on Wall Street during the 1790s in a house whose garden abutted Federal Hall, remarked in 1829 on the changes in the district:

> Pine Street is now full of blocks of many tall buildings, which overshadow the narrow passages between, and make it one of the gloomiest streets in New-York. The very bricks there look of a darker hue than in any other part of the city; the rays of the sun seem to come through a hollower and thicker atmosphere. . . . It was not thus thirty or forty years ago. Shops were on each side of the way, low cheerful looking two-story buildings, of light-coloured brick or wood, painted white or yellow, and which scarcely seemed a hindrance to the air and sunshine.

Though Verplanck complains of five-story buildings that we today romanticize, we cannot miss the modernity of the complaint. Dissatisfaction with living conditions was the motive for moving north. We must not, however, discount the rather large sum that one might obtain by selling one's home to a developer who wished to turn it or the site on which it stood to commercial uses. Philip Hone, who in 1836 fled the rapidly developing City Hall area for a new home on Bond Street, complained in his diary of having to move. Yet, as he put it: "I have turned myself out of doors, but $60,000 is a great deal of money."

When the middle and upper classes fled the downtown districts, they escaped the din of business in their domestic lives and they segregated themselves from the working class and impoverished populations who remained downtown. The privatization of family life was thus advanced, while the range of social experience inherent in everyday life was narrowed.

On another level traditional urban ways were complicated for the middle classes by the extension of the city beyond the tight, walking city of the eighteenth century. Commenting on his annual New Year's rounds in 1830, John Pintard told his daughter that "our city grows so extensive and friends so scattered that a pedestrian has enough to do to pay his compliments." The spatial reorganization of the city may also have encouraged the gender differentiation of cultural life. Men and women spent their time in different parts of town, and elite cultural organizations that were located downtown and depended on the participation of men and women, like the New York Atheneum, were dissolved, to be replaced by more specialized and gendered organizations.

While the middle classes were establishing themselves in a "suburban" pattern of living, which architectural critic Montgomery Schuyler noted in the 1890s probably provided the cheapest and most comfortable housing New York's middle classes ever had, the working classes and poor found it increasingly difficult to find adequate housing. In the late eighteenth century, apprentices and young journeymen still lived with their masters. But as apprentices were gradually depressed to the status of permanent wage-earners, and masters became manufacturers and capitalists, this pattern of social relations came to an end. Living with the master had been a stage in the life cycle of the young apprentice. By the time he was ready to marry, he would be a master himself, could obtain his own house—and take in other apprentices and journeymen. With the breakdown of this traditional pattern of expectations in the emerging capitalist market economy, workers who were low paid and who would remain so had to find cheap housing for themselves and the families they formed.

At first ordinary houses were subdivided. Several unrelated families might live in a house that had earlier housed an artisan's extended household. By the late 1840s, however, New York invented the tenement house, a new building type that acknowledged the new class structure. There were no tenements around the middle- and upper-class Square, but south of the Square, as Bleecker Street declined in the years following 1850, they emerged in numbers. The tenement replaced the second-rate genteel houses east of the Bowery and created on the Lower East Side a pattern of residence that would accommodate working-class and poor New Yorkers for a century to come. While middle-class residences rushed up the avenues after 1869 with the aid of elevated railroads, the immigrant poor were crowded into tenements. By 1876 50 percent of the city's population lived in tenements—residents who accounted for 65 percent of the city's deaths and an appalling 90 percent of the deaths of children under five.

It is no accident or mere coincidence that neighborhoods such as the one around Washington Square emerged at about the same time that the Lower East Side developed into a vast tenement district, extending from Cherry Street, where George Washington resided as president, to Mulberry Street, where Stephen Van Rensselaer in 1816 built a house that still stands, to once-fashionable Tompkins Square, which the *New York Herald* in 1860 described as having that "dusty, dirty, seedy, and 'all used up' appearance peculiar to the East Side of town." These developments are architectural expressions of the new social order. In a curious, perhaps even perverse way, something of the connection between the elegant row houses on Washing-

• • • •

ton Square and the emerging slums was captured in the oft-expressed desire of visitors to the city in the 1840s, including Charles Dickens, to see the houses on the north of Washington Square and the Five Points, the city's most notorious slum, near City Hall.

Beginning in the 1850s the class division of the city was further inscribed in the city's architectural styles. If the tenement was class specific, so was the brownstone. While the brick Federal or, later, Greek Revival house served both merchant and artisan as a residential type (though larger and more richly appointed for the former), the brownstone, which began to be built just north of the Square in the 1850s, as Manhattan moved north, was an exclusively bourgeois residential type. Thus the shift from red brick to brownstone, evident at Tenth Street as one walks north on Fifth Avenue, marks an important transformation in the city's social history.

When, after 1870, the city began to rise above five stories, Washington Square and the Village generally did not follow. Partly it did not for geological reasons, but it did not as well because the Village was isolated from downtown. Neither Fifth, Sixth, nor Seventh avenues then extended south of Bleecker Street, and the latter two (which do so now) did not until the 1920s and 1930s. Within the Village itself the peculiar street system inhibited circulation. All this limited its commercial appeal.

When New York became the administrative and financial as well as the shipping capital of an increasingly integrated national economy, a new urban building type was needed: the office building. Perhaps the first building constructed in New York exclusively for offices was the Trinity Building, erected by Trinity Church in the 1840s and located just north of the church. It was, however, only five stories high. The first office building to use a passenger elevator was the Equitable Life Assurance Building (1870), and, in the mid-1870s, the Tribune and Western Union buildings near Trinity Church were the first to challenge the church's spire for supremacy of the New York skyline. They marked the city's modernity, a point recognized by T. H. Huxley in 1876, when—spokesmen for Darwinism and modern science that he was—he happily noted upon arrival in New York Harbor that these buildings identified with modern communication and secular enlightenment ("centres of intelligence"), rather than the traditional church spire, defined the city's iconography.

By 1908 lower Manhattan had 550 buildings over ten stories high; dozens exceeded twenty stories. But with one notable exception—the Condict-Bayard Building on Bleecker just east of Broadway (Louis Sullivan's only New York building and one that expresses his artistic ideal for the tall building with remarkable clarity)—the skyscraper form bypassed the Washington Square area. Farther north at Madison Square, the new century saw the rise of the Flatiron Building and the Metropolitan Life Tower; before long, midtown became the site of a second and still-growing cluster of tall buildings.

· · · ·

New York's emergence as an administrative center, selling office space—indeed, exporting it as a sort of commodity to national and international corporations—seems to have made no mark on the physical form of the Village. And even today, relatively few employees of this corporate and financial New York have made the Village their home.

The creation of two separate clusters of towers on Manhattan, "sugar lumps," in F. Scott Fitzgerald's wonderful phrase, produces a striking visual image. To some the intervening district of low-rise redbrick houses offers a pleasant contrast. But to one of the twentieth century's greatest architects, the Village was an affront. In *When the Cathedrals Were White*, Le Corbusier noted of his visit to New York in the 1930s that "skyscrapers born out of national conditions in Wall Street multiplied . . . first on that site, establishing the mystically alluring city. . . . The skyscrapers then disappear in an area of several miles, an urban no man's land made up of miserable low buildings—poor streets of dirty red brick [only to] spring up suddenly in mid-town." Henry James, who by contrast was offended in 1904 by the "graceless" skyscrapers downtown that "so cruelly over-topped" his beloved Trinity Church, found the "salt that saves" at Washington Square, particularly in the "priceless" house that survived on the corner of Fifth Avenue and Washington Square until it was destroyed in 1950 to make way for the high-rise apartment building at 2 Fifth Avenue.

As people, fashion, and commerce moved up Broadway and Fifth Avenue, Washington Square rather quickly became, as Edith Wharton reminds us in *The Age of Innocence*, "old New York." In the decades following 1850, Fifth Avenue gradually came to be lined with brownstone homes, more charming perhaps in memory than they were in fact. From literature we get a sense of darkened interiors, and from old photographs a sense of a monotonous streetscape. Today, the Salmagundi Club at Twelfth Street, one of the first of the Fifth Avenue Italianate brownstones (and one of the larger ones), is the last survivor on the avenue. The scale and values of old New York that had established themselves on the Square were further distanced from changes in elite life in the city when the growing post–Civil War millionaire (and multimillionaire) class, led by the Vanderbilts and their architect, Richard Morris Hunt, built a series of houses on Fifth Avenue. With these limestone piles, the color of elite New York turned from brown to white, and the "bourgeois mansion" was, in the words of contemporary architecture critic Montgomery Schuyler, "expanded into a palace."

The growth of Greenwich Village stopped almost as quickly as it began. By the 1850s the rate of residential growth leveled off in the Village and below Fourteenth Street generally, save for the Lower East Side. In 1850 George Templeton Strong remarked in his diary: "How this city marches northward." As a young man in 1830, living down on Greenwich Street with his parents, he went on his evening walks to the edge of the city, no

• • • •

farther than Fourteenth Street. By 1871, however, the diarist recorded that these walks now took him up as far as the Seventies. By 1864 one-half of the city's population resided above Fourteenth Street. In view of the elite character of the Washington Square neighborhood, it is perhaps even more interesting that the rich moved above Fourteenth Street even faster than the general population. When, in 1851, the *New York Herald* published a list of the city's two hundred richest men, it turned out that one-half of them lived above Fourteenth Street, mostly on Fifth Avenue. An earlier list, published but five years before, listed only twenty of the two hundred men living north of Fourteenth Street.

If Washington Square thus became in some degree isolated from the latest tendencies of business and fashion during the second half of the nineteenth century, it had for this very reason a special appeal to some, an appeal that has not entirely vanished in the late twentieth century. An eddy in the northward flow of Manhattan life, Washington Square became the physical manifestation of collective memory, of history. In 1857 Alexander Lakier, a Russian visitor to New York, observed that history in the city ended with Washington Square. "It is remarkable," he wrote, "that the streets intersecting Broadway up to Washington Square have historical names but beyond there are numbered 1 to 131, as if history had become exhausted and refused to serve the imagination." What Lakier derived from street names, Henry James deduced from greater familiarity with, and a fuller appreciation of, the texture of the city. Uptown, he reflected in *Washington Square*, the "extension of the city" assumes a "theoretic air." At Washington Square, however, there was the appearance of "having had something of a social history."

In a city defined by movement, energy, and the struggle to be heard, the Square offered relief. Young Walt Whitman, lover of the sights, sounds, and smells of the city, nonetheless cried out in 1842: "What can New York—noisy, roaring, tumbling, bustling, stormy, turbulent New York—have to do with silence?" Three-quarters of a century later, Edith Wharton, so different from Whitman otherwise, similarly but even more succinctly exclaimed: "New York is overwhelming and I am overwhelmed." Speaking of Washington Square in 1880, James noted that "this portion of New York appears to many persons the most delectable. It has a kind of established repose which is not of frequent occurrence in other quarters of the long, shrill city." For Richard Watson Gilder, editor in the 1890s of the prestigious *Century Magazine*, the neighborhood of Washington Square stood as "an island of no pressure, a place to pull out for a while."

The quarter around the Square, known as the "American ward," began to receive an influx of immigrants at the turn of the century. The area had historically been a center of residence for Manhattan's black community, but now as blacks and some of the old white "Americans" moved north, they were replaced by immigrants, mostly Italian. Carmine Street, a historically black neighborhood, became Italian, as it remains, and an Italian church, Our Lady of Pompeii, arose on the site of an earlier black church. It was this Village, marked by both an older feel and new populations, that was so attractive to the city's famous bohemians, and it was this mixed neighborhood that was the subject of Caroline Ware's classic study, *Greenwich Village, 1920–1930*, published in 1935. The degree to which life in the Village diverged from the Protestant ideal of American culture made it all the more attractive to the cultural innovators who established themselves in the neighborhood before World War I. Enlisting modernism against modernization (with its large organizations and depersonalization), rejecting the genteel and provincial culture of brownstone New York, the self-consciously modern Greenwich Village intellectuals found in this homey atmosphere around the Square what the poet Floyd Dell called a "moral health resort"—right in the middle of the quintessentially modern city. Here they found space for cultural experimentation—in their understanding of the relations between the sexes, in art, and in politics.

This familiar identification of culture with the Village ambience suggests a concluding generalization. The Washington Square area in the nineteenth century was never a center of manufacturing or finance or any other key sector in the city's economy. It has, however, always been identified with urban cultural institutions and the sorts of cafés, magazine editorial offices, and clubs that, in cities, provide a place for creative spirits. One found in the Village all manner of cultural institutions: notable churches, such as Grace Church, the Church of the Ascension, and Judson Memorial; institutions of higher learning like New York University and Union Theological Seminary; learned societies, whether the New-York Historical Society, the New York Lyceum of Natural History (since become the New York Academy of Sciences), the National Academy of Design, or the Astor Library; the St. Nicholas and other fashionable hotels; luxury shopping at A. T. Stewart's fabulous department store on Broadway and Ninth Street; and places of amusement, from Charlie Pfaff's basement saloon on Broadway—where Walt Whitman, Henry Clapp, Ada Clare, and other early bohemians met in the 1850s—to Niblo's Gardens, to the Astor Place Opera. And it has always been in touch with other parts of the city, linking elite New York with ethnic neighborhoods and poorer populations to the east and west of the Square. It is a legacy we can cherish and nourish.

· · · ·

STRAIGHT DOWN CHRISTOPHER STREET

A TALE OF THE OLDEST STREET IN GREENWICH VILLAGE

Edited by Christine Boyer

From a report compiled by Ron Emrich, Clare Leary, Michael May, Kerry Moran, Cassie Murray, Judy Oberlander, Karen Rosenberg, Gary Sachau, and Carla Wiltenberg

Like an old parchment that has been written on over and over again, Christopher Street carries the traces of its historical past in the remnants and remains of its street pattern, block and lot formations, and its array of architectural forms. As careful observers we can travel down Christopher Street, sifting the evidence that tells us about the early beginnings of Greenwich Village and slowly exploring its development over time.

FROM FARMS TO BLOCKS AND LOTS: 1626–1821
• • • • •

The land in the vicinity of present-day Christopher Street was recognized by the Dutch as a valuable piece of real estate. Thus in 1629 an employee of the Dutch West India Company, Wouter Van Twiller, was granted two hundred acres near the Native American settlement of Sapponckanican, which lay close to the intersection of present-day Gansevoort and Washington streets. Arriving in New Amsterdam in 1633 as its third director general,

• • • •

Van Twiller lost no time in turning his land into a tobacco plantation he named Bossen Bouwery, or "Farm in the Woods."[1] Sometime before 1638, when Van Twiller was recalled to Holland, he transferred two large parcels of land to Francis Lastley (or Lesley) and to Jan Van Rotterdam. We know from studying later maps that the boundary between these two plantations eventually became known as "the road along Jan Van Rotterdam's to the Strand" and represents the exact trajectory of present-day Christopher Street.

When the English assumed power over Manhattan in 1664, they transferred the large tract of land on the south side of Christopher Street to the Crown. Hoping to make the Church of England the established church of New York, Queen Anne instructed her nephew, Lord Cornbury, to make a grant in 1708 of this Crown land to Trinity Church. The terms of the grant were exceedingly vague, and consequently it is unknown whether the grant extended as far north as Christopher Street or whether it stopped a short distance north of Canal Street. But conveyance records tell us that by the mid-eighteenth century, Christopher Street was the northern boundary of Trinity Church Farm. The property east of this farm and adjacent to Christopher Street was the Elbert Herring Farm. Directly to the north of these two farms, across the division of Christopher Street, lay the three-hundred-acre estate of Sir Peter Warren. As commodore of squadrons assigned during the 1730s and 1740s to capture French and Spanish vessels bound for the West Indies, Warren was reputed to have become exceptionally wealthy from the sale of this lucrative bounty. He used the proceeds in 1740 to build a country house two blocks north of Christopher Street, a site bounded by present-day Bleecker, West Fourth, Charles, and Perry streets. At this time Christopher Street was known as Skinner Road, named for the husband of Warren's youngest daughter, and it extended northeastward to the middle of the present-day block between Fifth and Sixth avenues. Sometime later it was renamed Christopher Street in honor of an heir of one of Warren's trustees.

On the death of Warren and his wife, his estate was divided among his three daughters. The lot adjacent to Christopher Street was granted to Charlotte Willougby, who, with her husband, the earl of Abingdon, subdivided the land as early as 1788. And so it happened that Richard Amos acquired the land to the north of Christopher Street between present-day Washington and Hudson streets, while David Mallows acquired the site to the east of Amos's land, between Hudson and Bleecker streets, and to the west between Washington Street and the river. By 1794 Mallows had transferred ownership of his land to Abijah Hammond, who in turn granted the riverside lots to the city of New York for the site of a new state prison.

Amos, Hammond, and their neighbors wasted little time in subdividing their holdings. Amos's land had been subdivided into blocks and lots

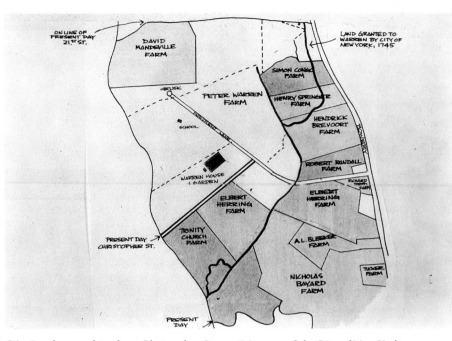

26. Land ownership along Christopher Street *(Museum of the City of New York)*

by 1789, and the Herring Farm, located on the south side of Christopher Street, was lotted in 1794. Hammond's property between Bleecker and West Fourth streets was platted in 1799, while his holdings between West Fourth Street and Greenwich Avenue were subdivided by 1807. The Thomas Ludlow Farm, situated to the east of the Herring Farm, would be lotted in 1826, and the Trinity Church lands in 1829. Eventually the entire length of Christopher Street was ready for development.

At the same time that these farmlands were subdivided, streets were surveyed, and Christopher Street was divided into blocks as well as lots. Amos surveyed the land for Charles, present-day West Tenth, and Greenwich streets in 1796. The same year a survey of the Hammond land located present-day Bleecker and West Fourth streets and Waverly Place, while surveys of the south side of Christopher Street done in 1799, 1809, and 1811 laid out present-day Bedford, Grove, Barrow, and Commerce streets. Although surveyed and located on maps, most of these streets were not officially opened nor their elevation regulated for some time to come. An application to the Road Committee was submitted for Christopher Street in 1810, for example, but it was neither regulated nor opened until 1817.

Throughout most of the eighteenth century, Greenwich Village was a rural hamlet and a popular resort for fashionable day-trippers. The rising tide of epidemic disease that repeatedly racked the population of Lower Manhattan in 1791, 1795, 1799, and 1805 transformed the bucolic, well-

• • • •

drained farmlands into a haven from pestilence, and the village into a town. "The demand for houses at Greenwich," reported a Boston newspaper in 1805, "is scarcely greater than the rapidity with which they are raised. On a spot where yesterday you saw nothing but a green turf, tomorrow you behold a store. . . . By night as well as by day, the saw is heard and the hammer resounds, and the consequence is that the village begins to assume the appearance of a town."[2]

Another impetus for development was the opening in 1797 of Newgate Prison, which extended northward from the foot of Christopher Street to Perry Street. One of the earliest reform penitentiaries in America, the Newgate was praised for its separate quarters for women, bathing facilities, and workshops training prisoners to be, for example, blacksmiths, nail makers, shoemakers, tailors, coopers, turners, spinners, and weavers. Because of a poor security system, however, revolts and prison breaks were frequent occurrences, and consequently the prison closed operations in 1827. Nevertheless, for thirty years the presence of the prison drew visitors during the summer months and spawned its own spontaneous development. The Greenwich Hotel opened its doors at the prison's doorstep in 1809, and within two years the Greenwich stage passed from the hotel to Federal Hall and back at least five times a day, keeping the West Village in constant contact with the city to the south.

By the 1820s Christopher Street was inhabited by modest craftsmen and tradesmen who also worked in Greenwich Village. Among the thirty-two names mentioned in Longworth's *American Almanac* of 1820 were the keeper and two assistant keepers of the state prison, five cartmen, six grocers or dry-goods men, and four members of the building trades. Twenty-seven of them lived on Christopher Street between Bleecker and Hudson streets. The oldest residence still standing is Number 133, on the north side of the street a few doors west of Hudson Street. Erected in 1819 for the cartman William Austen, the structure has since been widened and raised, but the outline of its original two and one-half stories can be determined by noting the change in the brickwork from Flemish to running bond. Sometime between 1802 and 1808, William Patterson erected a two-and-one-half-story house at the northeast corner of Bleecker and Christopher streets, devoting the first floor to his grocery store. The oldest structure on Christopher Street, it is still a grocery store.

Markets and churches always follow the growth of population. In the early months of 1804, two butchers put up a shed on the Greenwich Road, just south of Christopher Street. Four years later, in response to petitions from these butchers and local residents, and despite protests from licensed butchers in the public market on Spring Street, the city approved the construction of a public marketplace near the Newgate Prison. The Greenwich Market stood for twenty-two years on land donated by Trinity Church in

• • • •

1813. The greater width of Christopher Street on this block, where the Federal Archives Building now stands, is to this day a reminder of the wagons and carts that once crowded the site.

In 1821 Trinity made a second donation of Village farmland, on this occasion for the construction of St.-Luke's-in-the-Field, just to the south of Christopher Street on Hudson. In the same year, St. John's Church was built as a handsome stone-veneer structure then known as the Eighth Presbyterian Church.

FROM COUNTRY ROAD TO CITY STREETS: 1822–1865
· · · · ·

Although most of the land along Christopher Street had been parceled into lots and sold in the first two decades of the nineteenth century, the surrounding countryside remained predominantly open. The view eastward from Greenwich Street to the gallows standing in present-day Washington Square Park was unobstructed by development. In 1820 the expanse of open land that separated the Village from the city to the south was assumed to be a barrier that no pestilence could overcome. When an epidemic of yellow fever struck the city in 1822, Greenwich Village's reputation as a safe haven forced it to outgrow its narrow country form. One contemporary described the exodus from the city as having the appearance of a flight from a town under siege:

> From daybreak till night one line of carts containing boxes, merchandise and effects was seen moving toward Greenwich Village and the upper parts of the city. . . . Temporary stores and offices were erected, and even on the ensuing day (Sunday) carts were in motion and the saw and hammer busily at work. Within a few days thereafter the Customhouse, the Post-office, the banks, the insurance offices and the printers of newspapers located themselves in the village, and these places almost instantaneously became the seat of the immense business usually carried on in the metropolis.[3]

Many streets were built up with new residences for merchants and bankers, and temporary offices for employees fleeing the danger of Lower Manhattan. Although many businesses returned to the city after the fever subsided, abandoning structures that were eventually filled by immigrants and laborers, the gap between the city and the country had been closed once and for all. The *Commercial Advertiser* recorded this change in a January 18, 1825, article that noted: "Greenwich is no longer a country village. In three years' time, at the rate buildings have been built last season, Greenwich will be known only as part of the city and the suburbs will be beyond it."

City improvements quickly followed once the Village's isolation was ended. Christopher Street was paved and its sidewalks flagged in 1825. In the same year the city filled in the land between the present Washington and West streets that was underwater and extended Christopher Street to its full length. In 1825 the opening of the Erie Canal turned New York into a major seaport. Within three years a pier built at the foot of Christopher Street was the main entry for lumber and building materials targeted for the expanding city to the north.

With the closing of Newgate Prison in 1828, the city lotted and sold its grounds, setting aside space for a public marketplace on present-day Weehawken Street. Much to the surprise of real estate speculators, in 1833 the city decided instead to erect the Jefferson Market at the eastern end of Christopher Street. Following the vocal objections of property owners, however, the Weehawken Market opened as well one year later. Certainly three markets on one small street were too many, even at a boomtown location. Competition drove the Greenwich Market out of business within a year and denied success to the Weehawken Market, which closed in 1846. But the Jefferson Meat Market thrived, expanding in 1836 to include fishermen, poultrymen, and hucksters alongside the butchers.

The market's expansion spurred the development of the eastern end of Christopher Street. While shops and taverns clustered near the pier on the street's western extremity, town houses began to dominate its eastern stretch. The speculative building activities of Samuel Whittemore, a textile manufacturer and state assemblyman, reflect the pace at which lots were purchased and structures erected and sold. Whittemore purchased ten lots on the north side of Christopher Street between Greenwich Avenue and Waverly Place. By 1827 he had erected a row of ten two-story wood-frame houses with brick fronts. Although greatly altered, five of these houses—Numbers 13, 15, 17, 23, and 25—still stand today. In 1829 and 1830 Whittemore purchased the entire block on the south side of Christopher Street between Bedford and Bleecker streets, and the following year he added lots between Bleecker and Fourth streets. On the latter block two houses built for Whittemore in 1836 still survive.[4]

By 1830, as indicated by Longworth's *New York Register* of 1829–1830, remarkable growth had occurred along Christopher Street. The 102 residents surveyed now resided across the entire length of the street. Attesting to the city's northern growth, twenty-four residents were members of the building trades. Among the carpenters, masons, and painters were three stonecutters, one dock builder, and one street paver. By this time Christopher Street had also become home for those who serviced the expanding

• • • •
41

residential community. At least nineteen residents were involved with producing, delivering, or selling food, for there were six grocers, two butchers, and one baker as well as three watermen, two milkmen, and four individuals employed as porters. It is not surprising to discover that—in response to the needs of a residential community—inhabitants of Christopher Street were also engaged in the garment industry: six shoemakers, two tailors, and one hatter resided on the street. A professional class was also beginning to emerge, for a doctor, an attorney, an accountant, and a Spanish teacher could be found living on Christopher Street in 1830. The city's carting industry was yet another category in which a sizable percentage of the street's population found employment. In 1830 twenty-five cartmen, who carried hides, stones, coal, oysters, pipes and hogsheads, household furniture, and hollowware, resided on Christopher Street.

A change in the residential character of the street became apparent in 1830. While most of the buildings east of Fourth Street were apparently single-family residences, boardinghouses and multiple dwellings were springing up on the western end of the street. On the block between Bleecker and Hudson streets, for example, which contained the street's oldest structures, ten of fourteen houses surveyed in 1829–1830 contained two, three, or four different residences. A similar pattern was developing on the blocks west of Hudson Street.

The appearance of multiple-family dwellings by the 1830s suggests that the Village was beginning to experience the ills of overcrowding that haunted much of the city to the south. In 1835 fire destroyed houses that sheltered forty-one families and were described as "filthy, overcrowded, and disease breeding." Villagers petitioned for a park on the site, and in 1837 the city created Christopher Park (renamed Greenwich Park in 1856) through condemnation. Not far away the Northern Dispensary, a medical institute founded in 1827 to treat the poor living outside Lower Manhattan, had six years earlier erected a two-story triangular brick building. The need for this clinic, which still stands, is dramatically reflected by the fact that in its first year of operation, 3,296 patients were treated.

Often called "the year of the riots," 1834 marks the beginning of a new social consciousness among New Yorkers. As Daniel Walkowitz chronicles elsewhere in this volume, stonecutters rioted in Washington Square to protest the use of Sing Sing prisoners to cut the stone for the new buildings of New York University. Greenwich Village also honored one of the leaders of the abolition riots of that year by naming a street after Sidney Howard Gay, a New York lawyer and editor of the *Anti-Slavery Standard*. Gay Street had been opened a year earlier to connect Christopher Street and Waverly Place.

The growing social consciousness manifested in these events is hardly surprising. Artisans comprised a significant portion of the Village's population and were among the most politically active groups of the era. A survey

• • • •

of 162 residents of Christopher Street in Longworth's *American Almanac* of 1835–1836, for instance, underlines the increasing importance of the building trades. Eighteen carpenters, eight masons, three stonecutters, one turner, and one sawyer resided on the street. The number of Christopher Street residents working in the food services and the garment industry also continued to grow. The trend toward multiple housing continued: Forty-two of the ninety-four buildings surveyed in the *Almanac* contained multiple-dwelling units, and the area east of Fourth Street that had previously been predominantly single-family residences contained at least fifteen multiple dwellings.

Between 1840 and 1865 Christopher Street became increasingly commercialized, providing a service spine for the residential community located on its surrounding side streets. The reestablishment of the Hoboken Ferry at the foot of Christopher Street in 1841 prompted commercial interests to cluster near the riverfront: In 1845 a sailmaker's factory stood next to the Christopher Street Oyster Market, and in the next decade grocers, bakers, and blacksmiths all set up shop next to grain and feed warehouses, cigar dealers, and alehouses.

Two new trades were developing along the waterfront end of the street in the 1840s: an increasing number of residents (four in total) were now involved in the tobacco trade and a number of others found employment in shipping and dock activity. Christopher Street was home not only to a sea captain and numerous boatmen and seamen but also to a sailmaker, a ship carpenter, a boat builder, a ship joiner, a dockage man, and a wharfinger.

By 1860 the Hotel Christopher, known as the Great Eastern Hotel, was erected across from the ferry wharf. An ice company, a coal yard, a slaughterhouse, and several saloons joined the proprietors noted above, creating a hub of commercial activity at the western end of the street.

By the mid-1840s the commercial and manufacturing nature of Christopher Street was well established. The number of shopkeepers continued to rise and more and more structures that were once strictly residential now contained retail establishments. Two adjacent four-story buildings—Numbers 92 and 94—were representative of this shift toward commercial activity. Although built during the 1840s as traditional single-family houses, the two were exceptional because their original design included stores on the ground floor. All along Christopher Street, existing structures began to alter their first stories to include the addition of storefronts. In the city directory for 1845–1846, specific mention is made of stores, among them a milk store, a fruit store, a flour and feed store, and a toy store.

Other occupants listing Christopher Street as their business address included dressmakers, hairdressers, shoemakers, blacksmiths, tailors, tobacconists, and a clockmaker. The ranks of the cartmen had also expanded and now included such subcategories as hucksters, porters, night scavengers,

• • • •

express carriers, and a paper carrier. The dry-goods and grocery trade continued to expand: fifteen grocers; five porters; five bakers; five flour, feed, grain, or dry-goods merchants; two provisioners; and two butchers lived on the street. The garment industry was also represented in growing numbers. Simultaneously the presence of those employed in the building trades began to show both an increasing degree of specialization and a decline as the Manhattan building line pushed northward. Only one mahogany sawyer, one housepainter, one slater, and two whitewashers lived on the street in 1845.

The city directory of 1845–1846 also marks the first time that most of the residents along Christopher Street located their place of employment outside the immediate neighborhood. No doubt this shift resulted from the development of the omnibus, stagecoach, and horsecar system, which gave employees the freedom to live at a greater distance from their place of work. It was also an indication of the growing middle-class population that inhabited Christopher Street. As this class expanded, professionals began to find a place on the street. The architect J. B. Snook resided there in the 1840s and 1850s, and doctors, lawyers, accountants, brokers, and clerks began to fill out the professional profile.

At the same time the number of residents employed in the carriage trade rose. Since the Manhattan building line in the early 1850s lay somewhere between Fourteenth and Twenty-third streets, the numerous smiths, stage drivers, harness providers, saddlers, wheelwrights, coachmakers, and stagehands residing on Christopher Street no doubt reflected the early beginnings of the retail district that would center around Union Square and cater to the residential districts just to its north. Trow's *New York City Directory of 1860* recorded a decline in the number of cartmen living on Christopher Street, undoubtedly in response to the advance of the Manhattan building line beyond Twenty-third Street. The year 1860 also marked the moment when professionals disappeared and minor specialization spread to the lower rungs of the economic ladder.

The growth of commercialization and the resulting changes in the demographics of Christopher Street between 1845 and 1860 were mirrored by a significant change in the nature of residential housing. Although several new single-family residences were built along the street in the 1840s and 1850s, the construction of the Village's first tenement—Number 98—in 1856 by Samuel Taylor would dramatically change the character of the neighborhood. By reducing the height of each floor of this plain, six-story brick building, Taylor created apartments that, while crowded and dark, obtained a greater return on his investment. More tenements soon began to replace the two- and three-story town houses along Christopher Street. The transition from country resort to commercial city neighborhood was completed in 1865 when the old Warren mansion, which had been maintained as a country home by Abraham Van Nest from the time he purchased it in 1819 until his death in 1864, was demolished. The site and its surrounding grounds were replaced by the rows of town houses that stand there today. As the fashionable city began to stretch northward above Twenty-third Street, the profile of Christopher Street would change once again.

IMMIGRANTS, TENEMENTS, AND TRAINS: 1865–1910
• • • • •

After the Civil War, New York City's industrial base expanded and its population grew. By 1890 the city's population numbered 1.5 million. The retail center, called Ladies' Mile, moved into the blocks around Union Square and up the spine of Broadway to Twenty-third Street. Luxurious residences began to fill in the empty lots along Fifth Avenue above Twenty-third Street.

Christopher Street became part of a relatively quiet residential community. A report of the Council of Hygiene and Public Health, which had been formed to investigate the sanitary and living conditions in the city, noted in 1865 that Greenwich Village west of Sixth Avenue between Houston and Fourteenth streets was generally a neighborhood containing two-and-one-half- to three-story brick structures. More than 80 percent of these, or 2,850, were single-family houses. The remainder were private residences converted to lodge two or three families. In addition to these conversions, a few four- to five-story tenement houses were built along Christopher Street before the depression of 1873 froze all real estate activity in New York for nearly two decades.[5]

The ethnic diversity of Christopher Street increased markedly during the 1870s. Although forty-six residents had identifiable English surnames, twenty-six had Irish, and eighteen had German.[6] Many of these residents were employed in the sawmills, stone yards, breweries, and docks of nearby West Street. Others were shopkeepers whose enterprises were located on nearby Village streets, or clerks who worked in large downtown office buildings or the newfangled department stores along Ladies' Mile. One observer noted that new resident storekeepers "were content to take half a store and live in the rear of it, and to rise up earlier and stay up later than the old Village merchants."[7] Reuben May, who located his organ-making shop on Christopher Street in 1879, may have been one of these new storekeepers. Others may have included German saloonkeepers like Becker and Son, Theobald Scherrer, and Frederick Stock, all of whom located their establishments at the western end of the street near the riverfront.

• • • •

By 1871 a steam-powered elevated railroad had been constructed, with an elaborately simulated "Swiss chalet" station straddling the western end of Christopher and Greenwich streets. Dirty and incredibly noisy, the "el" was a nuisance, and housewives reportedly kept a pile of bricks in their kitchens to hurl at the trains when they passed within a few feet of their windows. Nevertheless it enabled the many clerks and office workers who resided in the West Village to be transported downtown rapidly by avoiding streets congested with trucks and carts that made overland travel a time-consuming affair. The popularity of this unique transportation in the sky, with its speed and efficiency, led in 1878 to the authorization of a competing line with a station located at the eastern end of Christopher Street. Just a few years before, Frederick Withers and Calvert Vaux had designed the colorful Victorian Gothic Jefferson Market Courthouse, with its tall watchtower, adjacent to the site of the new elevated station. These two railroad lines, in combination with the Central Park, North and East River Street railway, which had plied its way along West Street since 1860, and the Metropolitan Crosstown Railway, which traveled along Waverly Place from the East Village to Fourteenth Street, offered Village residents several rapid-transit options.

Although travelers had crossed the Hudson River from the foot of Christopher Street since the end of the eighteenth century, a formal ferry service seems to have been inaugurated only in 1838, after the Hoboken Land Improvement Company acquired the Barclay Street Ferry line. Little is known of the early ferry facilities, although in 1870 it was recorded that six million passengers per year were crossing from Hoboken to Manhattan and landing at either the Christopher or Barclay Street slips. In 1872 the Christopher Street Rail Road Company constructed a horsecar line from the Tenth Street Ferry on the East River, across Eighth Street, past Cooper Union, and along Christopher Street to the Hoboken Ferry. Its car barns and stables occupied the southern block between Washington and West streets, adjacent to the Great Eastern Hotel. The president of the Hoboken Ferry, Edwin Stevens, purchased the New Jersey State Pavilion building from the 1876 Philadelphia Centennial Exhibition, dismantled and shipped it to Christopher Street, and there had it reconstructed as the Hoboken Ferry Terminal. It was used until 1953 and subsequently demolished. With all this uptown, downtown, and crosstown commuting, it was no wonder that by 1879 ten different billiard and beer saloons could be found along Christopher Street.[8]

The largest landowners in this area of the Village after 1880 were William H. Beadleston and Ernst Woerz, the proprietors of the Empire Brewery. Their enterprise occupied the entire block between West Tenth, Charles, West, and Washington streets until it was demolished in 1937. Beadleston also began to speculate in real estate and in 1879 constructed a tenement on the corner of Christopher and Washington streets. In the 1880s

New York's population rose in tandem with the city's recovery from the severe economic depression of the previous decade. The arrival of a significant number of Catholic immigrants from Italy, Ireland, and Poland in New York and their subsequent settlement in the West Village led Father John Fitzharris to found St. Veronica's Catholic Church and School on Christopher Street near Greenwich Street in 1887. He celebrated his first mass on Palm Sunday in a renovated stable on Washington Street, while the church, designed by John J. Deery, was still under construction.[9]

With economic recovery a new cycle of housing construction began in the late 1890s, lasting until just before World War I. Perhaps the greatest alteration to the architectural fabric of the street was the construction, beginning in 1891, of the massive United States Appraisers Warehouse. Designed by Willoughby J. Edbrooke, it is now known as the Federal Archives Building. Although several city politicians and real estate speculators wanted to erect this structure near Bowling Green, the shipping and importing industry wanted an uptown location closer to the Hudson River piers. Consequently, Trinity Church farmland was selected as the site. According to an article of the time, the erection of such a massive and well-designed structure housing dozens of customs inspectors was expected to reverse the "depressed" real estate market in Greenwich Village.[10]

Although families with English surnames still made up the majority of residents on Christopher Street in 1890–1891, there were nearly as many families with Irish and German names. Within a decade, however, the picture had changed. By 1902 40 percent of the households on the street were of Irish parentage, 24 percent of American, and 16 percent of German.[11] Christopher Street's population was increasing as well, with many of the new residents living in large apartment structures that were usually seven stories high and sometimes covered several building lots. These new apartment buildings, often ornamented with a variety of stylistic motifs such as Romanesque Revival arches or fanciful terra-cotta elements, began to replace smaller brick houses along Christopher Street, especially along the blocks between Hudson and Bleecker streets. One tenement erected in 1900 and still standing has the "dumb-bell" floor plan (so named because of the shape of the building) that was mandated by the Tenement House Act of 1879 to allow light and air into every room.

BOHEMIAN TIMES: 1910–1945
• • • • •

By 1910 the Village had become a congested district whose maze of crooked streets were populated by Irish, Germans, Jews, Italians, and sailors as well

• • • •

as some old "New Yorkers." In 1904 the Municipal Arts Society proposed widening Christopher Street and extending it on a diagonal all the way to Union Square. Such a thoroughfare, it was thought, would open the Village to the flow of commercial and industrial activity.[12] Even without this scheme, however, manufacturers and wholesale merchants were moving to the West Village to take advantage of cheap land values and low rents. These new developers began to construct warehouses and loft buildings to house the expanding drug, leather, hardware, and ironware industries, as well as printing, publishing, and plumbing establishments.[13]

The Greenwich Village Improvement Society demanded more play space for children, better lighting, paved streets, and the installation of comfort stations. Greenwich Street in 1914, one report claimed, was "dark and dangerous" because the "el" obscured all the electric lights. Furthermore, there was "no record of when [Christopher Street] was last paved, but apparently it was many years ago."[14]

In 1910 several Village boosters selected "the psychological moment," when the city's planned cut-through of Sixth and Seventh avenues was assured, to propose that a new courthouse and law center replicating the Paris Opera House be located on a triangular plot of land formed by Christopher Street, Greenwich Street, and the widened Seventh Avenue.[15] A different approach was taken by reformers who argued that the city, which had demolished three hundred pieces of property for the cut-through of Seventh Avenue and dislocated at least one thousand families, should be charged with rehousing these former Village residents in new low-income structures.[16] Neither of these plans was adopted. Nonetheless, the alterations to Seventh Avenue drastically changed the appearance of the West Village. Three blocks on Christopher Street were plowed through, sawing off parts of buildings and offering the rear of some structures a new frontage on the Avenue. This cut-through, plus the construction of the new IRT subway line under Seventh Avenue and Christopher Street, only strengthened the growing division between the eastern and western parts of Christopher Street.

One Village resident "looked into the future and visioned squadrons of trucks racing down a new avenue, bound to and from warehouses. He saw the new subway disgorging thousands. In his jaundiced mind's eye, he visioned tall factory buildings on the sites of nineteenth century three-story dwellings."[17] Perhaps in anticipation of these new crowds, developers were busy constructing new six-story apartment houses, and Trinity Corporation announced in 1917 that they would replace 350 houses with modern structures in the Seventh Avenue section of their holdings. In spite of the incursion of warehouses and manufacturing establishments, the residential center of the Village was shifting westward. Furthermore, the conversion of homes into high-class rental apartments near Washington Square inevitably meant that cheaper apartments could be found in the Village near Sheridan Square and Seventh Avenue.[18]

• • • •

By 1916 the new zoning law heightened still further the distinction between the eastern and western sections of Christopher Street. West of Hudson Street, the waterfront blocks were left without restrictions, thereby permitting any type of building and land use. The Village to the east was a district from which all nuisance industries and large manufacturing establishments were excluded. The dividing line really lay along the new cut-through of Seventh Avenue: To the west, the ground floors of tenement houses were occupied by saloons and stores. These tenements and those on the streets immediately to the north and south were home to Irish longshoremen who crowded around hiring bosses on the waterfront in the early morning hours, at noon, and again at four in the afternoon, hoping to receive a brass check that meant a job unloading ships. The ships' crews also supported local businesses: In port for four to twelve hours a day, sailors patronized the street's speakeasies, poolrooms, cafés, and boardinghouses. To the east commercial establishments, such as Prohibition-style tearooms, nightclubs, bookstores, clothing shops, and gift stores, became the predominant activity. Two of the more notorious tearooms of the 1920s and 1930s, Romany Marie's and Bonnie's Stone Wall, were located on Christopher Street.

By the mid-1920s the expansion of Seventh Avenue, the opening of the subway, and a real estate building boom combined to transform Sheridan Square into the center of the Village and to make Christopher Street into a social and commercial attraction. The growing commercialization of Village activities highlighted the distinction between the Village's small coterie of bohemians, including their hangers-on, and the surrounding population. In her 1935 book *Greenwich Village*, historian Caroline Ware separated the residents of the Village into "locals" and "Villagers." "Locals," she claimed, were longtime residents located in the West Village and descended from immigrant families who settled there during the last decades of the nineteenth century. They were enthusiastic supporters of improvement schemes such as the Seventh Avenue cut-through, hoping that it would decrease the congestion of Village streets and improve their local businesses. The "Villagers" represented the new wave of sophisticated settlers, and their terrain remained the east side of Seventh Avenue.

On Christopher Street, consequently, there arose a neighborhood of different types. The working-class locals—longshoremen, butchers, saloon-keepers—lived in tenement houses to the west. The well-educated Villagers, a group that included socialists, poets, and writers, resided in high-rise apartments to the east of Seventh Avenue. These two groups shared no common ground, only a basis for suspicions.[19] A Village reporter noted: "Old Irish residents, and to a lesser extent the Germans . . . hated these strange Bohemians they did not understand. With prohibition, systematic raids were started which were rightly called the Slaughter of the Innocents."[20] The competition from speakeasies promoted by Italian racketeers and the frequent raids by Irish and German policemen prompted many tearooms either to sell liquor under "protection" or to close, thereby assuring the economic failure of many of the "Villagers'" gathering places.

By the 1930s bohemian Greenwich Village was fading away, for unemployment was rife among both the intellectuals and the locals. Although the neighborhood was being transformed into a sedate community, it continued to expand, largely through the construction of high-rise apartment buildings. On Christopher Street, two of the new apartment buildings rose sixteen stories tall. "Of late years," noted one 1932 account, "Greenwich Village has increased its regular popularity by leaps and bounds as a result of the many beautiful new apartment buildings that have replaced the old rattletrap shacks here, and are bringing in a more circumspect type of resident to the community."[21] But the Great Depression and then World War II soon brought an end to extensive redevelopment. Only one structure was built on Christopher Street between 1933 and 1945.

THE CONTEMPORARY LANDSCAPE OF CHRISTOPHER STREET: 1945–1990
• • • • •

Following World War II, Greenwich Village retained only faint remnants of its reputation as a bohemian enclave. In 1945 one local newspaper claimed that the Village epitomized "short crooked streets, . . . tiny antique shops, unusual signs everywhere . . . the last word in modern night clubs. . . . [the] suggestion of the quiet of a Paris street here and there."[22] By 1950, however, another local newspaper argued that "in trying to sum up the last seedy stronghold of Bohemia in New York one is forced to turn to the inevitable cliché: Greenwich Village is a state of mind. Once you are under its spell—the tiniest phoniest thinnest spell you can imagine, it is easier to unearth its attractions. When you come to it clinically the task of finding them is monumental."[23]

A shift in the character of the Village was apparent. Christopher Street had been rezoned in 1945, an act that accentuated the division between east and west by forcing all restaurants and industrial uses to move to the west of Seventh Avenue, and leading clothing stores and antique shops to settle to the east. Several Christopher Street tenements were demolished in 1953 to make way for St. Luke's School, and four years later the abandoned ferry terminal was torn down to make way for a new railroad freight depot.

The physical changes in the Village were accompanied by a steady decline in population during the 1940s and 1950s as people moved uptown or to the suburbs. By the late 1950s racial antagonism had also developed between the longtime Italian residents and blacks, referred to as "A-trainers," who had become the newest residents of the Village. Organized racketeering, an overabundance of nightclubs, and the presence of a large homosexual community also produced social friction and led to occasional street brawls.

One of the most notable instances of such street violence occurred in 1969. After a raid by plainclothes police at the Stonewall Inn, a Christopher Street bar frequented by homosexuals, many of the two hundred young men expelled from its premises transformed the immediate area into the scene of several protests and riots. On the boarded-up windows of the Stonewall Inn, graffiti called out to SUPPORT GAY POWER and LEGALIZE GAY BARS.[24] Christopher Street quickly became emblematic of the Gay Liberation Movement and a focal point for subsequent marches.

During the early 1970s crime seemed to increase steadily in the Village, as did the traffic from an exceptionally large number of private clubs. To add to the social tensions, a Village report estimated that between fifteen hundred and two thousand homeless men were sheltered in single-room-occupancy hotels like the Greenwich Hotel.[25] The catalyst for public debate over these mounting problems seemed to be the 1972 decision to demolish the Women's House of Detention at the eastern end of Christopher Street. Some Village residents wanted it replaced by the Urban Center of the New School, while many in the gay community wanted it turned into a community center with space allotted to local groups. It eventually became a community garden.

Amid the social tensions another movement was afoot. Buildings like the Northern Dispensary on Christopher Street, which had been labeled "obsolete structures" in 1946, were reevaluated and now called "interesting buildings." This trend gained momentum, and by July 1969 the Landmarks Preservation Commission found that Greenwich Village's architecture, the artistic life within its boundaries, and the sense of history throughout the area were qualities that warranted its designation as a historic district.[26] Impulses similar to the preservationists' also led to concern over the increasingly derelict condition of the Village's waterfront. A 1973 report called for the creation of a Washington Street Special District linking the new residential areas along Washington Street and Westbeth with other residential areas in the Village. Though the district had been zoned for industrial and manufacturing uses, it was proposed that residential and retail uses now be allowed. New construction, it was believed, should be sympathetic to the architectural character and building heights of the surrounding West Village. But most of all the report requested that the waterfront be reserved and improved for recreational purposes.[27]

After thirteen long years of struggle, the West Village Houses, located in part at the corner of Christopher and Washington streets, finally opened in 1974. The development of this cluster of five-story cooperative apartments, financed by the Mitchell-Lama middle-income housing program, was initially spearheaded by urban planning critic Jane Jacobs. Many felt that these walk-ups, rather than the proposed urban renewal towers in empty parkland, "would stimulate the neighborliness and preserve the character of the neighborhood by avoiding the cold impersonality fostered by high-rises."[28] But co-op sales never materialized, and in 1975 the city foreclosed on the mortgage and converted the buildings to low-cost rental apartments.[29]

By the 1980s the physical makeup of Christopher Street was relatively stable—stores would come and go as on any commercial strip, while new development seemed a thing of the past. When an architect sought permission to build an apartment house on a parking lot on Christopher Street, the Landmarks Commission rejected his design because it failed to harmonize with the existing streetscape.[30] The only major change to the street in the 1980s was the renovation and recycling of the Federal Archives Building, which, after the prolonged struggle, was converted into co-ops. And so Christopher Street—like the Village of which it is a part—remains, in the words of Paul Goldberger, both "a tranquil escape from the frenzy of the rest of Manhattan . . . [and] a lively alternative to the boredom of suburbia."[31]

· · · · ·

NOTES

1. Van Twiller's bouwery is located on the earliest known survey of Manhattan, the Manatus Map of 1639, and noted as Bouwery No. 10.
2. *Repertory* (September 20, 1805). Quoted in I. N. Phelps Stokes, *The Iconography of Manhattan Island: 1498–1909*, vol. 5 (New York: Robert H. Dodd, 1915), 562.
3. Quoted in Maud Wilder Goodwin, ed., *Historic New-York* (New York: G. P. Putnam's Sons, 1898), 290.
4. There are other Christopher Street residences from this period that still stand: two charming two-and-one-half-story Federal-style houses built by the carpenter Daniel Simonson in 1827, and a three-story town house erected the same year for the whipmaker and congressional representative Peter Sharpe. A two-story brick house was built for Elias Kent in 1828.
5. Citizens' Association of New York, *Report of the Council of Hygiene and Public Health and Upon the Sanitary Conditions of the City* (New York: D. Appleton and Co., 1866), 122.
6. Voter registration rolls for City of New York, 1874, and *Trow's City Directory and Business Directory* (New York: John F. Trow and Son, 1879).

· · · ·

7. Saxby Penfold, *The Spirit of Greenwich Village* (New York: Greenwich Village Cooperative, 1936), 9.
8. *New York Times*, August 8, 1870, p. 6; *New York Times*, October 4, 1873, p. 8.
9. "Wanamaker's Greenwich Village Guide," *The Villager* (1939): 11.
10. *New York Times*, December 7, 1890, p. 20.
11. *Trow's City Directory and Business Directory* (New York: John F. Trow and Son, 1890), and the Tenement House Department, *First Report* (New York: City of New York, 1902): 16.
12. *Municipal Art Proposal* (February 17, 1904): 9–14.
13. Raymond P. Roberts, "Rehabilitation of the Old Ninth Ward," *The Real Estate Record and Builder's Guide*, June 17, 1911, pp. 1140–1141.
14. Charles Lamb, "Report of the Greenwich Village Improvement Society" (New York: 1914), unpaginated.
15. "Greenwich Village as a Law Center," *Real Estate Record and Builder's Guide*, March 26, 1910, p. 667.
16. "Greenwich Village Investor's Mecca," *Real Estate Record and Builder's Guide*, April 11, 1914, p. 1.
17. "Old Resident Sees Visions Past and Future," *New York Times*, December 23, 1917, sec. V, p. 5, col. 4.
18. "Shift in Center of Greenwich Village," *New York Times*, December 23, 1917, sec. V, p. 5, col. 4.
19. Caroline Ware, *Greenwich Village, 1920–1930* (Boston: Houghton Mifflin Co., 1935), passim.
20. Charles Grandpierre, *History of Fourth Street* (New York: Greenwich Village Weekly News, 1940), 4.
21. Parker W. Chase, *New York: The Wonder Years* (New York: Wonder City Publishing Company, 1932), 266.
22. "The Village Is Our Beat," *Village Chatter* 4, October 12, 1945.
23. Mel Heimer, "Those Greenwich Village Yarns," *Greenwich Village Caricature* (December 1950), unpaginated.
24. "Four Policemen Hurt in Village Raid," *New York Times*, June 29, 1969, p. 33, col. 1; "Police Again Rout Village Youths," *New York Times*, June 30, 1969, p. 22, col. 1.
25. "Modern Perils Distress Old Village," *New York Times*, September 28, 1970, p. 1.
26. *Greenwich Village Historic District Designation Report* (New York: Landmarks Preservation Commission, 1969).
27. "West Side Highway," *Greenwich Village Waterfront Study Stage Two Report* (New York, 1972–1973).
28. Joseph P. Fried, "A Low-Rise Housing Co-op Opens in West Village," *New York Times*, July 23, 1974, p. 41, col. 3.
29. Fried, "Mitchell-Lama Housing Beset by Problems, but City Sees Progress in Solving Them," *New York Times*, December 8, 1974, p. 79, col. 2; Glenn Fowler, "Unsuccessful Cooperative Will Now Offer Rentals," *New York Times*, March 22, 1976, p. 29.
30. *Landmarks Committee Report* (New York: Landmarks Preservation Commission, 1979).
31. Paul Goldberger, "Walks Filled with Discoveries," *New York Times*, February 15, 1980, p. 17.

THE VILLAGE UNDER GROUND

THE ARCHAEOLOGY OF THE GREENWICH MEWS

Joan H. Geismar

When Thomas and Lewis Radford, grocers by trade, decided to build six brick row houses on Greenwich Street in 1844, they intended to sell them to members of New York City's growing middle class. In 1845 Samuel Furman, a dry-goods merchant dealing mainly in imported silks, moved his family from New Jersey to one of these newly finished houses. Furman's next-door neighbor was also his business partner, John G. Davis.[1] During the next five or six years the Furmans and Davises discarded enough broken crockery, bottles, garbage, and other refuse to enable us, more than 140 years later, to speculate about the lives of middle-class businessmen and their families in New York's mid-nineteenth-century Greenwich Village. Subsequent tenants during the ensuing thirty-five years left similar clues.[2]

The urban archaeologist prizes the refuse and debris of evolving cities, and what can be found in Greenwich Village is particularly intriguing. The neighborhood's centuries of development, coupled with building restrictions, make for an archaeological treasure trove. Here one can expect to find historical material and perhaps deposits left by prehistoric Native Americans. Coming forward in time, it is believed that a Native American village coexisted with Dutch farmsteads in the seventeenth century, and later, in the eighteenth, the British colonial elite chose to build its country estates here. In the nineteenth century, Greenwich Village became a middle- and working-class enclave. Since twentieth-century development

· · · ·

has been controlled by preservation laws, traces of these earlier times still remain, making the Village a unique place to study the process of urbanization.

The long settlement history of the Village ultimately created its modern aspect. The Dutch who first settled Manhattan called the area Bossen Bouwery, which means "farm in the woods," but the mid-seventeenth-century Indian name was one of several variations of *Sapponckanican*. This apparently meant "tobacco fields," or "land where the tobacco grows," and was more than likely a reference to what the Dutch, not the local Native Americans, were doing.

Sometime before 1629 Wouter Van Twiller, Nieuw Amsterdam's second Dutch governor, acting in character, appropriated a farm in the area that rightly belonged to the Dutch West India Company. On it he raised tobacco. The Indian name, *Sapponckanican*, first appeared in Dutch records in 1640, more than a decade after Van Twiller had established his tobacco plantation. These same records document the contemporaneous Native American settlement also known as Sapponckanican. Its location is thought to have been in the vicinity of the Hudson River and Gansevoort Street, near where the nineteenth-century Gansevoort Market was later built on landfill. By the time archaeologists Alanson Skinner and Reginald Bolton wrote about this village in the first decades of this century, all traces were long gone, and it was known only from historical sources. Bolton's reconstruction of Indian paths on Manhattan, based on these same sources, places the trail to the village along present-day Gansevoort Street.[3]

The village of Sapponckanican may have survived as late as 1661, just three years before the English first captured Nieuw Amsterdam from the Dutch. Since experts on the subject believe that an Indian village on Manhattan is unlikely before the Europeans arrived,[4] it probably dated to the historic rather than the prehistoric period and developed because of the economics of Dutch settlement. The fact that this settlement was gone long before it was known to archaeologists is typical of the Native American presence in Greenwich Village. Traces of these early populations on Manhattan were not likely to survive the changes made to the Greenwich Village terrain in the eighteenth and nineteenth centuries: Hills were leveled, shorelines altered, swamps dredged and filled, and streams filled or culverted, often wiping out original ground surfaces and with them evidence of aboriginal use. Most vestiges of Dutch and British colonial development were probably also obliterated, although some may remain in the yards of later houses or other structures.

The wealthy families who established country retreats in what became Greenwich Village were the cream of British colonial society, among them the De Lanceys and, for a short but critical time, Sir Peter Warren. (The De Lancey pedigree includes a lieutenant governor and a British colonial-

• • • •

army general. Warren married Susannah De Lancey in 1731.) Like other affluent New Yorkers, they made their homes in the city to the south in what is now Lower Manhattan.

• • • • •

Six Greenwich Village archaeological sites have been investigated since 1981.[5] Some have been wonderfully informative, others less so, but all have revealed something about the developing Village and the lives of its inhabitants. Not only is large-scale commercial development not allowed in this part of the city (so that archaeological material has a good chance of being preserved), but many who live here are acutely aware of their neighborhood's unique character.

One of these six sites, the Greenwich Mews located on Greenwich Street between Christopher and West Tenth streets, illustrates the motivation for archaeology and the methods and the findings of a Greenwich Village "dig." In this case the motivation was compliance with New York City's environmental review process, the methods included documentary research and field-testing, and the findings offered some practical, some political, and some touching aspects of urban life in the mid- to late-nineteenth century. Although Greenwich Mews is on the western periphery of the Greenwich Village Historic District, Manhattan's foremost landmarked district, it was Local Order 91 rather than the mews's location that flagged the site for investigation.

Based on the recommendation of the Landmarks Preservation Commission archaeologist, the developer was required first to conduct a search of municipal records and historical sources and then, once potential for nineteenth-century backyard features had been established, to implement a field-testing program. Only when this and several other unrelated conditions were met would the city grant a variance for underground parking and, ultimately, a certificate of occupancy for seven one-family town houses proposed for the site. At the time a one-story freight terminal stood on the L-shaped property that fronted mainly on Greenwich Street, its western boundary, but also included a lot on West Tenth Street.

Two sealed privy pits that produced details about tenant life in two of the Radfords' row houses built on Greenwich Street in the mid-1840s were major sources of archaeological information. Prior to the installation of running water, the outhouse, with its privy pit, was an urban necessity. These pits, subsequently abandoned and filled, have been found to contain extraordinary archaeological material. The main goal of the investigation was to determine when the privies were abandoned and when the houses might have been hooked into the city sewer system. But beyond this the artifacts, the historical records, and the privies themselves offered a study of urban-

• • • •

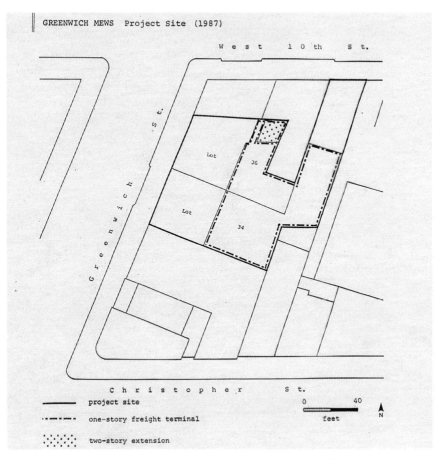

GREENWICH MEWS Project Site (1987)

W e s t   1 0 th   S t.

project site

one-story freight terminal

two-story extension

27. Plot map locating the Greenwich Mews site (*J. H. Geismar/K. Gregory*)

ization. Rather than concentrating on the life-styles of wealthy landowners, often the focus of archaeological inquiry, this investigation became a micro-study of tenant life. Among other things it revealed the attitudes of absentee owners toward amenities for their tenants in a middle- and working-class neighborhood. It also proved that delving into the history and archaeology of the not-so-rich and not-so-famous can be very rewarding.

In addition to discarded household trash, what has endured in the Village are the nineteenth-century dwellings, many of them, like the Radfords' row houses, originally occupied by tenants rather than owners. Often these were converted from single- to multiple-family homes as economic factors and social stratification changed some nineteenth-century neighborhoods for the worse. One element contributing to this decline in the vicinity of the Greenwich Mews site was the construction of an elevated train line in the late nineteenth century. When tracks rose above Greenwich Street, they altered its character and that of the neighborhood, blighting this part of the

• • • •

Greenwich Village suburb as they provided access to new, remoter areas of development. The building of the "el" coincided with double- rather than single-family occupancy of two of the site's row houses.

Archival research, which included a review of maps, municipal and federal records, city directories, library material, published histories, and unpublished reports, indicated that the property had little or no potential for prehistoric sites. Fresh water is a "must" for a long-term or reused Native American camp, and there was apparently none on or near the site. Yet the location of the Hudson River, a major waterway that flowed one city block away before landmaking moved its shoreline farther west, cannot be ignored. This would have made the site area accessible to Native American groups and it could have been used as a rest area or for temporary camps. But the presence or absence of prehistoric camps became a moot point when it was found that a hill that some maps show on the site and others immediately adjacent to it had been leveled early in the nineteenth century. This and later development would have destroyed any possible evidence of Native American use.

Although ownership can be traced from the Dutch period to that of Sir Peter Warren in 1744, no buildings were erected on the site until the second quarter of the nineteenth century. Warren's nearby mansion and its surrounding property were inherited by Warren's daughter, Lady Abingdon. In 1788 Richard Amos purchased nine acres of this inheritance, which included the site block. Little is known about Amos, but he is identified as a gardener in his land deed, and later his death notice in the *New York Evening Post* reported that he served in the Revolutionary War. Until 1858, West Tenth Street, the northern boundary of the site block, was known as Amos Street.

Amos built a dwelling near the site block sometime before 1807, but it stood partially on land he later granted the city for Greenwich Street. To replace this he built a new home directly on the block, but south of the site, at the corner of Greenwich and Christopher streets, where it stood from 1816 until just after the turn of the century. At about the time he built this second house, Amos surveyed his nine acres for subdivision but kept all his Greenwich Street lots on the site block and several on Amos Street; the site lots remained vacant during his lifetime. (Christine Boyer presents a detailed history of the development of Christopher Street earlier in this volume.)

• • • • •

Greenwich Village may rightly claim to be the first suburb on the island of Manhattan. Among the many reasons it evolved as it did were the natural expansion of a growing city, improved transportation, and—perhaps most importantly in light of the late-eighteenth-century yellow fever epidemics

• • • •

that plagued the lower city—its healthy aspect. As Boyer's essay details, the opening of Newgate, the state prison, on the Hudson River at the foot of Amos Street in 1797 helped Greenwich Village become a "bedroom community." It may not be entirely a coincidence that Richard Amos first registered his deed when construction of the prison began, eight years after he made his purchase.

Amos died in 1836, and after his widow's death in 1843, his children sold six of the Greenwich Street lots to Thomas and Lewis Radford, the aforementioned grocers. They had built three-story brick row houses on all their lots by 1845, three of them on the site under investigation. Amos's daughter Mary Hooker kept one site lot on Greenwich Street, one on Amos Street, and a lot on the corner of Amos and Greenwich streets that is not part of the site. After building some commercial sheds and shops, she ultimately built four- and five-story tenements on her site lots, but the Radfords' smaller row houses remained intact until 1907, when the two just south of the project site were replaced by a power station for the Port Authority–Trans Hudson (PATH) tubes. Today a sole survivor of the Radfords' row houses stands next to the power station. Although originally on Greenwich Street, it has been renovated into apartments and an architect's office, with its entrance on Christopher Street.

Two of the three row houses on the site[6] were one-family homes from the time they were built until they became two-family houses in the early 1870s, a change that coincided with the construction of the "el" that ran on Greenwich Street from 1870 until 1940. The third row house was always home to three or more families.[7]

By the early part of this century, two of these structures had become rooming houses with a single toilet or water closet in the yard or basement, but one remained a two-family dwelling. These buildings, and the tenements on the other site lots, were demolished in 1938. Seven years later a freight terminal was built on Greenwich Street over the former row house yards and across most of the tenement sites on Greenwich and West Tenth streets. Since the terminal had no basement, there was a good chance that earlier yard features, such as the row house privy pits and cisterns or wells, would remain under the one-story building. Although it was also conceivable that remnants of the early shops and sheds Mary Hooker had constructed on two of the lots might also exist, this was less likely since insurance atlases show that extensions to the tenements on these lots had encroached on the yards over time.

When the new Greenwich Mews town houses were first planned, soil borings were drilled to determine construction requirements, but these were found to be inconclusive regarding archaeological potential; an attempt was made to learn more by drilling through the terminal floor into former yards, but this too proved inconclusive. Based on the site's development history, a five-day field program was begun after the freight terminal was demolished.

• • • •

28. The sole survivor of six row houses built by the Radfords in 1844–1845 still stands at 681 Greenwich Street. (*J. H. Geismar, 1987*)

Beginning on November 9, 1987, under the author's direction (with the assistance of another archaeologist), a backhoe and operator and two construction workers helped test selected areas of the site. Fortunately the construction people were remarkably sensitive to the requirements of archaeological research. Testing entailed digging through debris from the demolished freight terminal and the site's earlier buildings to reach former yards. By digging eight trenches and three small test pits, all five site yards were explored, as was an area under the relatively shallow basement of the West Tenth Street tenement, where underground parking was planned.

Testing confirmed that the tenement yards had been completely eliminated as had traces of the earlier sheds and shops. But what remained proved to be a bonanza: Two of the row house yards contained circular, stone-lined privy pits filled with garbage-laden soil. One pit was completely intact, but the upper portion of the other had been partly damaged by construction of the freight terminal. The privy for the third site had apparently been totally destroyed by this same construction; no trace of it was found.

The privies turned out to be deep (each extended more than nine feet below the original yard surface and fourteen feet below the most recent yard grade), so the backhoe was used not only to find these features but also to lower the excavators into them and to lift out the artifacts. Approximately half the contents of each privy pit was excavated to provide a good sample of its deposit while leaving a section to be drawn or photographed.

Very soon after excavation began, it became apparent that the stability of the dry-laid stone privies was being undermined and that haste was essential. The refuse that was collected makes up a detailed record of mid-nineteenth-century urban life. Bottles and ceramics were the main components, but meat bones and shells—mostly oyster but some clam—were also recovered. Among the more exciting finds were Civil War–era photos—glass-plate collodion prints known as ambrotypes, three with images still intact. In addition there were fragments of other broken photographic plates, pieces of wooden frame cases with brass edgings, and a lock of blond hair that must have been enclosed with one of the photos. A great many embossed medicine bottles and unmarked vials, some with liquid still sealed inside, were also recovered, as were seven hair-dye bottles.

Samples of privy soil were collected for analysis, and the layers within the privy were drawn in section, creating a visual record of the fill—a "profile" in archaeological parlance. Since the instability of the soil made this difficult, photographs and written descriptions were also used to record the deposits, which were basically a dark gray sandy soil layered with ash and refuse.

When the pit bottoms were reached, the features were refilled with soil from the yard and the artifacts taken to a lab where they were washed, numbered, cataloged, and, when possible, mended. A very respectable sample of 3,009 artifacts was cataloged, and soil samples were sent to experts for seed, pollen, and parasite identification. The ambrotypes were treated to conserve them, and ceramics, glass, bone and shell (faunal material) and the contents of bottles were analyzed. Beyond the artifacts the excavation provided at least partial answers to questions about the construction and management of nineteenth-century urban privies, and the degree to which laws instituted to protect the health and well-being of the city's inhabitants were observed.

Identifying this extraordinary assemblage of glass and ceramics provided information about when they were made, where they came from, and, in the case of medicine bottles, approaches to such timeless concerns as treating illness. The producer's name and sometimes an address embossed on bottles, and the makers' marks found on the bottom of ceramics, helped determine their manufacture dates. When these clues were absent, the technique used to make the bottle or the decoration of the ceramics and the kind of clay or glaze used provided a less specific range of dates. Placing the artifacts in time established that privies associated with the row houses built between 1844 and 1845 were used for at least thirty-five years.

Although the earliest sewer assessment located for the site dates from 1886, city records indicate that sewers were installed on Christopher and Amos streets in 1853.[8] But regardless of when sewers became available, the artifacts suggest that the site houses were not hooked into a sewer system until about 1880. Information like this refines the documentary record, sometimes refutes it, and, in this case, expands it. For example, in the Greenwich Mews area, street sewers were an issue in the spring of 1853: The city's archives contain a petition made in March by local residents (none of them from the site) for such an Amos Street sewer and the remonstrance against it made in April by absentee owners, several of them Richard Amos's grandchildren. The records tell us that the petition for the sewer was successful, while the artifacts tell us that the owners of the row houses did not provide this amenity to their tenants for almost three decades.

If the original occupants of these Greenwich Street houses are an example, the mid-nineteenth-century row houses built on the site were certainly intended for the middle class. This is borne out by the 1865 *Sanitary Report of the Citizens' Association*, a district-by-district assessment of New York City's prevailing sanitary conditions. This groundbreaking report describes the eleventh district, which included the project site, as a middle-class enclave. For the most part it was the home of tradesmen, clerks, mechanics "of the better class," cartmen, and so on. In addition to the silk merchant, Mr. Furman, who was mistakenly described as a mechanic in the 1850 census, the occupants of the two Greenwich Street row houses between 1845 and 1880 included his partner, Mr. Davis, as well as a merchant, a butcher, a mason, a clerk, a coal merchant, and milk, oyster, fish, and mahogany dealers. These identified tenants are probably typical of the

• • • •

buildings' residents for most, if not all, of the nineteenth century and certainly while the excavated privies were in use.

These two houses appear to be examples of 1,721 classified as "private dwellings" in the sanitary inspection report. The report defines tenant houses, as opposed to private dwellings, as "all those originally designated as such and all others once used as private dwellings but now occupied by more than three families" (the tenement houses on the site built after 1877 meet this criterion).[9] Given this definition, the excavated privies were behind private, rented dwellings in 1865. The report goes on to document 484 buildings in the district that were considered "tenant-houses." Apparently the third site row house, which was home to three families from the time it was built, was one of them.[10] If this privy had been found, how interesting it would have been to compare its artifacts with those from the private houses.

In 1865 private Greenwich Village dwellings were not usually "first class" but were mostly "two and one-half and three-story brick dwellings . . . from 20 to 40 years old . . . supplied with Croton-water, most of them lighted with gas and heated by stoves; while about one-half have drains connecting with sewers. The water closets are almost always in the yard."[11] This description fits 691 and 689 Greenwich Street, but since their privies functioned until at least 1880, the artifacts tell us these houses were among those in the district not yet hooked up to sewers.

Based on ceramic and glass dates, it appears that at least the bottom levels of the two Greenwich Street privies may be associated with the buildings' first occupants, Samuel Furman and his family, and his partner and next-door neighbor, John G. Davis. Since their business was in the heart of the city on Pearl Street, these two men are examples of Greenwich Village suburbanites. Census information tells us that Furman, who was five years older than Davis, was from New Jersey, while Davis was born in New York. In this case the older man's household used more "old-fashioned" dishes than did that of the younger: Those recovered from the Furman levels of the privy were mainly traditional blue-and-white transfer prints, while the Davis family was partial to the newly fashionable white ironstone. Both were English imports, and the fact that Furman and Davis were importers may have made these wares particularly accessible to them.

While the archaeology of Greenwich Mews is not that of the wealthy, John G. Davis did ultimately become prominent. He continued in the silk dry-goods business with other partners both before and after Furman's death in 1862, and later became the vice president of the Merchants Exchange Bank. When he died in 1889, the *New York Times* printed a laudatory obituary. But when he rented his row house, Davis was a young, middle-class dry-goods merchant who lived with his wife, children, and two servants.

While a total of ten tenants can be identified in both Greenwich Street houses between 1845 and 1880, at least eight others remain unknown. Some were quite steadfast, staying up to fifteen years; others were decidedly less so, moving on within the year, a pattern found throughout the city during the nineteenth century. Examination of the garbage of the residents of this middle- and working-class enclave provided considerable insight into their life-style. They ate from blue transfer-printed whiteware and undecorated ironstone dishes, dining on beef cuts requiring long cooking and supplementing them with fish, shellfish, and fowl. Raspberries, strawberries, and grapes were consumed as fruits or jams, and corn or other grains were served as vegetables, breads, or cereals. They flavored their food with cloves and parsley (revealed by seed and pollen analysis). Some of the residents' maladies—including lung, stomach, and intestinal disorders—were determined by identifying patent-medicine bottles and analyzing soils for parasites. These analyses revealed the presence of egg casings from human whipworm parasites.

A concern with their personal appearance and that of their homes is suggested by artifacts such as bottles for black hair dyes and other hair preparations, cold creams, colognes, shoe polish, and furniture polish, as well as decorative vases and tableware. The images on the glass-plate ambrotypes provided some substance to the archaeological constructs, although none of the portraits, all of men, have been identified. The profusion of hair-dye bottles and the ambrotypes prompted a search to determine if there had been a hairdresser, wigmaker, or perhaps a photographer on the site, but no evidence was found. The growing availability of once-elite goods and the adoption of elite customs by the middle class are suggested by an increasing number of tea service pieces found over time. Cough medicines from the Furman household refuse seem appropriate since the silk merchant died of "phthisis," a wasting lung disease—probably pulmonary tuberculosis—eleven years after he moved from the Greenwich Street row house.

Bottled condiments, such as pickles and olives imported from France and England, and the number of English ceramics clearly show that imported goods were available to New York City's middle class. Prior to this investigation it had been thought that only domestic ceramics would be found, since the houses date from a time when American potteries were in production. Certainly the Furmans and Davises were fond of English blue transfer-print dishes, because sets with popular patterns were found in their refuse. Although most of the bottled goods appear to have been made and distributed in New York City, medicine bottles came from other cities such as Albany, Rochester, and Philadelphia as well as from the state of Massachusetts.

While much can be learned from a privy's artifacts, the privies themselves are also artifacts. Their size and placement on the site lots indicate that the Radfords had observed the laws governing their installation—they were built to required depths and their relationships to property lines were as mandated. Regulations meant to control the management of the privies, however, were not followed by the Radfords' tenants, for each one contained refuse prohibited by law.[12] And, although privies were to be cleaned prior to filling, this was done partially if at all, for had they been cleaned properly, there would be no artifactual record.

The archaeological investigation of the Greenwich Mews site illustrates that, though fragile, archaeological deposits are tenacious even in an urban setting.[13] Particularly in Greenwich Village where development has been limited, the backyards of nineteenth-century houses undoubtedly contain a wealth of information about the evolving neighborhood and perhaps relics of an even more ancient past. Depending on the location and development history, it is possible that Native American material may be found, even more possible that Dutch or British colonial deposits may remain, and certain that additional evidence of nineteenth-century life still exists.

While some Greenwich Village sites have been more fruitful than others, a great deal has been learned in a very short time. Using the Greenwich Mews site as an example, information has been recovered about the foods eaten by some nineteenth-century Village residents, about the medicines they relied on, about the domestic goods they chose, and about the measures taken to improve their personal appearance and that of their homes. Excavation of this site also revealed that laws meant to safeguard public health were only partly observed. In a broader sense, information has been amassed about the nature of nineteenth-century urban archaeological deposits and about the social and economic history of Greenwich Village.

•••••

NOTES

1. Samuel Furman lived at 691 Greenwich Street, John G. Davis at 689.
2. Much of the information presented in this essay comes from a report entitled *History and Archaeology of the Greenwich Mews Site, Greenwich Village, New York*, prepared for the Greenwich Mews Associates by Joan H. Geismar, Ph.D., May 1989.
3. Alanson Skinner, *The Indians of Manhattan Island*, Guide Leaflet Series, vol. 41 (New York: American Museum of Natural History, 1915; reprint, Ira J. Friedman, Inc., 1961), 51–52. Also Reginald P. Bolton, *Indian Paths in the Great Metropolis*, map 1, Museum of the American Indian (New York: Heye Foundation, 1922), and I.N.P. Stokes, *Iconography of Manhattan Island 1498–1909*, vol. 3 (New York: Dodd, Mead & Co, New York, 1918; reprint, Arno, 1967), 915.

••••

4. For example, the late Lynn Ceci, personal communication, Department of Anthropology, City University of New York, Queens College, 1988.

5. These six Greenwich Village sites, which include Greenwich Mews, have provided information that ranges from inconclusive to exceptional. All but one were excavated to learn about life in the Village during and after colonial settlement (the exception was the Sheridan Square site that might have contained earlier Native American material but where nothing conclusive was found). Three of the six were voluntary rather than mandated by city environmental laws, a rarity in New York City. (Usually the city's environmental review process triggers archaeological investigation. Local Order 91, instituted in the late 1970s and known as the City Environmental Quality Review [CEQR], subjects development requiring a variance or a rezoning application to review by city agencies. Its main purpose is to protect the quality of urban life, and to address such issues as air pollution or traffic flow, but it also applies to cultural resources. The New York City Landmarks Preservation Commission is the review agency that safeguards not only the city's historic structures but also, once an environmental review is initiated, its cultural resources.) One briefly explored the backyard of the Stuyvesant-Fish House, a New York City landmark built in the early nineteenth century at 21 Stuyvesant Street in the St. Marks Historic District of the East Village. A brick water cistern located in the backyard was found to be virtually empty and the yard around it disturbed.

The Sheridan Square excavation was undertaken in 1982 by professional archaeologists and local residents who volunteered their time in an attempt to find evidence of prehistoric Native American and historical use of an undeveloped triangle of land. Unfortunately no concrete evidence of Native Americans was found, but plow scars and postholes dating from historical times may have been uncovered. Two years later the Sullivan Street site, property owned and scheduled for development by the New York University Law School, was excavated. This research was more extensive and rewarding than previous excavations. Under the direction of the late Bert Salwen of New York University—one of the first in the Northeast to recognize the potential of urban archaeology—twelve nineteenth-century yard features, such as privies, cisterns, drainage sumps, and a well, were excavated. The features were associated with upper-middle-class and poorer, working-class houses and a tenement.

In 1987 the contents of a cistern located in a Barrow Street yard yielded artifacts and information that date from the 1860s when the house was occupied by middle-class families; in 1990 and 1991, a Twelfth Street privy was excavated. Reports on the Sullivan Street and Barrow Street findings are near completion, and the Twelfth Street report is in preparation.

I thank Dr. Anne Marie Cantwell and Dr. Diana Wall for information regarding all but the Greenwich Mews site. In addition Jean E. Howson, "The Archaeology of Nineteenth-Century Health and Hygiene: A Case Study from Sullivan Street, Greenwich Village, New York City" (M.A. thesis, N.Y.U. Department of Anthropology, 1987), provided information about the Sullivan Street site.

6. 691 and 689 Greenwich Street.

7. 687 Greenwich Street.

8. *Annual Report of the Croton Aqueduct Department* (New York: Spedon and Baker, 1857).

9. *Report of the Council of Hygiene and Public Health of the Citizens' Association of New York upon the Sanitary Conditions of the City* (New York: D. Appleton & Co., 1866), 120–121.

10. 687 Greenwich Street.

• • • •

11. *Report of the Council of Hygiene*, 121.
12. *Code of Health Ordinances and Rules and Sanitary Regulations* (New York: Metropolitan Board of Health, 1866); J. W. Amerman and George W. Morton, *Laws and Ordinances Relative to the Preservation of the Public Health in the City of New York* (New York: Edmund Jones & Co., 1860); *New York City Board of Health, extracts of Laws and Ordinances* (New York: New York Common Council, 1833), secs. 3–7.
13. Although there has been a great deal of post-field analysis, more information conceivably could be extracted from the artifactual record, particularly as our knowledge of these objects and their meaning increases. To this end Greenwich Mews Associates, the developer, has donated the collection to the South Street Seaport Museum, where the artifacts will be available for additional research and, ultimately, exhibition.

• • • •

GREEK AND GOTHIC SIDE BY SIDE

ARCHITECTURE IN THE VILLAGE

Sarah Bradford Landau

Nowhere are the intriguing—and sometimes puzzling—interconnections between people, period, and place better embodied than in the early-nineteenth-century architecture around Washington Square. During the 1830s and 1840s, when well-to-do and influential New Yorkers moved up to the Square and building activity flourished there, the Greek and Gothic Revival styles of architecture were in fashion. Many of the area's finest and most historically significant buildings, some extant and well known, others long demolished and all but forgotten, were built in those styles. Most are related—through patronage, the personalities involved, or style—to the founding of New York University (1831) and its Gothic Revival University Building.

The Greek Revival became popular in New York in the 1830s, coinciding with the intensive residential development of the streets around Washington Square. Stimulated by the publication in England of Stuart & Revett's *Antiquities of Athens* (1762–1816), the style was first practiced in America in Philadelphia around 1820. New York adopted it in the late 1820s, and in the 1830s it was disseminated throughout the country by such pattern books as Minard Lafever's *The Young Builder's Instructor* (1829) and *The Modern Builder's Guide* (1833). Like many of the Greek Revivalists, Lafever (1798–1854) was also adept at the Gothic Revival, in which style he designed the South Dutch Reformed Church. Not only was the Greek Revival ideologically well suited to a newly independent nation committed to a democratic form of government, it also appealed at a practical level. It could be easily employed by ordinary builders, who greatly outnumbered trained architects in America, and it could be adapted to all kinds of structures. Although Greek Revival buildings frequently bore little resemblance to ancient Greek buildings, the temple front and the rectangular temple form were favored for public and institutional buildings and for large houses.

In the case of the Thirteenth Street Presbyterian Church (1846–1847), rebuilt twice after fires in 1855 and 1902 and now converted to residential use, a Doric temple front inspired by the Theseum in Athens masks a rectangular, brick-walled building. The church has been attributed to the builder Samuel Thomson (1784–1850), who, as we will see, had previously been involved with other projects in the neighborhood. Thomson had constructed several buildings with temple fronts, among them his own house, Mount Washington (1839), in the Inwood section of Upper Manhattan, which had a similar Theseum-type porch. He had also served as the first builder of the New York Custom House in 1834 and 1835. The Custom House (1834–1842), designed by the firm of Town & Davis and now Federal Hall National Memorial, is based on the Parthenon, also a Doric temple. However, by 1846, when the Thirteenth Street Church was begun, the Gothic Revival had become the preferred mode for churches.

There were several Gothic Revival Presbyterian churches in the immediate vicinity, among them the new First Presbyterian Church on Fifth Avenue and Eleventh Street. The choice of the Greek Revival for the Thirteenth Street Church at this late date supports its attribution to a builder rather than an architect but may also have been influenced by the restricted midblock site and a limited budget. The Gothic Revival required a complex plan, stone walls, and elaborate carved ornaments, whereas the Greek temple front could be simulated with wood elements painted to resemble stone. (The porch of the Thirteenth Street Church is partly made of wood.)

In the case of more modest buildings, such as row houses, the Greek Revival elements were usually confined to columned doorways and classically inspired lintels and moldings. Numbers 1 to 13 Washington Square North, built in two groups from about 1832 to 1833, are typical Greek Revival row houses in respect to their plain brick fronts and spare Grecian trim; but they are exceptionally large houses, and their trim is marble rather than the more usual and less expensive brownstone. These houses, like the smaller-scale, more delicately detailed houses of the preceding Federal period, adhere to the model of London's eighteenth-century houses: Three windows wide and two or three rooms deep, they had deep backyards accessible from a private mews lane. In contrast to the pitched roofs and dormers of earlier Federal houses, these have a flat roofline and a full attic story. Deeply recessed doorways are framed by Doric or Ionic columns supporting plain entablatures, and high stoops—a standard feature in New York

· · · ·

from the Federal period until the 1890s—lead up to raised parlor floors identified by tall windows. Skylighted curving staircases grace the interiors of these spacious, high-ceilinged houses, and mahogany sliding doors framed by classical columns separate front and back parlors.

The length and homogeneity of The Row, as the group came to be known, are due to the fact that it was built on leased land in conformity to restrictions in the original deeds of 1831. The property owner was Sailors' Snug Harbor. According to the leases, "good and substantial" houses, their fronts "12 feet back of and parallel with" the street, had to be built on the land within two years. Among the original lessees were New York University council members James Tallmadge, who lived in Number 5, and John Johnston, whose house was Number 7. Samuel Thomson was the speculator-builder of Number 4, and he too played a role in the early history of the University. In 1832 he sold the University its land on the east side of the Square, apparently having acquired the property just for that purpose.[1] The Snug Harbor records do not name an architect for the Row, but for a number of reasons Thomson is a likely candidate. His firm, Samuel Thomson & Son, had previously worked for Snug Harbor. In 1831 the firm repaired some Snug Harbor properties on Eighth Street and by the late summer of 1832 was superintending construction of the Snug Harbor retreat on Staten Island, a famous Greek Revival group designed by Minard Lafever. The University Council minutes of December 24, 1832, record Thomson's offer to sell the University at cost some brick he had stored on their newly acquired land. Was this brick left over from the construction of his own and other houses in The Row? The houses could easily have been designed by a builder; in elevation and plan they conformed to earlier Greek Revival rows in the neighborhood.

Also unresolved is the question of who designed Colonnade Row (ca. 1831–1833) on Lafayette Place (now Lafayette Street). This group seems much too sophisticated in concept, proportion, and detail to be the work of a builder. The famous architectural historian Henry-Russell Hitchcock observed that Colonnade Row "equals in grandeur anything of the period that London or Edinburgh have to offer."[2] Also known as LaGrange Terrace, after the country house of General Lafayette, and as Lafayette Terrace, the row comprised nine marble-fronted houses linked by a continuous Corinthian colonnade two stories tall. Today only four of the houses, in lamentably shabby and altered condition, survive.

In the past Colonnade Row was attributed to the noted New York architect Alexander Jackson Davis (1803–1892). Davis, whose firm Town & Davis (briefly Town, Davis & Dakin) produced important Greek and Gothic Revival buildings of all types, did make a drawing of Colonnade Row; and Town, Davis & Dakin designed a rear balcony and interiors for the group. However, other evidence casts doubt on the Davis attribution. According to Fay's *Views in New-York*, the speculator-builder of the row was also the designer, Seth Geer, Samuel Thomson's chief rival in the building trade.[3] But that assertion is difficult to believe given the high quality of the design of this group. Moreover, it has been established that an Albany architect, Robert Higham, did some work for Geer in connection with Colonnade Row. And then there is still another personality to consider, James H. Dakin (1806–1852). Dakin joined Town & Davis in May 1832, not long after the row was begun, and his drawing of the row is the one reproduced in Fay's *Views*. In June 1832 Davis went to Washington, where he remained until September; surely Dakin was heavily engaged with the firm's work while Davis was away. All these circumstances suggest that Dakin was involved in the design of at least the interiors of Colonnade Row. Add to this the fact that in 1833 Dakin and Geer collaborated on the University Building, just a few blocks away. For both buildings Geer utilized marble quarried and tooled by Sing Sing prisoners. These interconnections are intriguing—and puzzling.

Colonnade Row was dubbed "Geer's folly" because it was so far north of the business district. Nonetheless the houses sold for high prices, and wealthy and socially prominent New Yorkers, among them the younger John Jacob Astor, lived there. The elder Astor had owned the land on which Colonnade Row was built as well as much of the surrounding land since the beginning of the century. For many years he had leased part of his

29.   University Building at New York University *(Museum of the City of New York)*

• • • •

property for use as the pleasure grounds known as Vauxhall Gardens. But in 1826, realizing that the time was ripe for residential development, he laid out Lafayette Place and began selling off his lots on both sides of the street. He held on to part of the tract, and later, through Astor family bequests, the Astor Library, now the Public Theatre, was built across the street. Colonnade Row may have inspired a pair of Ionic-columned houses, no longer extant, built in 1833 by Elisha Bloomer, a hat manufacturer and "infamous contractor" whose activities are detailed in Daniel Walkowitz's essay in this volume. These houses were at 714–716 Broadway, opposite Washington Place.

The Samuel Ward house, a freestanding mansion known as "The Corner," was indisputably designed by Town & Davis. Completed in 1833 on the northeast corner of Broadway and Bond Street, the mansion was brick with marble trim, and it was crowned by a diminutive cupola. Its chief distinction was its picture gallery, a windowless extension ornamented by Corinthian pilasters, at the rear of the house on the Broadway side. This gallery is said to have been the first private picture gallery built in America. In 1839 Ward commissioned the Hudson River School landscapist Thomas Cole to paint the famous *Voyage of Life* series for his gallery, but unfortunately Ward died that same year, before the series could be completed.

Ward was head of the eminent New York banking house of Prime,

30. Samuel Ward's mansion on the northeast corner of Broadway and Bond Street *(Museum of the City of New York)*

Ward, & King, and from 1830 to 1832 served as the first treasurer of New York University. Ward and John Delafield were the only members of the University Council to vote against the purchase of the land on the east side of Washington Square, perhaps because they believed the cost of forty thousand dollars was more than the University could afford. Both men resigned their council seats soon afterward.

Bond Street, where Ward built his house, was one of New York's most exclusive residential streets from 1820 to about 1850. Its impressive roster of residents included financier and statesman Albert Gallatin, who was the first president of the University Council (1830–1831). Gallatin lived at 5 Bond Street from 1820 to 1833. Succeeding occupants of the same house included Maj. Gen. Winfield Scott, later commander in chief of the army, and Circuit Court Judge William Kent. Most of the street's houses, including Gallatin's, were brick- or marble-fronted Federal row houses with high roofs and dormers. By 1850 Bond Street had begun to decline; business had overtaken this part of Broadway, and New York society had started to move farther north. In 1871 Numbers 1 to 5 were replaced by the cast-iron-fronted, mansard-roofed Robbins & Appleton store, rebuilt in 1879–1880 and still standing. In 1874 Brooks Brothers opened its new store on the site of the Ward mansion, and in 1875, the Colonnade Hotel opened in the five southernmost houses of Colonnade Row, bringing to an end the row's golden age. Those five houses were demolished soon after 1900, and the old Wanamaker warehouse was built on the site.

The Henry J. Brevoort, Jr., mansion, built on the northwest corner of Fifth Avenue and Ninth Street in 1834 and demolished in 1925, somewhat resembled the Ward house. Unlike the more commonplace brick face of the latter, however, the paneled facades of the Fifth Avenue mansion were apparently brick stuccoed to resemble stone. Considering its crisp geometric character and restrained ornamentation, the Brevoort mansion looks as if it might have been designed by Town & Davis, but no documentation exists to confirm that frequent attribution. Whoever the architect, he was obviously very good. The sensitively proportioned elements of the Fifth Avenue front, as well as the circular grand staircase inside and the huge drawing room with curved walls, attested to his competence.

By the 1850s lower Fifth Avenue had become one of the city's most elegant residential streets, built up with fine houses and, later, family hotels. Today almost entirely rebuilt with large apartment houses, it remains a highly desirable residential neighborhood. The Brevoort name—that of an early Dutch family who owned a vast tract of farmland in this part of the city—was commemorated first in Brevoort House, an "aristocratic" hotel, which opened in 1854 in three combined town houses at the northeast corner of Fifth Avenue and Eighth Street. Today the Brevoort, an apartment house built on the site of Brevoort House in the early 1950s, preserves the name of this notable Knickerbocker family.

• • • •

31. Middle Dutch Church, on the northwest corner of Lafayette Place and Fourth Street
(Museum of the City of New York)

• • • •

Still another superb Grecian building of the 1830s, long gone, was the Middle Dutch Church (1836–1839) on the northwest corner of Lafayette Place and Fourth Street, just down the street from Colonnade Row. The architect was Isaiah Rogers (1800–1869) of Boston, also responsible for the famous Astor House hotel (1832–1836), built by John Jacob Astor, and for the Merchants Exchange (1836–1842) on Wall Street. The Middle Dutch Church, which had a splendid Ionic temple front and a wooden steeple rising from a base inspired by the Choragic Monument of Lysicrates in Athens, is considered one of Rogers's finest designs. Its decidedly un-Greek combination of temple front and tower followed a well-established precedent set by a famous early-eighteenth-century London church, St. Martin-in-the-Fields. Later, Rogers designed the Astor Place Opera House (1847), which is remembered less for its architectural features than for the disastrous 1849 riots protesting the performance of English actor William Charles Macready and resulting in several deaths. A brownstone temple, more Roman than Greek in form, the building had interiors richly decorated by the Italian artist-craftsman Mario Bragaldi.

As witnessed by the old University Building and the many Gothic-style churches in the area, the Gothic Revival flourished around the Square from the 1820s through the 1840s. Again the source was England, where the style had evolved from a romantic and rather fanciful evocation of the Gothic in the eighteenth century to, by the 1840s, a serious, near-archaeological revival of the fourteenth-century English parish church. A similar progression, particularly well represented by New York's Episcopal churches, occurred in the United States. Not surprisingly, in view of its ecclesiastical associations, the style was never popular for city houses. The few built in New York usually had plain brownstone fronts sparingly decorated with Gothic detailing at doors, windows, and cornices. One of four contiguous Gothic Revival houses built in 1848–1849 by Henry Brevoort, Jr., Number 10 Fifth Avenue, retains its original crenellated parapet.

When St. Thomas's Church (1823–1826) was completed on the northwest corner of Broadway and Houston Street in 1826, it was considered the most genuinely Gothic structure yet built in New York. The architect of this Episcopal church was Josiah R. Brady (ca. 1760–1831), also credited with the second Trinity Church (1788–1791), predecessor of the present Trinity Church on Broadway at the head of Wall Street. While St. Thomas's was under construction, A. J. Davis was working in Brady's office. He and Dakin must have been impressed by the church's Perpendicular Gothic style and its architectural features. These included twin octagonal towers, crenellated parapets, a great ogee-arched window, and a ceiling said to have resembled that of London's Westminster Hall. Although more plausibly proportioned and more accurately detailed, the center section of the University Building may owe some of its inspiration to the church. The church burned in 1851

• • • •

but was rebuilt to look much as it had before. It was demolished in 1866; in order to escape the business district and slums that had grown up around it, the congregation had decided to rebuild farther uptown.

New York University's handsome white marble building on Washington Square (1833–1836) was the first important example of the English Collegiate Gothic in America and as such influenced later American college buildings. Its Gothic style was determined by the University authorities, not by the architects Town, Davis & Dakin. It is known that two University professors, David B. Douglass, professor of natural philosophy, architecture, and civil engineering, and Rev. Cyrus Mason, professor of religion, influenced the design of the building. Dakin was the principal architect, and his letters to Davis indicate that he was not entirely sympathetic with the University's choice of the Gothic style. The letters describe the preliminary design as "a half-barbarous thing" and as "a half-savage Gothic." Undoubtedly the University officials hoped people would associate the building and their new institution with England's venerable colleges of Oxford and Cambridge. The resemblance of the central section to King's College Chapel in Cambridge was immediately noticed, and everyone was impressed by the medieval collegial appearance of the whole.

The symmetrically planned building was about 180 feet long by 100 feet deep. In the center section a deeply recessed entrance opened onto a marble-paved hall 20 feet high. From there a wide flight of marble steps led up to a chapel on the second floor. Wings extending from the center terminated in towerlike projections at the four corners, the ones at the rear—on Waverly and Washington places—masking a pair of houses. Said to be "probably the most beautiful room of its kind in America," the three-story chapel interior was designed by Davis, who also supervised the construction of the building after Dakin left the firm late in 1833.[4] Davis's beautifully rendered study for the chapel might easily be taken for a drawing of an actual late-fifteenth-century English chapel. The pendant-vaulted ceiling was inspired by the choir of Oxford Cathedral. Except for George Templeton Strong, always a harsh critic, contemporary reviewers were enthusiastic. The great west window illuminating the chapel was widely admired. But Strong considered the "bright blue ceiling with big gold stars and the arms of the U.S. and likewise those of the university . . . rather out of place in a room that calls itself Gothic."[5]

The financial crash of 1837 hurt the struggling young University; from the beginning many rooms in the new building had to be rented out. A. J. Davis was among the first of many distinguished artist and architect tenants. The congregation of the South Dutch Reformed Church, whose minister, Rev. James M. Mathews, was University chancellor from 1831 to 1839, rented the chapel for several years before its new building was completed on the next corner. Another financial panic struck in 1873, and in 1874 the University subdivided the chapel into small rooms for rental. At the time of

· · · ·

its demolition in 1894, the University Building was badly in need of renovation and repair.

While the University Building was under construction, a Gothic Revival church also designed by Dakin was built nearby. This was the Mercer Street Presbyterian Church (1834–1835), later the Church of the Strangers, on the west side of Mercer between Waverly Place and Eighth Street. Built of stone laid in random fashion, the church had Gothic features similar to those of the University Building. Dakin probably had to exercise restraint in his use of Gothic detail, which may account for the building's extreme simplicity inside and out; at this time, some Protestant groups were still wary of the Gothic because of its Roman Catholic associations. The practical, squarish plan and boxlike proportions of Dakin's church identify it as still belonging to the early phase of the Gothic Revival.

If the Mercer Street Church (now demolished), the Church of the Ascension (1840–1841) by Richard Upjohn (1802–1878), and James Renwick, Jr.'s, still-later Grace Church (1843–1846) are compared, the evolution of the Gothic Revival is readily apparent—and so also are the differences in denominational preferences. All three are modeled on the type of the English parish church, but the two Episcopal churches, particularly Grace, are closer to the model and more sophisticated in concept than is Dakin's church.

Two other frontal-tower type churches built nearby also deserve mention. These are the brownstone First Presbyterian Church (1844–1846), designed by James C. Wells (d. 1860), and the demolished University Place Presbyterian Church (ca. 1845) by Upjohn. Wells's church, which is on Fifth Avenue between Eleventh and Twelfth streets, just a block north of the Church of the Ascension, reverts to the simplicity of Dakin's church. It may have been modeled on St. Saviour's (1829–1832) in Bath, England, an early Gothic Revival church; and beyond that, its tower was inspired by the famous late-fifteenth-century bell tower of Oxford's Magdalen College. For the University Place Church, Upjohn seems deliberately to have contrived a less correct Gothic than that of either the Church of the Ascension or his Trinity Church (1839–1846) downtown. But Wells and Upjohn were both English-born, so they may have looked to the early Gothic Revival as a way of distinguishing their Presbyterian churches from contemporary churches of the Episcopal denomination.

The congregation of the South Dutch Reformed Church engaged Minard Lafever to design its new building (1839–1840). The twin-towered church, Lafever's earliest-known Gothic Revival work, may have owed some of its inspiration to Brady's St. Thomas's Church, but a marked shift toward a more accurate Gothic style is evident. Lafever's sources have been identified as the Scottish Presbyterian Church (1824–1827) on Regent Square in London and the medieval York Cathedral.

The towers of the South Dutch Reformed Church were surely intended

32. Grace Church, on the east side of Broadway at Tenth Street *(Museum of the City of New York)*

to complement those of the University Building; together the two buildings contributed a romantic, picturesque skyline to the east side of the Square. Coloristically, however, the church's dark, rough-cut granite walls trimmed in reddish stone contrasted with the light marble walls of the earlier building. (Lafever was perhaps unwilling to sacrifice correctness for harmony.) In 1876, the South Dutch Reformed Church was sold to the Asbury Methodist Episcopal Church. In 1893 that congregation merged with the Washington Square Church, and in 1895 the old Dutch church was demolished.

Grace Church, despite the fact that its white limestone walls and plaster vaults were much criticized in the 1850s, is a masterpiece of the mature Gothic Revival. The building was purposely sited at a bend in Broadway at Tenth Street so that its graceful tower could be viewed from a distance. The original wooden spire was replaced by the present richly ornamented marble spire in 1883. Although Grace is not based on a particular English church and its ornament is a mixture of English and French Gothic rather than pure English, the whole effect is that of a jewel-like, fourteenth-century English parish church miraculously transported to New York. James Renwick, Jr. (1818–1895), won the commission, his first building, at the age of twenty-three. The fact that his mother was the sister of Henry J. Brevoort, Jr., surely helped him get the job, for the church is built on land purchased from the Brevoort estate in 1843. The young Renwick was clearly an excellent choice. The success of Grace led to his appointment later as architect of St. Patrick's Cathedral (1858–1879). Over the years Renwick and his firm created a harmonious setting for Grace. They added several compatibly styled, light stone buildings to its grounds as well as a Gothic backdrop, the recently renovated loft building on the north side.

• • • • •

Fortunately, many of the stately Greek Revival row houses built on Washington Square North are still with us today and are preserved in excellent condition. But with the razing of the old University Building in 1894 and the South Dutch Reformed Church a year later, the Gothic Revival disappeared from the Square. For a while the University had seriously contemplated moving the old University Building up to its proposed University Heights campus, whose first portion was purchased in 1891, and even tried to raise money for the purpose. McKim, Mead & White, the University Heights campus architects, made a drawing showing the reconstructed building at the center of the new campus flanked by complementary new buildings. But on June 5, 1893, the trustees decided that the cost of reerecting the building, estimated to be at least $250,000, was too high and that the same money would be better spent on the construction of four or five new buildings on its uptown campus. Demolition began on May 21, 1894.

• • • •

However, the University did not sell its land or vacate the Square. At first the trustees considered leasing the site and renting space in the new building that the lessee would erect on the property. Stanford White was asked to prepare a plan and may indeed have done so, because his firm, McKim, Mead & White, submitted a proposal for the new building in September 1892. Then the University apparently decided not to lease the land but instead to build its own new loft building and rent part of it to a commercial tenant. On February 5, 1894, the trustees agreed to accept the American Book Company as a long-term tenant;[6] and, at the same meeting, Chancellor Henry M. McCracken read a letter from Alfred Zucker (1852–?) presenting an estimate for a ten-story, fireproof building. Zucker, a German emigrant, was probably brought in by the American Book Company. He was an expert in the design and construction of commercial buildings and had designed many near Washington Square and below Houston Street. The University trustees accepted his design for Main Building (1894–1895) on March 12, 1894. In the next century, in need of more space on the Square, the University acquired or leased several Zucker-designed commercial buildings, among them the present Kimball Hall (1891–1892), East

33. Main Building, New York University, rendering by Alfred Zucker (*New York University Archives*)

Building (1892–1893), 19 University Place (1895–1896), and Shimkin Hall (1896–1897). Largely by chance Zucker succeeded Dakin as New York University's Washington Square architect.

Main Building's light-colored stone, brick, and terra-cotta-trimmed exterior may have been designed to correspond with McKim, Mead & White's new classically styled buildings on University Heights. A new, academic classicism inspired by the colonnaded white facades of the 1893 Chicago World's Fair buildings had come into fashion just in time to influence Zucker's conception. Stanford White's Washington Arch had already established the new classicism on the Square, and McKim, Mead & White were the leaders of the movement, so it is not at all surprising that Main Building follows their example. Zucker was also inspired by the Grecian elements of the houses on Washington Square North. The tripartite design of Main, like that of other commercial buildings of the time, was intended to suggest the three parts of the classical column—base, shaft, and capital—and also to reflect the mixed uses of the building. The top three floors, where the University had its quarters, form an Ionic temple, which originally carried the University's motto: "Perstando et Praestando Utilitati" (Striving and Excelling in Useful Pursuits). The five-story "shaft" that served as commercial space is suitably plain and businesslike. The combined first and second stories form a base embellished by the sturdy Doric order, which corresponds to the columns of The Row. On the Waverly Place side, the University's entrance (now altered) took the form of a double-storied temple, Ionic over Doric, reinforcing the symbolism of the top three floors. Unexpectedly, the Greek Revival had returned to the Square in the form of a ten-story loft building.

· · · · ·

NOTES

The author wishes to thank Jane B. Davies for generously providing information and criticism.

1. Thomson may have been acting as agent for the University. According to deeds on file in the Surrogate's Court, he purchased the land in three transactions, which took place in the fall of 1832. The sellers were the Second Associate Reformed Church and the Scotch Presbyterian Church, of which Thomson was a member, and the total cost to Thomson was $33,005. By September 27, 1832, Thomson had entered into negotiations with the University. The University paid him $40,000 and took title on November 26, 1832.

2. Henry-Russell Hitchcock, *Architecture: Nineteenth and Twentieth Centuries* (Harmondsworth, England: Penguin Books Ltd., 1987), 137.

· · · ·

3. Theodore S. Fay, *Views in New-York and Its Environs from Accurate, Characteristic & Picturesque Drawings* . . . (New York/London: Peabody and Company, 1831), 46.
4. *Francis's New Guide to the Cities of New-York and Brooklyn and the Vicinity* (New York: C. S. Francis & Co., 1854), 44.
5. Allan Nevins and Milton Halsey Thomas, eds., *The Diary of George Templeton Strong* (New York: Macmillan Co., 1952), 1:66.
6. The American Book Company occupied space in the building until May 1927.

· · · · ·

SELECTED BIBLIOGRAPHY

Brown, Henry Collins, ed. *Valentine's Manual of the City of New York, 1917–1918.* New York, 1917–1918.

Fowler, Dorothy Ganfield. *A City Church: The First Presbyterian Church in the City of New York, 1716–1976.* New York, 1981.

Hamlin, Talbot. *Greek Revival Architecture in America.* Oxford, 1944; reprint, New York, 1964.

Jones, Theodore Francis, ed. *New York University, 1832–1932.* New York, 1933.

King, Moses, ed. *King's Handbook of New York City.* Boston, 1892.

Kouwenhoven, John A. *The Columbia Historical Portrait of New York.* New York, 1953; reprint (with a new preface), New York, 1972.

Landau, Sarah Bradford. "Alfred Zucker, N.Y.U.'s Accidental Architect." *University: Academic Affairs at New York University* 7:2 (February 1988): 7–8.

Landy, Jacob. *The Architecture of Minard Lafever.* New York/London, 1970.

New York American. May 27, 1837 (description of the University building).

New York City Common Council. *Manual of the Corporation of New York* (1850–1870).

New York City Landmarks Preservation Commission. 2 vols. *Greenwich Village Historic District Designation Report.* New York, 1969.

New York Times. "New University Building." July 1, 1894, p. 8, col. 1.

New York University Archives. Building Committee Minutes (1833–1838); Buildings File; McCracken Papers; Minutes of the Board of Trustees (1892–1894); Minutes of the Council (1830–1834).

Pierson, William H., Jr. *American Buildings and Their Architects: Technology and the Picturesque.* New York, 1978.

Sailors' Snug Harbor Records, Library of State University of New York Maritime College.

Scully, Arthur, Jr. *James Dakin, Architect: His Career in New York and the South.* Baton Rouge, La., 1973.

Shepherd, Barnett. "Sailors' Snug Harbor Reattributed to Minard Lafever." *Journal of the Society of Architectural Historians* 35 (May 1976): 108–123.

Stanton, Phoebe B. *The Gothic Revival and American Church Architecture: An Episode in Taste, 1840–1856.* Baltimore, 1968.

Stewart, William Rhinelander. *Grace Church and Old New York.* New York, 1924.

· · · ·

WASHINGTON ARCH AND THE CHANGING NEIGHBORHOOD

Mindy Cantor

New York celebrated the two hundredth anniversary of George Washington's inauguration on April 30, 1989, with a flurry of festivities and patriotic pageantry. The centerpiece of the 1989 commemorative was the dramatization of Washington taking his oath of office at Federal Hall. Arriving at noon by horse-drawn carriage, the Washington impersonator was greeted by twenty-six costumed delegates from the original thirteen states and an array of dignitaries that included President George Bush. To conclude the pomp and circumstance, a parade with marching bands and marchers with placards bearing the likeness of each president proceeded up lower Broadway to Washington Square Park and the Washington Arch.

One hundred years earlier the centennial celebration of Washington's inauguration was no less flamboyant and ceremonial for its time. President Benjamin Harrison presided over a three-day extravaganza that included a gala parade that lasted two days. A temporary triumphal arch was erected for the parade, spanning Fifth Avenue about one hundred feet north of Washington Square between the residences of the Hon. Edward Cooper, former mayor of the city, and the Misses Rhinelander. William Rhinelander Stewart, who lived at 17 Washington Square North, had collected $2,756

• • • •

83

in funds from the residents of the neighborhood to erect the arch; Stanford White, of the architectural firm of McKim, Mead & White, had been commissioned to design it. The arch was built of wood and ornamented with a frieze of garlands and wreaths of laurels in papier-mâché. At night it was brilliantly illuminated by Edison's incandescent electric light, generated by a makeshift dynamo. On the jubilant day of the parade, April 30, 1889, a procession passed under the arch up Fifth Avenue to Fifty-ninth Street. The temporary arch was a great success, and praise was given to the residents of the neighborhood, who were said to have set a rare and worthy example of public spirit and patriotism.

A special committee, made up of William R. Stewart, Henry G. Marquand, Richard Morris Hunt, Richard Gilder, and others, was then formed for the purpose of erecting a permanent arch. Stanford White again designed the memorial. The architect intended the classical style of the arch to be distinctly Roman rather than reflective of the Italian Renaissance classicism that had been the popular style for upper-class New York homes since about the 1870s and that was regarded by White as "less robust and more fanciful." Even more, the Roman classic style of the arch embodied George Washington himself, who was said to have been a reincarnation of Roman Republican heroes.

The laying of the cornerstone on Decoration Day, May 30, 1890, was an impressive ceremony, conducted in accordance with Masonic ritual by the Grand Lodge. A copper box containing coins, medals, newspapers, and articles relating to the committee and the arch was placed in the cornerstone. The last block of marble was set on April 5, 1892, in a more informal ceremony, when a group of men, scaling ladders, assembled on the arch's roof. By June 1892, $128,000 for the completion of the arch had been raised by subscriptions from private citizens.

Set at the edge of Washington Square Park, across the street from where the temporary arch had been, Washington Arch is built of white marble from the quarries of Tuckahoe. Two marble eagles are perched on the keystones, and on the west pier there is a staircase of 110 steps. The trophy panels on the south front were carved in the autumn of 1892; those on the north front, in February 1893. The figures on the victory panels, War and Peace, were finished in February 1895. The inscription on the north facade reads: "To commemorate the One Hundredth Anniversary of the Inauguration of George Washington as first President of the United States." On the south facade is Washington's quote: "Let us raise a standard to which the wise and the honest can repair—the event is in the hands of God."

Huge crowds witnessed the dedication of Washington Arch on May 4, 1895. An imposing military pageant escorted the governor down Fifth Avenue to the Square: "marching regiments and blaring bands, ringing speeches and cheering crowds, high officials and glittering escorts."[1] Why was the event commemorating the centennial of George Washington and

34. Washington Arch with a view up Fifth Avenue, about 1900 (*Museum of the City of New York*)

the building of the Washington Arch marked with such fervor and ceremony over a period of six years? A speech given by Henry G. Marquand, chairman of the Washington Arch Memorial committee, at the ceremony for the laying of the cornerstone of May 30, 1890, provides a clue:

> The spot has been aptly chosen, and not a valid objection can be urged against it. It is true someone has remarked that the neighborhood in a

• • • •

few years will be all tenement houses. Even should this prove true, no stronger reason could be given for the Arch being placed there. Have the occupants of tenement houses no sense of beauty? Have they no patriotism? Have they no right to good architecture? Happily there is no monopoly of the appreciation of things that are excellent any more than there is of fresh air, and in our mind's eye we can see many a family who cannot afford to spend ten cents to go to the park, taking great pleasure under the shadow of the Arch. This is the Arch of peace and good-will to men. It will bring the rich and the poor together in one common bond of patriotic feeling.[2]

Washington Square in the nineteenth century was known as the "American ward," the part of New York that was a liberal model of cleanliness, good citizenship, and self-respect.[3] It was a neighborhood concerned with its patriotic duties and responsibilities to a growing city and nation. Developed in the 1830s with elegant Greek Revival homes, the Washington Square neighborhood had been the first fashionable residential area in New York and expressed a rising American nationalism and conservative middle-class taste. The east side of Washington Square North, known as The Row, was a unique example of community planning.

Greek Revival was also an economical style that could be adapted to both the wealthy houses on the Square and the less elaborate residences on Washington and Waverly places. This architectural style—classical columns, symmetrical alignment, and smooth, clean surfaces—created a dignified, graceful streetscape that expressed order, harmony, and simplicity. But by 1890 the order, simplicity, and harmony of the neighborhood had all but disappeared, and in their place were change, tension, and disharmony.

Until 1875 there was only a sprinkling of French, Italian, and Irish immigrants in the neighborhood. Toward the end of the century, however, the erection of tenements to the southeast and along the waterfront began to affect the Washington Square area.[4] Since the 1860s and 1870s, fashionable Bond, Lafayette, Great Jones, and Bleecker streets had lost their distinguished residential character. The difficulties of adjustment by growing immigrant populations, widespread poverty, and crime all took their toll on the Square. Breadlines formed at the once-fashionable Vienna Bakery next door to the ornate Gothic Grace Church at the crook of Broadway and Tenth Street. For ten cents a night, a homeless soul could get shelter and sleep in Mill House at 1 Bleecker Street.

Besides the rise of tenements to house the swelling number of immigrants close to the Square, another building type brought changes to the neighborhood. On the side streets near the University Building on Washington and Waverly places, West Fourth Street, and elsewhere, commercial buildings replaced the rows of Greek Revival houses. Made possible by the technological innovation of metal vertical supports, the typical commercial building provided large open spaces for stores, offices, and factories. By the

1870s, to the east and south of the Gothic University Building, a developing commercial and wholesale district of loft buildings brought workers and tradespeople to the area.[5] By the beginning of the twentieth century, these buildings were used for the manufacture of blouses, hats, and other fineries.

Much of the residential character of the south side of the Square was lost to little shops and cafés that catered to the bohemian community of artists and writers and the tenement population around Bleecker Street.[6] The old, Federal-style houses were deteriorating, and many of them became boarding-houses. Five-story apartment hotels were built on the west and southwest side of the Square. Only a few fine houses remained on the west side.

Washington Square Park opened as a military parade ground in 1828 and was used for that purpose until 1851. In 1852 a fountain (not the present one) was built in the center of the park with two thousand dollars appropriated by the Common Council of New York. The fountain was paved in brick, given a stone rim, and surrounded by an iron railing. Originally the park had been laid out in four quadrangles with four diagonal paths leading to the center where the new fountain was eventually built.[7] By 1870 the concern in New York was to provide picturesque open spaces that would give relief to the city's congestion and industrialization. In 1871 Washington Square Park was redesigned. M. A. Kellogg, the engineering chief, and I. A. Pillat, an assistant to the renowned landscape architect Frederick Olmsted, adapted Olmstedian principles when designing a more picturesque park with curvilinear plots of grass and paths, flowers, and shade trees. Scores of benches were provided, which in the 1880s were generally occupied by immigrants from nearby tenements.

Meanwhile the elegant and fashionable neighborhood of Washington Square was rapidly becoming, as Henry James said of his birthplace, a "reference to a pleasanter, easier and hazier past."[8] The old Knickerbocker families who occupied the brick and marble-trimmed houses on Washington Square North, steadfast to traditional values and bolstered by the continued richness of the eclectically styled houses on lower Fifth Avenue, struggled to maintain an air of dignified harmony. In this context the building of the arch by the residents of the neighborhood and its dedication in the spirit of liberalism and patriotism on May 30, 1890, may be viewed as a symbolic, if deeply ambiguous, gesture.

Insofar as it alluded to the grandeur of classical Rome, the arch reinforced the dignity and continuity of the Greek Revival homes and their owners on the north side of the Square. Yet in its monumental defensiveness and isolation at the edge of the park, the arch bears witness to the decline and tensions of the Square. Henry James called the arch "the lamentable little Arch of Triumph which bestrides these beginnings of Washington Square—lamentable because of its poor and lonely and unsupported and unaffiliated state."[9] Henry Marquand's address at the dedication ceremony may thus be seen as a patriotic gesture to the poor that at the same time betrayed his own and his neighbors' feelings of anxiety that the north side of the Square might be threatened with tenement houses in the near future.

As Washington Arch was being built on the north side of the Square, another memorial was under construction on the south side. Edward Judson, pastor of the Berean Baptist Church on Bedford and Downing streets since about 1880, and friend to such luminaries as Stanford White, John D. Rockefeller, and the Astors, wanted to build a church to commemorate the one hundredth anniversary of his father's birth. Adoniram Judson had been the first American foreign missionary to bring Christianity to Burma. The younger Judson wanted a massive and beautiful church to be situated in Lower New York "where the foreign nationalities, as they jostle each other, when they ask: 'What mean these stones?' may be informed that they commemorate the first American who carried the message of the Gospel to foreign parts."[10] Judson also intended his church to be on the borderline between the rich and the poor, to be expressive of the truth, to provide perpetually free seats and to be owned in such a way that it could never be mortgaged.

The southwest corner of Washington Square and Thompson Street— 130 feet wide and 100 feet deep—proved in 1886 to be the exact site for such a memorial.[11] Edward Judson felt the site for the new church was in a strategic position. It was close to a large tenement population and also "within reach of a most respectable and aristocratic neighborhood, from which it is hoped many will come to engage personally in Mission work."[12] As well as building a monumental church edifice, Edward Judson wanted to do "aggressive" missionary work in the area. His concern over the years was the relation of the church to the masses of people who were filling the lower portions of the city and determining the character of "our social and municipal life." He specifically wanted to attract the many Italians living around the Square. Since the 1880s Italians from southern Italy had been coming to New York in great numbers. Enrico Sartorio, an Italian Episcopal minister, claimed the Italians were going wild in America because they were out of reach of the clergy.[13] Judson wanted to reach the Italians with a library, gymnasium, a children's home, and "all the appliances needed in order to teach them to do good in lower New York."[14]

The old Baptist church was sold, and Judson raised funds all over the country: John D. Rockefeller contributed substantial sums of money. In 1890, the same year as the cornerstone ceremony for Washington Arch, a similar ceremony was held for Judson Memorial Church. Stanford White, the architect of Washington Arch, received the commission. His design called for a Romanesque church, strongly influenced by what White called an early basilica treatment. In actuality the church is more an early Italian Renaissance design than Romanesque. Just as White intended Washington Arch to refer to Roman classicism rather than the Renaissance, so he probably wanted the church to recall Roman construction. The brick and terra-

· · · ·

cotta design along with the small round-arched windows and geometric discs on the pediment make for a richly ornamented and impressive facade. Romanesque churches constructed of brick or stone with small round-arched windows were built all over Europe in the eleventh and twelfth centuries, during the time of the Crusades and Christian revival. Although in the twentieth century this building style has come to represent a period of tension and transition, it is more likely that Stanford White was interested in creating a classical Roman scene that could be seen through the arch and a church edifice that would be highly dramatic for a Baptist church. The Judson Hotel, a campanile, or bell tower, next to the church built layer by layer as money was raised, was to generate revenue by providing young men with furnished rooms and board.

While a monumental church was adorning the south side of the Square, the white-castellated Gothic University Building on the east side had become quite run down. Its decay and the deterioration of the neighborhood immediately to the east led New York University to decide in 1892 to retain McKim, Mead & White to design a new campus in the Bronx. Rather than abandon the site on the Square altogether, the University Council made the decision to replace the old Gothic building with a modern commercial structure (see Landau essay). The first seven floors of the new building were rented to the American Book Company, while New York University retained the top three floors for the professional schools of law and pedagogy.

The South Dutch Reformed Church, across the street from the original University Building at Washington Place East, was demolished in 1895 and replaced by the Celluloid Building, a typical commercial building with large arches atop the facade. The Benedick, studio apartments built in 1879, stood next door at 80 Washington Square East. Designed by McKim, Mead & Bigelow (the last was a partner from 1877 to 1879), the five-story redbrick building featured handsome bay windows, shops on the ground floor on either side of the central entrance, and the apartments themselves, which were intended as residences for single artists. In 1884 the home at 3 Washington Square North was converted into flats for artists, breaking the uniformity of The Row by the addition of another story. Thus, by 1895 the Square had undergone many changes, with the east and south sides retaining little or nothing of their original characters.

The Washington Square area lost its significance as a fashionable neighborhood as the city moved northward to horizontal residential palaces and vertical commercial empires. Although the area below Fourteenth Street was now considered largely beyond the social pale, the people who chose to remain kept up the spirit in which Washington Square had been founded. In the 1830s these well-to-do first families had carefully developed a structure of moral values and urban manners that were in keeping with the rising democratic spirit of Jacksonian America. Their Greek Revival houses provided the appropriate setting for and represented the harmony, dignity, and

• • • •

clarity they sought in the growing urban society. While the powerful mercantile magnates had now moved uptown, the second generation of upperclass residents around the Square upheld their moral responsibilities of service and duty, and above all their commitment to their conception of dignity and graciousness of character. They did this despite their anxiety that the immigrant population might infringe too closely on their personal lives. The second generation's social idealism and psychological repression were channeled into an intensification of missionary work.

Since their beginnings the churches in the area had always done a great deal of missionary work. The Presbyterian Church on University Place, which in 1918 merged with the First Presbyterian Church on Fifth Avenue and Twelfth Street, was founded in 1843 with an emphasis on missions for immigrants. George Griswold and James Boorman, wealthy men who lived on Washington Square North, were among its founders.[15] By 1889 a permanent home was found for the Bethlehem Mission at 196 Bleecker Street, with fifty thousand dollars subscribed to it by members of the church. In the 1890s the population around the mission became heavily Italian. Only about 3 percent of them were Protestant, but many, although baptized in the Roman Catholic faith, were without a church affiliation.[16] Bethlehem worked with this growing group of immigrants, and beginning in 1899, services were held for them in Italian.

The Church of the Ascension, at Tenth Street and Fifth Avenue, too, felt the need for increased missionary work. In a sermon given on Palm Sunday, April 2, 1882, Mr. Donald, rector of the church, said that the true glory of the church was to consecrate its present life and powers to the tasks that were growing out of new conditions. The Church of the Ascension moved to "preach the gospel to the poor; . . . to heal the brokenhearted; and . . . to set at liberty them that are bruised."[17] In 1895 the church removed the pew-owning barrier, making everyone welcome to worship. Grace Church, the fashionable Gothic structure designed by James Renwick, also initiated free pews at Sunday evening services, and in her will, Miss Catherine Lorillard Wolfe bequeathed $350,000 in the hope that Grace would become a free church.

Rather than changing addresses by moving uptown, these wealthy people remained around the Square, did their missionary work, and beautified their churches. Stanford White, Augustus Saint-Gaudens, and John La Farge, three friends who had close associations with the Washington Square neighborhood, were responsible for the changes made in the Church of the Ascension. White, who was born on Washington Place and whose father was a graduate of New York University, designed and supervised the work that was done on the chancel in 1888. La Farge, who lived in the Tenth Street Studios until his death in 1910 and whose father owned the La Farge House on Broadway, painted the famous mural of the *Ascension* above the chancel wall. Saint-Gaudens sculpted the angel figures below the

Ascension. At Grace Church, Catherine Lorillard Wolfe was the bene-factress for many of the improvements and additions during the years 1877–1883.[18] In 1894 La Farge and his partner, the Philadelphia-born George Louis Heins, built an extension to accommodate the Grace Church choir's school, New York's first.

The Gothic churches around Washington Square are today very much the same as they were in the 1890s, giving the neighborhood both conti-nuity and beauty. Washington Square, too, retains something of the unique character it had in the 1830s as well as reflecting the changes it underwent later in the century. The University has occupied all floors of its main building since 1927, and since the 1960s has taken over and adapted the commercial buildings around the Square to the requirements of higher edu-cation. Its campus is the neighborhood around the Square, which provides a potpourri of ethnic and artistic life for its students.

The facades of the Greek Revival houses on Washington Square North look just about the way they did in the nineteenth century; their interiors, however, have been converted to University offices and apartments. The south side, always vulnerable, has become home in the twentieth century to New York University's law school, student center, and library. The Elmer Holmes Bobst Library, a monumental structure designed by Philip Johnson in 1972, looms large over the Square, a modern, red sandstone, twelve-story cube. The west side of the Square maintains fine residential apartment houses, built in the 1920s, which replaced the five-story houses of the late nineteenth century.

Nevertheless the rapid expansion of New York University has not oblit-erated the past on Washington Square. The Greek Revival houses (or at least their facades), Judson Memorial Church, and Washington Arch still convey a reference to the ideals of the nineteenth-century neighborhood. It was thus fitting that the 1989 celebration honoring the bicentennial anni-versary of George Washington's inauguration ended at Washington Square. The dark, damp gloom of that Sunday turned magically into warm, bril-liant sunshine. Once again, for a few hours, Washington Square Park was a parade ground and the showpiece of New York City.

• • • • •

NOTES

1. *The History of the Washington Arch in Washington Square, New York* (New York: Ford and Garnett Publishers, 1896), 35.
2. Ibid., 40.

• • • •

3. Caroline F. Ware, *Greenwich Village 1920–1930* (Boston: Houghton Mifflin Company, 1935), 11.
4. Ibid.
5. Carol Herselle Krinsky, "150 Years of N.Y.U. Buildings," *New York University Education Quarterly* 12:3 (Spring 1981): 22–23.
6. I am indebted to Sarah Bradford Landau for this information.
7. Courtesy Heather Spoen, landscape architect, Parks Department, Flushing Meadow, N.Y.
8. Henry James, *The American Scene* (Bloomington/London: Indiana University Press, 1968), 87.
9. Ibid., 90.
10. Discussions with Arlene Carmine, archivist, Judson Memorial Church, including fund-raising letter from Edward Judson.
11. Ibid.
12. Ibid.
13. Enrico Sartorio, *Social and Religious Life of Italians in America* (Boston: Christopher Publishing House, 1981).
14. Judson Memorial Church, discussions.
15. Dorothy Ganfield Fowler, *A City Church, The First Presbyterian Church in the City of New York, 1716–1976* (New York: First Presbyterian Church in the City of New York, 1981), 102.
16. Ibid., 117–119.
17. James W. Kennedy, *The Unknown Worshipper* (New York: Morehouse-Barlow Co., Publishers, for the Church of the Ascension, New York City, 1964), 57–58.
18. William Rhinelander Stewart, *Grace Church and Old New York* (New York: E. P. Dutton & Company, 1924).

"BOURGEOISIE AND BOHEMIANS"
VILLAGE PEOPLES

Village Populations

"Greenwich Village" actually refers to three communities that evolved over the first half of the nineteenth century. The oldest, the West Village, was home to middle-class merchants and artisans who capitalized on the trading advantages of its proximity to the Hudson River. Beginning in 1820, the uniform blocks laid out near Broadway to the east, and the ensemble rows planned along Lafayette and Bleecker streets, emerged as residential enclaves for the affluent. Simultaneously Washington Square became the preserve of patrician New York, titled "the American ward" in recognition of its small foreign-born population.

As the new century approached, a variety of economic and demographic changes conspired to strip the Village of its dignified image. By the 1890s the district's housing stock had grown dilapidated. Slum tenements, drab manufactories, and brothels encroached the side streets running to the south and east of Washington Square, and per capita income plummeted, prompting nervous property owners and businesses to abandon the area. The newly arrived waves of Irish, German, and Italian immigrants took shelter in the boardinghouses and hastily partitioned flats that materialized in the homes vacated by the alarmed gentry.

The tolerance fostered by the Village's new ethnic diversity, the abundance of modest lodgings, and the privacy of the neighborhood's secluded alleys and culs-de-sac created an appealing climate to those at odds with mainstream society. Before 1900 pockets of bohemian activity had flourished intermittently in the Village, but it was the dawn of the twentieth century that ushered in a rootbound colony of bohemian rebels. It should not be forgotten, however, that this colony, despite its historical celebrity, never represented more than a tiny fraction of the Village's residential population.

35. Washington Square North As the twentieth century approached, the stately row of redbrick, high-stooped town houses defining the north side of Washington Square North remained the fortress of such venerable families as the Rhinelanders, Stewarts, Delanos, Van Rensselaers, and Joneses. *Harper's Magazine* in 1893 praised the persistence of "cleanliness, good citizenship, and self-respect" in this precinct of New York, captured that same year in this oil by Fernand Lungren. *(Collection of Hirschl & Adler Galleries, Inc., New York City)*

36. Immigrant children at Greenwich House Established in 1902 in modest quarters on Jones Street, the Village's first settlement house brought much needed social services. From the outset, Greenwich House dedicated its activities to helping immigrant families adjust to and improve their lives. Its staff, composed largely of middle-class female college graduates, appealed to this constituency by offering vocational training, free health and child-care clinics, and an array of educational and recreational programs. *(Greenwich House Papers, Tamiment Institute Library, New York University)*

37. Baby-feeding-clinic registration at Greenwich House By 1917 Greenwich House had acquired an additional facility on Barrow Street in order to accommodate the 2,200 people who weekly utilized the settlement's expanding menu of services. *(Greenwich House Papers, Tamiment Institute Library, New York University)*

38. Gay Street Greenwich Village was home to a sizable portion of New York's African American population beginning before the Revolutionary War. A stable alley that evolved into a byway of modest rowhouses in the 1840s, Gay Street had long been tenanted by black families, many employed as servants for the gentry of Washington Square. Prior to the Civil War, approximately a quarter of New York's black population lived in the vibrant ghetto known as "Little Africa," situated in the vicinity of Bleecker, Thompson, Sullivan, and MacDougal streets. *(The Schlesinger Library, Radcliffe College)*

39. Black-and-tan dive, Thompson Street Among Jacob Riis's recurrent photographic subjects were the "vile rookeries of Thompson Street and South Fifth Avenue" where the "old Africa (was) fast becoming a modern Italy." Emerging in the 1850s, the area southeast of Washington Square, known as Frenchtown, harbored the highest concentration of brothels, dance halls, and rough bars in the city. The so-called black-and-tan dives of Thompson and Sullivan streets were particularly notorious. *(Museum of the City of New York)*

40. Fleischmann's Model Vienna Bakery By day this fashionable bakery, located on the northeast corner of Broadway and Tenth Street, sold shoppers sweet rolls and aromatic coffees. In the evening its proprietors distributed unsold pastries to the poor, a nightly ritual that gave popular currency to the term *breadline*. *(Courtesy of The New-York Historical Society, N.Y.C.)*

41. MacDougal Alley In the early twentieth century, artists began to move into livery facilities out-moded by the advent of the automobile. MacDougal Alley, tucked behind Washington Square North, was nicknamed "Art Alley de Luxe" and was home to fashionable studio tenants such as the society sculptor and collector Gertrude Vanderbilt Whitney as well as painter Edwin W. Deming, whose young daughters are pictured here outside his studio. *(The Schlesinger Library, Radcliffe College)*

42. Revelers at the Kit Kat Ball in 1924 A variety of Village organizations founded in the teens seized upon costume balls as fund-raising vehicles that also promised some rowdy fun to all who attended. The element of disguise, which afforded anonymity to anyone who might revel to excess, led to imaginative theme costumes as well as skimpy outfits that on occasion included body paint. Indian loincloths and Roman togas were a sartorial mainstay because bedsheets were easily fashioned into such costumes at minimal cost. *(Delaware Art Museum, Wilmington, John Sloan Archives, Helen Farr Sloan Library)*

43. Domestic life on Bleecker Street Local development trends after World War I loosened the bohemian grip on Greenwich Village, luring a "more circumspect type of resident" for whom apartment houses with doormen, elevators, and other modern amenities held considerable appeal. By the 1930s the sight of bourgeois babies on Bleecker Street, once headquarters to the bohemian rag-tag, confirmed a new cycle of gentrification. *(Museum of the City of New York)*

· · · ·

Village Dramatis Personae

The emergence of Greenwich Village as a bohemian haven is commonly attributed to the district's allure for disaffected youth fleeing their small-town, middle-class origins. It is also true that the Village drew conscripts from Manhattan and other metropolitan areas in the United States as well as abroad. This pool of arrivals encompassed wide variations in age, social and economic background, and artistic aspiration. What gave these individuals a tribal identity was their perception of themselves as a generational movement. Although their points of entry into the community varied and their ideologies were often riddled with inconsistencies, they shared a contempt for conventional morality and modern materialism, and advocated radical change as the prerequisite to redeeming society from its corrupt and joyless condition.

During the mid-teens, a new breed of Villager made an appearance: the self-invented "character" or poseur who exploited the district's publicity as a seedbed of eccentricity by acting accordingly, often for a price. In conduct and concerns, this group contrasted sharply with the issue-oriented generation that had preceded them. Although newer recruits to the bohemian colony were accused of importing this form of hucksterism, some of the veteran avant-garde also modified their public personalities to run with this theatrical flow. After 1917 the cult of unconventionality for its own sake steadily gained converts.

44. Mary Kingsbury Simkhovitch Inspired by Chicago's Hull-House, Mary Simkhovitch targeted the slum areas around Jones Street as a base of operations for Greenwich House. Well bred and college educated, she fitted the profile of the young, urban idealist attracted to settlement work at the turn of the century. As the head of Greenwich House, Simkhovitch devoted herself to serving the immigrant poor and was baffled by the excitement their rookeries generated among the neighborhood's bohemian newcomers: "It was . . . astounding to us who had fought against cellar lodgings as unhealthful, damp, and unfit for human habitation, to see them revived as 'one room studios' and let . . . at six times the price of former rentals." *(Greenwich House Papers, Tamiment Institute Library, New York University)*

45. John Reed Raised on the West Coast in middle-class comfort, John Reed attended Harvard and spent a brief postgraduate sojourn on the Left Bank before heading to Greenwich Village to pursue his dual interests in journalism and poetry. He fell in league with the radical *The Masses* magazine and proceeded to hurl himself into the political controversies of the day. While covering the Eastern Front as a correspondent during World War I, Reed became an active supporter of the Bolsheviks, deserting the "adolescent Utopia" of Greenwich Village to devote himself to the Russian Revolution. *(The National Portrait Gallery, Smithsonian Institution)*

46. Mabel Dodge On moving to New York in 1912, Mrs. Dodge quickly established one of the Village's most noted salons. While not an intellectual, an artist, or a bohemian, she was an adroit hostess whose evenings brought together a provocative cross-section of social classes and ideological camps. The influence of Dodge's soirées was relatively short-lived. After relocating to quarters on Washington Square with her new husband, Maurice Sterne, in 1916, Dodge tried but failed to repeat her earlier social success and soon thereafter moved to New Mexico. *(Yale Collection of American Literature, Beinecke Rare Book & Manuscript Library, Yale University)*

47. Max Eastman As a contributing critic, poet, and essayist, Eastman came to embody the articulate essence of *The Masses*, steering its editorial course from 1913 through 1917 and that of its successor, *The Liberator*, from 1918 until 1922. Although he blithely sampled the Village's permissive practices, he also fought for many progressive Village causes and protested the bohemian tomfoolery that obscured these campaigns. A socialist at the outset of his Village career, Eastman eased into Wilsonian liberalism during World War I, rebounded as a Communist partisan and Trotsky supporter during the 1920s, and culminated his political odyssey by renouncing Soviet Russia in the 1930s. *(Yvette Szekely Eastman from "Enjoyment of Living")*

48. John Sloan at work One of the most prominent of the Ashcan School painters, Sloan is shown here in his studio overlooking Washington Square, painting the constant parade of open-air buses passing through Washington Arch. *(Delaware Art Museum, Wilmington, John Sloan Archives, Helen Farr Sloan Library)*

• • • •

49. Gertrude Vanderbilt Whitney in her Eighth Street studio Heiress to a great family fortune, Whitney surprised many of her society acquaintances by establishing a studio outpost in a remodeled stable on MacDougal Alley in 1907. Whitney's comfortable atelier soon became an informal drop-in center and exhibition hall for the "new" American art. Although her own sculptural style was conservative, Whitney appreciated the more progressive trends. Her advocacy of contemporary art extended to her purchases of it, thereby creating the nucleus of the art collection consolidated into the museum she founded on West Eighth Street in 1931. *(Collection of Whitney Museum of American Art, Archives)*

50. Marguerite Zorach with her son Tessim Marguerite Zorach and her husband, William, exemplified the adventurous "new spirit" in the Village following the 1913 Armory Show. William investigated lithography, art editing, and teaching before turning his attention to sculpture. Marguerite applied her interest in fauvism's vibrant colors and free treatment of form to textile designs and other decorative arts media. Their cross-disciplinary curiosity also led them to design sets, posters, and playbills and to paint scenery, sew costumes, and occasionally perform for the Provincetown Players. They also contributed ideas, illustrations, and odd writings to local radical magazines. *(Private collection)*

51. Theodore Dreiser in his apartment at 16 St. Luke's Place Camping out in a flophouse on Bleecker Street after his arrival from the Midwest in 1895, Dreiser supported himself as a magazine editor while completing *Sister Carrie* (1900). Shortly after its appearance, pressure was placed on the publisher to withdraw the book because of its ambiguous moral viewpoint. In 1915 Dreiser's frank portrayal of the sexual alliances of a young midwestern painter who moves to the bohemian Village, the semiautobiographical hero of *The Genius*, led to a temporary ban on that book's sale. The incident not only became a battle cry for the Village literati but also bolstered the author's literary reputation and earnings. *(Department of Special Collections, University of Pennsylvania, Theodore Dreiser Collection)*

52. Edna St. Vincent Millay As the precocious author of "Renascence," this slender, red-haired beauty established a metaphor for the bohemian generation by comparing youth with the lovely light of a candle burning at both ends. As a member of the Village's bohemian fold, Millay acted, wrote poetry, and captivated a string of competing suitors through the early twenties. Married to Eugen Boissevain in 1923, the same year that she won the Pulitzer Prize for poetry, she proceeded to host lively literary evenings and participate in local dramatic ventures until the couple left Greenwich Village for the Berkshires. *(Museum of the City of New York)*

53. Jane Heap Same-sex relationships were treated with much greater tolerance in the Village than in mainstream Manhattan. Since eccentric dress and unconventional gender behavior were keynotes of bohemian culture, gay couples enjoyed considerable latitude in their life-style, often being mistaken for "normal" nonconformists. Prone to wearing male attire, Jane Heap, with her mate, Margaret Anderson, editor of the progressive *Little Review*, held a salon at their Village home that drew many prominent lesbians and homosexuals from the local art community. *(Special Collections, University of Maryland at College Park Libraries)*

54. Elsa von Freytag-Loringhoven A woman of uncertain antecedents, the Baroness von Freytag-Loringhoven left her husband, a wealthy German businessman, to pursue a career as a cubist painter and Dadaist poet in the Village. Although she did publish work in the *Little Review* and pose as a life model for local artists, her primary vocation was that of high priestess to the bohemian cult of freedom of dress and behavior. *(Smith-Girard, Stamford, Connecticut)*

55. Adele Kennedy By 1916 Village tour guides had begun to advertise their expertise at squiring sightseers through the byways of bohemia. Adele Kennedy, who moonlighted as a tearoom hostess, was among the most popular. She obliged the expectations of tour parties by wearing an artist's smock, tam-o'-shanter, and flatsoled sandals, weather permitting. Like many of her fellow guides, she was careful to maneuver clients into local shops owned by friends. *(Alexander Alland, Sr., Collection)*

56. Miss Crump A typically itinerant Village tearoom, the Crumperie shuttled back and forth between a half dozen different addresses on or near Sheridan Square during its existence. Run by Mary Alletta Crump and her aged mother, this particular establishment geared its trade to an artistic and theatrical clientele. *(Museum of the City of New York)*

57. Clara Tice A pupil of painter Robert Henri, seventeen-year-old Clara Tice first entered the Village limelight in 1914 when a show of her delicately eccentric nude drawings at Polly's Restaurant was confiscated by New York's Vice Squad on suspicion of their "barely suggested naughtiness." She quickly became a star in Guido Bruno's stable of exhibiting artists and executed the impressive peacock curtain for his Thimble Theatre. She went on to dabble in costume design, act with the *Greenwich Village Follies*, and recycle the whimsical artwork that had earned her notoriety as a teenager. *(Billy Rose Theatre Collection, The New York Public Library at Lincoln Center, Astor, Lenox, and Tilden Foundations)*

58. Romany Marie Marie Marchand, a native of Moldavia affectionately called "Romany Marie" by her customers, launched the first in a series of Village eateries in 1912. In her guise as bohemian restaurateur, Marie wore exotic gypsy clothing laden with jingling jewelry and cultivated a mysterious air that belied her simple peasant ancestry. Although some wryly noted the ripening of her Romanian accent as tourist traffic through her taverns increased, so convincing was Marie's performance that many patrons sampled her well-advertised skills at tealeaf reading and palmistry. *(Portrait by John Sloan, Collection of Whitney Museum of American Art, Gift of Gertrude Vanderbilt Whitney, by exchange, 51.40)*

THE WASHINGTON SQUARE NEIGHBORHOOD 1830–1855

Bayrd Still

One of the earliest visual representations of the Washington Square neighborhood is Otto Boetticher's 1851 painting of Washington Square Park as a military parade ground. Only the east and south sides of the Square are visible, but the row of four-story, redbrick structures flanking the southern border typifies the uniformity of the dwellings that, by the mid-1850s, surrounded three sides of the Square. On the fourth, or east, side are the castlelike white marble University Building and the similarly neo-Gothic edifice of the South Dutch Reformed Church. Separating the two is a glimpse of Washington Place East, revealing additional uniform, redbrick structures, which suggest the appearance of the streets leading into the Square.

The Washington Square neighborhood began in the early 1830s as an extension of a residential enclave of the city's elite, who, by the 1820s, had begun to move northward to escape the noise and congestion in the vicinity of City Hall Park and the tip of Manhattan, once the city's most select residential quarters. By the 1820s Bond, Great Jones, and Bleecker streets were being lined with fine houses, and a grand Lafayette Place, to open in 1825, was in the planning stage.

As early as 1828 some houses had been built as far north as Fourth Street, which was to become the south side of the Square; but what really triggered

· · · ·
111

the development of a residential neighborhood focusing on Washington Square was the conversion, between 1826 and 1828, of what had been a potter's field (some 22,000 bodies had been interred there by 1826) into a military parade ground. Unattractive for residential use because of its subterranean occupancy, this open space nevertheless encouraged residential development of the surrounding area. The owners of farms and estates north of the parade ground now hastened to divide their properties into lots suitable for houses, and before long the Washington Square neighborhood was in the making. This neighborhood might be said to have included not only the streets abutting the parade ground and portions of the streets extending from it (that is, Fifth Avenue, University Place, Waverly Place, Washington Place East, Washington Place West, and MacDougal Street), but also Eighth (alternately called Clinton Place), Ninth, and Tenth streets on the north; Greene and Mercer streets on the east; and on the west, those portions of the streets from Fourth to Tenth that did not house commercial structures similar to those on Sixth Avenue.

•••••

Such was the neighborhood into which Henry James was born in 1843. His home at 21 (later 27) Washington Place East served as the setting for his novella *Washington Square*, published nearly forty years later. While James's absorbing story reveals some of the details of the neighborhood scene

59. *National Guard, 7th Regiment, Drilling on Washington Square (Museum of the City of New York)*

as recalled from his childhood, a somewhat more comprehensive picture of the community as it evolved from the mid-1830s to the mid-1850s can be reconstructed from such mundane sources as contemporary assessment books, city directories, a house-by-house map prepared in 1854 for the use of insurance companies, occasional personal recollections, and the returns of a state census of 1855, which provide details on the residents not theretofore officially recorded.

The first house on the north side of the parade ground (today's Number 20, later enlarged) was built in 1828–1829, in the middle of the block west of Fifth Avenue. The houses in the stately Greek Revival row east of Fifth Avenue were taxed for the first time in 1832 or 1833. As late as 1838, however, a number of lots in the block west of Fifth Avenue were still vacant, and the west side of the parade ground was still largely undeveloped. More completely occupied were the south side and the streets that radiated eastward from the Square and from Fifth Avenue and University Place, especially Washington Place East, Waverly Place, and Eighth and Ninth streets. The University Building on the northeast corner of the parade ground was first occupied in 1835; its neighbor across Washington Place, the South Dutch Reformed Church, was dedicated in 1840. By 1854 the parade ground was almost completely surrounded by dwellings, and the neighboring streets within the orbit of the Square were fully occupied save for some tracts on lower Fifth Avenue.

Viewing the neighborhood as it was when it was assessed in 1838 and again in 1854, its most striking feature is that the owners or renters, if male and not retired, had their places of business farther downtown and were obliged to commute to work. This was no hardship if one could afford the cost of travel by omnibus or owned one's own conveyance. Omnibus service on Broadway was available by the early 1830s. Philip Hone, writing shortly thereafter, said that he could walk downtown from his house on Broadway opposite Washington Place, but if he preferred to ride he could "always get an omnibus in a minute or two by going out of the door and holding up my finger."

A sizable number of the residents on the north side of the Square had coach houses and stables on their property and coachmen in their employ; commercial livery stables were available on Eighth Street between MacDougal Street and Sixth Avenue. Nathaniel Hubbard, a prominent commission merchant who resided on the north side of the Square from 1837 to 1866, kept horses and carriages "more particularly for the enjoyment of his family," but he used them also in his business operations. "My wagon . . . was always ordered to be at my door every morning. . . . I would call on my numerous customers around the city, and drive from thence to my store on Front Street, where I discharged my coachman, with orders to wait on my family for the remainder of the day."

Another striking characteristic of the neighborhood was the occupational

• • • •

uniformity of its residents. Among the twenty-four householders on the north side of the Square in 1854, at least fourteen were merchants, three were widows of merchants, four were bankers, and one came from a manufacturing family. To judge from the very considerable number of residents whose occupations could be identified, this overwhelming predominance of merchants characterized the neighborhood as a whole, though one could find among the householders a small number of bankers and exchange brokers, attorneys or "counsellors," judges, a few physicians and clergymen, a teacher, and the headmistress of an exclusive boarding school for girls. The merchant ingredient represented some of New York's most prominent firms, such as N. L. and George Griswold, Boorman and Johnston, G. G. and S. Howland, and Alsop and Chauncey.

In 1854 the houses on the north side of the Square were, as a group, the most highly assessed. Their value ranged from $17,000 to $35,000, with the average about $25,000, but elsewhere in the neighborhood individual dwellings were assessed at similar or even higher figures. The home of Cornelius Vanderbilt, 10 Washington Place East (between Greene and Mercer streets), was assessed at $25,000, and that of his neighbor at Number 12, Mathew Morgan, a banker, at $30,000. Between Tenth and Twelfth streets on Fifth Avenue, some of the houses were assessed at $28,000 to $38,000 in the mid-1850s; the home of James Lenox, on the northeast corner of Fifth Avenue and Twelfth Street, was assessed at $65,000.

Resident servants were very much a part of the Washington Square neighborhood in those years. In the most affluent homes, five to seven was not an unusual number. Bank president Shepherd Knapp, who resided at 2 Washington Square, employed a German-born hostler and a black coachman, a German-born waiter, and five female servants—three from Ireland, one from France, and one from Wales. Merchant George Barclay of 8 Washington Place East—whose family included his daughter, her husband, and their three children—had seven female and two male servants. Throughout the neighborhood, three to four servants, mainly female, probably constituted the average. Predominantly Irish born, these employees also included a considerable number of American-born blacks, as well as Welsh, Scots, Germans, a few French, and a Swede. Merchant-shipper George Griswold, at 9 Washington Square, had, in addition to a coachman, two male and two female black servants.

On Eighth Street, as the buildings approached the more commercial Sixth Avenue, a source of services existed beyond those supplied by live-in servants. Clinton Court was a complex of eight brick houses hidden in the interior of the block between Eighth Street and Waverly Place. Most of its occupants were mulatto or black workers. At 1 Clinton Court, for example, lived five black families, among whom were a laundress, a barber, a waiter, and a whitewasher, and one Scottish family whose breadwinner was a carpenter. On Eighth Street close to Sixth Avenue several structures housed a wide variety of workers. At Number 132 the census taker counted twenty-four families, mostly foreign born; among the occupants were a barber, a printer, a cartman, a coachman, a cooper, several shoemakers, seamstresses, tailors, a gas fitter, and a blacksmith. Nineteen of the twenty-one families at 116 Clinton Place (Eighth Street) were blacks or mulattoes.

For local shopping the residents of the Washington Square neighborhood could patronize the stores and shops that lined not only the western end of Eighth Street but virtually all of Sixth Avenue from Third to Tenth streets. Usually these were brick structures, often with sizable rear extensions. The store or shop was located on the street level; the proprietor and his family, and often boarders taken in by the family, occupied the upper floors. At 32 Sixth Avenue, for example, a German-born shoemaker, his wife, and six small children, with two male and two female boarders, lived above the shoemaker's ground-floor shop. Edward Carroll lived above his bookstore at 72 Sixth Avenue, nearly Waverly Place. He and his sizable family shared the space above with five other families, including that of a widowed dressmaker and her three daughters, all seamstresses. Near the corner of Waverly Place, at 80 Sixth Avenue, was a hardware merchant's store. The merchant, his wife, and four children lived above the store, with two Irish-born servants. In the middle of the next block, between Eighth and Ninth streets, a hairdressing establishment was located on the first floor, while above it lived the proprietor, Scottish-born Thomas Miller, his wife, four small children, and five barbers listed as boarders: three Germans, one Scot, and one Swiss. Miller employed two female servants, one Irish and one Scots, recently arrived in New York. On the opposite side of Sixth Avenue, in the vicinity of Greenwich Avenue, stood the Jefferson Market. The continuous succession of shops and stores on Sixth Avenue west of the Washington Square neighborhood supplied its residents with many of their day-to-day needs and services.

A remarkable conjunction of family and business ties characterized the relationships of members of the Washington Square neighborhood with one another in these early years. Both types of relationship—family and business—contributed to the development of the north side of the Square. For example, a considerable portion of the block extending from Fifth Avenue to MacDougal Street north of the parade ground had been part of a tract owned by John Rogers, Sr., a merchant whose home was downtown at 7 Beaver Street. This tract ultimately came into the possession of Rogers's heirs, two sons and a daughter, the wife of William C. Rhinelander. One of the sons, wealthy bachelor George P. Rogers, was responsible for the construction not only of the first house on the north side of the Square, today's Number 20, but of other houses too. In 1854 he was residing in what was then Number 16; at the corner, two doors to the east, was the home of his sister, Mary Rogers Rhinelander, who had a dwelling in the Greek Revival style built there in 1839–1840.

Business ties rather than blood ties figured in the construction of the imposing Greek Revival row built on the north side of the Square east of Fifth Avenue in the early 1830s. Among the prime negotiators with Sailors' Snug Harbor for the leasing of this property were John Johnston and his partner, James Boorman, of the merchant shipping firm of Boorman and Johnston. Boorman built and occupied 13 Washington Square and Johnston, Number 7. Families who had been neighbors downtown often wished to continue their association in the newly developing area. Before moving to Washington Square, Johnston had resided at 16 Greenwich Street. In 1837 his former neighbor, who had lived next door at 18 Greenwich Street, bought 12 Washington Square. This was Samuel Howland of the firm G. G. and S. Howland, famed for its involvement in the clipper-ship trade. Similarly James Tallmadge, first resident of 5 Washington Square, had lived at 99 Chambers Street in the old city, while James Boorman had occupied 98 Chambers. The records abound with examples of relatives or former neighbors who relocated near one another in the Washington Square neighborhood, and of business associates who elected to build or buy homes side by side in the new streets of the area.

The customary composition of the household in these years was responsible for close and enduring relationships within the family. In addition to husband, wife, and several children, the typical family frequently included an elderly mother or father, niece, nephew, or maiden aunt of the owner or his wife. And even in the most affluent families, it appears to have been the practice of unmarried sons, employed or not, to live at home. Thus, in the family of importer Elijah White were three sons listed in the census as merchants and a fourth, a lawyer, all living at home with their parents at 51 Fifth Avenue. The family of editor Evert A. Duyckinck, who resided at 20 Clinton Place, included his wife and three sons, eight to fourteen years of age, his brother George, his brother-in-law, and the brother-in-law's wife. A nearby dwelling at 49 Clinton Place was shared by broker Thomas W. Ogden and his brother Richard, a lawyer, together with their wives and nine children. Cornelius Vanderbilt shared his home with a married daughter and her husband.

A good bit of "neighboring" took place in the personal relations of this first generation of the Washington Square community, not only in terms of social contacts, but also in the cooperative assumption of responsibility for neighborhood institutions and the cooperative support for business ventures that members of the neighborhood promoted or in which they were involved. Emily De Forest, granddaughter of John Johnston, who in 1832–1833 built 7 Washington Square and was its first resident, reported

• • • •

that in her grandmother's day there was a "good deal of evening visiting among the ladies in the neighborhood." Mrs. Johnston would "run in" to see Mrs. John MacGregor at Number 8, Mrs. George Griswold at Number 9, Mrs. John Green at Number 10, or Mrs. Allen at Number 1. These informal calls were frequent except on Friday when Mrs. Johnston formally "received her friends, . . . Friday being Washington Square Day." A point of common interest among the wives was the beautiful gardens they maintained at the rear of their lots, separated by white grape-covered trellises with rounded arches. In time extensions of the houses replaced or reduced the size of these gardens.

Nathaniel Hubbard and his family, who resided at what was then 23 Washington Square, west of Fifth Avenue, were especially close friends of the family of Stephen Allen, a former mayor, who since 1835 had owned the house at 1 Washington Square. "My family, particularly the younger female portion of them, were almost in daily communication with the younger branches of his family, by his second wife," Hubbard recalled, "while my own sisters were more intimately associated with his daughters by his first wife."

The young ladies of the Washington Square neighborhood found their closest friends among the daughters of their neighbors as well as among their classmates at a finishing school for young ladies on Fifth Avenue. Margaret Johnston's "bosom friend" was Lydia Alley, daughter of commission merchant Saul Alley, who lived next door at Number 6. Phoebe Anna Thorne, who lived at Number 3, was another of her close friends, as was Frances Colles, who married Margaret's brother, John Taylor Johnston. Her friend Lydia Alley married the son of merchant George Griswold, whose family resided three doors away from Lydia's at 9 Washington Square. Griswold's sister married China merchant John C. Green, who in his youth had been one of her father's employees; in 1842 he bought Number 10, next door to the Griswold home, for their residence. Thus marriage as well as friendship flowered as a result of the closely interrelated Washington Square neighborhood from the 1830s to the 1850s. The predominantly Protestant, New York–New England origins of the neighborhood householders may have facilitated this development.

The close congeniality of the residents of the Washington Square community encouraged cooperation in both business and philanthropic ventures. Nathaniel Hubbard recalls coming to the financial aid of one of his neighbors, a fellow commission merchant, during the hard times of 1837. On another occasion, when his neighbors James Boorman and Thomas Suffern were raising subscriptions for the construction of the Hudson River Railroad, they appealed to Hubbard to "lend a helping hand," and he subscribed for twenty shares. It would be hard to exaggerate the importance of the role of this kind of neighbor-induced support in the economic advancement of New York City in these years.

A similar financial responsibility was taken by many members of the Washington Square neighborhood in assuring the permanence of the University of the City of New-York (now New York University). Among the largest donors through 1855 were George Griswold, John Johnston, James Boorman, John C. Green, Thomas Suffern, Samuel Howland, and Shepherd Knapp—all residents of Washington Square North—and donors of sizable sums were scattered throughout the neighborhood. In 1853, when the University sought to meet a deficit of $52,646, eight of the ten largest donors who came to the rescue were residents of the neighborhood. This group also figured prominently in the University's governing council. James Tallmadge of 5 Washington Square was president of the council from 1834 to 1846; the vice president was his neighbor at Number 7, John Johnston.

Thus the University was regarded not only as an ornament but also as a responsibility of the Washington Square neighborhood as a whole. In a different sense from the parade ground, it gave a focal point to this remarkably homogeneous enclave of the city's mercantile and financial elite. Indeed, in those pre–Civil War years the University might be said to have functioned as both lens and mirror—at once fostering and reflecting Washington Square's sense of community.

· · · · ·

SELECTED BIBLIOGRAPHY

A Note on the Sources

The effort to reconstruct a New York City neighborhood of the pre–Civil War period is complicated by the fact that in many instances house numbers were changed from time to time and that a given street occasionally went by two different names at the same time. Some houses still bear their original numbers today; for others, even nearby, the original number has been changed. The census takers of 1855 did not record the street numbers of the houses of persons on whom they compiled other significant data.

Autobiography of N. T. Hubbard, with Personal Reminiscences of New York City from 1798 to 1875. New York: John F. Trow and Son, 1875.

De Forest, Emily Johnston. *John Johnston of New York, Merchant.* New York: privately printed, 1909.

Greenwich Village Historic District Designation Report. Vol. 1, areas 1, 2, 3, and 4. New York: Landmarks Preservation Commission, 1969.

Longworth's American Almanac, New-York Register, and City Directory. New York, 1838.

· · · ·

Maps of the City of New-York Surveyed under Directions of Insurance Companies of Said City by William Perris, Civil Engineer and Surveyor. New York, 1854.

New York City. Municipal Archives and Record Center. Assessment books for the Fifteenth Ward. 1838, 1854.

New York State Census of 1855. Hall of Records. New York City. Data for the Fifteenth Ward, third, fourth, fifth, and sixth election districts.

Wilson, H., comp. *Trow's New-York City Directory for 1854–55.* New York: John F. Trow and Son, 1855.

CROSSROADS OR SETTLEMENT?

THE BLACK FREEDMEN'S COMMUNITY IN HISTORIC GREENWICH VILLAGE, 1644–1855

Thelma Wills Foote

The black presence in Greenwich Village dates back to colonial times. As early as 1644 several blacks owned land there: Domingo Anthony lived on a piece of land at the southwest corner of present-day Washington Square Park; Paul d'Angola lived on a lot between present-day Minetta Lane and Thompson Street; Christofell Santome owned a lot on the west side of the Bowery; Domingo Angola owned land on the west side of Fourth Avenue near present-day Astor Place; Willem Anthonys Portugies owned a lot on the east side of Fourth Avenue north of Domingo Angola's tiny estate and south of Astor Place; and Pieter Tamboer owned a parcel of land at the northwest corner of Old Sand Hill Road, now the intersection of Eighth Street and Fourth Avenue.

Several of these black landowners had been among the eleven men who made up the first documented shipment of slaves brought to Manhattan in 1626. These slaves arrived in a vessel of the Dutch West India Company, the leading carrier of slaves in the transatlantic trade during the seventeenth century and the monopoly trading enterprise that ruled Manhattan Island and the region between Buzzard's Bay and the Delaware River from 1624 to 1664. The original eleven managed over time to elevate their status from that of slaves to free blacks, and to acquire land.

In 1644 they petitioned the West India Company for their own freedom and their families' freedom. As dependents of the company, these slaves had

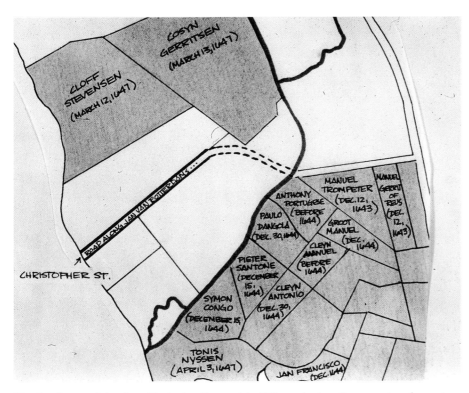

60. Land owned by free blacks in Greenwich Village during the seventeenth century (*Museum of the City of New York*)

become financially burdensome during that year, when a costly war against the Indians taxed the company's resources and the severe winter depleted its food supplies. Moreover, since the Dutch outpost at the tip of Manhattan Island was under threat of attack, the loyalty of its black inhabitants had to be assured. Slaves had been used in the recent war, and their services would perhaps be needed in the future. In any event this was a particularly dangerous time to have resentful slaves on hand, for a Negro uprising might have resulted in the destruction of the already enfeebled Dutch settlement. The Dutch West India Company therefore offered the black petitioners "half-freedom," manumitting them on condition that they labor for the company when called upon and that their offspring would be the company's property. When the company did not require their services, the "half-free" blacks would be at liberty to provide for their own subsistence.

Thus, by 1644 the area of Greenwich Village east of Hudson Street contained the so-called "free Negro lots," the modest homesteads of the "half-free" blacks. According to Isaac Newton Phelps Stokes's *The Iconography of Manhattan Island*, these lots were small, four-hundred-square-foot parcels, most of them situated within a triangular piece of real estate north of

• • • •

present-day Houston Street and south of Eighth Street between Lafayette Street and the Bowery.

In 1664 hardship required the West India Company to sell several of its Negro slaves in order to raise funds for the purchase of much-needed food supplies and to reduce the number of mouths it had to feed. Through a shrewd decision to capitalize on the company's predicament as they had in 1644, the "half-free" blacks seized the opportunity to improve their position in the Dutch settlement. At that time they petitioned the company for the removal of all limitations on their liberty, and the company, again eager to secure the blacks' loyalty during a crisis, granted the petitioners full freedom.

As already noted, the black petitioners had families of their own. In 1628 the company imported three Negro women slaves. Although no evidence suggests that the company intended to enter the business of breeding slaves, its records indicate that these women had been purchased for "the comfort of the company's Negro men" and that the conjugal relations between the company's slaves produced offspring, whose number cannot be determined. It is known that throughout the colonial period the Dutch Reformed Church in Manhattan sanctified unions between slaves and baptized slave children. On May 5, 1641, the first recorded marriage between blacks joined Anthony Van Angola and Lucie d'Angola. The black couple's surname—one they shared with many of the blacks in colonial Manhattan—suggests that they were natives of Angola, a likely conjecture since the company had established trading forts along the Angolan coast. Nevertheless the sources of slave imports into the Dutch settlement were varied, and, as the names of the original involuntary black immigrants indicate, the Congo supplied slaves, often by way of Brazil and even Portugal.

While the black petitioners were elevated to the status of free blacks, the remainder of the black population on Manhattan Island, numbering nearly seven hundred in 1664, were fixed in the position of chattel slaves. These slaves, mostly Negro men, labored on fortifications and other public works projects such as the construction and repair of roads. Located midway between the Caribbean and Holland and downstream from the fur trade along the Hudson River, Manhattan presented an ideal center for the collection and distribution of the company's beaver pelts as well as an excellent site for a naval depot to service Dutch vessels that plied the Atlantic. Using slave labor, the company erected a trading fort, a warehouse, and several crude highways on the island in order to facilitate its business ventures.

The company also used slaves to promote its meager efforts at land cultivation. Slaves worked the land, and the agricultural produce helped to feed the local inhabitants. In the 1620s the company established four "bouwerys," or farms, on the eastern shore and two similar units of agricultural production on the western shore of Manhattan Island—one of them

• • • •

situated east of Hudson Street in present-day Greenwich Village. Private residents and several of the company's employees—for example, Petrus Stuyvesant, director general of the Dutch West India Company's ventures in Manhattan—also owned and operated farms. Located adjacent to the company's farm beyond Hudson Street, in the sections of Manhattan now called the East Village and the Bowery, Stuyvesant's farm was being cultivated by forty slaves when, in 1664, the English took control of the island.

One of the first acts of the newly installed English authorities was to confirm all titles to slave property held by the inhabitants of the settlement, which the English called New York in honor of King Charles II's brother, the duke of York (later King James II). The Duke's Laws of 1665 included a law of slavery, but the status of Christianized Negroes remained ambiguous until 1706, when the provincial assembly stipulated that conversion to Christianity did not alter their status. By this means the English authorities foreclosed one of the blacks' few opportunities to elevate their position in the colonial settlement. Furthermore the assembly promulgated a number of additional antimanumission statutes and placed restrictions on the blacks who had obtained freedom under Dutch rule, laws endangering the survival of free blacks in Greenwich Village and elsewhere in New York.

A poignant illustration of the imperiled existence of free blacks under English rule can be found in the family history of Luycas Pieters, the owner of a lot located in Greenwich Village. Although Luycas Pieters had obtained freedom and land during Dutch rule, a descendant, also named Luycas Pieters, had by the 1730s been debased to the status of landless indentured servant. This impoverished black man was unable to support his ailing wife, and, in 1738, she turned to the public almshouse for aid. The pauperization of free blacks such as Luycas Pieters was closely followed by the near extinction of free people of African descent in New York. On the eve of the Revolution, most of "the free Negro lots" in Greenwich Village had fallen into the hands of white residents, and free blacks constituted only a tiny fraction of Manhattan's total black population.

Nevertheless, under English rule slavery was never a total system of domination in Manhattan. Black resistance took many forms, from the collective armed slave revolt of 1712 to the commonplace exodus of runaway slaves who, for the most part, escaped alone. Indeed, the survival of free blacks, if only an infinitesimal remnant, should in itself be viewed as a mode of resistance. Moreover, they also participated in the resistance by opening their homes to slaves and providing sanctuary for runaways. On March 7, 1671, Domingo and Manuel Angola, residents of "the free Negro lots," were brought before the Mayor's Court of the City of New York and charged with illegally sheltering slaves in their homes. These free black residents of Greenwich Village were ordered to stop their activities or forfeit their freedom.

· · · ·

Some white New Yorkers also resisted the slave regime. By manumitting their slaves, they frustrated the English authorities' desire to eradicate the free black presence in colonial New York. But because New York's anti-manumission statutes placed a prohibitive bond of two hundred pounds on voluntary manumissions, few benevolent slaveowners liberated their slaves during the English colonial period.

The abolition of slavery in New York was not a topic of serious discussion until the Revolutionary era. Following the Revolution, such prominent white New Yorkers as John Jay, Gouverneur Morris, and Aaron Burr favored abolition. In 1799 the New York legislature finally passed the Act for the Gradual Emancipation of Negro Slaves, which mandated that all slaves born after July 4 of that year were free. Male slaves born before that date would be emancipated when they became twenty-eight, females at twenty-four. Hence, because black children and young adults were bound to their masters under indentureships until they reached the age of manumission, New York slaveowners did not suffer the immediate loss of their most valuable slave property.

Nonetheless some slaveowners resented the 1799 act as an illegitimate exercise of governmental authority and an unlawful abridgment of their property rights. Rather than accept future losses in their human property, they illegally sold their slaves to buyers outside the state, most often to southern planters. This subterfuge had been outlawed more than a decade earlier, when in 1788, the legislature had prohibited the exportation of slaves for the purpose of sale. In 1817 the state legislators went one step further, declaring that *all* slaves would be free on July 4, 1827, thereby abrogating slaveholders' claims to the persons of Negro slaves after that date.

Disease, poverty, and the lack of political and economic opportunities were the disabilities black New Yorkers had to contend with on their passage from slavery to freedom. Then, of course, the abolition of slavery in New York did not settle all questions regarding the position of free blacks in New York's society. Some white residents were predisposed to continue to treat blacks as property, while others were skeptical of proposals that advocated placing blacks on an equal footing with whites. Such ambivalence on the part of the civil authorities rendered the newly emancipated blacks vulnerable to the hostile behavior of white residents who violated the rights of black freedmen. For example, Elias Boudinot, constable of the City of New York, was known as "the Negro Catcher" because of his ties to a notorious kidnapping ring that engaged in the illegal transportation and sale of free blacks outside the state. Boudinot was an ex-slaveowner and the descendant of a prominent New York family whose tradition of slaveowning had an enduring impact on his attitudes toward blacks. Similarly, many white residents had not yet fully accepted the free black presence in their midst.

· · · ·

The political contest between New York's competing parties further compromised the blacks' position in the new republic. After 1810 the dominant Democratic party expanded the boundaries of liberty to take in many more white inhabitants than the founding fathers had intended to include in the franchise. Between 1811 and 1821 the Democrats endorsed a platform of universal white male suffrage, which they obtained in 1821. At the same time New York's Democratic-controlled legislature placed a discriminatory property qualification of $250 on the Negro franchise, thereby denying most blacks the right to vote.

While the legislature was abridging the rights of black New Yorkers, black freedmen were engaged in a struggle for economic survival. The ordinary black workingman found employment as a day laborer at the shipyards, docks, and warehouses of New York, but the port's rise to a position of international preeminence after the War of 1812 did not guarantee the material welfare of the city's working class. The influx into the city of European immigrants in 1825 created an ample supply of cheap labor that depressed wages. At the same time discriminatory hiring practices barred most blacks from lucrative occupations in the skilled trades. As day laborers black workingmen could expect to earn only five dollars each week, while black women and children, who worked in such unskilled occupations as domestics and errand runners, could expect to earn only a fraction of the weekly wages of their adult male counterparts. Thus the combined income of a free black family barely added up to a subsistence wage, and during the frequent inflationary cycles and financial panics of the antebellum decades, the masses of black laborers were reduced to poverty.

Economic degradation produced a high rate of morbidity among the blacks of nineteenth-century New York City. The yellow fever epidemic of 1820, the smallpox outbreak of 1823, and the cholera plagues of 1832 and 1849 each carried away a disproportionate number of black city dwellers, whose low standard of living debilitated their health and rendered them especially susceptible to lethal diseases. Tuberculosis, a contagion generally associated with urban poverty, was a common ailment among the city's black residents.

During the period of gradual emancipation between 1799 and 1827, Manhattan's black residents began to remove themselves from the homes of their former masters, which were situated at the southern extreme of the island, and to relocate along the streets north of Chambers Street. By 1830 the heaviest concentration of black population had shifted northward from the older neighborhoods of the colonial port town, along a corridor of settlement east and west of what was at that time upper Broadway, and into Greenwich Village. Free blacks from the countryside joined this movement. The trek of recently emancipated blacks across Manhattan's landscape was

• • • •

significant on another plane of human experience from the demographic, for it was an aspect of the journey from slavery to freedom.

·····

By 1827 Greenwich Village had become populated by recently emancipated blacks who regarded it less as a neighborhood of choice than one of necessity. The Village was a place where the urban poor, both black and white, could find affordable housing. Unlike the black landowners of colonial times, who had owned "the free Negro lots," the vast majority of the free blacks who settled in Greenwich Village between 1799 and 1827 were landless laborers. These impecunious freedmen rented dwellings from white landlords. The typical abode was a two- or three-story brick or wooden dwelling, which was partitioned into smaller units with kitchens. The prototype of present-day apartments, these living spaces were typically cramped, inadequately ventilated, and damp shelters that cost black tenants from two to five dollars' rent each month. During the period of gradual emancipation, Greenwich Village showed a notable degree of racial segregation; boardinghouses in the neighborhood were segregated, and ordinary white residents rarely took black boarders into their homes. The black residents of the Village were therefore confined to inferior quarters on segregated streets, for the discriminatory practices of urban landlords left them with no choice but to accept poor housing.

By 1855 the social and economic composition of the residents in Greenwich Village had changed. The yellow fever epidemic of 1820 had precipitated the flight of wealthy city dwellers from the crowded sections of Lower Manhattan into the less populated area of Greenwich Village. As early as the 1820s the residences of affluent New Yorkers lined the streets in the vicinity of Washington Square Park. Over time the scarcity of cheap housing due to the rise in real estate values drove many black laboring families out of Greenwich Village and into other sections of the city where affordable housing could still be found. Some black families remained, but as the century progressed the proportion of blacks in the neighborhood's total population declined.

The state decennial household census of 1855 shows that the vast majority of black freedmen—approximately 80 percent of the total black population in Greenwich Village—secured housing in the homes of wealthy residents in exchange for their labor as domestic servants. Thus, despite their political emancipation, many free blacks lived in conditions of dependency. There were few autonomous black households in the Village on the eve of the Civil War, a fact that reflected the lack of economic opportunities for free blacks in the city at large during the antebellum decades.

Despite these circumstances, however, an enclave of struggling free

· · · ·

blacks had by 1855 settled within the borders of Greenwich Village on a narrow street, barely wider than an alleyway, called Minetta Lane. That street, which has survived the tremendous transformation of the city's landscape during the nineteenth and twentieth centuries, is now situated between Sixth Avenue and MacDougal Street, two blocks south of Washington Square Park.

The circumstances of the black families who lived on Minetta Lane reveal the familial arrangements and material conditions of the black freedmen's community in the Village in those years. Indeed, the ages, work, family backgrounds, and other contemporary census data can safely be extrapolated to serve as the basis for an examination of the conditions and circumstances under which many black freedmen lived in the Village.

The Hunsems, a rare example of an autonomous black family living in a single-family house, rented a brick dwelling on Minetta Lane. The household consisted of Joseph Hunsem; his wife, Elizabeth; his mother-in-law, Isabela; and his sister-in-law, Arabela. In 1855 Joseph was forty-two years old and worked as a porter. It is unknown if the forty-six-year-old Elizabeth was employed outside the domestic sphere. The Hunsems removed from New Jersey to New York City in 1835. Joseph and Elizabeth were old enough to have been born slaves, and they probably relocated in order to join Elizabeth's mother, Isabela Crowley, and to find work in the city. Isabela was born in New York City in 1796—a date that makes it likely that she, too, was an ex-slave. Isabela's other daughter, Arabela, was fifteen years old in 1855 and probably represents the first generation of free blacks in the Hunsem family.

The Thompsons—whose household included Edward Thompson; his wife, Anna; his son, Samuel; his daughter, Mary; and his mother-in-law, Edda Stout—rented a flat in a multiple-family brick dwelling at 25 Minetta Lane. In 1855 Edward Thompson was a fifty-five-year-old Methodist clergyman who had relocated from New Jersey to New York City in the same year as his neighbors the Hunsems. Anna Thompson, born in Virginia in 1802, had arrived in the city in 1837. She may have been one of the Virginia blacks whose masters had voluntarily manumitted their slaves after the Revolutionary War or a slave who had run away in order to reunite with her mother, Edda Stout, who had settled in the city in 1835. (With the exception of Anna Thompson and Hagar Hamilton, who could read but not write, all the Minetta Lane neighbors were literate.) Born in Virginia in 1775, Edda was eighty in 1855. Like her daughter, this ancient matriarch was in all likelihood either an emancipated Virginia black or a runaway. The Thompsons' two children—Samuel, fifteen, and Mary, eleven—were almost certainly the only members of the family who had been born free. (The passage of the Fugitive Slave Act of 1850 threatened many black Southerners living in the North whose ex-masters perhaps still held legal claim to them as property. The act was a major factor in the politicization of these blacks.)

Both mother and grandmother could have related memories of life under slavery in Virginia to these black children, while their father and their neighbors the Hunsems were in a position to remind them that Southern whites held no monopoly on man's inhumanity to man and that people of African descent had only recently been emancipated in the Northern states. And certainly no free black family in the North would have needed any reminder that four million Southern blacks remained in bondage.

Samuel and Maria Byard also rented a flat at 25 Minetta Lane. This black couple had moved from Delaware to New York City in 1853. In 1855 Samuel, thirty-nine, was a waiter. Like many black women in the Village—and in the city as a whole—Maria, who was twenty-eight in 1855, may have found part-time employment as a domestic in the households of wealthy residents or perhaps took in laundry in order to supplement her husband's wages. Relatively new to the city, the Byards could draw on the experience of their more seasoned neighbors for guidance on black life in Manhattan. All the members of the Guy family, also of 25 Minetta Lane, were native New Yorkers.

The household consisted of Aaron Guy; his wife, Melinda; and his seven children, who ranged in age from four months to twenty-one years. In 1855 Aaron Guy was a forty-one-year-old porter. Melinda Guy was also forty-one. Their eldest child, Philip, was a butcher, and his income doubtless helped to support his parents and siblings.

In 1855 Hagar Hamilton lived alone in a rented flat at 25 Minetta Lane. She had migrated from New Jersey to New York City twenty-five years earlier. Many of her neighbors had also been born in New Jersey and, like her, had left the place of their birth and resettled in New York City—another bond in the sense of community that linked the enclave of blacks on Minetta Lane. Hagar could read, but she could not write. With the exception of Anna Thompson, all of Hagar's neighbors were literate, and any one of them could have penned the letters Hagar perhaps sent to relatives and friends whom she had left in New Jersey.

Brigit Rauls, like Hagar Hamilton a widow, headed an extended family at 25 Minetta Lane that consisted of her married or widowed daughter Hester Polk, her granddaughter Lucy Polk, and her grandchildren Nelson and Anne Rauls. A review of the last names of Mrs. Rauls's grandchildren indicates that Hester Polk's husband as well as Brigit Rauls's son and daughter-in-law, the parents of Nelson and Anne Rauls, were absent. These black parents may well have died and left their children in Brigit's care, or, since none of the members of the Rauls household was employed in 1855, the absent family members may have lived and worked in the households of wealthy white New Yorkers and supported the Raulses of Minetta Lane from

• • • •

their wages. Three members of the Rauls household had been born in Virginia and arrived in New York City in 1835, the same year that their neighbor Edda Stout had removed from Virginia to the city. Pure coincidence may have brought these black freedmen to Minetta Lane, or perhaps their settlement on that obscure interstice of the growing metropolis was the intentional act of runaway slaves who had fled the Southern slave regime to freedom in the city of New York.

By 1855 four black West Indian women had also settled on Minetta Lane. Sarah Rogers headed an all-female household composed of her daughters Carolina, Anna, and Isabela, aged twenty-five, twenty-three, and twenty respectively. Sarah and her daughters had arrived in New York City in 1841 and may have been recently emancipated blacks who had migrated to the United States some time after the abolition of slavery in the British West Indies between 1834 and 1838.

As already noted, economic contingencies eventually forced many of the blacks who resided in the vicinity of Washington Square Park out of that section of the city. No longer able to afford the rising rents of that neighborhood, many of the surviving members of the freedmen's community were dispersed beyond the borders of Greenwich Village. Nevertheless a few exceptional blacks managed to rise above the masses of poor black laborers to become successful entrepreneurs. W. F. Brown and W. I. Scott owned an ice-cream shop at 70 Bleecker Street; the engraver Patrick H. Reason kept his shop at 56 Bond Street; and the restaurateur George T. Downing owned an oyster house at 690 Broadway. These black entrepreneurs were, however, degraded by the imposition of segregated public facilities and sometimes attacked by vindictive whites.

• • • • •

Although European travelers to New York City during the first half of the nineteenth century had been impressed by the equality of conditions among New Yorkers in contrast to the more stratified society of European cities, black city dwellers were, in fact, relegated to an unequal status in most areas of New York's society and culture. The city's Protestant churches, for example, reinforced the debased condition of people of African descent in their congregations by segregating blacks into separate pews or by imposing separate worship services for blacks. In response to these discriminatory practices, black ministers founded independent black congregations. Some of these black churches retained formal ties to the Protestant churches, while others established uniquely African-American religious institutions. The Shiloh Presbyterian Church on Prince Street is an example of the former type of black church. Shiloh Presbyterian became an important black church under the successive leadership of three prominent black

• • • •

ministers: Rev. J.W.C. Pennington, Rev. Theodore S. Wright, and Rev. Henry Highland Garnet. Shiloh's worship services and Sunday school no doubt drew adherents from the enclaves of black residents that were scattered throughout the Village and surrounding neighborhoods.

A variety of secular institutions also enhanced social solidarity among the blacks of Greenwich Village and elsewhere in the city. For example, black audiences congregated at the African Grove Club, a theater located at the intersection of Bleecker and Mercer streets that was in operation from 1821 to 1823. An all-black theatrical company performed such popular plays as Shakespeare's *Othello* and *Richard III*. Before each performance tea and ice cream were served to black patrons while they socialized in a garden adjacent to the theater. On June 21, 1823, patrons attended the final performance at the African Grove Club. The play, *The Drama of King Shotaway*—by Henry Brown, a black producer and playwright in New York City—depicted the 1795 slave revolt on St. Vincent. The choice of subject matter reveals something of the political consciousness of the blacks in nineteenth-century Manhattan.

The energies of some black city dwellers were channeled into political activism. By far the most active black organizations were those established to confront the recurrent crises that faced free blacks during the antebellum era. For example, the journeymen's riot of 1834, which culminated in an eight-day rampage, directed against the prominent abolitionists Arthur and Lewis Tappan as well as the homes of black residents, revealed the imperiled existence of free blacks in New York. In response to the turmoil and racial hostilities of the 1830s, black leaders formed the Committee of Vigilance (1837) and the Association for the Elevation and Improvement of the People of Color (1838). In 1850 a group of prominent black leaders formed the Committee of Thirteen in response to the Fugitive Slave Act, a law that threatened to erode even further the already compromised freedom of the city's black population. The committee supported the institutional apparatus of the Underground Railroad in New York City, and its aid to fugitive slaves sometimes transgressed the bounds of the law.

Complementing the activities of the formal political organizations were the black newspapers: *Freedom's Journal* (1827–1829), *The Rights of All* (1829), *The Weekly Advocate* (1837), *The Colored American* (1837–1841), and *The Ram's Horn* (1847). These periodicals provided an organ for the voices of black protest and disseminated crucial information to the urban black population that was dispersed in pockets throughout predominantly white neighborhoods such as Greenwich Village. *Freedom's Journal* reported on the commemoration of the final abolition of slavery in the state of New York, held on July 4, 1827. Along with its report, the black newspaper also printed the speech William Hamilton delivered on that occasion to the congregation of black freedmen who had gathered at the African Zion

Church, located between Leonard and Church streets within walking distance of the homes of the black residents of Greenwich Village. Hamilton greeted the newly emancipated citizens of color with these words of optimism and hope: "My brethren and fellow-citizens, I hail you all. This day we stand redeemed from a bitter thralldom. Of us it may truly be said, 'The Last Agony is O'er.'"

But the experience of the black freedmen of Greenwich Village and the blacks who lived elsewhere in the city during New York's postemancipation period revealed the limitations of political emancipation and suggested that in 1827 there were few sound reasons to believe that "the agony" had come to an end. No longer slaves in the households of local slaveowners, who for the most part provided for the subsistence needs of their slave property, the newly emancipated black freedmen began their life of independence in poverty, and as the century progressed, they continued to struggle for economic survival. There were, of course, a few exceptional blacks who became success stories, but the achievements of this infinitesimal, though talented, proportion of Manhattan's black population cannot obscure the hardships of those embattled black laboring families who lived in the shadow of poverty and whose material and political conditions gave the lie to expectations of a promising future.

In 1837, a decade after the abolition of slavery in New York, Samuel E. Cornish, the editor of the *Weekly Advocate*, wrote:

> 'Free man of colour' what an empty name! What a mockery! Free man indeed! When so unrighteously deprived of every civil and political privilege. Free indeed! When almost every honourable incentive to the pursuit of happiness, so largely and so freely held out to his fairer brother, is withheld from him. A freeman! When prejudice binds the most galling chains around him! . . . What a sad perversion of the term freeman! No man of colour, be his talents, be his respectability, be his worth, or be his wealth what they may, enjoys, in any sense, the rights of a freeman. That liberty, and those privileges which of right, and according to the principles of our constitution, ought to be his he enjoys not. Persecuted, and degraded, he wanders along through this land of *universal liberty and equality*, a desolated being. His, no station of honour, power, and fame! Too often the virtuous and intelligent man of colour must drag out an ignoble life, the victim of poverty, and sorrow. Then unwept for but by a few of his persecuted race, drops into the grave.

This indictment of the rhetoric of optimism and hope was Cornish's answer to the question: What difference did freedom make? His image of the citizen manqué, the black freedman who wanders along a tortuous road only to end in poverty and premature death, is simultaneously a poetic representation and a historically accurate description of the experience of the masses of free blacks in New York City in 1837.

The period following the abolition of slavery in New York in 1827 proved to be a time of testing for the blacks of Manhattan. It seemed that nowhere in the city could they secure "a safe dwelling place" and pursue "an honest calling." Where could these black freedmen settle? Forever at a crossroads, the black freedmen of Greenwich Village and others throughout the city who shared a similar experience were the most improper bohemians of them all.

•••••

SELECTED BIBLIOGRAPHY

Albion, Robert G. *The Rise of New York Port, 1815–1860.* New York: Charles Scribner's Sons, 1939.

Blackmar, Elizabeth. "Re-walking the 'Walking City': Housing and Property Relations in New York City, 1780–1840," *Radical History Review* 21(Fall 1979): 131–148.

Curry, Leonard P. *The Free Black in Urban America, 1800–1850: The Shadow of the Dream.* Chicago: University of Chicago Press, 1981.

Ernst, Robert. "The Economic Status of New York City Negroes, 1850–1863," *Negro History Bulletin* 13(March 1949): 131–143.

Freeman, Rhoda Golden. "The Free Negro in New York City in the Era before the Civil War." Ph.D. diss., Columbia University, 1966.

Gilje, Paul A. *The Road to Mobocracy: Popular Disorder in New York City, 1783–1834.* Chapel Hill: University of North Carolina Press, 1987.

Harris, M. A. *A Negro History Tour of Manhattan.* New York: Greenwood Publishing Corporation, 1968.

Litwack, Leon F. *North of Slavery: The Negro in the Free States, 1790–1860.* Chicago: University of Chicago Press, 1961.

McManus, Edgar J. *A History of Negro Slavery in New York.* Syracuse, N.Y.: Syracuse University Press, 1966.

Mohl, Raymond A. *Poverty in New York, 1783–1825.* New York: Oxford University Press, 1971.

Nash, Gary B. "Forging Freedom: The Emancipation Experience in the Northern Seaport Cities, 1775–1820." In *Slavery and Freedom in the Age of Revolution,* edited by Ira Berlin and Ronald Hoffman, 3–48. Urbana: University of Illinois Press, 1983.

Ottley, Roi, and William J. Weatherby, eds., *The Negro in New York.* New York: Oceana Publications, Inc., 1967.

Over, William. "New York's African Theatre: The Vicissitudes of the Black Actor." *Afro-Americans in New York Life and History* 3:2 (1979): 7–14.

Robinson, Armstead L. "The Difference Freedom Made: The Emancipation of Afro-Americans." In *The State of Afro-American History: Past, Present, and Future,* edited by Darlene Clark Hine, 51–74. Baton Rouge: Louisiana State University Press, 1986.

••••

White, Shane. *Somewhat More Independent: The End of Slavery in New York City, 1770–1810.* Athens: University of Georgia Press, 1991.

Wilentz, Sean. *Chants Democratic: New York City & the Rise of the American Working Class, 1788–1850.* New York: Oxford University Press, 1984.

Zilversmit, Arthur. *The First Emancipation: The Abolition of Slavery in the North.* Chicago: University of Chicago Press, 1967.

WASHINGTON SQUARE

A WOMAN'S WORLD

Carol Ruth Berkin

From Monday to Saturday, from early morning until sunset, Washington Square in the nineteenth century was a woman's world. With husbands, fathers, and adult sons at their offices six days a week, the only male intruders on this female enclave were the professors and students of New York University.

In truth the Square was not *a* woman's world but three, functioning side by side—or, more accurately, in concentric circles—distinguished from one another by class. At the center were the mistresses of the Square's households; around them, the nursemaids, cooks, waitresses, music teachers, seamstresses, and chambermaids whose activities the lady of the house directed; and, on the edge, almost invisible to the eyes of the others, the immigrant factory "girls," whose only contact with the domestic life of the Square were the brief moments of their arrival at and departure from work.

Here, then, in the neighborhood of Washington Square, is an excellent cross section of nineteenth-century urban America's "woman's sphere"—its myths, its paradoxes, and the rhythms of its daily routine.

THE GENTEEL WOMAN
· · · · ·

Henry James has fixed, for all time no doubt, the image of the genteel woman we wish to examine. Of Catherine Sloper, one of the main characters in *Washington Square*, James wrote: "She became an adorable old maid. She formed habits, regulated her days upon a system of her own, interested herself in charitable institutions, asylums, hospitals and aid soci-

· · · ·

eties; and went, gently, with an even and noiseless step, about the rigid business of her life."[1]

Catherine, of course, was a spinster. Yet in her public persona and in her passion for benevolent activity, she had much in common with the wives and mothers of her time and her class. As an unmarried woman, however, she was free from the main duties of the genteel woman of the nineteenth century. To her married sisters fell the tasks of managing the household and inculcating in their children the virtues their class admired.

The ideology of the day made much of the "sacred duties" of women. Proper wives were not simply to see that meals appeared on tables, clothes were made or bought, dust was banished from the mantelpiece, and the children were taught to behave in a mannerly fashion. Rather, the prescriptive literature of the day exhorted wives to create and sustain what one historian has aptly called "a haven in a heartless world," a home that offered husband and children the necessary illusion that life was orderly, aesthetic, and moral.

How many households met these idealized standards of the "cult of domesticity," and how many women embraced the ideology in more than superficial form, we do not know. Prescriptive literature by its very nature tells us what women were expected to be like, not what they were in fact like. However, we do know that, helter-skelter, women were standing this cult of domesticity on its head, turning their sex's acclaimed superior virtue, nurturing abilities, and religiosity into a justification, even a compulsion, for social action. "Social housekeeping"—or reforming the evils of the public sphere—was the logical or illogical extension of the century's insistence that women were the "superior sex." As early as the 1830s, New York women had battled prostitution. By the 1880s there were women's organizations to improve low-income housing, public health care, factory conditions, and the generally low morals of the city fathers. This reform activity should not be confused with modern forms of feminism. On the contrary, most activists found their strength of purpose in the belief that woman has a unique character. They wished to "feminize" their society, not participate with men in its corruption.

The motivation for women's active participation in reform, charitable organizations, and what Sheila Rothman has called the life of the "Protestant nun" was complex. Some historians have argued that reform and benevolent activity were means to a personal end. That is, the genteel woman received more—in the form of self-esteem, sense of accomplishment, and the testing of her skills and talents—than did the recipients of her attention and good intentions. Consciously or unconsciously "social housekeeping" may have been a rebellion against the restrictions that being genteel placed on a woman's activities. Other historians point to the very real social problems of the nineteenth century in a nation not ready to commit public

• • • •

61. A meeting of the Women's Central Association of Relief (*Museum of the City of New York*)

institutions and resources to the welfare of its people. Finally historians note the undercurrent of fear that motivated many of the post–Civil War genteel reformers, both male and female. They document a fear of immigrant "radicalism," life-styles, and moral depravity (real or imagined) and a fear that the standards of behavior and the code of morality they espoused were in need of protection through proselytizing. Perhaps benevolence was a form of social coercion, the velvet glove on the dominant culture's iron fist.

There is evidence from life on Washington Square to support each of these interpretations. Susan Pulsifer, daughter of a turn-of-the-century activist, recalls her mother's fear of neighborhood homes being turned into boardinghouses for immigrant workers. Yet she also remembers her mother's commitment to do what she could "to improve the home and family and childlife of this great jungle-like city."[2]

A few autobiographies and memoirs give us glimpses of the ladies of the Square, women encumbered by skirts so full they swept the ground, carrying a volume of Dickens in a picnic hamper on outings with the children or a copy of New York City's housing laws in a portmanteau en route to a meeting of the Washington Square Association.[3]

• • • •

These women left much of the routine care of their children to nurse-maids and nannies; they saw their role as that of exemplars and instructors, not caretakers. Thus they took care to preside over important daily rituals. "Reading aloud was a favorite habit and pastime with [Mother]," Pulsifer recalled, "and we children were usually read to for an hour after lunch and for several hours a day during the holidays."[4] Mothers also saw to it that piano or violin lessons and sessions with the seamstress were a regular part of the week's schedule. On winter afternoons they gathered their families to receive guests at a formal tea hour, passing on, through this ritual, the arts of polite society. In the same spirit they set the acceptable boundaries of their children's social life, forbidding daughters to invite girls who "live on the other side of Washington Square" to parties or gatherings inside their own homes.[5]

As observers we cannot fail to sense the contradictions between the social conscience of many of these women and the private world they created and sustained. Many demanded better working conditions for the factory girls yet resented the intrusion on their domestic serenity of the shrill blasts of the factory whistles. They campaigned for better immigrant housing but joined organizations to prevent the invasion of their neighborhood by tene-ments and boardinghouses for garment workers. They encouraged their daughters to organize groups like the "Acorn Club," which helped poor children aboard a floating hospital, but forbade them friendships with the daughters of the working class. Finally, Susan Pulsifer's mother worked to ameliorate the cruelties of the urban jungle, yet she felt no responsibility when her aged seamstress fell on the steps of the family home and was afterward "too frail to come again to sew." As historians of that period—and of this one—realized, class and sisterhood often pulled in different directions.[6]

DOMESTIC SERVANTS
• • • • •

The majority of women to be seen on the Square were not mistresses of the households in which they resided. They were, instead, domestic servants. To these women fell the task of keeping each home running smoothly and graciously. The typical Washington Square family of the 1880s employed cooks, waitresses (for serving meals), chambermaids, and laundresses. But the central figure in any household was the surrogate mother: the nurse or governess.

Every day, twice a day, the Square was filled with nurses and children, on their way to taking their constitutionals up Fifth Avenue. Dressed in

• • • •

uniforms with starched caps and aprons, the nurses looked as attractive as their well-dressed charges. Yet neither the nurses nor the children were necessarily happy with their lot. Nurses complained of their employers' vanity and concern for appearances. In words that would have delighted—or further depressed—Thorstein Veblen, one ex-nurse wrote: "The trouble is that almost every one of [the employers] wants to make a show, and it is more stylish to have the nurse in a cap and apron, and so she is ordered into them."[7]

The children had few complaints about their nannies' wardrobe but many about their personalities. Pulsifer asserts:

> Only for two or three in the long procession which came and went, did I have any genuine or lasting affection. On the whole, the name of "nurse" was anathema and represented a dominating and unwelcome personality to be studied for her weaker points and thereby got out of the way as much as possible.[8]

Nevertheless, a nurse with endurance came to wield great influence in such a family. Like the mammy figure of the Southern plantation, she was the continuous thread in the affective life of the family.

Women of the genteel class complained bitterly and often about the quality of domestic service in nineteenth-century New York. Even the socialist writer Charlotte Perkins Gilman voiced despair over the "servant problem" in her novellas and short stories. Her reform-minded heroines could not get about their important social tasks because maids, nurses, and cooks never proved "reliable."[9]

The immigrant women who worked as domestic servants agreed that there was a servant problem—but it was one they defined quite differently. When working women were interviewed in the 1880s, they readily explained why domestic service was the least desirable employment in New York.[10] The picture that emerges is a bleak one. Many women, for example, frankly disliked working for a genteel "sister." They preferred a male supervisor or employer in the factory. Possibly taking orders in the more intimate, personalized domestic sphere was more demeaning; a related complaint was that "we came to this country to better ourselves, and it's not bettering to have anybody ordering you around."

There was sometimes little harmony among the servants as well. Some women laid the blame upon ethnic or religious differences. As one chambermaid bluntly put it: "The cook and the waitress were just common uneducated Irish!" But it is likely that living arrangements strained everyone's patience and tolerance. Domestic servants had no privacy, either from the critical eyes of their employers or from their coworkers in the household. It was not uncommon for five servants to share one large room. "It's hard," one ex-domestic explained, "to give up your whole life to somebody else's orders and always feel as if you was looked at over a wall like."

Servants could rarely escape this enforced togetherness by solitary outings, for domestic workers had virtually no free time. Two household waitresses reported that they got only one afternoon a week off—and a "part" of every other Sunday. Despite the lack of privacy or leisure time, many women with experience in domestic service also cited the "awful lonesomeness" of the job. A domestic servant had to be, above all else, a single woman.

In the long run, the decision to enter or remain in domestic service seemed to rest on ethnic considerations. Irish, German, and Scandinavian women were more likely to fill the sewing rooms, kitchens, and servants' quarters on Washington Square, while Poles, Jews, and Italians entered the factories.

THE FACTORY "GIRL"
• • • • •

The factory worker was not, of course, an active or immediate participant in the life of the Square. The Square, nonetheless, loomed large in her life and livelihood; genteel ladies were an important part of the consuming public for the garment industry of New York. The benefits of this connection did not flow only one way. As one ladies' magazine editorial put it: the availability of "ready mades" meant that the genteel women had more time for "higher pursuits and the attainment of broader views." Thus, just as domestic servants made it possible for the genteel women to create a "haven in the heartless world," factory workers and pieceworkers helped make public benevolence a possibility.

The number of working women in New York City grew steadily during the century. The Bureau of Labor Statistics estimated that there were nearly two hundred thousand working women in 1885, excluding domestics.[11] Many of these garment workers, shopgirls, cigar makers, feather and artificial flower makers, and washers and ironers worked near Washington Square. Even before the Civil War, the work whistles at West's, Bradley's, and Carey's Hoop Skirt Works on West Twentieth Street could be heard piercing the silence of the early morning.[12] By 1908 large shirtwaist factories encircled the Square. With little variation from industry to industry and decade to decade, these working women trudged to work at six or seven o'clock in the morning and returned home well after dark. Many brought seven hours' work home with them as well. The poverty of these working

• • • •

women is a constant in the history of nineteenth-century labor. In 1835 women shirtmakers in New York earned "less in a week than a carpenter earned in a day and . . . the hardest working seamstress could not earn more than the cost of the bread she ate."[13] In 1872 the *New York Times* noted that unskilled women workers earned less than four dollars a week. "What kind of subsistence this pittance affords," the *Times* editorial added, "may be imagined in a city where the necessaries of life are higher than in any city of the world, where the meanest meal costs 15 3/8, the darkest cellar a dollar a week."[14] A year later, when the nation was struck by severe economic depression, a *Times* writer concluded a piece on working women with the comment: "How [they] continue to exist at all under the circumstances is a mystery."[15]

It was a question working women themselves could not answer. Discriminated against by sex, age, and, as recent historians point out, physical appearance as well, working women were beyond the pale of the "cult of domesticity." These women probably entered the consciousness of the Square only when they went on strike or did battle with local police. For example, on January 13, 1874, unemployed women and men, demonstrating for government action against the worst effects of the depression, were attacked by police at Tompkins Square.[16] Later, in May 1891, when striking garment workers held a mass rally at Cooper Union, the sounds of the crowd, which spilled over into the streets, must have been audible to the residents of the Square.[17] Rallies, held by the strikers from the nearby shirtwaist factories, might also have been heard or observed in 1909.[18] But when they were silent at their machines, women factory workers were probably little more than an abstraction for the residents of Washington Square; they were the "needy" of whom genteel women spoke.

•••••

NOTES

1. Henry James, *Washington Square* (New York: New American Library, 1964), 165.
2. Susan N. Pulsifer, *A House in Time* (New York: Citadel Press, 1958), 34.
3. Hamilton Fish Armstrong, *Those Days* (New York: Harper & Row, 1963), 9; Pulsifer, *A House in Time*, 34, 39.
4. Pulsifer, *A House in Time*, 49.
5. Ibid., 70.
6. Ibid., 83–84, 127.
7. Helen Campbell, *Prisoners of Poverty: Women Wage Workers, Their Trades and Their Lives* (Boston: Roberts Brothers, 1889), 229.

• • • •

8. Pulsifer, *A House in Time*, 26–27.
9. See, for example, Charlotte P. Gilman, "What Diantha Did."
10. The quotations cited in this section on domestic servants come from the interview materials in Campbell, *Prisoners of Poverty*, 224–230.
11. Ibid., 10.
12. Louis Levine, *The Women's Garment Workers: A History of the International Ladies Garment Workers Union* (New York: B. W. Huebsch Inc., 1924), 6.
13. Smith Hart, *The New Yorkers* (New York: Sheridan House, 1938), 78.
14. Philip S. Foner, *Women and the American Labor Movement* (New York: Free Press, 1979), 164.
15. Ibid., 165.
16. Ibid., 166–68.
17. Levine, *The Women's Garment Workers*, 61.
18. Foner, *Women and the American Labor Movement*, 326–330.

ITALIAN NEIGHBORS

Josephine Gattuso Hendin

Some were there when Washington Square was the burial ground of the poor and the wooden sheds that cluttered Washington Square South seemed to splinter at a sigh. By 1828, when the Square's potter's field was leveled to become a parade ground, nearly two thousand Italians had edged onto Bleecker, MacDougal, Sullivan, and Thompson streets, domains of the Irish whose clear hegemony had been honored even by the Church of Rome. On creating the diocese of New York in 1808, Pope Pius VII had named its first cathedral, a wine-red beauty at Prince and Mott streets, after *their* Saint Patrick. But Genoa would weave spells as magical as Dublin's or Galway's as its surrounding provinces in northwestern Italy sent stonecutters, chefs, musicians, and even a few intellectuals to New York.

As skilled craftsmen and merchants, these newcomers helped to save Village streets and shops from ugliness and incivility. Those Italians, noted an observer:

> [take] great pride in the artistic arrangement of fruit so that they will attract the eye; the Italian barber has transformed the appearance of the barber shop and has made it clean and attractive, displaying the sign of "Tonsorial Artist"; while the boot-black, beginning with a tiny box, rises to the established chair . . . , sparing no effort in his attempt to render satisfactory service and in making himself affable and agreeable. There is absolutely no doubt about this class being a permanent population, and it may be observed that their business success is notable and that they have brought their trade to a higher level than that in which they found it.[1]

The Church of Saint Anthony of Padua, built on Thompson Street, was dedicated to a saint who seemed to typify the northern sense of order.

• • • •

142

Known for his care of things that are lost, and sought for his ability to recover them, Saint Anthony was also a blissful protector of property against fire. Why were there so few fires in Italian streets? Because, it was said, of Saint Anthony's love for those who had built him such a fine church.

Intellectuals, composers, and men of letters and culture came in greater numbers as political turmoil in Italy fueled the flight to New York. Here they found a warm welcome. The affluent society that would be probed or satirized by Henry James and Edith Wharton smiled on these "ambassadors of European sophistication." Vincenzo Botta, who had been a member of parliament in Sardinia, became a professor of modern languages at New York University shortly before the Civil War, and played an energetic role in New York society as vice president of the Union League Club. Others, like the financier E. P. Fabbri, who became a partner of J. P. Morgan, combined their faith in culture with concern for labor. Fabbri helped endow the Italian School, a neoclassical building erected in 1855 on Leonard Street near Centre Street. There, in the heart of the Mulberry Bend district, the school devoted itself to implementing an American faith in upward mobility through education. However, Fabbri found his efforts thwarted by Catholic priests who resented the school's secular emphasis. Fearing that English lessons in the evening and secular reading would eclipse his importance and eventually turn the poor from Catholicism, one angry priest took to his pulpit to "utter fierce anathemas against those parents who permitted their children to attend the school."[2]

Such priests succeeded in closing the school several times. Having failed to close it for good, they made efforts to persuade their parishioners that contact with the school would be spiritually damaging. But the school's instruction, and especially its hospitality to music, proved irresistible to students who, after a day's toil, found relief in playing for the Italian School Band.

It was music that bridged the gap between scholars, craftsmen, and laborers. Opera was the link between Italians that would also leave its mark on the streets of the neighborhood. Fernando Palmo, known as "one of those Neapolitans who would give anything for an opera,"[3] opened a confectioner's shop and restaurant at 307 Broadway when he was twenty-nine.[4] Through years of making pasta and pastry, what sustained him was music. By the age of fifty, having amassed a comfortable fortune, he spent it all to build a splendid opera house on Chambers Street, between Broadway and Centre Street, delightedly attending its opening performance, Bellini's *I Puritani*. Palmo soon lost his shirt, though not his heart. Scarcely a year after that brilliant debut, Palmo was obliged to take a job as someone else's cook. Dying in poverty after age had left him unable to work at all, he was escorted to his grave by an impressive group of Italian music lovers and affectionately eulogized in the press. As *L'Eco d'Italia* sagely noted: "Had he

· · · ·

remained in the macaroni and ice cream business, today he would be a millionaire."[5]

Composer Luigi Arditi was another who tried to fuse an Italian sense of *bellezza* with the prevailing American taste. Undaunted by the sparse audience for *I Puritani*, Arditi based his opera *La Spia* on an American subject, James Fenimore Cooper's *The Spy*, a tale of political chicanery in the wilds and farms of Westchester during the American Revolution. Arditi enjoyed a limited success at the Academy of Music on Fourteenth Street, but it was not until 1847, when the wealthy of New York erected the Astor Place Opera House—eventually Cooper Union—that opera seemed to have arrived. Thanks to the codirection of Salvatore Patti, a Sicilian tenor whose greatest gift to music was his daughter, the soprano Adelina Patti, the Astor Place Opera's opening night was "so elegant and socially impressive a spectacle . . . as had not been seen before . . . in New York."[6] By 1852, however, it was clear that what makes a splash doesn't necessarily make a profit. To support itself, the elegant opera house was obliged to feature animal acts.

The twelve thousand Italians in Manhattan had to turn from music to meet the challenge of the American Civil War. Drawn by the dream of unification and freedom that had survived the vicissitudes of the *risorgimento*, many were devoted to the Union cause and took a stand against slavery. The Thirty-ninth New York Infantry, known as the Garibaldi Guard, actively recruited soldiers through the Italian press. These volunteers "carried into battle, next to the Stars and Stripes, a flag that had waved at the head of Garibaldi's columns when they fought the four powers that had destroyed the Roman Republic."[7] From their headquarters at 53–55 Franklin Street[8] they carried forth a banner bearing Mazzini's words: "GOD AND THE PEOPLE!"[9] On April 29, 1865, bearing "the flag of the new Italy side by side with that of the United States,"[10] they helped amass in the plaza in front of Cooper Union more than five hundred Italians from all walks of life for a funeral procession for President Lincoln. One of Lincoln's most distinguished Italian mourners was a man who had won the Congressional Medal of Honor for service in the Shenandoah campaign and whom Lincoln had appointed a brigadier general. Later to leave a lasting mark on New York City as a flamboyant arbiter of taste, in 1879 Gen. Luigi Palma di Cesnola became director of the Metropolitan Museum of Art, where his infatuation with the sculpture and artifacts of the ancient Mediterranean was indulged to his delight—and to the advantage of the museum's collection.

The love affair between New York City and its Italian citizens was severely strained in the 1880s, when a great flow of southern Italian immigrants, illiterate in their own dialects and unable to speak English, poured through Castle Garden, the Ellis Island of that time. These 307,309 poor

62. This statue celebrating Garibaldi attests to the Village's large Italian population during the late nineteenth century. (*Museum of the City of New York*)

contadini, or farm laborers, came through a Manhattan inhabited in 1880 by a mere 1.2 million people.[11] Enough Italian newcomers remained to alarm the established population. Their northern Italian compatriots, fewer in number, restrained in emotional style, and engaged in noncompetitive trades, had lived in relative peace with their immigrant, largely Irish neighbors. But the southerners, expressive and flamboyant, willing to work end-

• • • •
145

less hours at backbreaking labor for less pay, soon displaced the Irish in unskilled construction work and as longshoremen. In 1890 "New York's Inspector of Public Works testified before Congress that Italians constituted ninety percent of those involved in Gotham's public works." [12] According to Maine's Bureau of Labor: "It would be difficult at the present time to build a railroad of any considerable length without Italian labor," a comment that "applied to New York with equal aptness." [13]

Even as they crowded the Irish out of construction work, the *contadini* were themselves victims of economic exploitation. Most had received their jobs through *padroni*, fellow Italians who managed their passage, negotiated their wages, and arranged for their housing. As early as 1864,

> under special legislation, manufacturers and contractors were allowed to import foreign laborers under contract. The result was a huge speculation in cheap labor. Agents were sent throughout Europe seeking such persons as could be used for personal gain. The Southern Italian was the most easily hoodwinked. These poor, ignorant people, accustomed to receive from 12 to 25 cents a day for their labor, were offered 60 and 70 cents by these contractors and agents. [14]

Often these jobs actually paid $1.25 per day, a salary negotiated by the *padrone* and lower than the prevailing pay for the Irish and other groups. Appropriating the difference and then taking as much as half the acknowledged pay, the *padrone* further exploited his workers by forcing them to buy food in his store and at his price and overcharging for the hovels he compelled them to call home. Habituated to exploitation all their lives, the *contadini* toiled on, struggling to save money to send back to Italy.

Others in Mulberry Bend were even worse off. The most helpless victims of the *padroni* were children. The *padroni* would search the slums of southern Italy for children they could virtually buy from their parents for between nine and twelve dollars and promises of a better future. In fact, what the *padroni* "offered" these children was a future of virtual enslavement. The children were immediately forced to work for their "uncles." They had to walk all the way to ships docked in Marseilles and other seaports while begging, singing, and dancing to earn the money to pay their *padrone* for their passage to America in steerage. In New York they would beg, play, sing, and dance in saloons; many would discover in the slums of Manhattan a poverty more violent and abysmal than any they had previously known.

Mulberry Bend had the dubious honor of being perhaps the worst neighborhood in New York:

> Outwardly, a crooked three-acre lot built over with rotten structures, . . . the "Bend" lay within a maze of incredibly foul alleys. There the new arrivals lived in damp basements, leaky garrets, clammy cellars and

outhouses and stables converted into dwellings. . . . Half a dozen blocks up Mulberry Street, there is a ragpickers' settlement, a sort of overflow from the "Bend." . . . Something like forty families are packed into five old two-story and attic houses that were built to hold five and out in the yards additional crowds . . . are accommodated in shacks built of all sorts of old boards and used as drying racks by the Italian stocks.[15]

Here the *padrone* did his best to ensure that "his children" remained illiterate, ignorant of English, and utterly dependent on him.

How the exploitation of children by *padroni* was finally ended is a tribute to the effectiveness of New York City's social and legal institutions at the time, and to the successful assimilation of educated Italians into the city's administrative life. The combined efforts of the New York district attorney's office and the Children's Aid Society, in cooperation with the Italian government, produced sufficient evidence to indict Antonio Giovanni Anacarola in what came to be known as "the Italian Padrone Case."[16] Argued with eloquence and skill by Assistant U.S. Attorney William P. Fiero in 1880, the case against Anacarola aroused moral outrage against his mistreatment of children. Although the *padròni* system would continue to exploit adults, the decision against Anacarola articulated a policy of hope for the young. The nightmare of Mulberry Bend ended in July 1894, when legal and community efforts resulted in the city's condemnation and acquisition of the land bounded by Park, Bayard, Baxter, and Mulberry streets. The area was leveled, reclaimed, and became the first park constructed under the Small Parks Act of 1897. On its opening it was named, in a spirit of optimism, Columbus Park.[17]

Fighting to preserve what they knew to be their distinctive ways, the people of southern Italy tried to settle only with émigrés from their old Italian villages:

> Mott Street between East Houston and Prince held the Napoletani; the opposite side of the street was reserved for Basilicati. Around the corner the Siciliani settled Prince Street, while two blocks away the Calabresi lived on Mott Street between Broome and Grand. Mulberry Street was strictly Neapolitan, and Hester Street, running perpendicular to Mulberry, carried the local color of Apulia.[18]

Each group brought to the streets of New York visible evidence of the cultural faith that had sustained it through generations of exploitation and poverty.

Each September 19 the Neapolitans brought to Mulberry Street a feast in honor of San Gennaro (Saint Januarius). San Gennaro was martyred by the Romans at Pozzuoli in A.D. 306, but his enduring glory rests on more miraculous grounds: the "liquefaction" of his blood. Preserved in a glass bottle in the cathedral at Naples, the blood is said to liquefy and "freshen" eighteen times each year. In Naples San Gennaro's feast day is a public holiday distinguished by the joyful crowds who come to the cathedral to witness the miracle. In New York the feast is primarily an afternoon and evening celebration. An observer in the 1890s could see, as one still can in the 1990s, "the narrow street . . . arched with electric lights of varied colors, and a procession of worshipers following the effigy of the saint up and down the roadway between booths laden with candies, candles, votive offerings, and the like. There are fireworks to top off the festivities."[19]

The Sicilians of Baxter Street were not to be outdone in the celebration of their Saint Agata on her cherished day, February 5. Carrying her effigy down the street as though it were a charm against all disasters, they venerated and cheered the saint who, in the twilight of the sixteenth century, had stood facing the flow of lava streaming from Mount Etna toward Catania. With a flick of her veil, she miraculously turned the steaming fire away from the city and saved the lives of her people.

The importance of such feast days grew partly from the alienation of the southern Italians from the Roman Catholic Church as an institution. Occupying second-class status in the Irish-dominated American church, frequently relegated to church basements while Irish priests said mass for the "good people" upstairs, the Italians had also brought with them a history of exploitation by the church in Italy. Their experiences had not destroyed their faith but had given it a distinctive character, one focusing more on the miraculous intervention of an individual saint than on the efficacy or infallibility of the church. Jacob Riis, writing in the *Century Magazine* in August 1899, described the "artless joyfulness" the faithful could bring to their celebration of saints outside of churches. Here is his view of the people of Auletta, feasting their patron near Houston Street:

> The fire escapes of the tenement had, with the aid of some cheap muslin draperies, a little tinsel and the strange artistic genius of these people, been transformed into beautiful balconies, upon which the tenants of the front house had reserved seats. In the corner of the yard, over by the hydrant, a sheep, which was to be raffled off as the climax of the celebration, munched its wisp of hay patiently while barelegged children climbed on its back. Between birthdays the saint was left in the loft of the saloon, lest the priest get hold of him and get a corner on him, as it were. Once he got him into his possession he would not let the people have him except upon payment of a fee that would grow with the years. But the saint belonged to the people and they were not going to give him up.

Even as the Italians changed the look and feel of the streets of Greenwich Village, New York University transformed the look of the Square. If the southern Italians were criticized even by their northern brothers for too much ebullience, too much vulgar display of song, the University also received its share of censure for its Italianate excess. The *Evening Post* on July 16, 1833, reported the City Council's dismay over the design for a new building with showy buttresses projecting out on Washington Place. When the building was finished in 1835, *The Architectural Magazine*, a noted London journal, looked on the new building with patrician disdain: "The New York University building is a mountain of white marble and brick with Italian details, more incongruous than those of Westminster's Abbey. . . . In London it would be termed Carpenter's Gothic, but even that can give you no idea of its hideous abortions and monstrous absurdities." Not even such contempt could stop the neighborhood from becoming the home of an intellectual freedom and diversity that would have made Garibaldi proud.

The Italians who lived south of the Square were combining the charm of their native culture with American ambition and openness. Well before the 1920s they would find that their coffeehouses and restaurants were becoming the second home of students, artists, and intellectuals in search of Italian flavor. O. Henry would sentimentalize the wooden buildings on the south side of the Square as "houses of mystery," as Henry James had immortalized the graceful mansions on the north side in *Washington Square*. One day these neighborhoods and streets would produce journalists, novelists, scholars, and filmmakers who would see them through Italian American eyes. But meanwhile, in that devotion that outlasts mere patience, Italian neighbors underwrote the promise of their own active future in New York's cultural life by the sheer force of their imaginative love for the present, for ordinary days, for the pleasures of conversation, food, and song that continued to draw young scholars, painters, and poets to the Village. In the process Italian neighbors provided a generation of American writers with a glimpse of the sweetness of life as simple and intense as the taste of steaming cappuccino.

· · · · ·

NOTES

1. *Report of the Industrial Commission* (New York: 1903; reprinted in *Italians in the City: Health and Related Social Needs*, edited by Francesco Cordasco [New York: Arno Press, 1975]), 9–10, and commentary, Antonio Mangano, *The Italian Colonies of New York City* (Master's thesis, Columbia University, 1903; reprinted in ibid.).

· · · ·

2. "The New Italian School-House," *Harper's Weekly* (April 17, 1875), reprinted in Giovanni Schiavo, *Four Centuries of Italian-American History* (New York: Vigo Press, 1952), 159.

3. Ibid., 185.

4. Ibid., 182; *Directory of New York*, 1832; I. N. Phelps Stokes, *The Iconography of Manhattan Island* (New York: Robert H. Dodd, 1915), listing for Fernando Palmo.

5. Schiavo, *Four Centuries of Italian-American History*, 188.

6. Ibid., 188.

7. Michael A. Musmanno, *The Story of the Italians in America* (Garden City, N.Y.: Doubleday, 1965), 31.

8. Schiavo, *Four Centuries of Italian-American History*, 318; advertisements for volunteers in *L'Eco d'Italia*, July 26, 1862.

9. Musmanno, *The Story of the Italians in America*, 31.

10. Schiavo, *Four Centuries of Italian-American History*, 158.

11. Thomas Kessner, *The Golden Door* (New York: Oxford University Press, 1977), 48.

12. Ibid., 58.

13. Ibid.

14. Mangano, *The Italian Colonies*, 10–11.

15. Federal Writers' Project, *The Italians of New York* (New York: Random House, 1938), 19–20.

16. "The Italian Padrone Case: The United States of America against Antonio Giovanni Anacarola" (New York: New York Society for the Prevention of Cruelty to Children, 1880), transcript.

17. Stokes, *The Iconography of Manhattan*, Palmo listing.

18. Kessner, *The Golden Door*, 16.

19. Federal Writers' Project, *The Italians of New York*, 90.

LONG-HAIRED MEN
AND
SHORT-HAIRED WOMEN

BUILDING A GAY WORLD IN THE HEART OF BOHEMIA

George Chauncey

The gay life—and tolerance of the gay
life—are central components of Greenwich Village's reputation today. One
of the Village's central arteries, Christopher Street, is crowded with gay-
oriented bars, clothing stores, and bookshops and is so synonymous with
gay life that a well-known gay magazine is named after it. The Village as a
whole has a national reputation as a gay residential neighborhood, making
it a beacon for gay migrants fleeing small-town hostility and a rhetorical
target of antihomosexual politicians. And it was at a gay bar in the Village,
the Stonewall Inn, that patrons resisting a police raid in June 1969 provoked
a riot that launched the modern lesbian and gay liberation movement, an
event now commemorated every June throughout the Western world by gay
pride marches drawing hundreds of thousands of participants.

We tend to think of both the Village's gay reputation and its actual role
as a center of gay life as recent developments, products of the relative
openness of gay life since Stonewall. But the association of homosexuality
with the Village reaches back much further than this, to the years before
World War I, when the Village's growing bohemian reputation attracted

· · · ·
151

unconventional spirits from around the country and made it a national center of social, political, artistic, and sexual experimentation. Among those attracted by that reputation were numerous lesbians and gay men, some of whom played key roles in the bohemian community, whose presence soon added to the Village's notoriety. By the late 1910s a Village song included the line "Fairyland's not far from Washington Square," and by the early thirties the Village's gay reputation was so firmly established that a New York tabloid could quip that while a doctor had learned how to "switch the sex of animals, turning males into females, they beat the scientist to it in Greenwich Village!" The following pages examine why the Village became both a place where many lesbians and gay men lived *and* a place with a reputation as a gay neighborhood. The two are not synonymous, for in the twenties and thirties several other gay enclaves, which never attained the fame of the one in the Village, also developed in the city.

I
· · · · ·

The emergence of the Village as a gay refuge was closely linked to the development of the bohemian community there. Although Greenwich Village had originally been north of the city's borders, a safe haven for the rich from urban disorder and disease, by 1900 most of its elite residents had departed and the Village itself had been physically incorporated into a city whose borders had long since pushed far beyond it to the north. At the turn of the century the area was known simply as the Ninth Ward, dominated by working-class Italian immigrants. Only when native-born bohemian writers, artists, and radicals began to move into the neighborhood in the 1900s did it begin to be called "the Village" again—and then only by the self-styled bohemian "Villagers" who moved there, not the Italian "Ninth Warders."

The newcomers to the Village were attracted by the neighborhood's winding streets and Old World charm, by its relative isolation from the rest of the city, and above all by the social life its cheap apartments and services made possible. Indeed, although the Village became the most famous bohemian community in the country in the teens and twenties, subject to searching examination in the national press, similar residential districts were developing in large cities throughout the country. In many respects the Village was a prototypical furnished-room district, for it offered cheap rooms and restaurants to unmarried men and women who wished or needed to live without the domestic services conventionally provided in families by

· · · ·
152

the unpaid household labor of women, and who were thus freed both to develop social lives unencumbered by family obligations and to engage in work likely to be more creative than remunerative.

Cheap rents for single rooms attracted lesbians and gay men as well as struggling young writers and artists, as did the cheap restaurants and tea-rooms that proliferated to serve the nonfamily population living in those rooms. But a greater attraction was provided by the Village's reputation for tolerating nonconformity (or "eccentricity") and the impetus for social experimentation engendered in the district by the bohemians who originally settled there, for these held out the promise of making the Village a safe and even congenial place for homosexuals to live. Moreover, the particular forms of eccentricity attributed to the "bohemians" and "artistic types" who lived there made it unusually easy for gay men and lesbians to fit into Village society and also provided a cover to those who adopted widely recognized gay styles in their dress and demeanor.

Not only were many Villagers unmarried, but by becoming artists, free lovers, and antimaterialists (if not always anticapitalists), they had forsaken many of the other social roles and characteristics prescribed for their class and gender in ways stereotypically associated with homosexuals. Indeed, the unconventional behavior of many bohemian men—ranging from their long hair, flamboyant dress, and interest in art to their decided uninterest in the manly pursuits of getting married and making money—often led outsiders to consider them queer. Although not everyone thought their queer tastes extended to sexual matters, the arts world of the Village was often regarded as unmanly as well as un-American, and in some contexts calling men "artistic" became a code for calling them homosexual.

The frequent references by critics to the "long-haired men" and "short-haired women" of the Village sometimes constituted precisely such accusations of perversity, only slightly veiled, for the gender reversal implied by such images directly evoked the semiotic codes that denoted sexual perversion. The dominant images of gay men and lesbians, in this era, focused as much on their reputed gender role inversion as on their specifically sexual interests, and anyone who failed to conform to gender conventions risked being stigmatized as a homosexual (or "third sexer"). In 1929, for instance, a conservative Village paper attacked bohemian women for being "so ashamed of their sex that they do their best to appear like men, claiming, however, the privileges of womanhood just the same"; it went on to charge that "the majority of that type manifestly endeavor to create a third sex."[1]

This provided a useful cover to homosexuals, who could "pass" as bohemians, but it also threatened some of their avant-garde colleagues, who often were not so tolerant of homosexuals as their reputation might suggest. Indeed, there was often a considerable gap between the *representation* and the *actuality* of Village life and mores. As historians Ellen Kay Trimberger

• • • •

and Leslie Fishbein have shown, many of the leading self-identified male feminists of the Village remained deeply troubled or ambivalent about the independence of women and strove to protect their prerogatives and identities as men from the demands made by the ideologies of feminism and bohemianism.[2] In this context it is not surprising that many of them were troubled by the insinuation that their unorthodox behavior meant they were "queer" in a specifically sexual sense. In his 1934 memoir Malcolm Cowley recalled his fear that he and his fellow writers, intellectuals, and artists were being slandered as perverts. *Broom,* the little magazine he worked on in the early 1920s, he recalled, began receiving letters at its 45 King Street office addressed to "45 Queer Street" and "mention[ing] Oscar Wilde." "I came to believe," he added, "that a general offensive was about to be made against modern art, an offensive based on the theory that all modern writers, painters and musicians were homosexual. . . . I began to feel harried and combative, like Aubrey Beardsley forced to defend his masculinity against whispers." His reaction, as he frankly admitted, was to "hate . . . pansi-poetical poets"; he claimed to have had drunken dreams of a writers' revolution in the Village, when "you would set about hanging policemen from the lamp posts, . . . and beside each policeman would be hanged a Methodist preacher, and beside each preacher a pansy poet."[3]

The male artistic and political bohemians of the Village discussed sex more frankly than their middle-class contemporaries considered proper, and their "modern," scientific consideration of homosexuality sometimes disturbed the guardians of the old order. But their "frank" consideration of homosexuality was not necessarily positive, and it often simply condemned homosexuality in scientific rather than more *overtly* moralistic terms. Floyd Dell, for instance, defended "scientific" studies of sexuality against the censorship of the Comstock Society, but most such books were deeply anti-homosexual, as Dell himself emphasized. In Dell's own book, *Love in the Machine Age,* he argued that homosexuality was characteristic of patriarchal societies in which women were subordinated to men, and, in the modern age of free love, was a social anachronism and sign of personal regression.

Dell's critique and Cowley's anxiety hardly represented the entire range of bohemian opinion on the subject of homosexuality, however, and other bohemians—especially bohemian women—accepted the gay people in their midst with greater equanimity. The anarchist Emma Goldman, for one, defended the rights of homosexuals in some of her speeches, and according to historian Judith Schwarz, not only were numerous lesbians involved in the feminist club Heterodoxy, but the club's other members accorded lesbian relationships the same respect they granted heterosexual marriages.[4]

Indeed, even a cursory review of the intellectual and political ferment of the 1910s demonstrates that numerous homosexuals participated in the

· · · ·

bohemian milieu and that several played an important role in the construction of Village bohemia itself. Given the antihomosexual attitudes of many Villagers, as well as of the society at large, some gay Villagers felt obliged to remain circumspect. Carl Van Vechten, for instance, who played a key role in organizing Mabel Dodge Luhan's famous salons on lower Fifth Avenue in the teens and helped introduce the white public to the Harlem Renaissance in the 1920s, used his marriage to hide his homosexuality for many years. Others, such as the lesbians in Heterodoxy, were more open with heterosexual friends. Eugene O'Neill's companions in the Village and Provincetown included the noted gay painters Charles Demuth and Marsden Hartley, and, according to O'Neill's biographer Louis Sheaffer, the playwright based "Charles Marsden," the effete, implicitly homosexual character in *Strange Interlude*, on them.[5] Margaret Anderson and her masculinely attired lover, Jane Heap, championed James Joyce and published the influential *Little Review* from the Village, and they gathered other gay writers around them.

As these few examples suggest, individual homosexuals were tolerated and even accepted as friends by many Villagers in the 1910s, although they were scorned by others. But the very intimacy and small scale of the prewar Villager community, in which gay people were able (and sometimes required) to participate primarily as bohemians rather than as homosexuals and were, in any case, too few in number to do much more, mitigated against the establishment of distinctive gay institutions. The development of a gay enclave depended on the expansion and reorganization of the Villager community during World War I and the postwar years, the Village's integration into the city as a whole, and the development of a speakeasy demimonde in which gay locales might develop.

II
. . . . .

The rapid commercialization of the Village during World War I and the postwar years had an enormous influence on its character. The construction of the subway routes along Seventh Avenue in 1917 and along Sixth Avenue in 1927–1930 and the simultaneous widening and extension of both avenues transformed the Village from a remote, self-contained backwater into one of the most central and easily reached of the city's neighborhoods. Since the opening of the subway lines made the Village a more convenient place to live, growing numbers of businessmen, attracted by the Village's Old World charm, began to move there. They pushed rents up and some of the

. . . .

struggling artists out, real estate developers began building new apartment complexes in prime locations, and newly established taxpayers' associations launched campaigns to clean up some of the more disreputable aspects of the Village.

Moreover, just as the Village became more accessible, the advent of Prohibition made it a particularly attractive destination to men and women out on the town. The Italian restaurants, groceries, drugstores, and other shops that crowded its streets were the city's major sources of homemade Italian wine, and people flocked to the Village for their liquor supplies. Just as importantly, the Village's national reputation as a center of "free love" and other unconventional behavior made it an intriguing stop for tourists. The tearooms to the west and south of Washington Square had already enjoyed a boom during the war, when they became a major attraction to the soldiers and sailors passing through the city who were familiar with that reputation. In the years following Prohibition the area's speakeasies and clubs—known for their outlandish theatrical environments—attracted growing numbers of middle-class men and women out slumming, as well as men out to find the women known as "free lovers of the Greenwich Village type."

Most of the original "Villagers," the political radicals and bohemian artists who self-consciously identified themselves as members of a small-scale experimental community, lamented these changes. In their eyes the postwar Village seemed to have lost the intimacy, intellectual ferment, and genuinely bohemian character of its halcyon prewar days; the Village's incorporation into the city in the 1920s had turned it into another Coney Island, a cheap amusement center and playground for rich uptown slummers and poorer youths from the boroughs alike. Sociologist Caroline Ware, who published a study of the Village in 1935, reflected such misgivings when she dismissed the postwar generation of Villagers as "pseudo-Bohemians," interested less in intellectual creativity than in a mindless "escape" from the conventions of bourgeois society.

Nonetheless, the condescension of contemporary observers toward the newcomers should not be allowed to obscure the fact that the Village's reputation as a center of unconventional behavior—particularly of unconventional sexual behavior—had made it a beacon not only for rich slummers but also for increasing numbers of disaffected youths from the city's outer boroughs who wished to escape the constraints placed on their behavior by family and neighborhood supervision. Indeed, the Village became an even more important national symbol over the course of the twenties, as the cultural gap between Prohibition America and Jazz Age New York seemed to widen, as rural politicians pandered to prohibitionist and nativist constituencies by denouncing New York as the nation's Sodom and Gomorrah.

In this context the Village took on special significance for lesbians and

· · · ·

63. Charles Demuth's *Turkish Bath* subtly depicts the homosexual ambiance of a bathhouse in the Village. *(Courtesy of The Fogg Art Museum, Cambridge, Mass., anonymous loan)*

gay men around the country, and disaffected New Yorkers were joined in the Village by waves of refugees from the nation's less tolerant small towns. As one gay man wrote in 1924: "I have for the longest time tr[ied] so hard to make people understand me, and [it] was so very hard; my friends that I know don't care for people of that kind and I left them because I always thought they would find [me] out, then I went down the Village and [met] plenty [of gay people]." A hostile newspaper reporter made the same point when he asserted in 1931 that the people who flocked to Greenwich Village were "men and women taunted by their biologically normal companions in the small towns that ostracize those who neither eat nor sleep nor love in the fashion of the hundred percenters."[6] They fled to the Village, and in the 1920s their growing numbers allowed them to build an extensive gay world there.

Moreover, if the Village's reputation for unconventional sexuality attracted lesbians and gay men, their growing visibility in the district soon made homosexuality almost as much a part of the Village's reputation as free love. The presence of "fairies" and "lady lovers" (as gay men and lesbians were often called) in the Village was already sufficiently well known to have elicited press comment and attracted slummers by the beginning of World War I, and the Village's reputation as a gay neighborhood grew

• • • •

throughout the 1920s. One 1927 account of New York nightlife noted that two women dancing together in a Times Square club would elicit no comment, but in the Village it would be taken as a sign of their lesbianism. The "exposés" of the Village periodically published by the city's newspapers increasingly focused on the homosexual aspects of Village "depravity." In 1931 one series spotlighted gay meeting places in its "initial [tour] of the innermost stations of Greenwich Village's sex, pollution, and human decay."[7] In 1936 even the staid medical journal *Current Psychology and Psychoanalysis* published an article on the "Degenerates of Greenwich Village," which announced that the Village, "once the home of art, [is] now the Mecca for exhibitionists and perverts of all kinds." The gay scene in the Village became so prominent that it even made it into the movies. In the 1932 Clara Bow vehicle *Call Her Savage*, Bow's escort took her to a Greenwich Village dive patronized by artists, revolutionaries, and pairs of neatly dressed male and female couples, sitting in booths with their arms around each other. The waiters were two young men in frilly white aprons and maid's caps, each sashaying about holding a feather duster.

Caroline Ware noted the growing prominence of homosexual circles in the Village over the course of the twenties, although she dismissed it as a fad: "As sex taboos broke down all over the country and sex experimentation found its way to the suburbs, the Village's exoticism could no longer rest on so commonplace a foundation." The Jazz Age public's growing interest in homosexuality, she thought, simply provided the Village with a new angle: "The Village became noted as the home of 'pansies' and 'Lesbians,' and dives of all sorts featured this type." Villagers "pass[ed] on from free love to homosexuality . . . to mark the outposts of revolt."[8]

Throughout her study Ware regarded homosexual behavior and identity, particularly that of women, as nothing more than something "normal" people experimented with as part of a more general "revolt," rather than as part of a more authentic effort to shape a personal and collective identity. Indeed, she suggested that in the late 1920s homosexuality, and especially lesbianism, had become chic among Villagers, including numerous heterosexual women (whom she derisively termed "pseudo-Lesbians," as though they were a subcategory of pseudobohemians) who behaved like lesbians simply because it seemed the thing to do. Despite her cynicism, however, Ware's observations suggest that by the 1920s homosexuality had become more acceptable in Village circles and that lesbians and gay men had seized the opportunities the general bohemian revolt provided to construct a sphere of relative cultural autonomy for themselves.

The history of the Village dances, or balls, held at Webster Hall on East Eleventh Street near Third Avenue, illustrates how gay people used the openings created by bohemian culture to expand their public presence, as well as the commercialization and homosexualization of the Village's reputation. The first and most prominent of the balls were thrown in the mid-teens by the Liberal Club to finance its operations. But by the late teens the financial rewards of organizing a ball had become so evident that entrepreneurs unaffiliated with any community group began to sponsor them, competing to produce the most outlandish balls and attract the largest audiences. Floyd Dell, one of the organizers of the Liberal Club's first ball, later lamented that the balls had "finished the process [of betraying the Village's original ideals] which the restaurants [that drew slummers] had begun."[9]

Reports submitted by agents investigating "vice conditions" in the wartime Village confirm Dell's recollection that as the reputation of the Village as a bohemian enclave grew, increasing numbers of slummers from throughout the city visited the balls in order to get a taste of the unconventional life. As one agent reported in 1917: "Many of the people are advertising their dances as Greenwich Village dances in order to get the crowd, and it works." "These dances are getting quite popular," he added in a later report. The reason was obvious: "Most of those present at these dances being liberals and radicals, one is not surprised when he finds a young lady who will talk freely with him on Birth Control or sex psychology."

"Free love" was an important part of the attraction of the Village balls, but so, too, was homosexuality, as the same investigator's reports make clear. In 1918 he noted that an increasingly "prominent feature of these dances is the number of male perverts who attend them. These phenomenal men . . . wear expensive gowns, employ rouge[,] use wigs[,] and in short make up an appearance which looks for everything like a young lady." In another report he confirmed the importance of such "phenomenal men" to the allure of the Village balls, when he commented that a ball had attracted "the usual crowd who go expecting to find ["Homosexualists"] there. Some of the latter mocking [the "Homosexualists"], others actually patronizing them, associating with them during the night and dancing with them." "I mean," he added, "*men* with *men*."

Part of the attraction of an amusement district such as Greenwich Village was that it constituted a liminal space in which visitors were encouraged to disregard some of the social injunctions that normally constrained their behavior, allowing them to observe and vicariously experience behavior that in other settings—particularly their own neighborhoods—they might consider objectionable enough to suppress. The entrepreneurs who organized these balls were well aware of this and welcomed the presence of flamboyant gay men—sometimes making them a part of the pageants they staged—precisely because they knew that they enhanced the reputation and appeal of such events. Although some of the Village bohemians expressed reservations about the presence of such men, bohemian ideology encouraged the toleration of unconventional forms of sexual expression and identity. Gay people clearly took advantage of the opening created by this tolerance to claim their right to participate in Village affairs.

III
· · · · ·

By the twenties the presence of both gay men and lesbians in the Village was firmly established. No longer were they simply visitors to the Liberal Club's masquerade balls: By the mid-twenties they were organizing their *own* balls at Webster Hall, and had appropriated as their own many of the other social spaces created by the bohemians of the teens. Chief among these were the cheap Italian restaurants, cafeterias, and tearooms that crowded the Village and served as the meeting grounds for its bohemians. Gay men and lesbians seem to have become noticeable in such locales during the war, at about the same time they began attracting attention at the Liberal Club's balls. By the end of the war, the gay presence seemed to some worried observers to have become ubiquitous: An antivice agent investigating a MacDougal Street restaurant in 1919 commented that "In this restaurant, *as in all other Greenwich Village places* [emphasis added], there are all sorts of people among [the customers], many obviously prostitutes and perverts, especially the latter."

The gay presence became even more noticeable after the war, even though any commercial establishment that tolerated the presence of "obvious" homosexuals was subject to raids by the police and other forms of harassment. For the general cultural ethos generated in New York by Prohibition—and the general corruption of the police that accompanied Prohibition—tended to sanction the flouting of convention and made it easier for gay speakeasies to survive. Suddenly every tavern—not just the ones frequented by homosexuals—had to bribe the police and warn its customers to be prepared to hide what they were doing at a moment's notice. The popular opposition to enforcement and the systematic use of payoffs and criminal protection to protect speakeasies protected gay clubs as well.

Some speakeasies allowed lesbians and gay men to gather on their premises so long as they did nothing to draw police attention. More significantly, by the early twenties lesbians and gay men had begun opening their own speakeasies and tearooms, modeling their operations on those of the small-scale entrepreneurs whose establishments had played an important role in building the original Village community. Gregarious men and women whose personalities set the tone for their establishments, they attracted a

· · · ·

following and ensured that new patrons were welcomed and introduced to regulars; their restaurants and cafés, known as personality clubs, served as the salons of the Village intelligentsia. They sponsored poetry readings, musicales, and discussion groups and, above all else, offered a congenial environment in which regulars could maintain ties with their friends and meet other like-minded people. The best known of such locales in the teens was Polly's Restaurant on MacDougal Street. Run by Paula Holladay, the restaurant served as the unofficial dining club of the Liberal Club, which met in the rooms above it.

When several lesbians and gay men opened such places in the 1920s, they quickly became important centers of gay social life. Gay residents of the Village formed the core of their patronage, but they also provided a home-away-from-home for gay men and lesbians visiting the Village from other parts of town, a place where people who had no private space of their own in the neighborhood could gather nightly and construct a social world for themselves. This function was especially important for poorer men and women; Caroline Ware noted that many would-be Villagers forced by high rents to live with their relatives in the outer boroughs had succeeded in making the Village the core of their social world only by spending their evenings in its tearooms and cafeterias, and their number surely included gay men and women. While the patrons of the gay-run tearooms were not exclusively gay, they predominated and set the tone. By the late twenties, as Ware discovered, most "personality clubs" had closed, making it more difficult for newcomers to meet others and become a part of the Village community. But lesbian and gay clubs represented a notable exception to this trend, and even Ware had to admit that homosexuals and, most especially, lesbians found it easier than most other newcomers to gain an entrée into the Village community.

The best-known gay "personality club" in the Village in the 1920s was Paul and Joe's, whose development reflects the increasing prominence of gay clubs over the course of the decade. It had opened as an Italian restaurant at the corner of Sixth Avenue and Ninth Street in 1912, and during the war years, when the Village was crowded with soldiers on leave, it was considered a "tough place" reputed to host prostitutes who robbed their customers. Although some gay men and lesbians may have patronized it then, it did not have a gay reputation and only seems to have begun cultivating a homosexual following after the war, when it began hosting impromptu drag performances. By the early twenties the restaurant had established itself as a major gay locale in the Village: One man reported in 1922 that after a *very* late Saturday night of carousing, "On Sunday I always went to [Paul and Joe's], which is the main rendezvous for homosexuals." In 1924 Paul and Joe moved their restaurant up Sixth Avenue to a building on the corner of Nineteenth Street, thus removing it from the Village proper.

There they controlled the rooms upstairs, which patrons could rent for the evening for private parties. With the move Paul and Joe consolidated their position, quickly becoming, by one account, the "headquarters for every well-known Lesbian and Queen in town," who felt no need to hide their homosexuality and who were joined by numerous stage and screen celebrities, opera divas, and underworld figures. The restaurant also became publicly identified as a gay rendezvous: One gossip sheet mentioned its homosexual patrons several times in 1924, and in 1925 the writer and Village booster Bobby Edwards described it as the "hangout of dainty elves and stern women" in the pages of his magazine, the *Greenwich Village Quill*. It closed around 1927.

Although Paul and Joe's was located several blocks north of Washington Square, most gay restaurants and tearooms were located in the heart of the Village's bohemian commercial district just south and west of the Square, along MacDougal Street to the south and along West Third and Fourth streets as far west as Sixth Avenue and Sheridan Square. The arrangements made for the Fourth of July party held in 1922 at the Jungle, a "hang out for fairies" at Cornelia Street and Sixth Avenue, indicate the security gay men and lesbians felt in the area. The club advertised its party by distributing a handbill promising souvenirs, refreshments, a jazz band, and entertainment by "Rosebud" and "Countess." Rosebud and Countess were men—not female impersonators, but gay men, or "degenerates," as an investigator who had attended the event after seeing the notice described them—apparently with a local reputation strong enough to draw a crowd. Their audience consisted primarily of unattached men and women, the investigator reported, most of them apparently "fairies," many of them seemingly wealthy, "lady lovers of [the] Greenwich Village type" (by which, significantly, he meant lesbians), and, apparently, a few interested heterosexuals. The club had obviously made arrangements to ensure police protection—and protection from the police: The investigator noted that "a uniformed patrolman who is stationed in here was sitting with some of these fairies at one table and conversing with them and also entertained by them. . . . It appeared that he took a great interest [in] this performance and clapped his hands after [the] performance was over."

By the mid-twenties the MacDougal Street block south of Washington Square—site of the Provincetown Playhouse and numerous bohemian tearooms, gift shops, and speakeasies—had become the most important, and certainly the best-known, locus of gay and lesbian commercial institutions. Lesbians managed several of the speaks there in the twenties. The most infamous of the lesbian proprietors was Eva Kotchever, a Polish Jewish émigré who went by the name Eve Adams, an androgynous pseudonym whose biblical origins her Protestant persecutors might well have found blasphemous. Called the "queen of the third sex" by one paper, she ran the Black

Rabbit, "one of the Village's gay stamping grounds," popular with the after-theater crowd and apparently as well known for its lesbians in overalls as for its rum concoctions.

Although Adams's tearoom and the other gay-run clubs that succeeded it on MacDougal Street encountered opposition in the Village, this should not obscure the more important fact that the very existence of such clubs in a middle-class cultural milieu was unprecedented. Before the development of the bohemian community in the Village, middle-class gay life had existed but had always been conducted covertly, at private parties or at more public locales where the people involved strove to hide their identities and the significance of their interactions. The development of tearooms, restaurants, and dances publicly known to be frequented by gay people as well as by other bohemians represented an unprecedented expansion in the possibilities for gay sociability, different from previous patterns of working- and middle-class gay life alike.

The gay history of Greenwich Village suggests the extent to which the Village in the teens and twenties came to represent to the rest of the city what New York as a whole represented to the rest of the nation: a peculiar social territory in which the normal social constraints on behavior seemed to have been suspended and where men and women built unconventional lives outside the family nexus. Attracted by the Village's bohemian reputation, gay men and lesbians soon played a distinctive role in shaping both the image and reality of the Village, for they became part of the spectacle that defined the neighborhood's distinctive character, even as they used the cultural space made available by that character to turn it into a haven. Although their numbers continued to be small and their fellow Villagers did not always live up to their reputation for open-mindedness, in the 1920s gay people seized the opportunity provided by Village culture to begin building the city's most famous gay enclave.

• • • • •

NOTES

1. *Greenwich Village: A Local Review* (April 1929): n.p.
2. Ellen Kay Trimberger, "Feminism, Men, and Modern Love: Greenwich Village, 1900–1925," in *Powers of Desire: The Politics of Sexuality*, ed. Ann Snitow, Christine Stansell, and Sharon Thompson (New York: Monthly Review Press, 1983), 131–152; Leslie Fishbein, *Rebels in Bohemia: The Radicals of the Masses, 1911–1917* (Chapel Hill: University of North Carolina Press, 1982).
3. Malcolm Cowley, *Exile's Return* (1934; reprint, New York: Viking, 1956), 52.

• • • •

4. Judith Schwarz, *Radical Feminists of Heterodoxy: Greenwich Village, 1912–1940* (Lebanon, N.H.: New Victoria Publishers, 1982).

5. Louis Sheaffer, *O'Neill, Son and Playwright* (London: J. M. Dent & Sons, 1969), 352–353; idem, *O'Neill, Son and Artist* (London: Paul Elek, 1974), 242.

6. *Evening-Graphic*, August 28, 1931, p. 6.

7. *Evening-Graphic*, August 25, 1931, p. 3.

8. Caroline Ware, *Greenwich Village, 1920–1930: A Comment on American Civilization in the Post-War Years* (New York: Houghton Mifflin, 1935), 96, 238.

9. Floyd Dell, *Love in Greenwich Village* (New York: Doran, 1926), 299.

THE BEAT GENERATION IN THE VILLAGE

Barry Miles

American bohemianism is said to have started with Edgar Allan Poe, who, in his endless search for cheap lodgings, often found himself living in Greenwich Village. America's first Latin Quarter, New York's Montmartre, forever associated in the public mind with artists and bohemians—it was obvious that the stereotypical beatniks of the late fifties, with their bongos, flasks of cheap Chianti, berets, and sandals, would live in the Village. The original Beat Generation—Kerouac, Burroughs, Ginsberg, Corso, et al.—who were active in the forties and fifties, met in the Village bars and coffee shops, but the Village was already too expensive for them actually to live there.

In December 1943, a few days before Christmas, seventeen-year-old Allen Ginsberg, a freshman at Columbia, wrote to his elder brother Eugene: "Saturday I plan to go down to Greenwich Village with a friend of mine who claims to be an 'intellectual' and knows queer and interesting people there. I plan to get drunk Saturday evening, if I can. I'll tell you the issue."

His guide on this, his first visit, was Lucien Carr, a friend from St. Louis who lived on his floor at Union Theological Seminary, which was being used for student housing during the war. Carr first took Ginsberg to visit a hometown friend, David Kammerer, who had a room at 44 Morton Street, off Seventh Avenue. To Ginsberg, who grew up in Paterson, New Jersey, and had traveled little, the simple act of walking among the garbage cans

This essay is drawn from Barry Miles's Ginsberg, *a biography published in 1989 by Simon & Schuster. All quoted material is referenced in that volume.*

• • • •

64. Lucien Carr *(left)* and Allen Ginsberg in Washington Square on Easter Sunday, 1948 *(Allen Ginsberg Archive)*

and piles of dirty snow on those legendary streets was an exciting experience, made doubly so because he was aware of his homosexuality but had not yet revealed it to anyone, yet here he was "going down to the Village where all the fairies were. It was both romantically glorious and at the same time frightening and frustrating." After introductions had been made, they headed out, edging their way gingerly over the icy sidewalk of Minetta Lane to the Minetta Tavern—in those days one of the main bohemian watering holes in the Village—for Ginsberg's first drink in Greenwich Village.

A few days later Ginsberg and Carr again took the subway down to Christopher Street, but this time Kammerer was out. Undaunted, Carr led Ginsberg around the corner to 69 Bedford Street, where lived another hometown friend: William Seward Burroughs. He had one room on the second floor with French windows overlooking a small yard. Upstairs lived a lesbian friend of his named Louise. Burroughs liked Louise because, in his words, she was "straightforward, manly and reliable." (She eventually appeared as Agnes in the unpublished William Burroughs–Jack Kerouac collaborative novel *And the Hippos Were Boiled in Their Tanks.*) Ginsberg was delighted; the Village was proving to be everything he had hoped.

Littered with books but little else, Burroughs's room contained an old settee and an upturned log that served as both coffee table and chair. Carr told them about a fight he had been involved in after getting drunk at the Minetta Tavern with Kammerer. They had gone on to the studio of a gay portrait painter he knew, but the visit developed into a brawl that had demolished most of the painter's studio, and Carr had bitten off part of the painter's earlobe as well as sinking his teeth into Kammerer's shoulder. Recalling the event, Ginsberg said: "I thought it was pretty shocking and amazing. I never heard of *anything* like that because I was from East Side High School in Paterson, New Jersey. I didn't know people went around getting drunk and biting people's ears off!" The Village, even in wartime, lived up to its reputation.

Burroughs and Kammerer frequented the San Remo and Chumley's, as well as the Minetta Tavern, sometimes with novelist Chandler Brossard, then a reporter for *The New Yorker's* "Talk of the Town" column, who lived in Kammerer's building. Burroughs, whose grandfather had invented the adding machine and founded the Burroughs Corporation, was working as a bartender at the time, even though he was receiving an allowance of two hundred dollars a month from his parents in St. Louis. For someone like Burroughs, the Village was a refuge where he could live as he wished without encountering the disapproval of his fellow citizens.

Through Lucien Carr, Ginsberg also met Jack Kerouac, a merchant seaman living with his girlfriend, Edie Parker, near the Columbia campus. Parker was still at college, but Kerouac, who had attended Columbia on a football scholarship, had argued with the coach and left the college under less than agreeable conditions. He was officially "unwelcome on the campus."

Ginsberg, Kerouac, and Carr were romantic idealists, inspired by Yeats's "A Vision" and concerned with creating a "new vision" of their own—an inchoate version of what would become known as the philosophy of the Beat Generation. They read Paul Verlaine, Charles Baudelaire, Arthur Rimbaud, Jean Cocteau, and Percy Bysshe Shelley as well as the works of Samuel Taylor Coleridge, Edward Fitzgerald, and the Marquis de Sade. Sitting in the West End Bar, across from the Columbia campus, they created their own *vie de bohème:* Their Pernod became absinthe; shabby Broadway, the Boulevard St. Germain. Whenever possible, they made the trip downtown, where Greenwich Village provided the same artistic and tolerant atmosphere they imagined had existed on the Left Bank before the war.

David Kammerer was a homosexual who had become obsessed with Carr while teaching him in a grade-school play group. Although Carr was not gay, Kammerer pursued him relentlessly. Carr left St. Louis and attended Bowdoin College in Maine and several other schools, including the University of Chicago, but Kammerer followed him everywhere to pester him and demand his friendship. One night, while Carr and Kammerer were sitting in Morningside Park after the West End Bar had closed, matters came to a head: Kammerer threatened to harm Carr's girlfriend and lunged at him. "Dave wanted Lucien to stab him," says Burroughs, and that was what happened. Defending himself with a Boy Scout knife, Carr stabbed Kammerer twice through the heart, killing him. Jailed for two years, after his release, Carr kept a certain distance, at least in public, from the others. This "honor killing," as it was labeled by the newspapers, brought an end to the first phase of the Beat Generation.

• • • • •

The poet Harold Norse remembers meeting Ginsberg in 1944, on his way home to the Village on the subway at 3:00 A.M. There was one other person in the car, a young man wearing a red bandanna who was reciting French poetry to himself, aloud. The noise of the train prevented Norse from hearing what was being said until, at one stop, he caught enough to identify "The Drunken Boatman" and called out: "Rimbaud!"

"You're a poet!" exclaimed Ginsberg. Getting into conversation, they went to Norse's tiny apartment on Horatio Street near the meat market, where they read their poems to each other. "I found him sexy and appealing but had no idea of his poetic capacities," Norse recalls. "The poems he showed me were slight four-liners, and he seemed even shyer than I was." In Norse's autobiography, *Memoirs of a Bastard Angel,* he wrote: "For Allen, as for all of us, the Village was an oasis in the puritan desert, a watering place for the soul. The Village offered freewheeling sex. The closet cases of America were drawn to the bars and hangouts of Bohemia, longing to fulfill their secret desires."

The Beats first began experimenting with drugs, mostly morphine and benzedrine, in 1945, when Kerouac, Burroughs, Ginsberg, and several other friends shared an apartment on West 115th Street. Following Burroughs's lead, they explored the Times Square area, where the prostitutes, hustlers, junkies, jazz musicians, servicemen, jazz clubs, all-night bars, and Automats made it the most exciting place in the city. The twenty-four-hour neon lighting held a particular attraction for them, probably associated with the amphetamine they were using. Burroughs was thirty, but the others were still very young: Ginsberg was a teenager, Kerouac only twenty-three.

Slowly their ideas for a new society developed, and they began to meet like-minded people. The dropping of A-bombs on Japan and the revelation of the horrors of the concentration camps combined with the petty puritanism of bourgeois America to cause widespread disillusion with the established values of society and to lead them to seek another direction, away from hypocrisy toward honesty, truthfulness, and, they hoped, a new spirituality. Burroughs's particular interest in drugs led him to the society of petty criminals and hoodlums, among whom he met Herbert Huncke, the man who provided the key word *beat* for the sobriquet Beat Generation and the Times Square hustler who had first introduced Burroughs to morphine.

65. Hal Chase, Jack Kerouac, Allen Ginsberg, and William Burroughs *(left to right)* in 1945 *(Allen Ginsberg Archive)*

(Burroughs tells the full story in his autobiographical novel *Junky*.) Burroughs left New York to grow marijuana in Texas in June 1946, after a drug bust at the 115th Street apartment. From Texas he moved to New Orleans, where he again ran into trouble with the law. He continued south to Mexico City and did not return to New York until 1953.

Shortly after Burroughs left a young car thief from Denver named Neal Cassady appeared on the scene. Both Kerouac and Ginsberg were enchanted by him. Ginsberg fell in love and began a long-drawn-out, torturous relationship with him. Kerouac worshiped just as avidly, and spent much of the late forties journeying back and forth across the United States with Cassady at the wheel, later casting him as the hero, Dean Moriarty, in *On the Road*. When not in San Francisco or Denver with Cassady, Kerouac stayed at home with his mother in Ozone Park, living off her wages from the shoe factory where she worked. He had no apartment of his own.

In the late forties the most likely place to meet Ginsberg, Kerouac, and their circle of friends was the San Remo, at 93 MacDougal Street, on the northwest corner of Bleecker. A typically dark and smoky New York bar with a loud jukebox and crowded tables, the San Remo stayed open until 4:00 A.M. The alcoholic poet Max Bodenheim could often be found propping up the bar—above which hung a photograph of him in his younger days. Among its regulars were James Agee, Larry Rivers, Paul Goodman, John Cage, Merce Cunningham, W. H. Auden, Chester Kallman, Harold Norse, and virtually everybody associated with Judith Malina and Julian Beck's newly launched Living Theatre. Jackson Pollock, Willem de Kooning, Franz Kline, and many other abstract expressionists also hung out there when they weren't at the Cedar Street Tavern over on University Place.

"The only people for me," says Sal Paradise, Jack Kerouac's narrator in *On the Road*, "are the mad ones, the ones who are mad to live, mad to talk, mad to be saved, desirous of everything at the same time, the ones who never yawn or say a commonplace thing, but burn, burn, burn like fabulous yellow roman candles exploding like spiders across the stars."

This could easily have been a description of Bill Cannastra, a madcap Italian American lawyer, who despite poor attendance had managed to graduate from Harvard Law School. (He was also drunk when he took his bar examinations.) A regular at the San Remo, Cannastra was a friend of both Kerouac and Ginsberg, the leader of a large group of talented friends, most of whom were writers or artists of some sort, and one of the main players in the late forties Village scene. He lived three doors from Lucien Carr at 125 West Twenty-first Street, the site of frequent parties. Cannastra's many exploits were later featured in Alan Harrington's *The Secret Swinger*, in which he appears as Bill Genovese.

Cannastra enjoyed scaring his friends and passers-by by dodging through busy traffic and was knocked down on a number of occasions. Another trick was to lie down in the middle of an avenue before advancing traffic just as the lights changed a block away. A favorite party piece was to cavort drunkenly along the unrailed parapet on the roof of his building, taking greater and greater risks the more his friends pleaded with him to come down. He would encourage guests to take part in a competition to see who could hold his or her head the longest in the oven with the gas on and at parties he would dance barefoot across broken glass. Although he was mostly self-destructive, Cannastra sometimes turned his violence on others, once attempting to set fire to a friend who had passed out in a drunken stupor.

Alan Harrington's novel described the scene: "Genovese's loft was sometimes strewn with broken glass. People made love in the bathroom (often, without realizing it, for a circle of spectators looking down from the skylight). They made love on the fire escape and on the roof. . . . The loft was divided into sections by translucent hanging screens, and there were unmade beds and cots everywhere. The light of a bare bulb shone in the kitchen by the fire escape, but as you moved into the loft's interior smaller amounts of light filtered through the screens, until at the far end it was a dark place. Here young philosophers sat on a window ledge. Clutching dirty coffee cups filled with Tallyho beer, or drinking blended whiskey from old jelly glasses, they looked out over the low roofs of Chelsea, and back into the room where shadowy people were cutting their feet on glass fragments, and Bill Genovese ate glass and music roared out of the dark."

The broken glass also featured in Ginsberg's poem *Howl*: "(who) danced on broken wineglasses barefoot, smashed phonograph records of nostalgic European 1930s German jazz finished the whiskey and threw up groaning into the bloody toilet." To Ginsberg, Cannastra was another of the "best minds" of his generation, "destroyed by madness." Gerald Nicosia's biography of Kerouac, *Memory Babe*, says that "practically every gathering at the loft was planned to end as a sexual occasion. As much as these orgies gratified Cannastra's voyeurism, there was probably a deeper motivation involved, for a large part of Cannastra's life was a struggle to feel less like an outsider, to blend in with everybody else and relax. . . . At any rate, after getting thoroughly drunk, people climbed on top of one another on the beds, everyone groping everyone else. Actual sex acts when they occurred were virtually meaningless."

Between 1948 and 1950, Cannastra's alcoholism overcame him. He lost his job with a New York law firm, and his friends began to desert him. He was bisexual, and though his sexual preference seems to have been for men, in 1950 he was living with a twenty-year-old woman called Joan Haverty, who shared his enthusiasm for pranks and happily joined him in his escapades. Together they would roam the fire escapes, peering unseen into people's apartments and commenting on their mundane lives. Cannastra was fond of spying on people and had drilled peepholes into the wall of his bathroom so that he could watch his guests use it.

• • • •

Just after midnight on the morning of October 12, 1950, Cannastra was out on the town with a group of friends who were making their way to Carr's loft to borrow some money. They boarded the northbound Lexington Avenue IRT local train, heading for Twenty-third Street. At the Bleecker Street stop one of the party mentioned Winnie, the black bartender at the Bleecker Tavern, a favorite haunt. The doors closed and the train began to pull out of the station when Cannastra, as a joke, jumped to his feet and lunged out of the window on the platform side as if he meant to go to the bar. He misjudged his leap and found himself unbalanced, with his head and shoulders hanging too far out of the window. His friends rushed to save him, grabbing at his clothing, but his coat tore away in their hands. His shoulders were too far out of the window for them to reach. The train picked up speed, and he began to scream in terror but it was too late. As the train entered the tunnel, there was a thud and he was snatched from their hands, out of the window and onto the tracks. Someone pulled the emergency cord, but he was dragged for fifty-five feet before the train came to a halt. He was pronounced dead on arrival at Columbus Hospital.

After Cannastra's death Jack Kerouac devoted a tremendous amount of attention to Joan Haverty, Cannastra's girlfriend, who was still living in the loft. She was deeply impressed by the twenty-seven-year-old Kerouac. Within a few days he had moved into the apartment, and then to everyone's surprise, on November 17, 1950, only a month after Cannastra's death, Jack and Joan married. Afterward there was a party for two hundred at the loft. Attended by all the San Remo regulars, it was strangely subdued despite Kerouac's attempts to liven things up.

The marriage was doomed. Although in the early days it seemed to be a marriage based on love, Kerouac's views on marriage were old fashioned, even for 1950. Joan was not allowed to accompany him when he went visiting his friends, because Kerouac thought wives belonged at home with the dishes. She was not allowed to hold any opinions but those that Kerouac espoused; her role was to wash, cook, and clean for him as well as to keep them both from her earnings as a dressmaker. To earn extra money she took a job in a department store during the busy Christmas season, but Kerouac was lonely sitting at home writing and insisted that they give up the loft and move in with his mother in Queens. The move was a disaster: Kerouac and his mother spoke French together most of the time so that Joan was unable to understand them, and Kerouac spent a lot of his time going to parties and hanging out with his friends. Kerouac made her hand over her wage check to his mother each week, and Mrs. Kerouac regarded her as little more than a slave provided by her son to do all the housework.

It took only a few weeks for Joan to deliver an ultimatum: She was returning to Manhattan. Kerouac could either live with her or stay home with his mother. In January 1951 she found a new job and took an apartment at 454 West Twentieth Street, in the beautiful Greek Revival row that forms the south side of Chelsea Square between Ninth and Tenth avenues. She was at work when the moving men collected her things, but during her lunch break she went over to West Twentieth to see how the move was progressing. Sitting outside the building on his rolltop desk was Kerouac, his slippers in his hand. She took him in.

Among the items Joan had salvaged from Cannastra's loft was a pile of twenty-foot rolls of Japanese writing paper that provided the solution to one of Kerouac's problems. He did not believe in correcting his writing—a system he called "spontaneous prose"—and although he was a fast, accurate typist, he always felt stymied by the need to keep feeding his typewriter with paper. (A word processor would have suited him admirably.) Early in April 1951 he taped the rolls of paper together and fed one end into his typewriter. Writing continuously, often with little sleep, he had already written 34,000 words by April 9. By April 20 his masterpiece, *On the Road*—consisting of one long paragraph with little punctuation—was almost finished, with more than 86,000 words on a 120-foot roll. The latter part of the manuscript was written at Lucien Carr's Twenty-first Street loft, where one of the hazards was Carr's dog, who ate the last four feet of the roll.

Unfortunately his marriage to Joan had not been much improved by the move back to Manhattan. Jack's meanness—he wouldn't even share his cigarettes with Joan—his infidelities, and the fact that she was still a domestic slave at home after working all day at Stouffer's as a waitress, placed intolerable pressure on the relationship. Despite the fact that Jack often slept at Carr's loft, Joan managed to get pregnant, something that they had been trying hard for in the earlier days of their brief marriage. Now, as they were separating, Kerouac reacted with fear and anger at the news. She had revenged herself for his affairs by bringing a fellow worker at the restaurant home to her bed. Kerouac felt cuckolded and, despite his Catholicism, demanded that she get an abortion, claiming that the baby was not his. Joan refused and threw him out. After living at Carr's for a few weeks, he returned to live with his mother.

Jan Kerouac was born on February 16, 1952, but despite her uncanny physical likeness to her father, Kerouac denied paternity and went into hiding in California rather than pay child support. His daughter grew up desperately impoverished during the years of his greatest success. By the age of fourteen she was a heroin addict, selling herself on the streets to get a fix. She later recorded her experiences in *Baby Driver* and *Trainsongs*, two painfully honest autobiographical volumes of hippie life in the sixties.

• • • • •

Of the original members of the Beat Generation, Gregory Corso had the greatest claim to a Greenwich Village connection, having had the good fortune to be born above the funeral parlor on the southwest corner of

Bleecker and MacDougal streets. In 1930, when he was only six months old, his eighteen-year-old mother returned to her home in Italy. Thereafter his father boarded him with foster parents for most of his childhood. By the age of twelve he was out on the streets, where he was caught stealing food and sent to the Tombs. After his release the next year, he was arrested again almost immediately—having nowhere to go, he had broken into a youth center to sleep—and was returned to the Tombs. The next time he hit the streets he was fifteen and streetwise.

His conviction for organizing a robbery using walkie-talkies resulted in his spending the years 1947 to 1950 in Clinton Prison, at Dannemora, New York, near the Canadian border. It was there he learned to be a poet, reading his way through the prison copy of a 1905 standard dictionary, reveling in the obscure and archaic words. He studied history and, not knowing where to start, began with the Greeks. When he was released, just before his twentieth birthday, he had the beginnings of a classical education.

It was not long after he got out of prison that he met Allen Ginsberg. Corso was sitting at a table in the Pony Stable, a lesbian bar on Third Street at Sixth Avenue, enthusiastically telling some new acquaintances what a great poet he was. He had with him a sheaf of professionally typed poems. Ginsberg immediately recognized how good they were and soon introduced Corso to Jack Kerouac, Lucien Carr, and Ginsberg's other friends. The young poet quickly became the final member of the original Beat group.

The constant mobility of the Beats meant that whoever had an apartment invariably had many of the other members of the group staying with him. Kerouac, for instance, never had an apartment of his own. Throughout his entire life, he either stayed with friends or lived with his mother. Ginsberg was the only member of the group who actually took regular jobs for a living, working as a copyboy, typist, and for six years as a market researcher. Having a job meant that he had an apartment, and there was a time in 1953 when Burroughs, Corso, and Kerouac were all staying with him. Ginsberg moved into his first apartment near the Village, an eighteen-dollar-a-month, two-room attic with dormer windows at 346 West Fifteenth, between Eighth and Ninth avenues, in December 1951. It is still there, a nondescript brownstone dwarfed by the huge bulk of the Port Authority warehouse, which occupies the entire block on the north side of Fifteenth Street. His feelings about the place are expressed in the poem "Walking Home at Night," which ends: "Remembering / my attic I reached / my hands to my head and hissed / 'Oh God how horrible!'" While he was there he worked on many of the poems that later appeared in his book *Empty Mirror*.

Ginsberg was using his marketing skills in another direction. While in Texas and Mexico City, Burroughs had written a novel about his experiences as a heroin addict in New York, New Orleans, and Mexico City that

Ginsberg had been trying to sell for him. After seeing virtually every editor in town, he turned to his friend Carl Solomon, who worked at his uncle's paperback publishing company, Ace Books. Solomon was enthusiastic about the idea of publishing something other than the usual run of westerns and whodunits, and Burroughs was enthusiastic about a paperback original. Out of concern that they might be advocating the use of drugs by publishing a junkie's memoirs, Ace hesitated before finally putting *Junky* on the news-stands in the summer of 1953. It had a lurid cover of a woman in a red dress struggling with a man for possession of a hypodermic syringe, and was bound back-to-back with *Narcotic Agent*, by Maurice Helbrant, described as "a gripping true adventure of a T-man's war against the dope menace." Burroughs published the book under the pseudonym of William Lee because he didn't want his parents to read it and cut off his allowance.

Kerouac was not having comparable luck in getting his books into print. His first book, *The Town and the City,* a conventional Thomas Wolfean novel, had been published in 1950 but had not set the world on fire. No one wanted the more radical *On the Road* or his subsequent books *Dr. Sax* and *Maggie Cassady.* Ginsberg managed to get an advance for him from Ace for *On the Road*, but the text as Kerouac presented it, though no longer on one long roll of paper, was still too far out for them, and they dropped their option.

Kerouac had written *Dr. Sax* while staying with Burroughs in Mexico City. It was unfinished when he returned to New York, where he and Ginsberg had finally come up with an ending while leaning on a fence in the Village at West Fourth Street and Sixth Avenue in the summer sunshine. *Dr. Sax* is a novel of awakening youth based on Kerouac's upbringing in Lowell, Massachusetts. It explores the demons and monsters of his fantasy-ridden adolescent world. Memories and dreams give way to an apocalyptic vision of a huge snake emerging from the center of the earth, but Kerouac did not know how to go on. Ginsberg proposed a Shakespearian solution: "Ah! 'twas a husk of doves," suggesting that the snake, representing all the evil in the world, was nothing but a dry husk surrounding a flock of beautiful doves. Kerouac liked the idea and wrote: "His Snake would not destroy the world but merely be a great skin of doves on coming-out day." Years later Ginsberg arranged for *Dr. Sax* to be published by Grove Press.

By October 1952 Ginsberg was earning enough money as a free-lancer in market research to enable him to move to a bigger apartment on the Lower East Side, an area in which he has lived ever since. Located at 206 East Seventh Street, between Avenues B and C, a half block from Tompkins Square Park, Ginsberg's apartment was, as usual, a gathering point where the other, more itinerant Beats could stay. Gregory Corso was the first to move in. In the summer of 1953 Ginsberg took a forty-five-dollar-a-week job as copyboy at the *New York World-Telegram*, which offered shorter hours

· · · ·

than his job in market research in the Empire State Building. Corso lived off his wages, but Ginsberg did not complain because he enjoyed having Corso around. Kerouac, who had been living in California with Neal Cassady, now returned to his mother and made frequent visits to the city to stay with them.

They hung out at the San Remo, still largely populated by a collection of Village types Ginsberg referred to as "subterraneans." Kerouac later appropriated the name for his book about the bohemian scene in Greenwich Village and the Lower East Side around 1952–1953. Although certain unconvincing cosmetic changes were made in the published text to relocate the book in San Francisco to avoid charges of libel, the book is peopled by many of the same characters that appeared in Burroughs's *Junky* and Ginsberg's *Howl*. One of them, Adam Moorad (Ginsberg's name in the book), is credited with inventing the name. "The subterraneans," wrote Kerouac, "is a name invented by . . . a poet and friend of mine who said, 'They are hip without being slick, they are intelligent without being corny, they are intellectual as hell and know all about Pound without being pretentious or talking too much about it, they are very quiet, they are very Christlike.'"

In the summer of 1953 William Burroughs, who had returned to New York City for the first time in seven years while en route to Tangier, displaced Corso from Ginsberg's apartment. While Burroughs was in New York, he was mildly addicted to Dolophine, an early form of methadone and the pill of choice to replace junk in the early fifties. His habit did not trouble him at all, because he could always score "dollies" at Joe's Luncheonette on Cornelia Street, the subterraneans' favorite place to eat.

Ginsberg and Burroughs did a great deal of work while Burroughs was in town. Burroughs had been on an expedition to South America in search of the telepathic, hallucinogenic *yage*, and his letters from there were filled with anecdotes, routines, and hilarious descriptions of his tribulations. Together they assembled the material into the third book in a projected trilogy—*Junky, Queer,* and *Yage*—and hired Alene Lee, Jack Kerouac's new girlfriend, to type it up. Sections from all three books were later incorporated into a text known as *Interzone*, which for a time had the working title of *Naked Lunch*. *Yage* was never published as conceived in 1953, but many of the letters were used in *The Yage Letters*, a volume of correspondence City Lights Books published in 1963. It was a creative period for Burroughs, and many of the ideas that appeared later in *The Naked Lunch* were first thought of at East Seventh Street. The futuristic vibrating city of Interzone, with its levels connected by a web of catwalks, was inspired by the fire escapes and washing lines in Ginsberg's backyard.

The mid-1950s was a time of exodus for the Beats. Burroughs left New York in December 1953 for Tangier. Apart from a short stay in 1965, he did not live in the United States again for more than twenty years, returning as a prodigal son in 1974 when he felt the atmosphere was finally amiable enough for him to live here peaceably. Kerouac continued to shuttle back and forth across the country, spending most of his time in California or Mexico City. He made a brief trip to Tangier in 1957 but did not like it and was back in New York for the publication of *On the Road*. Corso moved on to Cambridge, Massachusetts, where his first book, *The Vestal Lady on Brattle*, was published. Then he joined Ginsberg in San Francisco, traveled with him to Mexico City and from there on to Paris.

Ginsberg also left the city for an extended period. Apart from a four-month stopover en route to Tangier, he did not return to the city until August 1958. He first explored the jungles of Chiapas, Mexico, for six months before spending almost three years in San Francisco. Thereafter he toured Europe before living with Burroughs and Corso for a year or so in the Beat Hotel in Paris. When Ginsberg returned to New York City, he found that everything had changed. The publication of *On the Road* in September 1957 had made Kerouac famous and much in demand for television talk shows and interviews. Kerouac's sojourn in Europe had been short, and he was living with his girlfriend, Joyce Glassman, at her midtown apartment when the book came out and became an immediate best-seller. His unsuccessful attempts to handle the resultant fame and media attention are related very effectively in her autobiography, *Minor Characters*.

Kerouac used the money from *On the Road* to set up house with his mother in suburban Northport, Long Island, but she refused to return from Florida, where she was then living, unless Ginsberg and Burroughs were banned from the house. Kerouac's preference for his mother over his friends and literary associates effectively ended his participation in the group, although he often came into New York for drunken weekends until his death from alcoholism in 1969. Kerouac covered his shyness by drinking, but alcohol made him loud and sometimes belligerent, often resulting in barroom scuffles and fights.

On the Road caught the public imagination, and Greenwich Village began to fill with "weekend beatniks," a term coined by Herb Caen of the *San Francisco Chronicle* when writing about North Beach, San Francisco. But the original Beats had long gone. A decade had passed since the events chronicled in *On the Road* and *Howl*. Some of the players were already dead or had moved to the country. Others, like Burroughs and Corso, were expatriates, and the small-time gangsters and hoodlums Burroughs had hung out with in the forties were never part of the Greenwich Village scene. Herbert Huncke stuck to an uptown beat. The hero of *On the Road*, Neal Cassady, lived in California and had always made only short visits to New York. California was also the home of most of the second-generation Beats: Gary Snyder, Philip Whalen, Lawrence Ferlinghetti, Bob Kaufman, and the other heroes of Kerouac's books.

· · · ·

New York had a few home-grown second-generation Beats of its own, most notably LeRoi Jones (now Imamu Amiri Baraka) and Diane diPrima, two poets influenced by Ginsberg. But Ginsberg's own favorite New York poets were Ed Marshall and Frank O'Hara. Ginsberg made contact with all these new poets when he and his lover, Peter Orlovsky, passed through New York on their way to Europe in the winter of 1956–1957. They returned in August 1958 and found an apartment on the Lower East Side, between Avenues A and B at 170 East Second Street, overlooking an all-night Jewish bakery. Ginsberg enjoyed the sound of the noisy trucks coming and going all night, collecting fresh bagels and rye bread. The bakery also had a big clock in its front window, which was useful since Ginsberg didn't own one. It was here that Ginsberg wrote his greatest work, *Kaddish*, an elegy for his dead mother.

The poem had its inspiration in an all-night visit with his friend Zev Putterman, who lived on the corner of West Fourth and West Tenth streets—one of those anomalous Village addresses that so confuse tourists. They sat up talking, playing Ray Charles records, and taking morphine and Methedrine, a form of amphetamine new to Ginsberg. As the night wore on, Ginsberg chanted the verses of Shelley's *Adonais*. Then Putterman produced his old bar-mitzvah book of Hebrew ritual, and together they read aloud the central passages of the Kaddish, the Jewish prayer for the dead. Morning came and Ginsberg left, walking home to the Lower East Side.

He reached Seventh Avenue and walked south, through all the surreal empty streets, past all the familiar clubs and bookstores, groceries and delis, all closed and shuttered. The rhythms of the Kaddish rang in his head, and on reaching home, he sat down to write. *Kaddish* was written in one long thirty-hour session, beginning with an account of its genesis: "Downtown Manhattan, clear winter noon, and I've been up all night, talking, talking, reading the Kaddish aloud, listening to Ray Charles blues shout blind on the phonograph . . . / I go out and walk the street, look back over my shoulder, Seventh Avenue, the battlements of window office buildings shouldering each other high, under a cloud, tall as the sky."

•••••

By the end of 1958 the Village was being overrun by weekend beatniks. Ginsberg reported to his publisher, Lawrence Ferlinghetti: "God, reporters all over, all asking the same questions and no end in sight, it's getting stranger and stranger, life. Beginning to get invites from TV programs but have been holding out for scene where I can read poetry rather than discuss Beatnikism. The world is really mad."

The Village streets were filled with tourists and weekend beatniks in beards and berets. Beatnik cartoons appeared in *The New Yorker*, television

••••

companies made documentaries, and poet Ted Jones and photographer Fred McDarrah set up Rent-a-Beatnik, charging the squares steep fees to have their parties attended by a scruffy beatnik carrying bongo drums and a sheaf of bad poetry. The *New York Post* ran a twelve-part series on beatniks, and *Life* and *Time* worried whether America would survive this attack on its moral values. The situation was summed up very succinctly by Ted Jones in his poem "Let's Play Something":

> Let's play something. Let's play anything. Let's play bohemian, and wear odd clothes, and grow a beard or a ponytail, live in the Village for 200.00 a month for one small pad and stroll through Washington Square Park with a guitar and a chick looking sad.

Corso fled back to Europe, first to Athens and then to Paris, where he was joined in 1961 by Ginsberg and Orlovsky, who were slowly making their way to India. Kerouac moved to Florida with his mother. Burroughs remained in Tangier. The transition from Beat to beatnik was complete, and it would not be long before the tolerant streets of Greenwich Village and the Lower East Side were filled with a new crop of bohemians: the hippies.

"RADICAL AGENDAS"
VILLAGE POLITICS

Complacency Challenged

The acute social conscience and reforming impulses credited to Greenwich Village were embedded in community traditions, institutions, and charities organized to respond to neighborhood problems as well as larger injustices. Beginning in 1834, when local masons rioted in Washington Square to protest New York University's use of building stone cut by Sing Sing prisoners, demonstrators wishing to publicize a cause often appropriated this historic park to stage message-based marches and rallies. Built in 1857 with the expectation of promoting free debate, the Great Hall of Cooper Union also emerged as a controversial theater of opinion. From its podium moral crusaders and other firebrands exposed the nineteenth-century public to a wide spectrum of progressive ideas, including women's rights and the interests of labor.

By the early twentieth century, the mounting strife of the labor movement in New York had stimulated the concern of many Village intellectuals. The Triangle Shirtwaist Factory Strike of 1909 and the catastrophic fire that ravaged the sweatshop two years later provided a powerful catalyst in inciting the Village community to seek constructive political action.

66. Cooper Union Built by the prosperous iron merchant Peter Cooper, Cooper Union provided a forum for new social and political ideas. As early as 1858, a local lyceum committee had taken charge of the institute's imposing auditorium "for the purpose of rendering the popular lecture an institution for the masses in this city" at a nominal admission. *(Museum of the City of New York)*

67. **Samuel Gompers at Cooper Union** In the fall of 1909 owners of the Triangle Shirtwaist Company on Washington Place locked out employees who had joined the International Ladies Garment Workers Union. At an emotional rally held in the Great Hall, Samuel Gompers, president of the American Federation of Labor, endorsed the ensuing strike. The walkout proved successful in winning gains for workers in more than 350 shops, although management succeeded in crushing the union at the Triangle Company. *(Brown Brothers)*

68. Triangle Shirtwaist Factory Fire on March 25, 1911 Tragedy struck the Triangle Company two years after its failed strike, when the top three floors of the ten-story loft building burst into flame. Finding the exit doors bolted by management to deter employee theft and early departures from shifts, 146 female garment workers died in the conflagration, many by leaping to the street below. Victor Gatto, an eyewitness to the fire, later painted this scene from memory. *(Museum of the City of New York)*

69. Police in charge of the bodies The Triangle Fire left an indelible impression on the nation's social conscience and on the Greenwich Village community. The sidewalks on Washington Place and Greene Street were converted into a makeshift morgue for the victims' charred bodies. For several days after the disaster, mourners assembled in Washington Square to express their outrage at the unnecessary loss of life. Although the sweatshop's owners were indicted and tried, they were acquitted. Village activists played an influential role in the resulting campaign to reform building codes and insurance laws, and to draft legislation requiring safer conditions in the workplace. *(Greenwich House Papers, Tamiment Institute Library, New York University)*

70. **Labor Day demonstration in Washington Square** In the aftermath of the Triangle Factory Fire, Washington Square served as a base of operations for an ever-increasing number of public demonstrations. In 1912 female marchers in New York City's Labor Day parade rallied in the Square to proclaim their rights as workers and citizens. That year marked the first participation of the Women's Trade Union League in the festivities. (*Brown Brothers*)

The Radical Rendezvous

The radicals who colonized Greenwich Village before World War I subscribed to the bohemian creed of informality, spurning on principle all traditions of structured socialization. In practice, however, they proved unusually adept at consolidating their scattered ranks in order to exchange, clarify, and promote their revolutionary aims. At first this bohemian underground commandeered select taverns, boarding hotels, and restaurants to use as companionable clubhouses. By 1913, three new depots had joined this network of neighborhood meeting centers: the Liberal Club on MacDougal Street, Mabel Dodge's salon at 23 Fifth Avenue, and the editorial offices of *The Masses* magazine on Greenwich Avenue. Each of these intellectual crossroads helped to focus and strengthen the hitherto diffuse voice of the Village vanguard, supplying critical voltage to its reforming crusades.

71. **Interior of Mabel Dodge's apartment on Washington Square** The conversational bill of fare served at Mabel Dodge's ranged from discussions of Freud and birth control to talks on cubism, socialism, and syndicalism. Her strategic location at the base of fashionable Fifth Avenue helped to connect uptown resources with a variety of bold Village projects. Rarely voicing strong opinions of her own, the hostess is said to have presided over these evenings with regal inscrutability. *(Yale Collection of American Literature, Beinecke Rare Book & Manuscript Library, Yale University)*

72. A session at the Liberal Club Relocated from Gramercy Park to 137 MacDougal Street in 1913 as a "Meeting Place for Those Interested in New Ideas," the Liberal Club sponsored programs spanning the gamut of "advanced" Village interests, from examinations of the tango and slit-skirt fads to weightier inquiries into eugenics, modern art, imagist poetry, and left-wing politics. The club also consolidated the functions of a pub, art gallery, dance hall, gaming room, and laboratory theater for neighborhood intellectuals. Members co-opted Polly's Restaurant below the club as their private dining annex, and used the Washington Square Book Shop next door as a lending library. (*Museum of the City of New York*)

73. Emma Goldman The most outspoken exponent of anarchist philosophy in early twentieth-century New York was Emma Goldman, a refugee of czarist Russia and adoptive citizen of the Village by way of the Lower East Side. Her fearless attacks on organized religion, American business, and conservative morality impressed many Village radicals, as did her missionary teachings on birth control, trade unionism, free love, and tolerance of homosexuality. At the pinnacle of her influence on Greenwich Village, she lived in tenement quarters on East Thirteenth Street that doubled as a publishing office for the anarchist journal *Mother Earth*. (*Tamiment Institute Library, New York University*)

• • • •

74. Alexander Berkman In his seven-year tenure as editor of *Mother Earth*, which began in 1908, the radical agitator Alexander Berkman enjoyed a high profile among Village revolutionaries because of his prolific anarchist writings and lectures, and his formative role in the organization of the Ferrer School on St. Marks Place. In 1919 he was deported to the Soviet Union during the height of the Red Scare, a fate shared by his anarchist colleague and former lover, Emma Goldman. *(Museum of the City of New York)*

75. Henrietta Rodman Best remembered for her role in acquainting the "university crowd, the social settlement crowd, and the Socialist crowd" with "the Liberal Club crowd," Rodman orchestrated the 1913 revolt that resulted in the Liberal Club's relocation. Her principal commitments were to the Feminist Alliance, a coalition she organized in 1914 to pressure for the removal of all social, political, and economic discrimination based on sex, and to secure cooperative housing for professional women of the Village. Rodman also courted notoriety as an early champion of dress reform. *(The Schlesinger Library, Radcliffe College)*

• • • •

76. *The Masses*'s office The descendant of a muckraking socialist organ that ceased publication in 1912, *The Masses* moved from Nassau Street to Greenwich Village in June 1913. Setting up editorial offices in a converted storefront at 91 Greenwich Avenue, the magazine emerged overnight as a meeting ground for revolutionary labor and the radical intelligentsia. Although propagandistic in intent, *The Masses* avoided allegiance to rigid party lines by adhering to an open publications policy and collective ownership. *(Tamiment Institute Library, New York University)*

77. Defendants and supporters outside the courthouse during *The Masses*'s first conspiracy trial; *left to right*: Crystal Eastman, Art Young, Max Eastman, Morris Hillquist, Merrill Rogers, Floyd Dell With the outbreak of World War I, *The Masses*'s strident stand against American involvement proved lethal to its economic survival. The Department of Justice twice indicted and brought the editors to trial under the Espionage Act. Although no convictions resulted, the government muffled the magazine by banning its sale from newsstands and revoking its second-class mailing privileges. Denied access to its postal subscribers, *The Masses* ceased publication in December 1917. *(National Archives, Washington, D.C.)*

• • • •

78. Architects of the Paterson silk strike Among the labor agitators summoned to Mabel Dodge's salon were Elizabeth Gurley Flynn, hailed as the Joan of Arc of American labor; her companion, Carlo Tresca (*at left*), lionized by Max Eastman as "the most pugnaciously hell-raising male rebel I could find in the United States"; and the IWW leader "Big Bill" Haywood, whose imposing figure and rough-hewn sincerity endeared him immediately to his Greenwich Village audience. (*Yvette Szekely Eastman from "Enjoyment of Living"*)

79. Paterson Strike Pageant program Village writers and artists first learned of the violent confrontation that had erupted between mill owners and factory operatives in Paterson, New Jersey, at Mabel Dodge's salon, for New York's major dailies had mounted a news blackout of the dispute. As the union funds available to sustain the early 1913 walkout dwindled, Village sympathizers formulated a plan to call attention to the workers' plight by staging a colossal pageant that would reenact pivotal incidents in the strike. (*Robert F. Wagner Labor Archives, New York University*)

80. **"Picketing the Mills" scene from the pageant** With start-up costs covered by Mabel Dodge, scenery painted by John Sloan, sets designed by Robert Edmond Jones, and a script and direction supplied by John Reed (whose recent eyewitness account of the strike had riveted readers of *The Masses*), the pageant was presented in Madison Square Garden on June 7, 1913. More than five thousand people attended the spectacle, which featured a cast of fifteen hundred striking silkworkers. Although the strike itself collapsed one month later, the pageant was hailed as a dramatic triumph and attracted considerable publicity for its Greenwich Village organizers. *(Robert F. Wagner Labor Archives, New York University)*

The Radicals' Concerns

During the height of its iconoclastic celebrity, Greenwich Village contributed talent and energy to "anything, so long as it was taboo in the Middle West," as one partaker joked. The array of progressive causes ranged from the modern suffrage, birth control, and left-wing labor movements to more trailblazing territory such as radical feminism, psychoanalysis, and free love. Village intellectuals also experimented incessantly with new educational methods, new domestic arrangements, and new ways to oppose American militarism. This endemic spirit of dilettantism prompted leading critics to complain that Village activists lacked the stamina to sustain their involvement on these diverse fronts. Intoxicated by the drama of political predicament, their enthusiasm tended to lag once the immediate crisis had passed. For many Village radicals the article of faith that underlay their agenda was the belief in revolution as an end in itself and the only means by which individuals could acquire real freedom, justice, and self-awareness.

81. **Inez Milholland Boissevain** The statuesque figure of Inez Milholland was a familiar sight among those who paraded for the vote. A Vassar graduate with a law degree, Milholland earned wide admiration from her Village colleagues for her tireless support of the radical labor and women's rights movements. On her death in 1916 from pernicious anemia, following a draining lecture tour undertaken to boost the cause, she was regarded as a martyr and peerless lobbyist for women's suffrage. Her husband Eugen Boissevain, whom Milholland had married in 1913, later wed Edna St. Vincent Millay. (*Yvette Szekely Eastman from "Enjoyment of Living"*)

82. Suffragists demonstrating in Washington Mews The long battle to secure voting rights for American women was fought with particular vigor by Greenwich Village activists in the teens. Washington Square served as the launching platform for extravagant parades that attracted between ten to fifty thousand participants who continued north up Fifth Avenue. The corps of Village personalities who devoted funds, propaganda, and organizational abilities to the cause cut across traditional class and sex lines, creating a coalition that encompassed the radical left-wing as well as old-line society. *(The Bettmann Archive)*

83. Ida Rauh and Max Eastman in their Greenwich Village apartment Trained as a lawyer, Ida Rauh was also an actress, sculptor, poet, birth control advocate, labor agitator, and more improbably, a wife and mother. When she married Max Eastman in 1911, the couple caused a public uproar by flouting convention and listing themselves on their mailbox as "IdaRauh/Max Eastman." Like many Village men with advanced social views, Max Eastman, who for a time headed the Men's League for Woman Suffrage, endorsed in principle the aspirations of radical feminism while fretting in private about its amatory practices. *(Yvette Szekely Eastman from "Enjoyment of Living")*

Army Medical Examiner: "At last a perfect soldier!"

84. Army Medical Examiner: "At Last a Perfect Soldier!" The outbreak of World War I in 1914 compelled the Village intelligentsia, in Malcolm Cowley's words, "to decide what kind of rebels they were. If they were merely rebels against puritanism they could continue to exist safely in Mr. Wilson's world. The political rebels had no place in it." Foes of "preparedness" found allies in the American Union Against Militarism, co-founded by the Village peace activist Crystal Eastman. On the literary front *The Masses* emerged as potent voice of protest for those opposed to the war. *(Tamiment Institute Library, New York University)*

85. Will Durant and his pupils of the Modern School on East Twelfth Street Founded in honor of Francisco Ferrer, the Spanish educator and anarchist executed for alleged subversion in 1909, the Modern School was staffed mainly by anarchists who renounced rigid pedagogical methods and sought instead to instill a love of learning through a governing philosophy of "Free Order." Initially a day school for the children of workers, the institution quickly bloomed into an innovative laboratory for adult education, offering evening courses in literature, history, foreign languages, and modern arts. In 1912 the school relocated to a brownstone facility in East Harlem. *(Special Collections and Archives, Rutgers University Libraries)*

86. **"Did you know that I am an Anarchist and a Free-lover?"** By the mid-teens, Freudian jargon was so prevalent in Greenwich Village that, as playwright Susan Glaspell noted, "you could not go out to buy a bun without hearing of someone's complex." Freudianism's principal use to the Village was its validation of the libertarian ideals of free love. Ironically, many bohemian couples who scorned bourgeois marriage discovered themselves bound by the same expectations of conjugal fidelity. *(Tamiment Institute Library, New York University)*

87. **A Greenwich Village Prohibition protest parade** Parades protesting the Volstead Act filed through the streets of Greenwich Village with some regularity during Prohibition. The payoff system that bought protection for establishments that could afford it led to the collapse of many less affluent tearooms, which were raided intermittently by enforcement agents on the suspicion of brewing bootleg. *(Museum of the City of New York)*

• • • •

88. Margaret Sanger entering the courthouse Experience as a nurse on the Lower East Side and important contacts with Village radicals in the early teens reinforced Margaret Sanger's belief in a woman's right to regulate her own reproductive life. Her crusade to supply the public with practical contraceptive advice led first to her indictment for mailing "obscene" materials, which was dismissed, and later to her conviction for founding the country's first birth control clinic, in Brooklyn, and a thirty-day sentence for "operating a public nuisance." *(Sophia Smith Collection, Smith College)*

THE ARTISANS AND BUILDERS OF NINETEENTH-CENTURY NEW YORK

THE CASE OF THE 1834 STONECUTTERS' RIOT

Daniel J. Walkowitz

Greenwich Village has had a rich historical association with political dissenters, cultural rebels, and oppositional groups, and New York City's flourishing trade-union movement has been a related and integral part of this history. Since the middle of the nineteenth century, striking workers have gathered in mass rallies at Union Square, on the northern edge of the Village. Many national and local unions have long had offices in the area. In Village cafés radical groups with a commitment to a working-class movement—communists, socialists, and anarchists—have debated strategies for organizing factories and workshops on the nearby Lower East Side.

Labor's struggles in the Village are representative of the conflicts punctuating the history of American industrialization and the growth of the labor movement. In an often ruthlessly competitive marketplace, manufacturers sought ways to lower costs and gain an edge, introducing machines and speedups or lowering wages and lengthening hours. In entrepôts such as New York, metropolitan industrialization was characterized by seasonal labor on the dockyards and in the finished goods workshops, making for especially harsh and tumultuous working and living conditions—which, not surprisingly, engendered heated worker responses. Sometimes workers manifested their anger in well-organized strikes, such as the 1909 "uprising" of between twenty and forty thousand women shirtwaist makers, or the strike of the sixty thousand cloakmakers the next year. At other times, however, their response took the form of what social elites saw as irrational rioting. Since bosses pitted immigrants—Irish, Italian, and Jewish—or black laborers against one another for jobs, much of this protest was expressed in racial or ethnic conflict. In New York the 1846 Astor Place Riot pitted Irishmen against Americans of English descent; the 1863 Draft Riot, against conscription into the Union army of anyone who could not afford to pay three hundred dollars to have someone take his place, incited working-class Irish crowds, fearful of cheap labor competition, to attack blacks. Indeed, employers had been using such black labor on the dockyards to undermine the fragile position of Irish longshoremen. Other riots, such as the 1902 Kosher Food Riot in which Jewish women ransacked merchant stalls over dramatic price increases, reflected pressures on the household economy of the working class.

The earliest New York riot rooted in the social tremors accompanying industrialization, the Stonecutters' Riot, took place in 1834 in the heart of Greenwich Village around Washington Square. Unlike many subsequent crowd activities, it was not a racial or ethnic conflict but a struggle over the use of free versus convict labor. The 1834 disturbance dramatically reflected the emerging social transformations wrought by new wage relations, frustrated artisanal yearnings for entrepreneurial opportunities, and the pressures of competition on struggling manufacturers and on working people. For New Yorkers the Stonecutters' Riot was an unsettling introduction to the American industrial revolution: Events surrounding the riot marked one of the first activities of the new citywide trade-union movement in New York, and the violence foreshadowed the tumultuous character of industrial relations in the city.

Writing in 1872, a historian of New York explained how the city had "fairly distanced all competitors" by 1842. The signs of the city's commercial and physical growth were everywhere. Gas was introduced to the city in 1825; the magnificent Merchants Exchange and the Custom House were built in 1827; the Gothic Revival building of the University of the City of New York had been erected along the east side of the new Washington

Square parade ground by 1835; and by 1842 both the Croton Aqueduct and the telegraph had come to the city. "Nothing was wanting to her temporal prosperity; her civil freedom was all that could be desired."[1]

At the same time wealthy mercantile families erected stately residential symbols of the city's (and their) preeminence around the new Washington Square Park, thus transforming a potter's field that had been a final resting place for the destitute and poor. The park's north side stood as an impressive testimony to the fortunes that were made as the city became a commercial center for a burgeoning national market. The row of simple yet imposingly formal Greek Revival buildings represented a bold assertion by an expansive bourgeoisie that the park was now elite territory and symbolized the bourgeoisie's authority and power. Yet the buildings also served as a reminder of another social fact: as the city expanded commercially, its working population was increasingly subject to the new social relations of the competitive economy.

The park and the brick-and-marble elegance of its north side were not the only signs of social transformation. The history of the 1834 Stonecutters' Riot and details of its participants tell us about worker resistance to competitive restraints imposed on labor and capital during this era, providing a social context for the building of the park that is much more complex than the physical images of material progress might otherwise convey.

89.   Southwest corner of Washington Square (*Museum of the City of New York*)

• • • •

The stonecutters' grievance stemmed from a decision made by the governors of the old University to introduce economies in the erection of its first building. After selecting a site for the building on what is now Washington Square East between Waverly and Washington places, the University council acquired the land for $40,000. On January 28, 1833, the council authorized its building committee to contract with the state prison at Sing Sing for the purchase of marble that would be hewn by the prisoners.[2] In theory prison labor would help rehabilitate the prisoner, teach him a trade, and, not incidentally, produce goods at a low cost.[3] In fact, according to the University's centennial historian: "The marble from Sing Sing would cost about $10,000; but 'influential men in the State encourage us [the Council] to believe that ultimately the marble will be given to the State [and then to the University].'"[4] The University certainly could have used the money. When construction began in late June 1833, its treasury balance was $66.46.[5]

Stonecutters, however, could also have used the money, and later that year, both the Manufacturers of Marble Mantels and 325 journeymen marblecutters sent petitions to the state legislature addressing that very point. The highly unusual participation of a manufacturers' association in such a petition suggests the ambiguous class position of the manufacturers caught up in the transition between the artisanal and industrial worlds. The petitions opposed prison labor, which, the stonecutters later explained, "took the bread out of their mouths."[6] The legislature, however, chose not to act. The ensuing anti-prison-labor campaign, joined by trade unionists who had been organized in the General Trades' Union, was led by the stonecutters.

In July 1833, they again gathered to address the issue, passing a series of resolutions condemning the "State Prison Monopoly." The journeymen vowed "as mechanics and freemen, to protect our rights (if the 'collective wisdom' of the State neglect or refuse so doing), and prevent their being monopolized by the convicts, or agents of a State's Prison." Furthermore, they resolved not to work on any marble that convicts had dressed or to employ anyone who worked on any contract prison marble from any state. Eighty journeymen signed the resolutions.[7]

Meanwhile, work on the University Building proceeded, the governors either oblivious to or unmoved by the journeymen's complaints.[8] On Friday, October 24, after a series of lengthy parades in which banners and placards proclaimed their rights and denounced the local men who contracted for the prison work, a group of between 100 and 150 men decided to bring their protest to the marble works of the contractor himself.[9] The contractor was none other than Elisha Bloomer, the man who had introduced the practice of using prison labor to manufacture silk hats, marble chimneypieces, grates, and locks.[10]

Between nine and ten o'clock that evening, the stonecutters walked

• • • •

up Broadway in a "quiet and orderly manner, creating no suspicion, as it were supposed by those who passed them that they were returning from Church."[11] When they reached Bloomer's shop at 160 Broadway, near Fourth Street, their anger boiled over. Bloomer was then "petitioned" with rocks and brickbats. For the third time that year, the mayor had to call out the Twenty-seventh Regiment of the New York State National Guard to disperse the crowd.[12] (The guard had never been used as a public police before 1834.) In the attack on Bloomer's shop, doors and windows had been smashed and some marble mantels destroyed. He estimated the damages at $2,000 and offered a reward of $250 for the apprehension of anyone responsible.[13] Apparently no one was arrested, and what has been passed down in historical accounts as the Stonecutters' Riot seems to have ended.

For the stonecutters, however, dispersal of the crowd did not solve the prison labor issue. While tempers cooled the military remained on guard in Washington Square Park. The Square was adjacent to the University construction site and to Bloomer's marble works, a territory familiar and congenial to the Twenty-seventh Regiment. Only three days earlier, it had held its annual inspection and review of troops there.[14] Lest the irate stonecutters, whose grievances were disparaged by most men of commerce, should reassemble in what the authorities could only understand as a "mob," the regiment remained encamped on duty for four days and nights.

The University Building was completed with prison stone, without any further disruptions, but the question of prison labor did not die. In fact, the continued and intense agitation by stonecutters against contract labor had a real impact: The University Building and two houses then under construction on the northwest corner of Eighteenth Street and Fifth Avenue were the last buildings erected with marble quarried by prison labor.[15] In 1884 the state legislature finally abolished contract prison labor, but only after considerable trade-union agitation.[16] However, the immediate events surrounding the riot only begin to illuminate the stonecutters' concerns about the changing world in which they lived and worked: a fuller explanation lies in the history of changing modes of work in the trade, changing relations between journeymen and manufacturers, and in the new market pressures of the emerging commercial and industrializing economy. Finally, there was an important and revealing sequel to the riot: a stonecutters' strike the following year.

In the early years of the nineteenth century, the fraternity of stonecutters retained long artisanal traditions. Masonry, stonecutting, and marblecutting were related trades, and the masons' early credo conveys these trades' sense of their rights, dignity, and idea of justice:

> . . . I pay my debts,
> I steal from no man; would not cut a throat

To gain admission to a great man's purse,
Or a whore's bed; I'd not betray my friend,
To get his place or fortune: I learn neither to flatter
A blown-up fool above me, nor crush the wretch beneath me.[17]

Relations between apprentices and masters reflected this code: They were honor bound and close, almost familial. They lived together and remained in contact after the apprenticeship, occasionally working together and always identifying with each other's problems. Apprentice stonecutters served a seven-year term, often beginning as masons and later learning to cut the more expensive marble. Dressing and laying the brick or stone were the more common crafts. But an artisan who possessed the ability to draw and was skilled with a chisel—and had the opportunity—might gain some experience doing the ornamental marble work traditionally associated with Italian craftsmen. Such was the experience of John Frazee, a trained stonecutter who actually rose to become one of the country's first native-born sculptors.[18]

Born in Rahway, New Jersey, in 1790, Frazee received little help from his father, Reuben, a carpenter by trade but a rather dissolute alcoholic. The grandparents who raised young John taught him most domestic crafts and farming, but he early gained the appellation "limner," which was given to strolling portrait painters, for his drawings on doors and walls. At the age of fourteen he followed in his brother's footsteps and was bound over to a bricklayer and plasterer, William Lawrence, for whom his father also worked at the time. So began what Frazee later described as his apprenticeship in the "great art and mystery of the dirty helter-skelter occupation of a country bricklayer and plasterer!"[19] His apprenticeship under Lawrence provided him with a solid training, unusual opportunities for advancement, and a familial intellectual environment. Frazee remembered those years fondly:

> When Lawrence had all his boys at home and seated around his winter evening's fire, we constituted a sort of debating club and could Newton and Archimedes have heard our wild and heterogeneous disquisitions and arguments upon science and laws, I am sure they would have been highly and laughingly amused, if not enlightened.[20]

In 1810, in the last year of his apprenticeship, Frazee was hired out to work on a bank and Queens College (now Rutgers) in New Brunswick. Again his employer, John Sandman, a stonecutter, received him "with particular courtesy and attention," as much like a friend as an employee, taking him about town and securing accommodations for him. Frazee had observed some New York stonecutters at work two years earlier and had been enraptured with the mallet and chisel. Confident of his ability to engrave, Frazee arranged to work eleven hours a day for Sandman as a mason and then spend his lunchtime and four hours' overtime learning to hew and chisel stone. The next year, on his last job before the expiration of his apprenticeship, Frazee put his new craft to work. While employed on a masonry job in Nyack, New York, he convinced Lawrence to let him tackle a mantelpiece that would have required importing another stonecutter from New York City. Frazee did the work and did it well, gaining the admiration and envy of the other masons, in part for what he himself recognized were privileged work conditions: "sheltered beneath the cool bower and under no other direction and dictation than that of my own taste and judgment."[21]

The years after his apprenticeship were not easy for Frazee. Construction trades were traditionally seasonal and keenly affected by economic depression. During the War of 1812, he got by in the winter months running choral programs for the local Rahway churches. He then hit upon the idea of engraving gravestones for his parishioners. Lawrence agreed to provide his former apprentice with stone in exchange for half the profits of the venture, and the two became partners. In the boom after the war, Frazee was able to parlay his skill with stone engraving and his contacts with church-going society into an independent livelihood sufficient to support a young family. Increasingly well-known and respected for his outstanding letter style, around 1829 Frazee moved his family to New York City, where the aspiring artisan-artist shortly made his mark in the fine arts, first as a fine tombstone and ornamental mantelpiece stone- and marblecutter, and later as a sculptor.

Though Frazee's success was not typical, his career illustrates the traditionally close relationship between artisan journeymen and masters. Frazee, too, in 1831, took one of his own former apprentices, Robert E. Launitz, into partnership in the execution of ornamental marblework. But by 1833, when the stonecutters of New York were petitioning the legislature against prison labor, Frazee was already in Boston completing a bust of Daniel Webster for the Atheneum. Nonetheless, Frazee's family was touched by the prison labor issue: The 1834 petition carried the name of Anson Frazee, undoubtedly a nephew or brother.

By the 1830s there was substantial continuity with the traditional work patterns of the previous generations, but new market pressures and divisions between different classes of work in the trade had begun to erode the commonality of interests between journeymen and masters and to jeopardize the economic position of the craft. The strains were everywhere evident. For instance, in the newspaper reports on the 1834 petition, the men who employed stonecutters are referred to as both masters and manufacturers—the Master Marble Manufacturers—a title that quite accurately reflected their own double, and often contradictory, identities midway between the artisanal and industrial worlds. As masters, they were themselves artisans; as manufacturers, they were employers, bosses of others dependent on them for a wage.

In 1834, however, the association of master manufacturers joined with the journeymen on the issue of prison labor, expelling from their society two manufacturers of marble mantels who used convict labor. The expelled manufacturers, Joseph Phillips and Henry C. Webb, defended their use of prison labor, blaming instead the availability of cheaper marblework from Italy for putting New York journeymen out of work. The stonecutters nonetheless insisted that the prison monopoly deflated wages and divided the masters and journeymen. Webb and Phillips, they complained, "endeavored to create dissentions [sic] between them and us, by endeavoring to reduce the value of our labor." The journeymen publicly proclaimed that they "highly approve[d]" of the society's expulsion of the offending manufacturers. [22]

But journeymen stonecutters had come to recognize that the master manufacturers might side with them on the prison labor issue for the present, but the tendency within the industrial world was toward disharmony of interests. Thus, early in the prison labor controversy during the previous summer of 1833, journeymen artisans and mechanics of New York had established the General Trades' Union of the City of New York. [23] The group took a strong stand against prison labor and organized collective trade-union opposition to it. The scope and appeal of the movement could be seen from a list of some of the unions represented: stonecutters, cordwainers, weavers, coopers, rope-makers, builders, typographers, chairmakers, hatmakers, bakers, tailors, bookbinders, sailmakers, house carpenters, brushmakers, silk hatters, and ladies' cordwainers. The preamble to their constitution made clear their understanding of the dramatic shifts taking place in the nature of work and social relations:

> We the JOURNEYMEN ARTISANS and MECHANICS of the City of New York, and its vicinity, therefore, believing as we do, that in proportion as the line of distinction between the employer and employed is widened, the condition of the latter inevitably verges toward a state of vassalage while that of the former as certainly approximated towards supremacy; and that whatever system is calculated to make the many dependent upon, or subject to the few, not only tends to the subversion of the natural rights of man, but is hostile to the best interests of the community at large, as well as to the spirit and genius of our government. [24]

The problem of dependence focused stonecutters' concerns on the wage. As highly skilled craftsmen, they made a relatively good daily wage. But construction workers' pay was seasonal and, even in the best of times, did not provide a high living standard. Unskilled laborers might earn only seventy-five cents a day, while a stonecutter received between fourteen and sixteen shillings per day in 1834 (about two dollars). An annual income of four hundred dollars, however, was below the estimated subsistence level of nearly six hundred dollars for a family of five.[25] Economizing, taking in boarders, and relying on the labor of children and wives were all necessary survival strategies. Such problems were aggravated by heavy inflation in the speculative atmosphere of Jacksonian New York. Furthermore, the gradual decline of such artisanal practices as residential apprenticeship, together with the rise of the rental market, meant that rent gouging complicated the problem of inflation.[26]

> "The expenses of living, and supporting a family in this city," reported the *National Trades' Union*, "are annually increasing at the rate of ten or twelve per cent. . . . Rents are enormously high; and in many cases, especially in the lower part of the city, owners of houses demand, for the ensuing year, an advance of twenty-five or thirty, and even as high as forty percent on the rent of the current year. The grocer must add the amount of the advanced rent to the price of his articles—every other dealer must do the same; and the mechanic must pay more than he did last year for everything which he or his family eat, drink or wear."[27]

By 1835 the use of prison labor remained a contested issue for New York stonecutters, but they saw themselves, their families' economy, and their independent work culture assaulted on several fronts. In response they organized and fought to have wages in their industry equalized.[28]

This fight, too, related to the changing conditions of work. There was a growing division of labor in the trade and increasing pressures toward lower wages. And again the struggle illustrated the continuing identification of different branches of the trade with one another. At the time the stonecutters were divided into two classes, a third who worked at the two-dollar-a-day rate, and two-thirds who earned by the piece whatever the market would pay surplus labor. In April 1835 the journeymen who were paid by the day went out on strike on behalf of the more poorly paid piece-rate stonecutters. "As free and independent people," the journeymen complained that "unprincipled, uncontrolled competition" would "deprive us of that which we consider it our undoubted right to receive, *an equivalent for our labor.*"[29] By early June the Association of Journeymen Stonecutters of New York and Brooklyn had won acceptance by the manufacturers of a list of prices, according to which any stonecutter who worked the full ten-hour day would receive two dollars. Obviously even the better-paid journeymen stood to benefit from the victory, as cheap labor would no longer threaten to undermine their position in the industry. But in point of fact the strike had *not* been to increase their own wages and was fought at considerable personal cost. Though there is no evidence that any other trade gave the strikers more than moral support, the *National Trades' Union* recognized the extraordinarily heroic character of their brotherly action: "They deserve, and we trust will receive, the hearty thanks of all their brotherly mechanics."[30]

All, however, was not as rosy as this portrait of craft solidarity suggests. The prison-labor issue persisted, and its reemergence in 1835 exposed strains in the shifting relationships between journeymen, masters, and manufacturers that riddled urban Jacksonian America.

At a general meeting of the Association of Journeymen Stonecutters of New York and Brooklyn on March 14, a committee of five was unanimously chosen to renew opposition to the prison monopoly. In the 1834 elections, both Democrats and Whigs had voiced support of the association's position, but in February 1835, the state legislature had accepted a subcommittee report recommending that the practice be continued. Now the stonecutters reiterated their opposition in strong, unequivocal language. "To effect the speedy annihilation of the diabolical system," of the "detested material" manufactured by it, and of the men who contracted for such labor from "the den of thieves," the committee urged all brothers and others who might be members of the fire companies "not to assist at the extinguishment of any fire, wherein, on or about the said fire may in any way be composed of goods manufactured in the State prisons."[31] The committee that drafted the resolutions was composed of five men, two of whom, Gilbert Cameron and James Hughes, would reappear in quite a different role scarcely four months later.

On July 18 Cameron and Hughes wrote to the *National Trades' Union* to complain against the same stonecutters' association they had so recently served. As entrepreneurial journeymen, they took ideas of republican rights to which the stonecutters had so frequently referred in the past year and recast them in behalf of free trade—in the right to establish a manufactory and to subcontract with whomever they pleased. They had built a shop at Nineteenth Street and employed ten to twelve stonecutters; the problem was that they contracted with Elisha Bloomer, the infamous prison-labor contractor whose work on the New York University Building had precipitated the protest the preceding fall.[32]

So, in 1834 and 1835, at the same time that master-manufacturers were throwing other prison-labor manufacturers out of their association, and, while journeymen struck on behalf of less-well-paid piece-rate workers, two journeymen—themselves outspoken leaders of the anti-prison-monopoly movement—had seen their own identities and interests shift dramatically. Upset by the journeymen's opposition to their use of the prison labor, Cameron and Hughes completed their intellectual and political somersault. When the journeymen convinced the blacksmith not to sharpen the offending shop's tools, Cameron and Hughes pressed criminal charges that "ultimately end[ed] in the committal of three of the conspirators to prison."[33]

In the Jacksonian city, journeymen and manufacturers confronted very different worlds. For entrepreneurs a volatile free market offered the chance for fortune, security, and power, although many also suffered significant business failures. For artisan-masters and journeymen, however, such flux only ensured the worrisome fate of dependence and marginality.

In contrast to this confusion stood the new Washington Square parade ground, with its stately mansions to the north and proud new edifice, the University Building, to the east. Washington Square was the site of the first efforts by New York's mercantile elite to separate itself out from the helter-skelter residential mix of the downtown colonial city. The beginnings of transport systems—omnibuses and horsecar railroads—facilitated the move; fear of contamination by the poor compelled it. The division of labor, the growing gulf between journeymen-masters and master-manufacturers, and the burgeoning army of poor associated with metropolitan industrialization together encouraged the elite to establish segregated residential enclaves. Washington Square served that purpose, but it served a cultural and political purpose too. In a world of disorder and increasing inequity, with riotous and increasingly dependent social relations, the park as an elite space asserted the hegemony of bourgeois authority and power, as it projected a metropolitan image of orderly progress and economic achievement.

The events surrounding the Stonecutters' Riot make it clear that both military authority and the economic achievement of the mercantile class were real, but that the image of enduring order they attempted to project and defend was only that—an image. Faced with the National Guard, rapacious contractors such as Bloomer, and a legislature unwilling to redress their grievances, the stonecutters "petitioned" the authorities with the only weapons they had left to them—stones and brickbats. Subsequent struggles would often have an ethnic or racial cast, but control of the workplace would remain a fundamental issue and the New York labor movement would henceforth stand organized. The repression of the stonecutters in 1834 was not the conclusion of an era, but rather the beginning of the urban workers' modern struggle for social justice.

· · · · ·

NOTES

I would like to thank Sean Wilentz for graciously directing me to many of the sources for the Stonecutters' Riot. His book, *Chants Democratic: New York City and the Rise of the Working Class* (New York: Oxford University Press, 1982) amplifies this history. I would also

· · · ·

like to thank Carl Prince, Ed Countryman, Molly Nolan, Carroll Smith Rosenberg, and Judith R. Walkowitz for their comments on an early draft.

1. William L. Stone, *History of New York City, From the Discovery to the Present Day* (New York: Virtue & Yoeston, 1872), 507.
2. Theodore Francis Jones, ed., *New York University, 1832–1932* (New York: New York University Press, 1933), 41–42.
3. See, for example, Michael Ignatief, *A Just Measure of Pain: The Penitentiary in the Industrial Revolution* (New York: Pantheon Books, 1980).
4. Jones, *NYU*, 42.
5. Ibid.
6. Benson John Lossing, *History of New York City*, 2 vols. (New York: A. S. Barnes & Co., 1884), 341; *The Man* (New York), June 7, 1834.
7. *The Man*, June 7, 1834.
8. According to Lossing, 341, the stonecutters' grievances had not yet been publicly aired.
9. *Commercial Advertiser* (New York), October 27, 1834.
10. *The Man*, November 3, 1834.
11. *Commercial Advertiser*, October 27, 1834.
12. J. T. Headley, *The Great Riots of New York, 1712 to 1873* (New York: E. B. Treat, 1873), 67–78; (Col.) Emmons Clark, *History of the Seventh Regiment of New York, 1806–1889*, 2 vols. (New York: Seventh Regiment, 1890), 214–215; and, Stone, *History of New York City*, 456–460.
13. *Commercial Advertiser*, October 28, 1834; *The Sun* (New York), October 29, 1834; *Transcript* (New York), October 27, 1834.
14. Clark, *Seventh Regiment*, 225.
15. Stone, *History of New York City*, 466.
16. For discussion of later efforts to abolish contract prison labor, see Daniel J. Walkowitz, *Worker City, Company Town: Iron and Cotton-Worker Protest in Troy and Cohoes, N.Y., 1855–1884* (Urbana: University of Illinois Press, 1978), and Brian Greenberg, *Worker and Community: Response to Industrialization in a Nineteenth-Century American City, Albany, New York, 1850–1884* (Albany: SUNY Press, 1985).
17. *City Directory for New York*, 1805–1806, 138–139.
18. John Frazee, *Autobiography*, unpublished manuscript, ca. 1850, New-York Historical Society.
19. Ibid.
20. Ibid.
21. Ibid.
22. *The Man*, June 7, 1834.
23. *National Trades' Union* (New York, weekly), 1834–1835.
24. Ibid., August 9, 1834.
25. Sean Wilentz, *Chants Democratic: New York City and the Rise of the American Working Class* (New York: Oxford University Press, 1982).
26. Elizabeth Strother Blackmar, "Housing and Property Relations in New York City, 1785–1850," Ph.D. diss., Department of History, Harvard University, 1980.
27. *National Trades' Union*, April 4, 1835.
28. According to Wilentz, *Chants Democratic*, New York City labor had already largely secured ten hours by 1832, but the movement pressed on elsewhere.
29. "An Appeal," in *National Trades' Union*, May 9, 1835.
30. *National Trades' Union*, June 6, 1835.

31. *National Trades' Union*, April 11, 1835. Political party support of antiprison labor is described in Paul O. Weinbaum, *Mobs and Demagogues: The New York Response to Collective Violence in the Early Nineteenth Century* (Ann Arbor: University of Michigan Press, 1979), 64.

32. Letter "To the Public" from Gilbert Cameron and James Hughes, in *National Trades' Union*, July 18, 1835.

33. Ibid.

THE CULTURE
OF CONTRADICTION

THE GREENWICH VILLAGE REBELLION

Leslie Fishbein

Intellectuals who lived in Greenwich Village before World War I ran a genuine risk of cultural schizophrenia. In the days before the Bolshevik Revolution imposed a standard of political orthodoxy on the Left, the Village rebels were free to explore competing and contradictory ideologies, ignoring concerns about intellectual consistency, to create new elixirs brewed out of personal desire. If, as Ralph Waldo Emerson argued in "Self-Reliance," "A foolish consistency is the hobgoblin of little minds," the Village rebels suspected that *any* consistency might betray a lingering attachment to bourgeois values, and they were firmly committed to demonstrating their own iconoclasm. The result was not chaos but creativity and a rich, if flawed, exploration of the arts, politics, and life-style that drew nourishment from the Left's unprecedented freedom.

Contradictions abounded. Many of the bohemians and radicals who flocked to prewar Greenwich Village like poet Floyd Dell; founder of the little theater movement, George Cram Cook; and author Theodore Dreiser were alienated from the restrictions and stultifying conformity of the small-town existence into which they had been born and eager to embrace cosmopolitanism. Yet ironically the Village to which they journeyed retained many of the charms of small-town life. The Village had resisted the sterile grid pattern of streets that efficiency had imposed on the rest of Manhattan, and its rents were attractively cheap because its twisted maze of streets repelled commercial traffic. While artists and writers, including Edgar Allan Poe, Walt Whitman, and Mark Twain, always had inhabited Greenwich Village, they had lived isolated from each other in separate cliques, and their presence had had little impact on their neighbors. In contrast the pre-war Village witnessed an invasion of newcomers, not only artists and writers but social workers, university professors, schoolteachers, and journalists. They embraced picturesque poverty without reckoning on the impact that their presence might have on the Irish, Italians, and other immigrants whose poverty was less a matter of choice, whose rents were driven up by the more affluent new arrivals, and whose traditional Catholic and conservative mores were offended by the rebels' behavior. Although many of the Village rebels fancied themselves socialists, anarchists, or syndicalists, they remained blithely impervious to the plight of their less privileged neighbors and instead celebrated the exoticism and élan of the ethnic life they had discovered.

While the rebels had presumably chosen to live in the Village on account of its cosmopolitan tolerance of behavior tabooed in their hometowns, one would hardly know that from their subsequent testimonials, which emphasized the high moral tone and respectability of the area. Poet Floyd Dell actually claimed that genuine Villagers scorned being dubbed bohemian and instead were highly respectable citizens with solid virtues:

> Those Greenwich Villagers were schoolteachers, college professors, social workers, doctors, lawyers, engineers and other professional people. As for artists and writers who then lived in the Village—such as John Sloan and Art Young, Mary Heaton Vorse, Inez Haynes Gilmore, Susan Glaspell, Theodore Dreiser—they already had positions of importance in the realm of art and letters. None of these Villagers were what I call poor; some of them owned houses in the country, in Westchester County, in Connecticut, New Jersey, or on the Massachusetts coast. They had most of the familiar middle-class virtues, and in addition, some of their own; they were an obviously superior lot of people.[1]

If Paris was famed for its aesthetic bohemia, New York appeared to be creating an ethical one as reformers and social workers with more explicitly moral and political concerns began to displace local artists.

But such lofty commitments did not always translate into local social action. Mary Simkhovitch, founder of the social settlement Greenwich House, noted the supreme irony of the conflict between theory and practice: "It was certainly amusing and astounding to us who had fought against cellar lodgings as unhealthful, damp and unfit for human habitation, as they were, to see them revived as 'one room studios' and let often at six times the price of former rentals."[2] The contrast between the ethical and

* * * *

bohemian impulses is revealed in the poetry of John Reed, whose "Forty-two Washington Square" exposed the poverty of his Italian neighbors:

> There spawn the overworked and underpaid
> Mute thousands;—packed in buildings badly made,—
> In stinking squalor penned,—and overflowing
> On sagging fire-escapes.

while it celebrates the freedom their Village residence offered to "young men of spirit":

> But nobody questions your morals,
> And nobody asks for the rent,—
> There's no one to pry if we're tight, you and I,
> Or demand how our evenings are spent.
> The furniture's ancient but plenty,
> The linen is spotless and fair,
> O life is a joy to a broth of a boy
> At Forty-two Washington Square![3]

By embracing picturesque poverty, these Villagers had won for themselves a temporary reprieve from adult economic responsibilities that might confine their creativity. An interlude in bohemia afforded them a reprieve from mature commitments—a chance to explore life, to be spontaneous and free prior to the assumption of family obligations that would dictate more cautious behavior. These rebels celebrated childlike pleasures: swimming in the nude, attending fancy dress balls, playacting in Provincetown, playing children's games. But such pleasures were the fruits of privilege. Well educated, talented, and charming, these rebels could leave bohemia at will by opting for respectability and economic stability, whereas their neighbors were victims of capitalist exploitation with no readily available means of escape. And it was the very exploitation that rendered the Village a low-rent area that simultaneously offered its artists and intellectuals unprecedented creative freedom.

With social critic Randolph Bourne as its apostle, these Villagers celebrated the cult of youth. If adulthood implied the necessity of making and abiding by hard choices, the Village radicals preferred the plasticity of childhood and intentionally retained its virtues in all aspects of their life. For example, the anarchist Hippolyte Havel visited an editorial board meeting of the socialist magazine *The Masses* and expostulated against putting questions of art to a vote determined by the bourgeois majority. "But," Floyd Dell argued, "even anarchists must decide things by some kind of method." "Sure—sure," replied Havel, "we anarchists make decisions. But we don't abide by them."[4] Bourne opposed the tyranny of the aged that stifled youth-

90. Randolph Bourne, one of the most penetrating essayists of his generation, wrote regularly on education, politics, pacifism, the right to dissent, and the rejuvenating quality of the "cult of youth" in the radical journals read by the Village intelligentsia. He died in 1918, a victim of the influenza epidemic. (*Randolph Bourne Papers, Rare Book and Manuscript Library, Columbia University*)

ful creativity. But, since he believed that the cult of youth would liberate the older as well as the younger generation, Bourne thereby burdened the young with sole responsibility for revitalizing American culture:

> The ideas of the young are the living, the potential ideas; those of the old, the dying or the already dead. This is why it behooves youth to be not less radical, but even more radical, than it would naturally be. It must be not simply contemporaneous, but a generation ahead of the times, so that when it comes into control of the world, it will be precisely right and coincident with the conditions of the world as it finds them. If the youth of today could really achieve this miracle, they would have found the secret of "perpetual Youth."[5]

However, the cult of youth was a concept that often contradicted the socialist beliefs of its adherents. They failed to recognize the ephemeral nature of the challenge that the cult posed to the older generation, since the rebellion of the young did nothing to undermine the social institutions that their elders had created. If the cult of youth treated youth as a special class, its apostles failed to realize that youth never would be a class in the Marxist sense, because its members were not bound by class interests. The cult of youth simultaneously ignored the social and economic distinctions that divided the young from one another and the inadvisability of separating youth from their elders in the class struggle.

• • • •

The cult of youth had implications of cultural nationalism. In a January 1917 editorial, poet James Oppenheim, one of the founders of *Seven Arts* magazine, described America as a naturally adolescent nation noteworthy for its flux and possibility. It was precisely this youthful openness to new experience that appealed to Village intellectuals engaged in an effort to create a new American culture. Ironically, the very writers and critics who embraced Friedrich Nietzsche, Sigmund Freud, Henri Bergson, and other European thinkers simultaneously spearheaded the demand for a new American culture. It is true that their flirtation with European thought had been strikingly American. Randolph Bourne employed Nietzsche as a pagan liberator useful in Bourne's own attack on domestic puritanism. And Isadora Duncan hailed Nietzsche as a source for her invention of modern dance; she dubbed him "the first dancing philosopher."[6] Clearly Villagers were transforming an elitist and pessimist into a democrat and optimist, recasting Nietzsche's message in language that could appeal to American evangelists of pagan freedom.

Seven Arts sought to become the catalyst for creating a new American culture. Lacking what they deemed any viable indigenous literary tradition, the magazine's authors argued instead that the essence of Americanism was adolescent flux. Editor James Oppenheim concludes his paean "America" with a Whitmanesque affirmation of poet as prophet:

> This is my city, this is my land. . . .
> What care I if it have no past?
> I have a Past. . . . I bequeath it to America. . . .
> Is it dreamless? I bring it a dream!
> Lacks it vision? It shall have mine![7]

Ironically Oppenheim's vision is a sublimated version of the puritanism the Village radicals had repudiated, because it implicitly argues that America is a "city on a hill," a land untrammeled by the dead past that can offer a fresh vision to humankind. And the vision that Oppenheim shared with other exponents of a new American culture was an inherently elitist one: an aristocracy of thought that would guide American labor toward radical social and economic change. Thus, despite their commitment to socialism, men like Bourne, Oppenheim, and Walter Lippmann viewed the intellectual as best able to control and analyze political events, to exert leadership over the masses.

Despite their commitment to a new American culture, these Village intellectuals remained intrigued by European thought. In particular many of them turned to the work of Freud. Freud's popularity in America coincided with a startling new frankness in discourse regarding sexual matters. Among Freudianism's earliest converts were Village intellectuals, who flocked to its ranks as both patients and popularizers. The socialists among them should have been troubled by the immense cost of psychoanalytic treatment, but Villagers greeted the practitioners of Freudianism with arms—and purses—wide open.

The Villagers' interpretation of Freudian doctrine reflected an American optimism and faith in progress that neglected Freud's pessimism and ambiguity. Max Eastman, for example, presented the Freudian notion of sublimation to a popular audience as a panacea designed to remove troublesome animal impulses from the unconscious and channel them neatly into a "socially, or professionally, or artistically, creative sphere" where they would make "*no* trouble" at all.[8] The feminists among them should have been disturbed by Freud's notion that anatomy is destiny, with its corollary that feminine physiology dictated a passive role for women. Although Mabel Dodge was a member of Heterodoxy, a Village club for unorthodox women, she did seek treatment with Smith Ely Jelliffe and A. A. Brill and serialized an account of her therapeutic experiences for the Hearst newspapers. She found both Jelliffe and Brill dogmatic and domineering, seeking to control her life rather than to allow her to express herself, yet she lingered in treatment, allowing them to undermine her decisions about love, politics, and life-style.[9]

Village intellectuals embraced psychoanalysis because it promised to free them from neurotic symptoms, depression, writer's block, and sexual repression. And it enlivened one's repertoire when entertaining friends; Dell even wrote an article for *Vanity Fair* entitled "Speaking of Psycho-Analysis: The New Boon for Dinner Table Conversationalists." Both Dell and Eastman were so eager to be cured that they presented their psychoanalysts with none of the resistances traditionally associated with therapy. Dell even managed a preemptive strike, confessing to the prescribed litany of Freudian sins before his analyst had the chance to discover them during the course of treatment: "My psychoanalyst gave me no interpretation of my dreams, but let me interpret them myself; nor did he tell me I had a terrific mother-complex, and was narcissistic, had a great deal of unconscious homosexuality, and a variety of other frightful-sounding traits; I found all that out myself, and told him."[10]

Dell championed Freudianism to his Village compatriots because he believed that psychoanalysis had dissolved his writer's block and allowed him to love deeply and to begin a novel. He therefore enthusiastically embraced a Freudian worldview that many socialists deemed antithetical to orthodox Marxism's emphasis on historical materialism. By the thirties Dell was willing to confess that the Freudian impulse in his life always had been more vital than the Marxian one: "It is not politics, ever, which has set my pen flowing across paper—it is and always has been a different motive, the pursuit of some kind of psychological rather than political truth."[11]

. . . .

While Max Eastman had less faith in the psychoanalytic method per se, believing that it was applicable largely to people who were truly sick, Eastman did profit from his attempts at analysis with Freudian psychiatrist Smith Ely Jelliffe and advice from A. A. Brill to undertake a self-analysis aimed at explaining his reluctance to commit himself to his wife, Ida Rauh. Accordingly, during the summer of 1914 Eastman took to his boathouse loft in Provincetown: "Thus during the approach and outbreak of the First World War, this international revolutionist, 'cultural leader of socialism in the United States,' was engaged in a search within the tiny corridors of his own brain for his own wish."[12] Not only were early Village popularizers of Freudianism like Dell and Eastman prone to view Freudian theory through personal prisms of desire, with scant reference to any notion of Freudian orthodoxy, but they also neglected the challenges Freudian theory posed to their Marxism: its implicit conservatism; its emphasis on adjustment to the status quo; its focus on the mental rather than the material; and its concern with individual rather than social pathology.

Village radicals were constantly torn between personal imperatives and political beliefs, because for them the political and the personal were one. Although the prewar rebels believed that their lives should serve as a testimonial to their political beliefs, it often proved difficult to integrate art, politics, and life-style. The anarchist Emma Goldman chose lovers who were resentful of women's political activities, like the Austrian photographer and anarchist Edward Brady, or who were charming but deceitful and untrustworthy with movement funds, like hobo doctor Ben Reitman. Goldman was shamed by her inability to dedicate herself as fully to the movement as male anarchists did: "To the end of my life I should be torn between the yearning for a personal life and the need of giving all to my ideal."[13] Despite his dedication to poetry, John Reed found himself obliged to sacrifice that passion in order to redeem himself as a revolutionary in the wake of the Bolshevik Revolution. Upon his return from the new Soviet state, Reed confessed to Max Eastman that his own success at political work had been purchased at the price of his art: "You know this class struggle plays hell with your poetry."[14]

And Village radicals were torn between their personal desire to celebrate the paganism or exoticism of the other cultures flourishing in New York City's cosmopolitan environment and their political commitment to ameliorating the lot of the disadvantaged, whose charming idiosyncrasies might vanish in the egalitarian blandness of the socialist commonwealth or even in the more modest economic improvement offered by the concessions of capitalism purchased at the price of acculturation and sameness. Journalist and social observer Hutchins Hapgood always regretted his white Anglo-Saxon Protestant heritage and bemoaned the fact that he had not been born into a more exotic and cosmopolitan culture. Yet when he chronicled Jewish immigrant life on the Lower East Side, he was torn between his artistic desire to preserve their quaint and charming way of life, with its intellectual stimulation and respect for age, and his commitment as a socialist to modernizing and ameliorating their lives, thereby posing the threat of the materialist destruction of the spiritual heritage that had preserved the Jews for centuries in the Diaspora.[15]

Hapgood also sought to escape from the sterile respectability of his heritage by prowling city streets in search of members of the "submerged tenth," so that he could live vicariously in the realm of pure feeling he believed they had created. Hapgood populated his book *Types from City Streets* (1910) with a panoply of Lower East Side types: Bowery bums, ex-thieves, Tammany men, "spieler" girls (confidence women and card sharps), bohemians, and artists who fascinated him because of the authenticity of life lived at "de limit" and because of their implicit value as exemplars of nonconformity. The fact that such exotics lived outside the working class and in many instances preyed on its members did nothing to undermine Hapgood's obsession with the challenge their way of life posed to bourgeois mores.

What Village rebels were looking for in others—particularly in blacks, exotic white ethnics, prostitutes, and criminals—was a new paganism that would undermine the puritanism of traditional American culture. Villagers sought help in exorcising the puritan demon from vastly different sources. Some turned to the ideals of ancient Greece. George Cram Cook, the founder of the Provincetown Players and a mainstay of the little theater movement, hoped to transpose the Dionysian "madness" of the ancient Greeks to the American stage and devised plays in an Hellenic setting. A socialist and a mystic, Cook moved to Greece, even donning the bucolic attire of a peasant shepherd.[16] Adopting the Greek tunic as a costume for modern dance, and basing her choreography on her study of dancers on Greek vases, Isadora Duncan came to embody the pagan spirit for many radicals. Max Eastman elegized her years after her tragic death as the modern embodiment of the Hellenic spirit: "She rode the wave of the revolt against puritanism; she rode it, and with her fame and Dionysian raptures drove it on. She *was*—and perhaps it is simplest to say—the crest of the wave, an event not only in art, but in the history of life."[17]

Similarly Villagers regarded blacks as natural pagans who had not been blighted by Victorian sexual repression as whites had. Carl Van Vechten, a music critic, novelist, photographer, and art patron, served as the catalyst of the cultural exchange between Harlem and Greenwich Village. His own novel about Harlem, *Nigger Heaven* (1926), was preoccupied with exotic and bizarre sexuality, with characters like Lasca Sartoris and the Scarlet Creeper, a seductress and a pimp, portrayed as more intriguing than Mary Love and Byron Kasson, representatives of the black bourgeoisie. Untrammeled by the genteel tradition, blacks could revel in dissipation and vice while their white counterparts sullied their amusements with guilt. During the teens Van Vechten decided to bring a glimpse of Harlem nightlife to the Village. He persuaded Mabel Dodge to invite two black entertainers to her salon at 23 Fifth Avenue for her first "Evening." The hostess alternated between revulsion and voyeuristic pleasure:

> An appalling Negress danced before us in white stockings and black buttoned boots. The man strummed a banjo and sang an embarrassing song while she cavorted. They both leered and rolled their suggestive eyes and made me feel first hot and then cold, for I never had been so near this kind of thing before, but Carl rocked with laughter and little shrieks escaped him as he clapped his pretty hands. His big teeth became wickedly prominent and his eyes rolled in his darkening face, until he grew to somewhat resemble the clattering Negroes before him.[18]

While Dodge's evening may have been a precursor to whites' slumming parties that toured Harlem in the twenties, frequenting the Cotton Club and the gin joints in search of pagan rhythms and steamy sex, these white patrons of exotic culture remained indifferent to their own psychological exploitation of black art.[19] However, since Harlem blacks lacked the capital to nurture indigenous culture, this patronage had the salutary effect of encouraging black artists, musicians, actors, dancers, writers, and singers while infusing the dominant culture with new vitality by allowing it to draw on the inspiration of previously neglected indigenous art.

By the twenties Van Vechten would become the leading white patron of the Harlem Renaissance. His celebration of primitivism found a receptive white audience. It was an era in which popularized Freudianism and disillusionment with the sterility of material affluence that had reached even the American hinterland, as witnessed by the popularity of Sinclair Lewis's *Babbitt* and *Main Street.* Basking in his role as a cultural catalyst, Van Vechten never questioned whether such black freedom was, in fact, merely an escape from oppression or whether the drunken revels and bizarre orgies he chronicled in Harlem could compensate blacks for the deprivation that American racism had imposed on their daily lives. Nor did Van Vechten consider whether such black art represented an indigenous attempt to return to black roots and to create authentic black culture or whether it was simply a response to white cultural imperatives.

If Hapgood and Van Vechten were engaged in a visceral search for excitement and vitality among exotic cultures, on a more intellectual level Randolph Bourne proselytized a new transnational America, a cosmopolitan interweaving of distinctive ethnic cultures to produce a new sense of world citizenship. Bourne viewed this transnationality as America's last chance at

• • • •

salvation from the threat of homogeneity and cultural conformity.[20] Villagers like Hapgood, Van Vechten, and Bourne never recognized the patronizing nature of their position. While they personally profited from their exposure to other cultures, thereby enriching the dominant cultural tradition, they failed to acknowledge that the smug parochialism of the dominant culture condemned the members of those exotic subcultures to remain in poverty in a society that provided no economic rewards for the preservation of ethnic identity.

The Villagers also romanticized criminals for their freedom from bourgeois conventions. By blaming capitalism rather than the criminals themselves for the existence of crime, radicals viewed criminals as society's victims rather than as its scourge. Many of the Villagers, including hobo poet Harry Kemp, black poet Claude McKay, journalist Lincoln Steffens, and John Reed, consorted with tramps, thieves, and prostitutes. In a January 1917 poem in *The Masses* titled "Heavenly Discourses," Charles Erskine Scott Wood tweaked bourgeois sensibilities by noting that Jesus Christ, too, had consorted with publicans and sinners. Lawlessness provided vicarious pleasure for the timid and the respectable. But in celebrating criminality and vagabondage, the new radicals too often effaced the distinction between the individual defiance of tramps and outlaws and the disciplined resistance of those who engaged in the class struggle. While the radicals profited from their association with criminals by relaxing the pressure toward conformity exacted by civilization and by questioning the value of civilized morality, they failed to recognize the fact that criminals were not simply exemplars of social freedom but also exploiters of the poor and helpless members of society on whom they preyed.

Religion also evoked mixed emotions from Village radicals. As Marxists presumably they should have eschewed religion in all its forms as an opiate of the proletariat, but they were drawn to religion because they desired a life of intensity and commitment. While many of the Village rebels remained critical of organized religion as an institution, they applauded the strength of the religious impulse. They noted the wealth and corruption of the church; its total disregard of the needs of the poor, a neglect rendered more dramatic when the Church of Alphonsius called in the police to arrest Frank Tanenbaum, a youth leading a band of homeless, unemployed men into the church to ask for food and shelter. The church's betrayal of its original mission of supplying charity to the poor and protection for suppliants became a *cause célèbre* in the radical press.[21]

Yet if radical critics of Christianity found the church corrupt, its rituals devoid of personal meaning, and its sympathies entirely with the rich, these same critics nevertheless celebrated Christ as the "first Socialist," emphasizing "not his divinity, but his carpentry."[22] Since many of the Village radicals, including Eastman, Hapgood, poet Horace Traubel, Walter Lipp-

· · · ·

mann, Clarence Darrow, and McKay, had been raised by families of free-thinkers or by parents plagued by religious doubts, they had no difficulty in distancing themselves from institutional religion. And their repudiation of church ritual and doctrine made good sense in a bohemian milieu that scorned dogma in whatever form it appeared. But they found consolation in religion and even at times refuge in prayer. And Christ remained for them a potent revolutionary symbol. Bouck White, head resident of Trinity House, devoted an entire book, *The Call of the Carpenter* (1912), to a depiction of Christ as a workingman-agitator who forbade charity because it took the insurrectionary edge off poverty and who identified himself with his fellow workers in their struggle against industrial despotism. Christ was invoked as a friend of criminals, an apostle of the cult of youth, an iconoclast. Margaret Sanger went so far as to enlist him as a supporter of contraception in her 1931 autobiography, *My Fight for Birth Control*. Village rebels showed remarkable flexibility in their adaptation of Christ to their personal needs. As the first socialist, this renovated Christ allowed bohemians and radicals to fuse their old religious faith with their newly acquired political ideology. The fact that orthodox Marxism had repudiated religion as inimical to the class struggle did not deter Village rebels from finding inspiration and strength in it.

It is ironic that while the Village rebels self-consciously advocated paganism, the religious hero they celebrated was himself celibate, and Christianity as a religion preached chastity rather than ecstasy. But it is not altogether clear that the Villagers themselves were comfortable with the sexual revolution they presumably led. Although Freud was actually no disciple of the cult of free love, many of his radical American believers *were* and invoked his name to buttress their exploration of alternative life-styles. But their commitment to a free-love ideal foundered on the rock of their own jealousy: Monogamy offered too much emotional security to be abandoned for an ideal that was more abstract than real. If anything, Villagers had replaced the old slavery of wedlock with a newer form of bondage that may have been even more demanding. When Floyd Dell decided to end his three-year affair with a longtime Villager, he faced as much recrimination from friends as if he had severed a conjugal union. And when Villagers—like Max Eastman and Ida Rauh, John Reed and Louise Bryant, Hutchins Hapgood and Neith Boyce, Susan Glaspell and George Cram Cook—did marry, their unions involved expectations of sexual fidelity that, when thwarted, caused them to founder and, in some cases, to dissolve.

The sexual revolution was abetted by Margaret Sanger's crusade for birth control. But Sanger's mixed motivation in leading the crusade was indicative of the confusion of many of birth control's most ardent supporters. As a socialist Sanger viewed birth control as a means of enabling lower-class women to preserve their health and control their fate. She assumed that if workers could control their fertility, they would thereby deny the military and industry a steady stream of exploited labor. If workers were to improve their lot, Sanger believed, they would have to restrict their numbers and demand higher wages, thereby rejecting the notion that only the increasing misery of the proletariat would lead to revolution.

Despite her initial concern for the poor, Sanger believed that birth control would free its more affluent practitioners from a sexual repression that prevented the expression of women's distinctive sexuality. Ironically, her misconceptions of Freudian theory and the personal inspiration she derived from Havelock Ellis led her to believe in a yin-and-yang view of sexuality that defined feminine sexuality as rigidly as the Freudian maxim that anatomy is destiny. Nor was Sanger particularly aware of the irrelevance of the quest for sexual liberation to the working-class women she sought to serve. If the sexual revolution failed to bring the social revolution in its wake, the new preoccupation with sexual expression proved injurious to political militancy by encouraging a retreat into the haven of personal life. In sexuality, as in other dimensions of personal experience, the bohemian and radical impulses warred inconclusively for control, and the fragile hope of unifying the personal and the political in a coherent ideology faded into oblivion.

Another focus of struggle between the personal and the political was the feminism of the Village rebels. Many of them were militant feminists, marching in suffrage parades, fighting with Henrietta Rodman on behalf of the right of schoolteachers to marry without losing their jobs, going to jail for illegally disseminating birth-control information or devices. But many of these same women were themselves slaves to love, dismissing the importance of their other achievements when they failed at romance. Mabel Dodge presided with sphinxlike splendor over the era's most important salon at her home at 23 Fifth Avenue, yet she admitted her total dependence on men to wrest her from the "fatal inner immobility" she had suffered since childhood. She had a passionate affair with John Reed in the wake of the Paterson Strike Pageant (a dramatic reenactment of the Paterson Silk Strike of 1913 staged in Madison Square Garden and intended to provide publicity and funds for the strikes) and was so jealous that she resented his withdrawal of attention even to read a newspaper. Dodge won a temporary respite from her jealousy only when Reed fell ill with diphtheria and became helplessly dependent on her. She dismissed her own importance as a cultural catalyst and stripped her autobiography of ultimate significance by writing: "That I have so many pages to write signifies, solely, that I was unlucky in love."[23]

Greenwich Village nurtured modern feminism and permitted its female rebels the possibility of successfully merging their personal and professional lives, combining marriage, motherhood, and a career without loss of femininity and charm. Rose Pastor Stokes, Susan Glaspell, Neith Boyce, and Mary Heaton Vorse had husbands committed to feminism, and Emma

Goldman's lover Alexander Berkman and Elizabeth Gurley Flynn's lover Carlo Tresca viewed women's equality as essential to their revolutionary ideology. However, while Village feminists gladly welcomed male support, that support might be self-interested and patronizing, even if male feminists were themselves unaware of the implicit arrogance of their position. For example, Floyd Dell's primary interest in feminism lay in its benefits for men. He argued that feminism would exempt men from the claims of economically dependent women and children and so would free men from the thralls of capitalism.[24] Dell viewed the modern women's movement as proof of feminine willingness to adapt to masculine demands:

> Men are tired of subservient women; or, to speak more exactly, of the seemingly subservient woman who effects her will by stealth—the petty slave with all the slave's subtlety and cleverness. So long as it was possible for men to imagine themselves masters, they were satisfied. But when they found out that they were dupes, they wanted a change. If only for self-protection, they desired to find in woman a comrade and an equal. In reality, they desired it because it promised to be more fun.[25]

Village feminists also divided on the implications of domesticity for modern feminism. Some of the more traditional socialists argued that socialism would permit women the economic freedom requisite to devoting themselves exclusively to marriage and motherhood, failing to recognize that some women actually found fulfillment in work outside the home, or at least an escape from domestic drudgery. More radical professional women sought means of escaping from the trammels of domesticity. Henrietta Rodman, a high school English teacher and ardent feminist, championed a totally mechanized apartment house with a central kitchen in the basement and a rooftop kindergarten for preschool children, both staffed strictly by professionals in order to cater to the needs of professional women with families. However, Rodman neglected the implicit elitism of her scheme, whose exorbitant cost rendered it inaccessible to nonprofessional women, and scorned child raising as a task unsuited to exceptional women, thereby undermining any overarching sense of sisterhood.[26]

Again it was Emma Goldman who provided a lone critique of the superficiality of the Village feminists' belief that women's economic emancipation could provide them with personal freedom. Unless women freed themselves from the tyranny of public opinion, unless they demanded work comparable to that available to men, economic independence would offer working women few rewards outside the small professional elite:

> As to the great mass of working girls and women, how much independence is gained if the narrowness and lack of freedom of the home is

• • • •

exchanged for the narrowness and lack of freedom of the factory, sweat-shop, department store, or office? In addition is the burden which is laid on many women of looking after a "home, sweet home"—cold, dreary, disorderly, uninviting—after a day's hard work. Glorious independence! No wonder that hundreds of girls are so willing to accept the first offer of marriage, sick and tired of their "independence" behind the counter, at the sewing or typewriting machine. They are just as ready to marry as girls of the middle class, who long to throw off the yoke of parental supremacy.[27]

As long as women were relegated to alienating and gender-typed work outside the home, they would experience no greater freedom than they had when confined to domestic drudgery.

While the prewar Village may have been short on ideological consistency, it was even shorter on rigidity and dogma of any kind. The absence of the kind of political orthodoxy spawned by the Bolshevik Revolution and its aftermath left Villagers free to explore issues of art, politics, and life-style with an openness and creativity that would vanish in the postwar years. The revolution demanded hard choices, and John Reed gave up his poetry and Robert Minor his art. Reed journeyed to Russia and engaged in a frenzied round of political activity on behalf of the Bolshevik Revolution despite his prewar reservations, and Minor became active in Communist party political work. Even as many American literary intellectuals expatriated themselves to Paris and dissolved their ties with radicalism, Eastman continued to defend communism as the "science of evolution" and eventually adopted Leon Trotsky as the defender of the faith.[28] Ideology gained ascendancy in the Village in the postwar years, but only among the stalwarts of the teens.

The Village itself could no longer nurture a community of rebel spirits in the postwar world. Its isolation from the rest of the city dissolved as Sixth Avenue was cut through south of Carmine Street to Canal Street, permitting the flow of commercial traffic, and in the thirties the opening of the IND subway beneath Sixth and Eighth avenues further diminished the Village's ability to cloister itself as a haven from the rest of the city.[29] By the twenties the Village had become a popular place for tourists eager to catch a glimpse of bohemian frolics:

> The tangle of crooked streets would be pierced by a great straight road, the beautiful crumbling houses of great rooms and high ceilings and deep-embrasured windows would be ruthlessly torn down to make room for modern apartment-buildings; the place would become like all the rest of New York City—its gay, proud life would be extinguished. This was inevitable. But a worse and swifter doom than we could guess was to fall upon Greenwich Village. It was to become a side-show for vulgarians, a commercial exhibit of tawdry bohemianism.[30]

• • • •

225

Not only was the Village flooded by voyeuristic tourists in search of titillation. Worse yet, Greenwich Village standards, with the aid of business and advertising, seemed to sweep the country as women bobbed their hair and took to smoking cigarettes, as men in their forties committed adultery and discussed their neuroses, as homes throughout the country were furnished to resemble studios. By the end of the twenties the older bohemian Village of the teens was moribund. As Malcolm Cowley announced:

> If, however, the Village was really dying, it was dying of success. It was dying because it became so popular that too many people insisted on living there. It was dying because women smoked cigarettes on the streets of the Bronx, drank gin cocktails in Omaha and had perfectly swell parties in Seattle and Middletown—in other words, because American business and the whole of middle-class America had been going Greenwich Village.[31]

In the old Village bohemianism and radicalism had coexisted, but the newcomers who flocked to the postwar Village were far more cynical and no longer needed to crusade against puritanism because it did not interfere with their personal lives. The old idealism of the prewar Village was gone, dissolved by World War I and a draft law that left the rebels against puritanism free to survive and crushed the political rebels. The freedom of the prewar Village, as Cowley noted, was commercialized and trivialized as its message reached the American hinterland. But to the privileged few who had lived in the prewar Village, that freedom had an incandescent, if ephemeral, glow. And with that glow these bohemians and rebels, with their naïveté and charm, hoped to light the world.

· · · · ·

NOTES

1. Floyd Dell, "Rents Were Low in Greenwich Village," *American Mercury* 65 (December 1947): 663.
2. Mary K. Simkhovitch, *My Story of Greenwich House*, quoted in Edmund T. Delaney, *New York's Greenwich Village* (Barre, Mass.: Barre Publishers, 1968), 104.
3. John Reed, "Forty-two Washington Square," quoted in Mabel Dodge Luhan, *Movers and Shakers, Intimate Memories* (New York: Harcourt, Brace and Company, 1936), vol. 3, 175–176.
4. Louis Untermeyer, *From Another World* (New York: Harcourt, Brace and Company, 1939), 48–49.

· · · ·

5. Randolph S. Bourne to Prudence Winterrowd, 18 May 1913, Bourne Papers, p. 1, reprinted in Randolph Bourne, "Letters, 1913–1916," *Twice a Year* (Fall–Winter 1941): 85; Randolph Bourne, *Youth and Life* (1913; reprinted Freeport, N.Y.: Books for Libraries Press, 1967), 15–16. Quotation appears in latter.

6. Isadora Duncan, *My Life* (New York: Boni and Liveright, 1927), 341.

7. James Oppenheim, "America," *Seven Arts* 1 (March 1917): 471.

8. Max Eastman, "Mr. -er -er -Oh! What's his Name?" *Everybody's Magazine* 33 (July 1915): 103.

9. Luhan, *Movers and Shakers*, 143–144, 439–457, 505–512.

10. Dell, *Homecoming: An Autobiography* (New York: Farrar and Rinehart, 1933), 295.

11. Dell to Elizabeth Lancaster (1937), Dell Papers, quoted in George Thomas Tanselle, "Faun at the Barricades: The Life and Work of Floyd Dell," Ph.D. dissertation, Northwestern University, 1959, p. 445.

12. Eastman, *Enjoyment of Living* (New York: Harper & Brothers, Publishers, 1948), 490–495. Quotation appears on p. 495.

13. Emma Goldman, *Living My Life*, vol. 1 (New York: Alfred A. Knopf, 1931), 152–153.

14. Eastman, *Heroes I Have Known: Twelve Who Lived Great Lives* (New York: Simon & Schuster, 1942), 223.

15. Hutchins Hapgood, *The Spirit of the Ghetto*, ed. Moses Rischin (1902; reprinted Cambridge, Mass.: Belknap Press of Harvard University Press, 1967), passim, particularly 9–43.

16. Van Wyck Brooks, *The Confident Years, 1885–1915* (New York: E. P. Dutton & Company, 1952), 540.

17. Duncan, *My Life*, 254; Eastman, *Heroes I Have Known*, 86.

18. Luhan, *Movers and Shakers*, 79–80.

19. Nathan Irvin Huggins, *Harlem Renaissance* (New York: Oxford University Press, 1971), 84–136; Harold Cruse, *The Crisis of the Negro Intellectual* (New York: William Morrow & Company, 1967), 26; Carl Van Vechten, *Nigger Heaven* (New York: Alfred A. Knopf, 1926); Van Vechten, *Peter Whiffle* (1922; reprinted New York: Modern Library, 1929); Michael Gold, "Notes of the Month: Negro Literature," *New Masses* 5 (February 1930): 3.

20. Bourne, *War and the Intellectuals: Collected Essays, 1915–1919*, ed. Carl Resek (New York: Harper & Row, 1964), 125; Bourne, *History of a Literary Radical and Other Essays*, ed. Van Wyck Brooks (New York: B. W. Huebsch, 1920), 296–297, 299.

21. Eastman, "The Tanenbaum Crime," *The Masses* 5 (May 1914): 6–8.

22. Walter B. Rideout, *The Radical Novel in the United States, 1900–1954: Some Interrelations of Literature and Society* (Cambridge, Mass.: Harvard University Press, 1956), 77–78.

23. Luhan, *Movers and Shakers*, 228, 263, 285–286.

24. Dell, "Feminism for Men," *The Masses* 5 (July 1914): 14–15, 19.

25. Dell, *Women as World Builders: Studies in Modern Feminism* (Chicago: Forbes and Company, 1913), 19–20.

26. June Sochen, *Movers and Shakers: American Women Thinkers and Activists, 1900–1970* (New York: Quadrangle/New York Times Book Company, 1973), 37–38, 40; William L. O'Neill, *Everyone Was Brave: The Rise and Fall of Feminism in America* (Chicago: Quadrangle Books, 1969), 132–133.

27. Goldman, *Living My Life*, vol. 1, 371; Goldman, *Anarchism and Other Essays*, 177–178, 222. Quotation appears on p. 222.

28. Eastman, "Political Liberty," in *Freedom in the Modern World*, ed. Horace Kallen (New York, 1928), 159–182, quoted in John P. Diggins, *Up from Communism: Conservative*

Odysseys in American Intellectual History (New York: Harper & Row, Publishers, 1975), 24.

29. Edmund T. Delaney and Charles Lockwood, *Greenwich Village: A Photographic Guide*, 2nd, rev. ed. (New York: Dover Publications, Inc., 1976), viii.

30. Dell, *Love in Greenwich Village* (New York: George H. Doran Company, 1926), 296.

31. Malcolm Cowley, *Exile's Return: A Literary Odyssey of the 1920s* (1934; reprint, New York: Viking Press, 1962), 65.

• • • •

DISTURBERS OF THE PEACE

RADICALS IN GREENWICH VILLAGE, 1920–1930

Daniel Aaron

A fuller title of this essay might read something like this: "A Highly Selective and Impressionistic Glance at the Literary Left, Loosely Defined, in Greenwich Village, circa 1920–1930, With a Backward Look at Its Antecedents." By "Antecedents" is meant the interlude between roughly 1910 and 1917 sometimes referred to in literary histories as the "Little Renaissance" or the "Joyous Season." It came to a close the year the United States declared war on Germany.

A vast amount has been written about the men and women who flocked to the Village in the prewar years: histories, novels, memoirs, autobiographies, and volumes of correspondence. Legends and apocryphal stories have accumulated around them. That isn't so surprising given such heroes and heroines as Max Eastman, Mabel Dodge, Floyd Dell, Emma Goldman, Art Young, Hutchins Hapgood, Elizabeth Gurley Flynn, John Sloan, Dorothy Day, and Margaret Sanger. A few of them—Randolph Bourne and John Reed come to mind—were already legends when they died: Bourne (hounded by Secret Service agents for his antiwar views) in the 1918 flu epidemic; Reed in the Soviet Union two years later. Legends are part of the true history of the Village, if "truth" be defined as what people choose to remember, however imperfectly, however drenched in nostalgia.

The young Edmund Wilson wrote in 1922:

> When I think of Greenwich Village, it is almost with tears. For there this battered battalion dress their guns against the whole nation. Where

• • • •

Floyd Dell

7 a.m. Sunday, July 27, 1911.

F. Dell.

91. An archetypal Village bohemian, Floyd Dell juggled the part-time careers of playwright, novelist, essayist, sexual theorist, and community commentator while paying his rent with the modest salary he earned as associate editor of *The Masses*. *(Floyd Dell Papers, The Newberry Library, Chicago)*

the traffic, gnashing iron teeth, no longer oppresses the pavement, where the toned red bricks of low houses still front an open square. . . . From the darkest corners of the country they have fled for comfort and asylum. You may think them feeble and ridiculous—but feebleness is always relative. It may require as much force of character and as much independent thought for one of these to leave his Kansas home and espouse the opinions of Freud as for Wagner to achieve new harmonies or Einstein to conceive a finite universe. . . . Let me return: I shall not cease from mental fight nor shall my sword rest in my hand until intolerance has been stricken from the laws, till the time-clock has been beaten to a punch-bowl![1]

As the cliché has it, Greenwich Village was not only a place; it was also a state of mind. Lewis Mumford pictured it as an idyllic backwater to a dynamic city, "so well defined, so individualized, that the city planning commissioners of 1811 did not dare to make it conform to the gridiron pattern they imposed with geometric vigor on the rest of the city."[2] Perhaps that was one of its attractions for nonconformists and mavericks. The Village was enclosed physically, open intellectually. It tolerated eccentricity and intransigence. It provided cheap lodgings, cheap food, and entertainment. It was a refuge for free spirits from all over the country, restless people who felt plagued by small-town snooping, smugness, and hostility to the arts. At least that's the legend.

Serpents always lurk in Edens. It goes without saying that charlatans and crazies flourished in the Village along with the gifted and the pure of heart. All the same, for a brief time, say from the launching of *The Masses* in 1913 until its suppression by federal authorities in 1917, the Village was home to men and women who had similar political and cultural affinities. Many of them were socialists of the utopian or pragmatic schools; few if any were prepared to subordinate art to ideological formulas or to act as disciplined adherents of a party, no matter how revolutionary their feelings. Yet for all the differences in their programs and prejudices, they did constitute an entity of sorts until the war and the Russian Revolution exposed its fragility.

In the middle and late 1920s, however, a small number of writers and intellectuals moved toward communism and opted for a radical reconstruction of America. This coincided with the moment when a majority of former Village bohemians, in Floyd Dell's words, "put aside with a kind of shame [their] broken and shattered ideals."[3] What follows will be a small phase of that complicated, poignant, and comical story. I shall stick to the years between the armistice and the stock market crash of 1929, and focus on five writers who reflected in idiosyncratic ways the social and cultural climate of the postwar Village: E. E. Cummings, John Dos Passos, Michael Gold, Edmund Wilson, and (briefly) Floyd Dell.

Of the five only Mike Gold came close to Arthur Koestler's definition of the "earnest revolutionary . . . [the] bureaucrat of Utopia,"[4] and he didn't start out that way. The other four were radicals in varying degrees, although *rebels* would be a more accurate term to describe them. The directional signals—Left, Right, Center—are at best only relative and subjective designations. So it is enough to say here that the five writers differed in their political affiliations, aesthetic values, and personal tastes, but that in the 1920s each positioned himself to the "left" of the national consensus. Each in the Menckenian sense was a disturber of the peace, seeking his own way, choosing his own targets. And each had links, whether strong or tenuous, with the prewar radicals.

E. E. Cummings arrived in the Village in 1918 after a stint with an ambulance unit on the Western Front. Two other Villagers, Malcolm Cowley and John Dos Passos, had also served as "gentlemen volunteers" and, like Cummings, returned to the States convinced antimilitarists, but Cummings's foreign adventure was a touch unusual. He and his sidekick, Slater Brown, had been arrested and thrown into a French military prison because of some imprudent antiwar letters Brown had written to his parents. In them he had more than hinted at declining morale in the French army and observed that shooting the officers on both sides might be a practical way to end the war. Although he wasn't directly implicated by the censors, Cummings refused to repudiate his pal's views and went to jail.

Out of that experience came *The Enormous Room*, a classic of prison literature and a splendid testimony to human resilience and the will to survive—indeed, to flourish—under the bleakest conditions. A dark and comic *Pilgrim's Progress*, Cummings's novel isn't intentionally "political," but it is animated by an undoctrinaire anarchism and a strong sympathy for the underdog that betray an affinity with the prewar libertarians of *The Masses*. So does his humor and his love of paradox.

But Cummings (and the same could be said of the new Villagers of comparable age and background) was more sophisticated, hard-boiled, sardonic, and scatological than the prewar Village pacifists and more of a smart-alecky scoffer. He parodied the "Hundred Percent" patriots ("next to of course god america i / love you land of the pilgrims' pride and so forth") who extolled "these heroic happy dead / who rushed like lions to the roaring slaughter / they did not stop to think they died instead / then shall the voice of liberty be mute? / He spoke. And drank rapidly a glass of water";[5] he celebrated the young idealists going off to war with "trumpets, clap, and syphilis"[6] and paid a savage tribute to a "conscientious object-or." Olaf, "whose warmest heart recoiled at war," is beaten up and tortured by the military, but he won't yield to his tormenters. "I will not kiss your f-ing flag," he tells them (even Cummings couldn't flout the censors, Mencken's "smut-hounds"), and Olaf endlessly repeats before he dies in prison, "there is some s. I will not eat."[7]

• • • •

What is new in these verses and in some of the writings of his fellow transient Villagers, Dos Passos and Wilson, is not so much anger and bitterness but a feeling of impotence. Unlike their hopeful predecessors, they no longer believed it possible to change society, as Malcolm Cowley said, "by any effort of the will." The war was a swindle, Woodrow Wilson a fraud, and Warren Gamaliel Harding (the only man, Cummings observed in his mock elegy, who could write a simple declarative sentence with seven grammatical errors) a big joke.

This feeling of disenchantment and frustration was implicit in the cynicism that underlay the frenetic gaiety of the twenties. Cummings wasn't in revolt against anything in particular; he was against authority, censors, the military, the police. The enemy was against "you and I." The enemy was "they," "mostpeople," "the Others," "Mankind," Emerson's "agglutinated masses" who had sold their individuality to the collective.

But Cummings was no amateur bohemian. He and his circle took their writing very seriously. They were professionals who scrabbled for their livings, took on editorial jobs, wrote novels and plays and poems, sold pieces to *The Dial, Vanity Fair, The New Republic,* or *The Freeman.* They worked to perfect their skills and were more concerned with self-expression than social redemption.

In the early 1920s the Village was a temporary oasis as well as a jumping-off point for Paris, where a number of literary refugees camped from time to time. In fact Paris became a kind of Greenwich Village suburb—what the editors of *Secession* (one of the avant-garde "little" magazines first published abroad) called in 1922 "the present literary capital of America." The antics and achievements of the so-called expatriate group have been endlessly recounted. Suffice it to say that they were never more American than when they were belaboring America's cultural blight. Their diatribes against "civilization" in the United States, George Santayana remarked, inadvertently demonstrated its crude vitality. As Cummings expressed it in a Gertrude Stein–like sentence: "France has happened more than she is happening, whereas America is happening more than she has happened."

H. L. Mencken, widely read in the Village throughout the decade, relished the wonderful nonsense of the times. He didn't expect much to happen in the "happening," but he stayed put in the United States, he said, because America was as amusing as a zoo. On the other hand, Edmund Wilson and Kenneth Burke, two of the more thoughtful surveyors of the twenties scene, did expect something to happen and entertained hopes for a revitalized national culture. And they weren't alone. One senses in their articles and reviews and in their private letters that while keenly interested in the technical experiments of the modernists, they were less ready than the debunkers to trash America and less eager than the experimenters to junk the old and glorify the new.

• • • •

Veterans of the prewar rebellion particularly distrusted the emphasis on form and technique at the expense of content and fundamentally disagreed with the younger artists and writers on the definition, meaning, and purpose of art. As Meyer Schapiro has pointed out in his brilliant essay on the Armory Show of 1913 (where many Americans got their first glimpse of post-impressionist art), "socialist leaders were most often conservatives in art."[8] They favored "easily legible images of misery, class struggle, and the radiant socialist future," or if not that, "relaxing pictures of nature's beauty"—an art that was robust, in the American vernacular, and above all representational. Not surprisingly, then, they deplored what seemed to them willful and perverse in the new art—imageless, esoteric, private—and hardly differed from genteel critics in the intensity of their opposition to cubism and abstraction and to what Van Wyck Brooks called the "unholy alliance" between literature and the plastic arts in modernist literature and criticism.

"However it may be in the plastic arts," wrote Brooks in 1922, "in literature the subject, the content dictates the form. The form is an inevitable consequence of the thing that is to be said and rises out of it as naturally as the flower rises out of the seed. To seek forms, therefore, is to confess that one lacks things. It is the frankest sort of acknowledgement of a complete literary insolvency." Brooks went on to charge the young "barbarians" or "patricians," as they were sometimes referred to, with fetching up "the rags and tatters of a badly assimilated erudition . . . the fruits of a parvenu intellectuality." He attributed the preoccupation with form and technique to the postwar generation's preference for "questions that were concrete and hard when so much that was human seemed treacherous, dubious, and soft."[9] The accusation, if not baseless, was simplistic. Brooks was so fixed in his own moral and aesthetic groove that he failed to appreciate sufficiently how and why the new writing shook up and energized a stale literary culture. Nor did he ever convincingly explain why a delight in Joyce and Eliot and Proust—or, for that matter, in jazz, skyscrapers, burlesque shows, comic strips, and advertising copy—necessarily implied "an indifference to everything else."

Brooks's "barbarians"—the Dadaists, surrealists, formalists, or whatever—had never extinguished in themselves the social and moral idealism they jeered at. More often than not, they conveyed it profanely. Surely he exaggerated when he said that Greenwich Village "had lost its symbolic meaning" and that the "old circle of Randolph Bourne had also all but vanished from the literary mind." Admittedly the tone of Village life had changed; no doubt the higgledy-piggledy radicalism of the Little Renaissance had begun to separate into distinct strains. Terms like *liberal, anarchist, socialist, communist*—once of no great moment—now defined oppositions. Yet the old dichotomy, them and us, still obtained. The bourgeoisie, the middle-class establishment, was still a prime target even as its representatives from

• • • •

uptown invaded the Village enclave. Most of the unclearly designated Left continued to snipe at the vestiges of the genteel tradition and what was subsumed under the rubric of puritanism, prohibition, censorship, or repression of any sort.

All the same, Brooks had a point. The composition of the Village artists and literati was no longer what it had been, thanks to the influx of young college graduates. The war had widened their social vistas and made them impatient with their Victorian nurture without eliminating their ethnic and racial prejudices. There was no equivalent among them of Max Eastman or Floyd Dell or Jack Reed or Randolph Bourne. Try as they might, they never quite managed to feel at ease (as *The Masses* circle had been) with unclassifiable eccentrics, with blacks, Italians, and Irish, and with Jewish radicals from the wrong side of the tracks, many of whom had been strongly affected by the Russian Revolution and were soon to be attracted to the Communist party. For the most part, they took the side of the "downtrodden," but they were also likely to sentimentalize them, to see them as exhibiting a life force noticeably lacking in their own class.

At first glance John Dos Passos would seem to be an exception to this generalization. His background was similar to those of other Ivy League rebels (he was educated at the Choate School and Harvard), but from an early age he felt himself to be an outsider, perhaps because of his father's Portuguese ancestry, perhaps because of his own illegitimacy. In any event, by the time he graduated from Harvard, he was an admirer of John Reed and a sympathizer of the anarcho-syndicalist International Workers of the World (IWW). He dreamed of "vengeful guillotines" set up on Wall Street and of a revolution that would end in "the wholesale assassination of all statesmen, capitalists, war-mongers, jingoists." To be sure, he expressed these bloody thoughts exuberantly, but he was more than half serious when he wrote that the capitalists—"swag-bellied gentlemen," he called them— were in the saddle and likely to remain so. His radical friends shared this conviction until the prospects of a benevolent world communism momentarily beguiled them—but not Dos Passos.

Having already absorbed the antiwar animus of the old Village radicals, he had no illusions about the Allied cause when he sailed for France in 1917 to drive an ambulance in a Norton-Harjes unit.[10] Crossing the water was a literary act, not a patriotic one. It was also a way, Malcolm Cowley wrote at the time, to break out of a "fixed orbit," to see Paris, to take part in "the great common experience" of one's generation "without which one will be somewhat of a stranger to the world of the present and the future."[11] Dos Passos didn't put it in quite those terms, but he immediately started to "suck up the stream of sensation" as it flowed by. "All the cant and hypocrisy," he wrote in his journal, "all the damnable survivals, all the vestiges of old truths now putrid and false infect the air, choke you worse than German gas—the ministers from their damn smug pulpits, the business men—the heroics about war—my country right or wrong."[12]

Still pessimistic about the future at the war's end, he remained a party of one, spokesman for every oppressed minority, and as suspicious of monolithic organizations as Cummings, his collegemate and traveling companion. "Organization," he declared, "is death." At the same time he made an earnest effort to divest himself "of class and the monied background" by throwing himself into the struggle against "privilege." Off and on he lived in the Village and joined his friends in their random dissipations—but more as an observer than participant. He was never really a Villager.

Dos Passos appears as a character in Edmund Wilson's *I Thought of Daisy*, a novel in which Village types figure prominently. Here he is Hugh Bammon, a roving investigator always on the point of departing for Russia or Mexico or any exotic spot in the process of upheaval. Hugh is shy and stuttering (Dos Passos couldn't pronounce his *r*'s—"strike" would come out "stwyke," a handicap for a would-be tribune of the working class); he wears thick glasses and doesn't really enjoy the drunken parties and the bold "new women" he encounters in the Village. So he sneaks off to little oases of respectability and old-fashioned middle-class manners. But he continues his experiments in fiction and reportage. He paints and writes poetry and incorporates into his fiction and plays what he has learned in his fight against exploitative capitalism.

Wilson's novel came out in 1929. By that time Dos Passos was already looking back fondly to the innocent bohemians of prewar Greenwich Village and its mouthpiece, *The Masses*. Callow, ineffective in its rebelliousness, or so he described it, the Village stood for something missing in postwar America, "a community of feeling with the common men who did the work," and he identified more than ever with its libertarian credo. The war killed the dream of the common man striding "forward out of the welter of the past, happy, powerful, and inventive, and willing for his neighbor to be happy and powerful too." Although Dos Passos conceded the advances in personal freedom—writers had recovered "the use of unbowdlerized English, and the national capacity to see painting and drawing [had] enormously increased"—in respect to social ideas, he found that "the time was one of defeat, sectarianism, and reaction."[13]

In this mood he wrote his first important novel, *Manhattan Transfer*, a pessimistic overview of a corrupt New York City "both marvelous and appalling" in which Dos Passos indulged his talent for fierce and funny social satire. Following that came several plays, experimental in form and revolutionary in content, for the New Playwrights Theatre on Grove Street. At the end of the decade, he was, if anything, an unattached anarchist of sorts, suspicious of organized socialism in any form.

Dos Passos's political vagaries and especially his strong reservations about the Soviet Union troubled Michael Gold, himself a contributor to the New Playwrights Theatre. He was also one of the founders of *The New Masses*, ostensibly a revival of the old one. In 1926 the editors, Dos Passos among them, represented a spectrum of Left opinion from liberal to communist. Three years later the magazine had become, in effect, an organ of the Communist party. It would not be long before Gold sorrowfully denounced his friend Dos Passos as a class enemy.

A onetime protégé of Max Eastman and Floyd Dell, Gold hero-worshiped Jack Reed, the inspiration of his proletarian rhapsodies. He had written for *The Masses* and, after its suppression, for *The Liberator*. Rather than fight in what he considered an imperialist war, he hid out in Mexico. Thus he had better revolutionary credentials than did Cummings, Dos Passos, and Wilson and represented, as they did not, an authentic Village type: the radical bohemian, author of one-acters for the Provincetown Players, a familiar figure at the Village watering holes—where he drank with Eugene O'Neill and talked about Tolstoy and revolution with Dorothy Day, later the editor of *The Catholic Worker*. By his own account his conversion to socialism occurred in 1914 as he listened to Elizabeth Gurley Flynn orate in Union Square, an incident he made the culminating scene in his novel *Jews Without Money*.

Gold exemplifies the immigrant strain among the Village literati or what might aptly be described as the downwardly mobile Jew. The persona he adopted early was the open-shirted proletarian roistering with his working-class comrades, half Walt Whitman, half Jack Reed. He saw himself as the antitype of the intellectual as "bastard" and of the "careful men with perpetual slight colds" who wrote for *The New Republic* and *The Nation*. A theatrical self-portrait appeared in a letter to Upton Sinclair in the mid-1920s, in which he explained that while he admired Sinclair's books and was grateful for his generosity, he couldn't collaborate with him on a magazine project. To do so, he said, would be tantamount to

> being asked by a pure girl in marriage when one is a battered old roué with five or six affairs on hand, I am immoral, Upton, I drink, smoke, swear, loaf, sneer, shoot pool, dance jazz, shake the shimmy, ride box-cars, do most everything. I would rather hear a good joke most of the time than a Communist speech. I would rather take a long walk into the country with a bunch of roughnecks than write a novel. I cannot be pious and love Jesus. I used to, but I don't anymore. After I have been with good people, formal people, however revolutionary, for a month or two, I want to bust loose and do something wild, etc. I am not boasting about all this; I just don't want you to labor under any misapprehension. I am a good Red, etc., and take that seriously enough, but it might get on your nerves if you found me smoking six or seven cigars a day, and hanging out in bootlegging joints with a

bunch of Wobblies. I cannot be as pure, fervent, and Puritanical as yourself, Upton, and would not want to be. The mass of humanity, stupid or intellectual, is fond of any kind of fun, sensuality, relaxation, sport and frivolity, and I am one of them.[14]

Gold's outburst—pure Whitman, of course—was consistent with the bohemian-anarchist-Red: sentimental, tough, funny, inventive, earthy, spontaneous. This was the Gold who as early as 1921 prophesied the downfall of bourgeois art and literature. "The old ideals must die," he proclaimed. "But let us not fear. Let us fling all we are in the cauldron of the Revolution." Few writers in the debunking twenties paid much heed to his call, but they found him refreshing. Friendships between writers of opposing ideological and aesthetic camps were still possible in the uncommitted 1920s—much less so in the sectarian thirties. In that decade Gold changed from the "happy determined warrior" into the literary hatchet man of the Party, an unsuitable role for one who was by nature friendly and generous and at bottom (although he felt impelled to deny it) a romantic anarchist. Gold fiercely espoused the Communist party "line" during the thirties and lashed out at former "fellow-travelers" who had turned against the Soviet Union. Among them he included Edmund Wilson whose brief involvement with the Party he compared to "a myopic, high-bosomed Beacon Hill matron entering a common street car."[15]

The image has a certain validity. During the 1920s Wilson lived fleetingly in the Village—for a time he had an apartment on Bank Street—but he was never really *of* it. He had come there on his return from France, where he had endured the war in a gruesome medical depot. Living in the Village allowed him to detach himself from the confines of his family and old associates without losing contact with them. His "people," the ones he felt most at home with, were likely to be classmates and social equals whose America had little in common with Mike Gold's. In the Village milieu Wilson became as bohemian as he ever would be. He conquered his sexual inhibitions, drank excessively, mingled with types he had seldom encountered at Princeton, yet retained his reserve and kept himself at a distance from the undisciplined revelers.

I Thought of Daisy, together with his letters and notebooks, best convey his ideas and feelings in this decade. Among other things they dramatize the tug of war going on in his mind between the past, with which he associated the honorable traditions and values of his father's generation, and the iconoclastic, liberating, and destructive ethos of the 1920s.

The poet Edna Millay, "Rita" in the novel—free, unconventional, impulsively promiscuous, but sternly committed to her art—objectifies for him the ardor of the Village. Through this priestess the spirit of the Village is revealed to him. After meeting her, the narrator feels as if he has been

• • • •

translated into a higher plane. Like Miles Coverdale in Hawthorne's *The Blithedale Romance*, intoxicated by his first contact with the carefree communitarians, he is ready to turn his back, he says, "on all that world of mediocre aims and prosaic compromises; and at that price—what brave spirit would not pay it?—I have been set free to follow poetry."[16]

Something of a Brook Farm idyll is suggested in his notebook entries. He describes pretty girls in batik dresses; Washington Square after rain, "freshened with tender green and swimming in milky pallors"; Bank Street in June, ailanthus trees swaying: "The child always crying in the backyard,— Music: highbrow piano and jazz accordion.—Appetizing smell of dinners cooking in the late afternoon." In these moods he envies "the Greenwich Villagers proper," even though he finds them insipid and underbred because they belonged to an earlier and braver day.

But the idyll has its dark underside. The diarist contrasts the fresh green Village, the Village as Arcadia, with the dirty and dingy Village, the Village as Waste Land: Varick Street strewn with rubbish, "here and there a grimy little knot of Italians," the "taxis scooting around like cockroaches when you go into the kitchen at night."[17] The parties the narrator of *I Thought of Daisy* is drawn to but despises are attended by "young journalists cheapened by their work; pottering young writers, like myself; debauched or epicene young poets, with neither genius nor self-respect; mediocre middle-aged literary men, with bald heads and stale reputations; and all that odd mixed company of lawyers, contractors and brokers." He has found "the pit of ashes at the bottom of the gin-bottle."

Politically Wilson stayed in the liberal camp until the late twenties, attentive and not unsympathetic to the anarchists and communists, but more observer than activist and still hopeful about American vitality and cultural promise. It goes without saying that he disdained the business class— in his eyes a vulgar greedy lot totally devoid of public spirit—and spurned their mean ambitions. But he was also troubled by the hostility of his literary contemporaries toward their country. Edith Wharton, Van Wyck Brooks, Dos Passos, Sinclair Lewis, Thornton Wilder—all seemed to regard America as a terrible place filled with Yahoos. He thought this was especially true of his friend Dos Passos, who wrote, Wilson said, as if he had had a bad egg for breakfast every morning. Nonetheless, Wilson was becoming increasingly at odds with the managers of the nation, if not the nation itself, and, with some other socially conscious intellectuals, he moved closer to the politics of Gold and Dos Passos.

One of the causes for this shift, it has frequently been said, was the trial and execution of Sacco and Vanzetti, a world-reverberating event that had a special resonance in the Village. Wilson had been and remained critical of both Dos Passos and Gold for allowing their biases to falsify reality. Some "deeply buried streak of hysteria," he suspected, lay behind their "misap-

• • • •

plied resentments." He particularly condemned Gold's overemphasis on the "economic and political factors" in judging a work of art. After the execution of Sacco and Vanzetti he grew even more critical of writers (he cited Hemingway, Fitzgerald, and Wilder) who cultivated their "own little corners" and ignored "the situation as a whole."

Wilson didn't join Dos Passos, Dorothy Parker, Katherine Anne Porter, Edna Millay, William Gropper, Paxton Hibben, and others who went to Boston to protest the execution. He had been too lazy or insufficiently aroused to demonstrate, despite Dos Passos's appeal, but the aftermath left him shaken and reflective. In one of his pieces he mentions meeting Cummings in an Italian restaurant and asking him if he'd been in Boston on the day of the execution. Cummings replies:

> Of course my attitude toward this whole thing—I mean it's just unfortunate—it's a bore, like somebody losing his pants—it's embarrassing, but it oughtn't to be a surprise to anybody—what surprises me is that they managed to stay alive for seven years! Why I've seen them shoot people first and search them afterwards—and if they've got any bullets in them, they arrest them for carrying concealed weapons.[18]

It was far from being a bore or an embarrassment to Wilson. He now believed that the electrocution of the two anarchists had atomized American life "with all its classes, professions, and points of view and raised almost every fundamental question of our political and social system." A conviction was growing in him that the liberal ideas of his boss, Herbert Croly, editor of *The New Republic*, had been tested and found wanting.

The Sacco-Vanzetti case brought Dos Passos closer than he ever had been or would be again to a revolutionary position: a United States of two conflicting nations. It inspired Mike Gold's polemic against the "lynching bee" conducted "by well-known Harvard graduates in frock coats" and underscored the break (in his own mind) between the old *Masses* (which he now called "a more brilliant but a more upper class affair") and a militant *New Masses*, crude but vital and going after a "kind of flesh and blood reality." To Kenneth Burke, who professed to be negative in his radicalism, the fate of Sacco and Vanzetti was important emblematically. "Perhaps it is too important for a symbol," he wrote Cowley, "perhaps it incites less adequately than a downtrodden flag or a shoe on a stick, but it will serve."[19] In retrospect, Cowley called this event and the Russian-German agreement of 1939 "the two heaviest blows that American liberalism had ever suffered."[20] It coincided with, and perhaps triggered, his leftward course.

By the 1930s, Greenwich Village had become synonymous with a defunct bohemia, and the term *Greenwich Villager*—for the leftists at least—

· · · ·

an epithet. The buoyancy and hope that colored the prewar dreams of Randolph Bourne and those of a few postwar kindred spirits were pretty well gone. The most reliable memorialist of Village vicissitudes during the period discussed above is Floyd Dell, its historian, interpreter, critic, and defender.

Dell left Chicago in 1913 for the Village, where he helped Max Eastman edit *The Masses*. An exemplary Villager, he enacted and celebrated the "play-spirit" of prewar radicalism. He equated political and sexual freedom, Lenin and Freud, and welcomed and defended the Russian Revolution, although he never managed to reconcile his allegiance to socialism with his subversive individualism. The conflict can be traced in his brushes with officialdom, his plays and novels, his literary theories, and his sexual adventures. He was one of the few radicals capable of judging himself and his times with a kind of bemused disinterestedness, and who acknowledged his emotional and intellectual follies without bitterness or remorse.

Dell got it in the neck from many quarters in the twenties and thirties. Some Villagers resented his loving but stern critique of what he called "intellectual vagabondage," his name for irresponsible escapism. He was one of the first of the left-wingers to point out "the neurotic origins" of much of the political radicalism of the day. In fact, as he replied to one of his attackers in a private letter, he might have become a successful satirist of the Left had he not resisted the temptation out of loyalty to the radical cause. For his unforgivable deviations—among them his refusal to agitate for Sacco and Vanzetti—and his resignation from the editorial board of *The New Masses* in 1929, he was savaged by his former protégé, Mike Gold. According to Gold, the Greenwich Village "playboy" had always been more devoted to the female anatomy than he was to the class struggle. [21]

Dell took such attacks in his stride and stayed out of the ensuing ideological wars. At least his alleged preoccupation with sex, he wrote, had freed him "from the bondage of a preoccupation with a grand Economic Explanation of Everything, which is rigor mortis to the mind." [22] He retained his social idealism and continued to resist what he described in a letter to Eastman many years later as "the constricting influences of emotional disillusionment." [23] This was at a time when political confessions were in vogue and ex-radicals were being pressured to apologize for their past political sins. Tolerant of other people's self-deceptions as well as his own, Dell reminded his old friend that becoming a socialist, supporting the Russian Revolution, and fighting the capitalist system involved emotional rather than rational processes. These "great idealistic enthusiasms" were bound to end in disillusionment "as the smug wiseacres on the sidelines knew all along, damn them." [24]

Even so, he concluded—and here he spoke for the Greenwich Village

· · · ·

community as well as for himself—"there are some follies worth undergoing because they exercise to the utmost the humane, generous, and more or less heroic parts of our nature."[25]

· · · · ·

NOTES

1. Edmund Wilson, *The New Republic* 30 (March 8, 1922): 76–77.
2. Donald L. Miller, ed. *The Lewis Mumford Reader* (New York: Pantheon Books, 1986), 192.
3. Daniel Aaron, *Writers on the Left* (New York: Columbia University Press, 1992), 106.
4. Arthur Koestler, *Arrow in the Blue, an Autobiography* (New York: Macmillan, 1952), 272.
5. E. E. Cummings, *Complete Poems* (New York: Harcourt Brace Jovanovich, 1972), 268.
6. Ibid., 273.
7. Ibid., 339.
8. Daniel Aaron, ed. *America in Crisis* (New York: Alfred A. Knopf, 1952), 229.
9. Van Wyck Brooks, *The Freeman* 8 (August 8, 1923): 527.
10. Organized at the beginning of World War I by a Bostonian, Richard Norton, and Henry H. Harjes of Morgan, Harjes and Company, Paris. See Charles Norman, *The Magic Maker* (New York: Macmillan, 1958), 73–75.
11. Paul Jay, ed. *The Selected Correspondence of Kenneth Burke and Malcolm Cowley, 1915–1981* (New York: Viking, 1988), 50.
12. Townsend Ludington, *John Dos Passos. A Twentieth-Century Odyssey* (New York: E. P. Dutton, 1980), 130.
13. John Dos Passos, "Grandfather and Grandson," *The New Masses* (September 15, 1936): 19.
14. Gold quote from undated letter in the Upton Sinclair Papers, Lilly Library, University of Indiana, Bloomington.
15. Michael Gold, *The Hollow Men* (New York: International Library, 1941), 68.
16. Wilson, *I Thought of Daisy* (New York: Farrar, Straus & Giroux, 1975), 296.
17. Wilson, *The Twenties*, ed. Leon Edel (New York: Farrar, Straus & Giroux, 1975), 296.
18. Ibid., 185.
19. *Selected Correspondence of Kenneth Burke and Malcolm Cowley*, 179.
20. Ibid., 229.
21. Quoted in *Writers on the Left*, 216.
22. Ibid., 218.
23. Floyd Dell to Max Eastman, Nov. 1954, Newbery Library, Chicago. I am indebted to Professor John P. Diggins for calling this letter to my attention.
24. Ibid.
25. Ibid.

· · · ·

THE RADICAL WOMEN OF GREENWICH VILLAGE

FROM CRYSTAL EASTMAN TO ELEANOR ROOSEVELT

Blanche Wiesen Cook

Greenwich Village has been New York's main center of freedom, creativity, permission, and anonymity and the spiritual home of artists, writers, and radicals throughout the twentieth century. A neighborhood of brilliant talk, festive dress, and full-blown masquerades, it is also a village of quiet, underpopulated alleys and mews, with low buildings, tall trees, and narrow winding streets and lanes that make no sense and form no pattern. It has been and remains an ideal place to live and enrich one's life with good food, noble ideas, and great friendships.

For many, it was the place to be when we were growing up in order to meet the kindred folk who allowed us to know that we were not alone and that we were not crazy. During the 1950s we would come at night, in the dark, often after midnight—after school and work—to drink coffee and listen to poetry or folk songs or to go to a bar and dance with each other—women together or women and men, black and white.

We could hold hands in the Village, and think reckless thoughts, and read banned books and forbidden magazines, and look ardently into each other's eyes. We were sure we were not alone, but we really did think we

• • • •
243

were the first. And for so many years there were no books, no articles, no poems to tell us differently.

Twenty years ago virtually nothing was written about the radical feminists of the pre–World War I era, nothing about the women of the peace movement; and nothing about the extraordinary networks of friendship and work the political women living in Greenwich Village during the first decades of the twentieth century had created with imagination, ardor, and, yes, even lust.

An example of how completely the great women of our history were erased may be found in Albert Parry's classic, *Garrets and Pretenders: A History of Bohemianism in America.* Like so many of his contemporaries, Parry dismissed the contributions of women, and instead credited their closest male relatives for their achievements. So, for example, he devotes entire paragraphs to Max Eastman and Wallace Benedict, Crystal Eastman's first husband of several years, for virtually all of her work. He does not mention Crystal Eastman at all. This is merely typical, and would not be so grievous did he not have the gall to credit the introduction of the charming custom of putting flower boxes in windows to "Max Eastman's brother-in-law," Wallace Benedict.

Now, you may think this a simple thing, but I consider it the essence of our history. It explains why I have chosen to be and remain a historian: to right the wrongs, to do justice by the virtuous, and to celebrate the righteous. And so the truth is as follows: Crystal Eastman moved to the Village after she graduated from Vassar in 1903. She worked as a recreation leader and counselor at the Greenwich Settlement House in the evenings while she studied for a master's degree in sociology at Columbia University during the day. After her graduation in 1904, she entered New York University Law School and graduated second in the class of 1907. Until 1911 she lived communally, first with several friends, and then with her friends and her younger brother Max, whom she had persuaded to join her.

At first Eastman's primary community included three friends from Vassar and law school: Ida Rauh, Inez Milholland, and Madeleine Doty. Their apartment became one of the major communication centers for labor and suffrage activities. Their work and friendship endured hardships, political disagreements, and sundry changes. Ardent suffragists and reformers, all subsequently married progressive and supportive men equally involved in their great concerns. Rauh married and later divorced Max Eastman. Inez Milholland, known as the great Amazon of the suffragist movement after her dazzling appearance at suffrage parades astride a white horse, married Eugen Boissevain, who "commanded a whole fleet of merchant ships." After Milholland's sudden death during a suffrage campaign in 1916, Boissevain lived communally in still another Village house with Eastman and her circle until he married Edna St. Vincent Millay. And Madeleine Doty mar-

· · · ·

92. Crystal Eastman *(The Schlesinger Library, Radcliffe College)*

ried and subsequently divorced social worker and civil libertarian Roger Baldwin.

Their home always featured fresh-cut flowers and window boxes, and Wallace Benedict had nothing to do with it. When Crystal Eastman agreed in 1910 to marry Benedict, a robust and athletic outsider from Milwaukee

• • • •

who was without political commitment or intellectual pretensions, the re-
actions of her friends and her brother ranged from puzzlement to horror.
No one could understand it. A chronological coincidence may offer an explanation. Just prior to agreeing to marry "Bennie," Eastman went to see
New York's first Freudian psychoanalyst, Dr. A. A. Brill, to "get her libido
down." And Benedict, an insurance salesman, seemed to have as his one
significant virtue a virile and handsome physique. Unfortunately, he made
it a marital precondition that Eastman move back to Milwaukee with him.
Before their marriage she got so sick she took to her bed, from where she
wrote Max:

> I've been feeling very scared about getting married all through this sick-
> ness. Getting back to New York and living with you was the hope I fed
> my drooping spirits on—not Milwaukee and the married state. Your
> suggestion that if I can't stand it, you'll know it's not for you, gives me
> a humorous courage. Perhaps after we've both experimented around a
> few years, we may end up living together again.

Although she ran the famous women's suffrage campaign in Wisconsin
in 1912, Eastman's career was in New York, which represented the center
of a great network of political change and excitement. Bored by Milwaukee
and by Bennie, within two years she left him and returned to the Village.
Soon thereafter she was appointed to a federal commission on work accidents and compensation and commuted regularly to Washington throughout 1913–1914.[1]

Now, this may seem very removed from window boxes in Greenwich
Village, but flowers are merely the topside of many things for which women
have failed to get credit. Until I wrote my book about Crystal Eastman she
had virtually disappeared from history. She was also the founder of the
Woman's Peace party, which became the Women's International League
for Peace and Freedom. The first meeting of the party was held in November 1914, in Greenwich Village. British suffragist and pacifist Emmeline
Pethick-Lawrence journeyed to New York to galvanize concerned women
into a massive movement of resistance against the madness of war.[2]

In January 1915 Eastman and Pethick-Lawrence traveled to Chicago,
where they helped to found the national Woman's Peace party, with Jane
Addams as president. Eastman remained president of the New York branch
throughout the war and ensured its status as the most militant and activist
branch in the United States. She presided over its journal *Four Lights*,
which was patterned on *The Masses* and was gay, impulsive, and entirely
disrespectful of authority.

Jane Addams disapproved of its tone, and over time came rather to disapprove of Crystal Eastman as well: She was too direct, too forthright. She

represented "impulsive radicalism," and her "casual sex life" confused the issues and seemed threatening to the antiwar movement. The women of Greenwich Village campaigned for birth control, took lovers, and got divorced. They not only opposed the draft, they campaigned for free speech in wartime, supported anarchists and socialists, picketed with striking union women, and were themselves arrested. Until the Red Scare placed all activists in the same discredited boat, discretion seemed preferable to Addams and the more conventional leadership of the progressive peace movement.

Perhaps it was the habit of freedom caused by living too long in Greenwich Village; perhaps it was the habit of freedom promoted and enabled by a loving, supportive, and dedicated radical family—including a mother who was a minister and also a suffragist and feminist. Whatever the origins of her worldview, Eastman was neither conventional nor discreet. In the first issue of *Four Lights*, published in January 1917, she promised that the new journal would be "the voice of the young, uncompromising peace movement in America, whose aims are daring and immediate."

The Woman's Peace party of New York was also the home of many of the women of Heterodoxy, a Saturday-afternoon luncheon club that was likewise founded in 1915 and survived until 1940. The group comprised Eastman's closest friends—the bohemian women of the Village. The Heterodites' basic message was simple: "It is the aim of women not to hate, but to love one another," and to respect all the differences between us. One of the most interesting aspects of Heterodoxy was that its membership included radicals and conservatives—Democrats, Republicans, and Socialists. Creative work and feminist concerns were the criteria for admission. Members worked for money; called themselves socialists, anarchists, or free thinkers; believed in free love; read erotic and exotic books; wore amazing costumes; and dressed for each other. They honored their friendships and themselves. "What a seamless shining robe [Heterodoxy] . . . has been weaving . . . the garment of comradeship and loyalty, courage and charity, trust and faith and love." They were the "New Women" of a new time in a world they did much to create: Margaret Lane, Anne Herendeen, Freda Kirchwey, Katherine Anthony, Elisabeth Irwin, Madeleine Doty, Marie Jennie Howe, Agnes Brown Leach, Mary Heaton Vorse, and many others.

In the beginning the Woman's Peace party, and the American Union Against Militarism, over which Crystal Eastman also presided as executive director, had several real successes. In 1916 their efforts helped avert a war with Mexico. But as the war in Europe raged, and business and imperial interests organized and began to control the media and regulate public opinion, their efforts to keep America neutral failed. They then turned their attentions to a campaign for democracy in wartime and struggled to keep the United States from becoming a militarist, "Prussian-like" power. They held free-speech rallies, opposed the draft, and sought to keep profits out of munitions making. After the United States entered the war in April 1917, one group of Union activists, led by Crystal Eastman—member in charge and leading attorney—founded the National Civil Liberties Bureau, which has had a long and honorable life as the American Civil Liberties Union. They proposed to fight for the survival of constitutional liberties in wartime, especially the right to dissent, to speak and write, to assemble, to protect conscientious objectors, and generally, Eastman explained, "to maintain something over here that will be worth coming back to when the weary war is over."

There were men in the American Union leadership, just as there were men in the suffrage movement. Indeed, in 1909 Crystal Eastman had urged her brother to organize the Men's League for Women's Suffrage. But whenever men are involved, they tend to get all the credit, and to this day the women involved in the World War I–era peace movement get short-changed. Eastman ran the American Union Against Militarism, and Lillian Wald was president. They worked with Max Eastman, Roger Baldwin, John Haynes Holmes, Jane Addams, Zona Gale, Emily Greene Balch, Amos Pinchot, Oswald Garrison Villard, and many others, but in study after study the women are rarely celebrated.

In 1916 Eastman divorced Bennie, from whom she had been separated, to marry Walter Fuller, a British antimilitarist, poet, and musical impresario. This time her brother and friends approved: Fuller was ardently political and seriously intellectual. He also made her laugh, and they had fun together. When she took several weeks off to have her first child, Geoffrey Fuller, Eastman asked her good friend Roger Baldwin to come to New York from St. Louis and temporarily run the Union office.[3] Within six weeks Eastman was back in the office to continue her work as director and attorney in charge until after the war, when she resigned to move to London with her husband.[4]

On March 24, 1917, *Four Lights* ran a banner headline to hail "the Russian Revolution with mad glad joy." The journal warned of the death of democracy, doomed to drown in a sea of militarism, and called for a genuine peace that was free of forcible annexations and punitive indemnities and that encouraged the free development of nationalities. But the end of the war heralded the Red Scare. The women associated with the Woman's Peace Party and *Four Lights*, who now also condemned racism, lynchings, and the violent race riots led by men in uniform that followed the armistice, were singled out in particular by the antiradical, anti-antiwar, "anti-Bolshevik" crusade.

The Red Scare shattered the progressive antimilitarist coalition. After 1918 the Woman's Peace Party seemed united only by the condemnation of Attorney General A. Mitchell Palmer and the various local "Red" squads that were formed in every major American city. However much liberals, radicals, and conservative reformers might have disagreed individually about politics and political strategy, their reactionary enemies were united in their opposition. Both Crystal Eastman and Jane Addams, formerly the nation's "conscience," were labeled enemies of America. They and all their allies were condemned as "Reds"—dangerous, un-American members of a pernicious "spider web" that threatened to devour the country and all its traditions.

During and after the Red Scare of 1919–1921, Addams, Eastman, and their allies continued to pursue their feminist vision, despite the attentions of J. Edgar Hoover's newly formed Federal Bureau of Investigation and other Wilsonian agencies of intimidation. Their speeches were recorded, their writings copied or suppressed, their journals banned from the mails, and their political efforts subverted in a massive campaign of distortion. Some of the more prominent women, including Eastman, were blacklisted. The Red Scare splintered the radical movement, and strengthened the anti-democratic forces that ushered in twelve years of Harding–Coolidge–Hoover Republicanism.

In 1919, as her last action as president of the New York chapter of the Woman's Peace Party, Eastman organized the "First Feminist Congress" of the United States. In her keynote address she assessed the deplorable political status of women and reviewed the variety of restrictive laws placed on women's bodies throughout the country. In "Now We Can Begin," one of her most vigorous feminist statements, she called for a bold new movement fired by a spirit "of humane and intelligent self-interest." Women, she argued, must embark on a bold new crusade for their own freedom. For revolution to succeed, women had to forge an independent and nonpartisan campaign for the liberation of all women who were everywhere under male rule: "We will not wait for the social revolution to bring us the freedom we should have won in the nineteenth century."

During and immediately after the war Eastman had lived communally in Greenwich Village, sharing two houses and a collective flower-filled court-yard with Max; his new lover, actress Florence Dershon; their childhood friend Ruth Pickering, who was soon to marry Amos Pinchot; and Eugen Boissevain.

According to Max, Crystal had engineered this "delightful half-way family," which also included several servants and featured a collective kitchen, to promote companionship and economy. They spent their weekends in the country at Croton-on-Hudson, where they also lived communally amid a circle of Village friends that included the artist Boardman Robinson, activists Margaret and Winthrop Lane, writer Floyd Dell, Harlem Renaissance poet Claude McKay, and—until they left for Russia—John Reed and Louise Bryant. In 1919 McKay was hired as the associate editor of *The Liberator*, the new journal of revolutionary art and protest Crystal Eastman co-owned and -edited with her brother.

Eastman has failed to receive due credit from historians for her role in creating and sustaining *The Liberator*. According to Max, "as joint editor [Crystal] really ran the magazine." Until she had to remove herself for health reasons after the difficult, premature birth of her second child, her daughter Annis, she earned ninety dollars a week; Floyd Dell, seventy-five dollars; and Max, sixty dollars. Her husband, Walter Fuller, who edited *The Freeman*, earned fifty dollars a week. But in 1922 he left for England for a better job and new opportunity, all of which seemed closed off to him in the United States. He began a literary agency and eventually produced musical programs for the BBC. His sudden departure left Eastman distraught and feeling abandoned. She soon followed her husband to London, where she spent the last years of her life working for equal rights for women and regularly commuting between London and New York. Her famous *Cosmopolitan* article "Marriage Under Two Roofs," written largely for money, was not meant as spoof. She and her husband lived under separate roofs in two different countries between 1922 and 1927, when Fuller died.

Wherever Eastman lived during these years, she battled to help organize the Anglo-American women's movement and to ignore the symptoms of her own rapidly failing health. She was a workaholic who for more than ten years had worked from ten to twenty hours a day on behalf of peace, women's rights, and justice. Her health was wrecked and her spirits were low. She was blacklisted and could not understand her inability to find work. Everyone knew of her talents as an attorney, journalist, orator, and administrator, and everyone understood her views. She was an equal-rights socialist, of whom there were virtually no others. As one of the four authors of the Equal Rights Amendment introduced in 1923, she fully appreciated the opposition to that simple paragraph. We can, she noted, assess the importance of the ERA by the intensity of the opposition: "This is a fight worth fighting even if it takes ten years."

Her activities as the first self-declared socialist journalist to visit Communist Hungary to celebrate Béla Kun's revolution were no less startling to potential employers. As coeditor of *The Liberator*, she published John Reed and Louise Bryant from Moscow; a regular column of international news by Alexander Trachtenberg, the founder of International Publishers; and contributions by such liberals, radicals, anarchists, and communists as Helen Keller, Dorothy Day, Norman Thomas, Roger Baldwin, and Lenin.

Her great friend Paul Kellogg, who had first hired her to study work accidents and the law, tried to explain her inability to find work. There were "practical difficulties" that could not be minimized, for the United States was not as "tolerant" as the United Kingdom: "We still have a lot of beating up of bugaboos, and you will get a touch of that in any public work . . . and your various espousals—such as the Woman's Party—would not help in some of the few quarters where industrial research is still carried on."

As a result of her notoriety, Crystal Eastman spent most of her last years unemployed, in exile in England. She wrote steadily, and Margaret Thomas,

Lady Rhondda, gave her a regular column in *Time & Tide,* England's most militant feminist newspaper, which also featured work by Nancy Langhorne Astor and Rebecca West. But it was not enough, and Eastman soon became bored and impatient. In 1927 she returned to the Village and her New York friends and allies, and soon got a temporary job organizing *The Nation's* tenth anniversary celebration. But that year her husband died of a stroke, and within ten months Crystal Eastman too was dead, of nephritis. She was forty-eight. Her last thoughts, written in a letter to her friend Ruth Pickering Pinchot, were of her children and all the work she would leave undone.

Agnes Brown Leach adopted Annis and Geoffrey, then aged seven and ten. A member of Heterodoxy, she was one of the most consistent supporters of the American Union Against Militarism and treasurer of New York's branch of the Woman's Peace Party. Agnes Brown Leach was also a member of the executive committee of the National Woman's Party, one of the few progressives among the equal rights activists in the United States, and subsequently one of Eleanor Roosevelt's close friends.

Crystal Eastman was mourned by many. Claude McKay believed that she joined in "her personality that daring freedom of thought and action—all that was fundamentally fine, noble and genuine in American democracy. Crystal Eastman was a greathearted woman whose life was big with primitive and exceptional gestures. She never wrote that Book of Woman which was imprinted on her mind. She was poor, and fettered with a family. She had a grand idea for a group of us to go off to write in some quiet corner of the world, where living was cheap and easy. But it couldn't be realized and so life was cheated of one contribution about women that no other woman could write."

Eastman's contemporaries considered her a great leader. Freda Kirchwey wrote that when she "spoke to people . . . hearts beat faster and nerves tightened. . . . She was simple, direct, dramatic. Force poured from her strong body and her rich voice, and people followed where she led. . . . In her personal as in her public life her enthusiasm and her strength were spent without thought; she had no pride or sense of her own power. . . . Her strength . . . her rich and compelling personality—these she threw with reckless vigor into every cause that promised a finer life to the world. She spent herself wholly, and died—too young."

•••••

For several years before Crystal Eastman's death, rumors circulated that Greenwich Village was dead; that after the war it had become a "bogus and lewd bore," a philistine swamp filled with lesbian harems and other licentious things. That interpretation, at once misogynist and mean-minded, ignores the continued dynamism of the Village as a haven for creativity and the home of choice for independent radical women. Interestingly, many

••••

women who were not part of Heterodoxy or any organized circle chose the Village as their home and—like their spiritual predecessors—created communal, ever-expanding, and inviting environments.

During the height of the Red Scare in the early 1920s, when few progressives could get elected to office, a generation of the radical "New Women" of the prewar years survived and indeed flourished. Throughout the 1920s the prewar suffragists continued the long struggle for political and social change. Though many of them were Crystal Eastman's contemporaries or friends, some of them were new to the struggle.

In 1921 Eleanor Roosevelt, at thirty-six two years younger than Eastman, joined a circle of Village women she came to love, trust, and depend on for direction and companionship. They encouraged her to continue the feminist fight for progressive politics and civic decency, and offered her a new community after her marriage had become a limited and lonely partnership. For all their progressive and unconventional convictions, the women Eleanor Roosevelt joined rarely used such words as *socialist, communist, anarchist,* or *free love.* Unlike Eastman's circle they represented a more closeted and, in some ways, more conventional environment. They published journals of political information like *City-State-And-Nation,* rather than revolutionary journals like *Four Lights* or *The Liberator.* Still, they belonged to the Birth Control League, picketed with unionists, worked vigorously for change, and were themselves free spirits who dedicated their lives to peace, justice, and the advancement of women.

Eleanor Roosevelt's romance with Greenwich Village began when she returned to New York after eight years in Washington as the wife of the Assistant Secretary of the Navy and recently defeated vice presidential candidate Franklin Delano Roosevelt. Eleanor Roosevelt was aggrieved in 1920, having learned that her husband was in love with another woman, Lucy Mercer. She offered him his freedom and entertained thoughts of divorce. But she was the mother of five children, ranging in age from three to thirteen, and her mother-in-law threatened to cut FDR off without a cent if he divorced his wife to marry another woman. And so they made an agreement and sought to rebuild their lives and their spirits. Above all Eleanor Roosevelt now longed for work of her own—new purpose and serious activity.

Greenwich Village became the headquarters from which Roosevelt began to pursue her long career as an independent political activist after 1920. On her return to New York City, she was introduced to the work of the City Club, the League of Women Voters, and the activist women associated with the Women's Committee of the Democratic party. The League's first president, the prominent Republican Narcissa Cox Vanderlip, and such cofounders of the organization as Esther Lape, Elizabeth Read, and Agnes Brown Leach, were progressives who had been ardent suffragists and who now sought through the League to make the vote meaningful in terms of women's rights and needs. Divided over the issue of the Equal Rights Amendment, they joined with Crystal Eastman's circle to lobby for industrial safety and health measures and an eight-hour day for all workers. Although their views differed from Eastman's in some respects, Eleanor Roosevelt and her allies were condemned with equal gusto by A. Mitchell Palmer and New York's Lusk Committee during their investigation of "Revolutionary Radicalism and Bolshevism." Among the specific allegations leveled against the activists of the League of Women Voters was their supposed intention to weaken America by destroying the family. Eleanor Roosevelt's massive FBI file, kept by J. Edgar Hoover throughout her life, actually began with a February 1924 entry concerning her activities with Esther Lape, Elizabeth Read, and Narcissa Cox Vanderlip on behalf of that "un-American" body, the World Court.

Esther Lape and Elizabeth Read were Roosevelt's political mentors and became her best friends. Over the years, and until her death, she turned to Lape for advice and emotional support. Read, who became Eleanor Roosevelt's attorney and financial adviser, died in 1941. Throughout the 1920s Roosevelt spent several evenings every week in their home at 20 East Eleventh Street, often at dinners that sparkled with conversation, strategy, poetry, and politics. The three women worked together on issues that ranged from the World Court to the Sheppard-Towner Law, which provided maternity and health care for mothers and infants. During the 1930s Roosevelt rented an apartment for herself in their home. Throughout the White House years her Eleventh Street home was a haven for herself and her own company, a secret place hidden away from the glare of newspapers and photographers.

Like most of the postsuffrage "New Women" of the 1920s who lived in Greenwich Village, Lape and Read were committed to personal and emotional freedom as well as political and social reform. Privileged and affluent, they gave their time and their money to causes they believed in and movements they helped to organize. They smoked, drank champagne, and lived in a world of elegance and daring they had created for themselves. They followed no blueprint or tradition, answered to nobody, and acknowledged no established order. Their dinners were formal and splendidly served, their costumes dashing, unusual, and bold.

Fashion and ceremony were important to Esther Lape and Elizabeth Read, and everything in their life-style harmonized entirely with their own vision and chemistry. Their cats, a series of cats actually, were called Ariel and Pan. At the entrance of their 147-acre Connecticut estate called Saltmeadow, purchased in 1927, was a double-size doormat, painted in green letters, "Toujours Gai." Above the door Elizabeth Read carved Plato's invocation to the god Pan, ruler of woods and fields: "Beloved Pan, and all ye other gods that haunt this place / give me beauty of the inward soul. . . ."

Harmony and temperance, unity of being, wisdom and purpose: "No

• • • •

other way of life could we more fervently ask for," Esther Lape concluded in her unpublished memoir of Saltmeadow, written for friends toward the end of her life. Esther Lape and Elizabeth Read believed that life could be crafted, and made a work of art. Their friends were central to the world of "beauty and the gaiety of life" they created at Saltmeadow and in Greenwich Village, and Eleanor Roosevelt was at the heart of that world.

Empowered by the knowledge that she could rely at all times and under all circumstances on the support of her friends and a wide-ranging network of activist women, Eleanor Roosevelt became nonconformist and consciously followed the impulse of her own vision and the needs of her own heart. She was particularly grateful to Lape and Read, and she fully appreciated the ways in which her friends emboldened her. In her memoir *This Is My Story*, she wrote: "We all of us owe, I imagine, far more than we realize to our friends as well as to the members of our families. I know that in my own case my friends are responsible for much that I have become and without them there are many things which would have remained closed books to me."

During the 1920s Roosevelt became close to Nancy Cook and Marion Dickerman, two other women with whom she shared a great part of her life. Together they bought the Todhunter School on East Eightieth Street and Val-Kill, a new home two miles away from FDR's mother's home at Hyde Park. Their lives were entwined for twelve years, and they did much of their political and life-enhancing work together. Unlike Crystal Eastman, Eleanor Roosevelt was not forthright about her private life. Indeed, her three volumes of memoir are a monument to discretion, a sarcophagus filled with unspoken words. Because virtually all the correspondence between Roosevelt and Cook and Dickerman, and between Cook and Dickerman, has disappeared (stolen, I suspect), we have no idea of the nuances or the nature of their friendships. We know that Eleanor Roosevelt loved Nancy Cook, because Marion Dickerman said so. We also know that Cook and Dickerman, like Lape and Read, were a couple. There was a fourth partner in their collective business enterprises—the Todhunter School and Val-Kill furniture factory—and their political work. Caroline O'Day, an artist, philanthropist, and political activist, served three terms as a member of Congress at large representing New York, the only woman ever elected to a position that was tantamount to a Senate seat. All her papers, even those related to her public career, have disappeared. (Her lost papers are one of the strangest facts of this history.)

Cook and Dickerman were also Villagers. They shared an apartment at 171 West Twelfth Street, near that of Lape and Read and just across the hall from Molly Dewson, one of the greatest women leaders of the Democratic party, and her life partner, Polly Porter. Although Porter avoided partisan politics, she was considered a radical and "poetic anarchist;" and was very close to two leading Communist party leaders, Grace Hutchins and Anna

· · · ·

Rochester, who were also neighbors in the Village and in Maine. Indeed, most of the twenty-four apartments at 171 West Twelfth Street during the 1920s (and until the 1950s) were occupied by political women in Eleanor Roosevelt's circle.

Roosevelt's friendship with Cook and Dickerman ended unhappily during the 1930s, in part because of her friendship with Lorena Hickok, the Associated Press's top woman political reporter, who was assigned to cover the first lady–elect in 1932. Roosevelt began to prefer Hick's company, and the reporter could not abide what she regarded as the arrogant presumptions of Cook and Dickerman, refusing ever to be in their company. While she considered them stuffy snobs, they considered her outrageous, flamboyant, and tough. Although Hick never lived in the Village, she seemed far more "downtown" than the "uptown" ladies of West Twelfth Street. But Eleanor Roosevelt loved Hick, and her closest friends, Lape and Read, welcomed her cordially into their company.

Toward the end of FDR's third term, Eleanor Roosevelt began to consider life after first ladyhood and decided to move into a larger space at 29 Washington Square West, where on occasion her husband might join her—but only on occasion, for after 1920 Eleanor and Franklin Roosevelt, like Crystal Eastman and Walter Fuller, lived under two roofs. Like many Edwardian couples, the Roosevelts led separate lives and had separate courts. In addition to Val-Kill, Eleanor Roosevelt chose the Village for its attractive environment and its free-thinking anonymity—as seems only appropriate given the hectic nature of her free-thinking, heterodox life.

· · · · ·

NOTES

1. Her appointment resulted from her research work for the Russell Sage Foundation several years earlier, when she investigated the mines and mills of Pittsburgh. Her compelling book, *Work Accidents and the Law*, was published in 1909 and led New York Governor Charles Evans Hughes to appoint her as the first woman commissioner on Employer's Liability and Causes of Industrial Accidents. In that capacity she authored New York's first workers' compensation law, which became the model for the entire nation. While working for the federal commission, Eastman prepared her reports, only recently declassified, and drafted legislation that resulted in the United States' first federal worker's compensation law.
2. She and Eastman had become friends during the Seventh Congress of the International Suffrage Alliance in Budapest in 1913, and Eastman shared Pethick-Lawrence's conviction: "There is no life worth living, but a fighting life."
3. The American Union Against Militarism's office was located in the Village at 70 Fifth Avenue, in a building that housed several of America's more radical movements.

· · · ·

4. Not until my book party for *Crystal Eastman* in 1978 did Roger Baldwin admit publicly that Eastman had actually founded the ACLU, an act for which he had always been credited.

· · · · ·

SELECTED BIBLIOGRAPHY

Today we celebrate the radical women of Greenwich Village with new knowledge, and a new level of anguish at all the work that for so many decades distorted their lives and our history. I write this with gratitude particularly for the brilliant research done by Judith Schwarz on the women of Heterodoxy, and the recent and splendid biographies of Mary Heaton Vorse by Dee Garrison and of Molly Dewson by Susan Ware. My own work on Crystal Eastman and Eleanor Roosevelt has introduced me to a world of women few have yet studied— Eastman's many political friends who, with her, organized the Women's International League for Peace and Freedom, and Eleanor Roosevelt's closest friends and colleagues, Esther Lape and Elizabeth Read. Every one of these women deserves her own biography, and it is our great good fortune that virtually every one of them has an astounding FBI file, and a Greenwich Village address.

My own understanding of Greenwich Village has been enhanced by a lifetime of friendships and sparkling experiences. I am, however, particularly grateful to Clare Coss and the late Audre Lorde for twenty and thirty years of the most incomparable Village times.

See especially:

Coss, Clare. *Lillian D. Wald: Progressive Activist*. New York: The Feminist Press, 1989.
Lorde, Audre. Especially "The Old Days." In *The Black Unicorn*. New York: W. W. Norton, 1978. "Everyone wants to know / how it was in the old days / with no sun or moon / in our colorless sky / to warn us / we were not insane. . . ."

See also:

Cook, Blanche Wiesen. *Crystal Eastman on Women and Revolution*. New York: Oxford University Press, 1978.
———. "Female Support Networks and Political Activism." *Chrysalis*, 1977. Reprinted in *Women's America: Refocusing the Past*, edited by Linda Kerber and Jane DeHart. New York: Oxford University Press, 1986.
———. "Feminism, Socialism, and Sexual Freedom: The Work and Legacy of Crystal Eastman and Alexandra Kollontai." In *Women in Culture and Politics: A Century of Change*, edited by Judith Friendlander, Blanche Wiesen Cook, Alice Kessler-Harris, and Carroll Smith-Rosenberg. Bloomington: Indiana University Press, 1986.
———. "'Women Alone Stir My Imagination': Lesbianism and the Cultural Tradition." *Signs* (Summer 1979).
———. *Eleanor Roosevelt: A Life, 1884–1933*, vol. 1. New York: Viking, 1992.
———. "The Real Eleanor Roosevelt: A Centennial Celebration." *Ms.*, September 1984.

———. "Eleanor Roosevelt and Human Rights: The Battle for Peace and Planetary Decency." In *Women and American Foreign Policy,* edited by Edward Craypol. Westport, Conn.: Greenwood, 1987.

———. "Turn Toward Peace: Eleanor Roosevelt and International Affairs." In *Without Precedent: The Life and Career of Eleanor Roosevelt,* edited by Joan Hoff Wilson and Marjorie Lightman. Bloomington: Indiana University Press, 1984.

O'Neill, William. *The Last Romantic: A Life of Max Eastman.* New York: Oxford University Press, 1978.

For conventional histories of Greenwich Village, see:

Parry, Albert. *Garrets and Pretenders: A History of Bohemianism in America.* 1933. Reprint. New York: Dover, 1960.

Ware, Caroline F. *Greenwich Village, 1920–1930.* 1935. Reprint. New York: Harper Colophon, 1965.

For feminist analyses, see especially:

Garrison, Dee. *Mary Heaton Vorse: The Life of an American Insurgent.* Philadelphia: Temple University Press, 1989.

Schwarz, Judith. *Radical Feminists of Heterodoxy: Greenwich Village, 1912–1940.* Norwich, Vt.: New Victoria Publishers, 1986.

Ware, Susan. *Partner and I: Molly Dewson, Feminism, and New Deal Politics.* New Haven: Yale University Press, 1987.

"A SPIRITUAL ZONE OF MIND"
VILLAGE CULTURE

Cultural Citadel

With the nineteenth-century migration of an aspiring citizenry to Greenwich Village, institutions essential to serving the spiritual, educational, and entertainment needs of this expanding community quickly materialized. Prestigious church congregations put down roots there. The arrival of New York University in the 1830s lent an intellectual tone to the development around Washington Square. Private art galleries, art academies, libraries, literary salons, a cluster of erudite societies, and an opera house soon contributed to the area's cultural fabric. Entering its Victorian heyday, Greenwich Village stood secure in its identity as a prospering domestic stronghold.

93. New York University New York University's new Gothic Revival headquarters rose on the east side of Washington Square in 1837, six years after the nonsectarian college was chartered to spread practical as well as classical education among the "artisan" classes. Staffed by a faculty of six, this academic facility incorporated a chapel, classrooms, laboratories, and crenellated towers with rooms set aside for rental income. Local artists and writers, as well as the New-York Historical Society, were among the early tenants. (*Museum of the City of New York*)

• • • •

94. **Astor Place Opera House** One of the most prominent cultural landmarks in nineteenth-century Greenwich Village, the Astor Place Opera House was in 1849 the scene of a riot between the feuding fans of English actor Charles Macready—then appearing in a production of *Macbeth*—and his American rival, Edwin Forrest. The rampaging mob cost forty-three lives and forced the new opera house to close. It reopened after extensive repairs as Clinton Hall and later housed the Mercantile Library. *(Museum of the City of New York)*

The Pfaffian Circle

Consensus points to Pfaff's Beer Hall, opened in the 1850s at 653 Broadway, just north of Bleecker Street, as the birthplace of New York's first bohemian sect. Aspiring authors, journalists, and actors, joined by initiates to bohemianism from staider professions, comprised the freethinking crew who regularly drank at Pfaff's. Their fellowship was strengthened by *The Saturday Press*, which made its debut in 1858 and operated as a house organ. Filled with fresh, often irreverent perspectives on contemporary literature, drama, art, and politics, the controversial weekly also showcased the newest American writing.

Although the Civil War decimated the ranks of those who congregated at Pfaff's, the reputation of nineteenth-century Greenwich Village as a bohemian safe port endured. Shortly before Pfaff died in 1890, the tavern moved uptown to Twenty-fourth Street, and the original Broadway site was demolished to make way for W. & J. Sloane's Department Store. *(Museum of the City of New York)*

• • • •

95. **Pfaff's Beer Hall** *(Courtesy of The New-York Historical Society, N.Y.C.)*

AS THEY WERE SAID TO BE BY A KNIGHT OF THE ROUND TABLE.

BOHEMIANS AS THEY ARE—DESCRIBED BY ONE OF THEIR OWN NUMBER.

96. The Bohemian War Seated in a private alcove reserved for their use, the bohemian patrons of Pfaff's fomented conversational rebellion while dining on sausage, cheese, and hearty ale well after midnight. This pair of cartoons from the 1864 *New-York Illustrated News* alludes to a schism that developed in 1864 among the Pfaffian regulars when a splinter group formed an alternative club called The Round Table and proceeded to leak lurid tales about the saloon to the popular press. As exposés of this sort became more common, outsiders converged on 653 Broadway to behold these strange underground "doings." (*General Research Division, The New York Public Library, Astor, Lenox, and Tilden Foundations*)

97. **Ada Clare, the "Queen of Bohemia"** Few women risked the notoriety associated with Pfaff's, but propriety mattered little to Ada Clare. An actress, feminist, and author, she was crowned "Queen of Bohemia" during the height of her celebrity. After her only novel was savaged by the critics, she abandoned the literary world to resume acting in a provincial stock company. Her career ended in a grisly death from a dog bite suffered in her theatrical agent's office. *(Harvard Theatre Collection)*

Bohemia's Moorings

Well before the turn of the century, artists and writers had been attracted by the Village's existing studios, rooming houses, and "bachelor" flats concentrated around Washington Square. The modesty of these accommodations—private cookstoves, plumbing, and adequate heat were the exception rather than the rule—lent a public dimension to bohemianism, spurring occupants to rummage for food and warmth in local restaurants and saloons. Predictably patronage tended to center on those establishments where good cheer cost little, portions were plentiful, and character came free on the house. Together these boardinghouses, taverns, and eating establishments provided cooperative solutions to surviving on limited means while helping to foster communal identity and camaraderie.

98. The House of Genius Beginning in the 1890s the most celebrated of the inexpensive boarding hotels along Washington Square South was Number 61, managed by Katherine Blanchard and home to a *de facto* art colony that included painters, journalists, dramatists, and authors. Among those who found shelter and stimulating company there were the writers Frank Norris, Stephen Crane, O. Henry, and the young poet Alan Seeger. This roster of creative lodgers earned the address acclaim as the "House of Genius." *(Museum of the City of New York)*

• • • •

99. Café Bertolotti Bertolotti's on West Third Street was one of the most popular of the trattorias frequented by the bohemian art crowd. Historic charm pervaded the place: poet Edgar Allan Poe and his child bride once occupied the building; sawdust littered the floors; and cod-oil lamps glowed from the tables. Proprietor Angelo Bertolotti wore a derby, collected walking canes, and shared an endless supply of anecdotes with patrons. Signora Bertolotti—affectionately known as "Mama"—served a famous lunch of thick minestrone soup, bread and butter, and red wine for fifteen cents, tip included. Those who couldn't pay were often fed on the house. *(The Schlesinger Library, Radcliffe College)*

The New Literature

The Village atmosphere nurtured authorship as a privileged profession. By 1850 this quarter of New York sheltered a disproportionate share of the city's writers, editors, and publishers. An infrastructure of local salons, libraries, clubs, booksellers, and large- and small-scale presses materialized over the latter part of the century to bolster their solidarity as an artistic community. Enticed by these conveniences as well as the area's history as a sanctuary for unconventional genius, literary adventurers began to gravitate to the Village after the turn of the century. In addition to its liberating intellectual milieu, the Village scene offered endless literary possibilities and, not surprisingly, recurred as a theme and backdrop in the "new" fiction by resident authors.

100. Anne Charlotte Lynch In the mid-nineteenth century, New York's literati flocked to the fashionable salon hosted by Anne Charlotte Lynch at her home on Waverly Place in Greenwich Village. An aspiring poet and teacher of English, Miss Lynch convened her weekly receptions in a spacious parlor warmed by double fireplaces. Among the guests who accepted her hospitality were William Cullen Bryant, Herman Melville, Horace Greeley, and Edgar Allan Poe, who gave his first public reading of "The Raven" at one of her gatherings. *(Museum of the City of New York)*

101. Willa Cather (wearing a necklace given to her by Sarah Orne Jewett) Renowned for her evocative stories about the immigrant experience in America's Middle West, Willa Cather was a literary personality rooted in Greenwich Village. Her arrival in 1906 antedated the district's bohemian heyday, and as a mature writer she remained aloof from the Village's radical maelstrom. In 1917 Cather and her companion, Edith Lewis, revived a Village tradition by designating Fridays as their "salon" afternoon when guests could drop by for tea, literary chat, and delicacies prepared by Cather's French cook. Ten years later the brick house she occupied was demolished to make way for the Seventh Avenue subway, and she moved uptown. *(Willa Cather Pioneer Memorial Collection, Nebraska State Historical Society)*

102. Samuel Clemens hosting a dinner for Maxim Gorky In 1906 Samuel Clemens, then living at 3 Fifth Avenue, hailed the arrival in New York of Maxim Gorky with a gala dinner at Club A, a cooperative rooming house and meeting spot that catered to socialists, suffragists, and writers of leftist leanings. The charismatic Russian novelist and agitator used the occasion to plead the cause of democratic revolution in his homeland and was showered with praise until the press disclosed that the "wife" he had in tow was not Madame Gorky. Ostracized by polite society, he turned to the presumably more liberal Village for acceptance. Ironically the Brevoort Hotel deemed his liaison "bad for business" and offered him private dining privileges but denied him lodging. *(Culver Pictures)*

103. An editorial meeting at the *Ink-Pot* magazine The *Ink-Pot* was one of a short-lived crop of literary magazines published out of Sheridan Square in the teens. Typically run on a shoestring budget by amateurs, whom one veteran periodical editor characterized as "Village poets whose temporary lack of employment has become a permanent feature of their conversation," the magazines' formats often fluctuated from issue to issue because of the necessity to shop among different printers for the best typesetting bargains. *(Culver Pictures)*

WASHINGTON SQUARE BOOK SHOP
GREENWICH VILLAGE
NEW YORK

JESSIE TARBOX BEALS N.Y.

35

104. The Washington Square Book Shop Founded and managed by Charles and Albert Boni, the original Washington Square Book Shop was (despite its name) located at 135 MacDougal Street, next door to the Liberal Club. Around 1914 the wall separating the two was broken through to create a space large enough to house plays and lectures sponsored by the club and to entice its membership to browse through and purchase the literature for sale. Instead of buying books, however, in-house bibliophiles merely borrowed them, spoiling potential sales because of the thumbprints they left. By 1918 the shop had relocated to West Eighth Street, its operation passing into the hands of the Village publisher Egmont Arens (shown with back to the fireplace). *(The Schlesinger Library, Radcliffe College)*

The New Art

From the mid-nineteenth century on, Greenwich Village nurtured a vigorous art colony whose legacy endured in the form of private picture galleries, schools of art, studio workshops, and an enclave of models trained to pose. By the turn of the century, the depressed condition of housing in Greenwich Village enticed artists of less secure means and reputations to take up residence. Relishing the cheap rents, useful amenities, and colorful environs they had inherited, these newcomers immediately set to work. Although the body of paintings, sculpture, drawings, and prints they produced was often more radical in mood than in style, it bore the imprint of experimental energy then astir in the district. Two separate but not unrelated developments helped to propel the cause of progressive art in the Village: the seminal 1913 Armory Show, which engaged the passions of the local avant-garde, and the founding of the Whitney Studio Club to showcase cutting-edge works by contemporary artists, which matured into the Whitney Museum of American Art in 1931.

105. Tenth Street Building The innovative Tenth Street Studio Building was the catalyst most responsible for transforming the Village into a hub for the visual arts. Designed with a Parisian flair by Richard Morris Hunt and completed in 1858, this imposing redbrick structure had the distinction of being the country's first centralized facility for artists constructed to service their needs for light, space, privacy, and showrooms. The Tenth Street Studios, in which New York's art elite quickly seized power, became a magnet that lured influential critics, affluent patrons, and the curious public alike to its well-publicized exhibitions and "visiting days." (*Museum of the City of New York*)

· · · ·

106. **Visiting day at the Tenth Street Studios** *(Museum of the City of New York)*

107. The Tile Club at work In 1877 a group of New York artists began to meet informally each week to paint pictures on Spanish tiles. The host of each session supplied food and entertainment in exchange for the right to retain that night's production of tiles. The "Tile Club" was organized to give additional structure to the evenings, to sponsor occasional sketching trips outside the City, and to offer a forum for discussing new art ideas its members had acquired while studying abroad. During its ten-year existence, the club numbered among its members William Merritt Chase, Winslow Homer, Stanford White, Edwin Austin Abbey, and Augustus Saint-Gaudens. *(General Research Division, The New York Public Library, Astor, Lenox, and Tilden Foundations)*

108. William Merritt Chase's studio The *sanctum sanctorum* within the Tenth Street Studios was the suite of workrooms occupied by William Merritt Chase, the acknowledged "dean" of American painters in the late nineteenth century. In his studio Chase conducted art classes, engineered sales, held exhibitions, and hosted dinners, balls, and other entertainments. Guests were dazzled by its nonchalant opulence and exotic clutter, the latter called into service as props for Chase's paintings and for exercises he assigned to students. *(Museum of the City of New York)*

109. Frenzied Effort at the Whitney Studio Club Between 1915 and 1930 Gertrude Vanderbilt Whitney and Juliana Force, her chief lieutenant, launched a series of organizations intended to bolster contemporary American artists by exhibiting and marketing their works. In 1918 the Whitney Studio Club—featuring galleries, a library, and a billiard room—opened to serve this purpose. Evening sketch classes like the one captured here by Peggy Bacon (the ponytailed figure with glasses at the far back of the class), were added in 1923. *(Collection of Whitney Museum of American Art)*

110. Sixty-ninth Regiment Armory on Lexington Avenue   Although staged considerably north of Greenwich Village, the International Exhibition of Modern Art, or "Armory Show," brought the Village art community to the forefront as champions of the "new art." The intellectuals who frequented Mabel Dodge's salon and Gertrude Vanderbilt Whitney's studio were pivotal in gaining support for the event, marshaling an audience, and promoting the exhibit's revolutionary significance. Some contributed financially to the exhibition; others coaxed loans out of private collections. *(Walt Kuhn Papers, Archives of American Art, Smithsonian Institution)*

The New Drama

The so-called "little theater" movement in Greenwich Village was inaugurated in the fall of 1913, when amateur thespians associated with the Liberal Club began to stage short, experimental skits. The popularity of these informal programs brought into being such important nonprofessional dramatic troupes as the Provincetown and Washington Square players. Influenced by the vibrant ethnic theaters of the Lower East Side, these casual collectives matured into innovative repertory companies whose production theories ran entirely counter to the predictable froth and spectacle of Broadway.

The plays, typically one act in length, required minimal props and costuming, were inexpensive to produce, and focused on topics of interest to contemporary Village audiences such as birth control, the Freudian fad, left-wing politics, and labor unrest. Although professional ambition overtook the more successful of these ventures, and operational expansion and underfinancing led to the collapse of others, the adventurous spirit that fed the little theaters of Greenwich Village in the teens helped to free the possibilities of American drama from the stranglehold of Broadway's commercial influence.

The Washington Square Players

Bandbox Theatre

111. **The Washington Square Players** Founded in 1914, the Washington Square Players were committed to mounting productions by new American playwrights and modern European dramatists. Failing to find a playhouse in the Village that was both cheap and small enough for amateurs performing only on weekends, the Players turned instead to the Bandbox Theatre on East Fifty-seventh Street. The move uptown proved an astonishing success, and by 1917, the players began to hire professional actors and soon moved their operation to a Broadway theater. Although overexpansion and internal differences caused them to disband in 1918, the players formed the nucleus of the Theatre Guild. *(Museum of the City of New York)*

112. Upstairs at Christine's—133 MacDougal Street It was a postperformance custom for the Province-town Players to gather in the theater's upstairs dining canteen. Christine Ell, the canteen's manager, was an anarchist, onetime model, and former tearoom keeper who periodically slipped away from her meal preparations to perform as an extra. She is here depicted with James Light, a director for the Players; Charles ("Hutch") Collins, occasional actor for the company; Jig Cook, its executive director, and Eugene O'Neill, major contributing playwright. Charles Ellis, a painter, set designer, and actor associated with the troupe, recorded the gathering. *(Oil painting by Charles Ellis, ca. 1920, courtesy of the Estate of Norma Millay Ellis)*

113. Playwrights' Theatre The first playhouse leased by the Provincetown Players in Greenwich Village was the parlor floor of a MacDougal Street brownstone next to Polly's Restaurant and the Liberal Club. In 1918 they moved three doors south, where they transformed a property originally built as a riding stable into an auditorium that seated 184. After the original troupe's dissolution in 1922, the Playwrights' Theatre endured changes in management during the 1920s, stood "dark" from 1930 to 1936, and reopened under the aegis of the WPA as the Studio Theatre. *(Museum of the City of New York)*

• • • •

114. Charles Edison's Thimble Theatre Opened in July 1915, the Thimble Theatre was the collaborative undertaking of Village publisher Guido Bruno and his protégé Charles Edison, a dilettante poet and occasional inventor in the mold of his famous father. Occupying space above the Edison Diamond Disc Shop at 10 Fifth Avenue, this intimate playhouse seated one hundred and featured a stage curtain emblazoned with peacocks and butterflies designed by Village artist Clara Tice. *(Museum of the City of New York)*

115. Scene from "Hobohemia" Adapted from a story by Sinclair Lewis originally published in a 1917 edition of the *Saturday Evening Post, Hobohemia* was one of the first shows to test the commercial viability of subjecting Village bohemianism to comic scrutiny. The three-act farce poked fun at Freudianism, feminism, anarchism, cubism, and several other "isms" held sacred by the Village vanguard. Criticized for its amateurishness, the production, mounted at the Greenwich Village Theatre, soon closed. *(Museum of the City of New York)*

116. John Murray Anderson and Barney Gallant Anderson, a talented young producer, director, and lyricist, created the *Greenwich Village Follies* in 1919. Barney Gallant *(standing)*, his partner in this venture, was a jack-of-all-trades who served as business manager and press representative for the Greenwich Village Theatre, ran the Greenwich Village Inn, and operated a series of successful Village speakeasies and nightclubs. Gallant achieved special renown as the first New Yorker to be imprisoned for violating the new Volstead Act in 1919. *(George Eastman House)*

117. Julian Beck and Judith Malina In 1946 Julian Beck and his wife, Judith Malina, formed the Living Theatre to present poetic drama in innovative ways. After performing at the Cherry Lane Theatre for a number of years, they relocated to Sixth Avenue and Fourteenth Street and produced Jack Gelber's *The Connection*, a play about addicts that was to make the theater famous and lead the Becks to create extraordinary and shocking new connections between politics and their art. The Becks now began to perform for audiences around the world. Although they returned to Fourteenth Street at various times until they were evicted from their theater by IRS agents in 1963, the company had in fact outgrown its Village roots. *(Museum of the City of New York)*

· · · ·

281

CULTURAL MOORINGS IN THE NINETEENTH-CENTURY VILLAGE

Paul R. Baker

In its day (1835–1894) the old Gothic Revival building of the University of the City of New York (New York University) housed, at one time or another, the New-York Historical Society, the New York Academy of Medicine, the American Geographical Society, the Chess Club, and the Women's Library. That the school should derive additional income from renting rooms had been part of the initial planning for the building, and these and other organizations influenced the early development of the Washington Square area. But what gave the building and its neighborhood their distinctive flavor was the group of scientists, artists, and writers who made the new University their home.

When the building was opened in 1835, the well-known artist Samuel F. B. Morse took four rooms as studios for his students and two for himself as both studio and laboratory space to conduct experiments on the telegraph. At the time Morse was president of the National Academy of Design and professor of the literature of the arts of design at the University. Among those who studied painting with him were Daniel Huntington and William Page, both of whom had workrooms in the building. In a glass-roofed studio atop the Gothic structure, Morse also worked on daguerreotypes, collaborating with Chemistry Professor John W. Draper. While living at the University, Morse gave instruction in daguerreotype to Mathew B. Brady, later

118. Allegorical landscape, by Samuel F. B. Morse, showing New York University (*Courtesy of The New-York Historical Society, N.Y.C.*)

famous for his Civil War photographs. Morse's evocative painting *An Allegorical Landscape Showing the University*, completed in 1836, provided a highly romantic interpretation of what was his home for seven years.

The University numbered many other talented people among its tenants. The architect Alexander Jackson Davis rented quarters there soon after the building was opened. Samuel Colt, who lived in the southwest tower room for a time, did work on the design of the revolver there. And Henry James, Sr., rented a room in the building from 1838 to 1840. James, who was married in 1840 at the home of his bride's mother, Elizabeth Walsh, at 18 Washington Square North, later lived on Washington Place, in a house between the University Building and Greene Street, where Henry James, Jr., was born in 1843.

By mid-century, although it was already beginning to look somewhat seedy and run down, the building had many artist-residents. Here in 1856 Richard Morris Hunt, the first American to be trained at the École des Beaux-Arts in Paris, took a studio and commenced a long and successful career as an architect and teacher that would eventually bring him a reputation as "the dean of American architecture" and as an influential educator in his field. Hunt filled his second-floor domain with paintings and drawings, antique furniture, and countless art objects. And there were his many books, which already formed one of the largest and most comprehensive collections on art and architecture in America—a library that Hunt made readily available to others.

• • • •

Highly energetic and a vigorous talker, Hunt always struck those about him vividly. He became a well-known figure around the University Building within a short time—so well known, in fact, his longtime friend Theodore Winthrop even portrayed him in a melodramatic Gothic novel, *Cecil Dreeme*, set there. From its inception in 1857 until 1861, the American Institute of Architects had its headquarters in the University Building. In later years Hunt—a founder of the institute—and his family resided at Number 2 Washington Square North.

With such painters as Eastman Johnson, George Harding, Eugene Benson, and Winslow Homer also living there, the University Building was a very special community in which artists worked, taught, and socialized in close association with each other. Homer, whose studio was the place to gather for "jolly evenings" with friends, used the flat roof to pose models in daylight, completing there his famous *Prisoners from the Front*. When the illustrator Edwin Austin Abbey moved into a third-floor studio in 1875, the artistic associations of the place were commemorated by old tin signs in the halls that indicated where well-known painters and writers had lived. A few years later the painter George Inness commuted regularly to a studio in the building from his home in New Jersey.

Artists found life at the University useful as well as congenial, for there they could come to know people influential in the city, men who would themselves become patrons or clients or who could introduce them to others who might. The room next door to Hunt's was rented by Joseph Howland, the unemployed son of a wealthy merchant. Howland, who had grown up in a house on the north side of Washington Square, would one day be Hunt's brother-in-law and patron.

By the 1860s the University Building had deteriorated further. The writer Thomas Bailey Aldrich reported in 1866 that "the University is one of those buildings that have lost their enthusiasm. It is dingy and despondent, and doesn't care." A visit to the "gloomy structure," wrote Aldrich, was made worthwhile only by seeing the pictures under way in Homer's small tower studio and the splendid view over the Square toward the river and the hills beyond. By the 1880s the building was considered decidedly "old fashioned," and, in 1894, it was torn down to make way for the present Main Building. At that time many New Yorkers felt that they had lost an endearing if somewhat bedraggled old friend.

• • • • •

Two other structures, now part of the New York University complex, were also important in the neighborhood's artistic development. To the south of the University Building, the Tuckerman Building at 80 Washington Square East, designed by McKim, Mead & Bigelow, was completed in 1879.

• • • •

Popularly called the Benedick, because the apartments were designed for bachelors, the redbrick building attracted many artists, among them the painters J. Alden Weir, John H. Twachtman, and Albert Pinkham Ryder, who lived there for over ten years beginning in 1880. Number 3 Washington Square North, a Greek Revival house that dates from the 1830s, was remodeled and enlarged in 1884 and named "the Studio Building." Among its first tenants were the painters Thomas W. Dewing and Will H. Low. In the twentieth century the painters Ernest Lawson, Rockwell Kent, William Glackens, Guy Pène Du Bois, Walter Pach, and Edward Hopper lived and worked there.

• • • • •

The most significant nineteenth-century artistic center near the Square was completed in 1858 at 15 (later 51) West Tenth Street, just east of Sixth Avenue. Commissioned by James Boorman Johnston, son of a wealthy merchant who had been both a founder and an officer of New York University, and designed with a Parisian flair by Richard Morris Hunt specifically for artists' quarters, this studio building was the first such structure erected in the United States. Upon completion of the three-story, redbrick-face building, Hunt himself moved his working office there. The building's ample, well-lighted, and pleasant rooms were quickly occupied by some of the best-known painters, sculptors, and writers of the day.

Many of those renting rooms at the Tenth Street Studios were already well-established artists, several associated with the Hudson River School and most of them members of the National Academy of Design. The roster of residents includes some of the most talented American painters of the nineteenth century: Frederic Church, John La Farge, Homer D. Martin, William S. Haseltine, Sanford R. Gifford, Worthington Whittredge, Jervis McEntee, William M. Hart, Albert Bierstadt, Eastman Johnson, Emanuel Leutze, John F. Weir, and William Page, among others. Launt Thompson, a sculptor, occupied a studio cluttered with statuary, busts, and medallions, everything usually coated by marble dust. The authors Theodore Winthrop, Henry T. Tuckerman, and Thomas Bailey Aldrich found living in the building helpful to their writing. Some of the artists stayed on for years: La Farge took his studio in 1858 and kept it until his death in 1910, and Gifford rented his for twenty-two years. When Winslow Homer moved there from the University Building in 1872, he commented on the "atmosphere of comradeship" at his new home.

It was this friendly character of the Tenth Street Studios that residents mentioned again and again. On Saturday afternoons, except during the summer, most of the artists opened their workrooms to visitors, and three or four times each winter big evening receptions were held in the building,

• • • •

with good food and wine on hand. Connecting doors between the rooms were opened so that guests could wander from one studio to another, viewing works recently completed or in progress and taking in the bohemian atmosphere of the artists' cluttered studios. Albert Bierstadt collected Indian objects, such as peace pipes, war clubs, and wampum, while Frederic Church filled his rooms with tropical plants gathered on his travels. Artists who wanted to show a new painting frequently organized public viewings. When Church exhibited *The Heart of the Andes*, more than twelve thousand paying visitors came to see it during the seven weeks it was shown. These open houses, receptions, and exhibitions obviously stimulated public interest in, and helped sell, works of art. And the many purely social affairs encouraged feelings of fellowship and a sense of community among those who lived and worked in the building.

Yet the atmosphere of the Tenth Street Studios was not wildly bohemian; indeed, some judged it constrained and overly concerned about the proprieties. The wife of the painter Jervis McEntee, for a time in the 1860s the only married woman in the building, often acted as chaperone for bachelor artists when they entertained women visitors; and young artists occasionally complained that they were not welcome at the studios except as paying pupils. Many of the residents in fact, including Richard Morris Hunt, used their studios for teaching purposes.

Later in the century the largest room in the building, a spacious, domed studio formerly used for general exhibitions, was occupied by the painter William Merritt Chase and became a focal point for artistic life in the city. Chase frequently opened it for receptions, musicales, and lavish parties. The Music Club, an elite social group, gathered monthly, and for many years art societies used the large room as a meeting place. Chase's painting *Tenth Street Studio* shows his luxurious quarters crowded with art objects. Despite its colorful history, however, the remarkable studio building was razed in 1956 to make way for an apartment house.

In the 1880s the prestigious but short-lived Tile Club had its headquarters almost directly opposite the studios at 58-1/2 West Tenth Street in a small, picturesque dwelling standing in a courtyard behind the street-fronting house, where the painter Francis Hopkinson Smith lived. The Tile Club was organized in 1877 by several prominent New York artists to provide fellowship and professional stimulation to its twelve (later thirty) members. Each club night, a "host" was designated who presided at supper; afterward the "guests" drew or painted, often on tiles, then presented their work to the host. Among the club members were Stanford White, Augustus Saint-Gaudens, Homer, Vedder, Chase, and Twachtman.

Another cultural organization—the most famous and long-lived in the city for those engaged or interested in the fine arts and letters—the Century Association was located for a few years (1852–1857) at 46 East Eighth Street (formerly 24 Clinton Place). The Century was a bastion of wealth and prestige, its success pointing to the social recognition of artists in the United States. Nearly all New York City's leading painters, sculptors, architects, and writers became members.

By the mid-nineteenth century the area around Washington Square was firmly established as an artistic and cultural center. In 1849 the National Academy of Design acquired the property at 663 Broadway near Bleecker Street for its exhibitions. Galleries located in a building on Fourth Avenue and Tenth Street were later used for exhibitions by the academy and other groups. Contributing to the character of the neighborhood were the Cooper Union Art School, established in 1859; the Salmagundi Club, organized for artists in 1871; and the Astor Library on Lafayette Street, which attracted both general readers and professional writers.

In the same period, the Hotel Albert and the Hotel Lafayette on University Place were frequented by many who had achieved prominence in the artistic and literary worlds. A few literary salons in the Washington Square area also provided centers of sociability and intellectual stimulation for artists and writers during the mid- and late nineteenth centuries. In the 1840s Anne Charlotte Lynch regularly held literary evenings for authors and editors at her house, which stood at 116 Waverly Place. Such well-known writers as Edgar Allan Poe, William Cullen Bryant, Catherine Sedgwick, Herman Melville, Fitz-Greene Halleck, Horace Greeley, Bayard Taylor, and Margaret Fuller gathered at her residence to exchange ideas about new works. The minor writer Evert A. Duyckinck also held literary gatherings at his home on Clinton Place (Eighth Street), which Melville attended regularly. Later in the century Richard Watson Gilder, editor of the *Century Magazine*, and his wife, Helena de Kay Gilder, hosted a literary salon in their houses, first a remodeled stable on East Fifteenth Street and later at 13 East Eighth Street (formerly 55 Clinton Place). The Gilders' Friday evenings attracted such notables as Mark Twain, Saint-Gaudens, William Vaughan Moody, and William Dean Howells. Howells, who lived for a time on the north side of the Square, used the area as a setting for some of his stories.

The closest thing to a bohemian gathering place in mid-nineteenth-century New York was Pfaff's Saloon, a beer cellar located at 653 Broadway, just north of Bleecker Street. Its presiding spirit was Henry Clapp, who in 1858 founded the *Saturday Press*, a literary journal. Ada Clare, a minor poet and actress, known as the Queen of Bohemia, added a certain flamboyance to the gatherings there. Walt Whitman frequented Pfaff's, as did many other writers and painters, self-consciously trying to re-create there, in the 1860s, an atmosphere reminiscent of the bohemian cafés of Paris.

Another favorite gathering place for artists was Martinelli's, a small Italian restaurant on Third Avenue near Tenth Street. Close by, many studios were located in older commercial buildings along Broadway north of Houston Street, often on the skylighted attic floors. The Vienna Bakery Building, adjacent to Grace Church, had several studios for artists, while some painters took over former photograph galleries along Broadway. Ireland House, at the corner of Washington Square South and West Broadway, was also used for artists' studios.

Increasingly, by the end of the nineteenth century, the pre–Civil War dwellings to the south of the Square, turned into inexpensive rooming houses, were populated by young writers. Number 61 Washington Square South became known as "the House of Genius" on account of the many well-known writers—Frank Norris was one—who were said to have resided there. The Judson Hotel's cheap rooms also drew many aspiring writers and artists. By the end of the century, the scene was being set around the Square for the bohemian literary and artistic renaissance that enveloped "the Village" by 1910. The nineteenth-century developments thus provided a stimulating atmosphere and a rich foundation for the considerable achievements of the early twentieth century.

GREENWICH VILLAGE WRITERS

Alfred Kazin

Long before I came briefly to live there myself, Greenwich Village exercised a spell on this provincial from Brooklyn. Physically it was so different from most of Manhattan's gridiron plan—long, straight, numbered avenues and sharply regular numbered streets. As O. Henry (William Sydney Porter from North Carolina) noted in a story called "The Last Leaf," in the little district west of Washington Square "the streets have run crazy and broken themselves into small strips called 'places.' These places make strange angles and curves. One street crosses itself a time or two."[1] O. Henry disrespectfully noted of "the Village" that "the art people soon came prowling, hunting for north windows and eighteenth-century gables and Dutch attics and low rents. Then they imported some pewter mugs and a chafing dish or two from Sixth Avenue and became a 'colony.'"[2]

Although O. Henry tried here to sound superior about the place, pretended to be a real Manhattanite with better things to do than inhabit a "colony," "The Last Leaf" betrays his real affection for the Village. An elderly embittered painter, unsuccessful all his life, works all night painting a leaf on a wall in the backyard. This is for a dying bedridden girl who cannot bear to see "the last leaf" disappear from the tree in the yard that is her sole remaining link with life. The painter dies of pneumonia as a result of his heroic exertion. And it seems that in New York such a noble artist could have lived nowhere but in "the Village."

In the same spirit the first important American writer to live in the Village, if only at the end of his life, was the English-born rebel Tom Paine.

· · · ·

Grove Court — Scene of O. Henry's story "The Last Leaf"   *Josephine Barry*

119. William Sydney Porter, popularly known as O. Henry, was intrigued by Greenwich Village's mysterious culs-de-sac and back alleys. Grove Court—a group of attached brick houses on a gated courtyard canopied by shade trees—furnished the background for "The Last Leaf," one of the writer's most poignant tales. *(Museum of the City of New York)*

Paine's fiery pamphlets *Common Sense* and *The Crisis* helped save the American Revolution. He was extraordinary in every way. With little schooling, first apprenticed to a corset maker, he successively became a schoolteacher, tobacconist, grocer, and excise man. Forced into bankruptcy after unsuccessfully pleading with Parliament to raise the wages of excise men, he found a new life for himself in America, with the support of Benjamin Franklin. And thanks to Tom Paine's unique literary services in behalf of the colonies in their sometimes desperate struggle, the war for independence took on a new life.

A revolutionist in religion as well as in politics, Paine was a revolutionist everywhere. In France, after being elected to the Convention with the relatively moderate Girondin party, he lost such power during the Terror that, already outlawed by England, he was arrested by France as an enemy Englishman. In jail for almost a year, 1793–1794, he wrote *The Age of Reason*, his great affirmation of deism.

• • • •

Jefferson praised Paine as the only writer in America who could write better than himself. William Blake said Paine was in a class with Jesus as "a worker of miracles." No doubt thinking of *Common Sense* (1776), Blake said Paine "had been able to overthrow all the armies of Europe with a small pamphlet." After the war Paine movingly wrote in *Thoughts on the Peace & the Probable Advantages Thereof* (1783): "Never, I say, had a country so many openings to happiness as this."

Where could a rebel and freethinker have settled in his old age but in Greenwich Village? Although New York State presented him with a farm in New Rochelle in recognition of his services to the Revolution, his conservative neighbors made attempts on his life. As Susan Edmiston and Linda Cirino note in their invaluable *Literary New York* (1976), a book to which I owe many specific details of writers' lives in Greenwich Village, Paine gave up the farm in 1806 and went to live permanently in the city. He was taken in by the portrait painter John Wesley Jarvis at 85 Church Street: "His somewhat Bohemian manner of life apparently did not disturb the neighbors when he and Jarvis sat up late discussing religion, government, and the rights of man."[3]

Paine moved up to Herring Street (now Bleecker) when the Village was open country and a favorite refuge for New Yorkers fleeing regular epidemics. It was becoming a country village of estates and small wooden houses. Bedridden, Paine begged an old friend, Madame Bonneville, to take care of him. She rented a house just a few yards away, on the site of the present 59 Grove Street. Carried to it in an armchair, Paine died a month later in the back room.

• • • • •

Edmiston and Cirino place the first literary salon in America, directed by Anne Charlotte Lynch, at 116 Waverly Place. Although James Fenimore Cooper had lived at 145 Bleecker in 1833, and Edgar Allan Poe lived at 85 West Third Street and 130 Greenwich Street, the connection of these "outsiders" with the Village does not seem so significant as that of the native New Yorkers Herman Melville and Henry James.

Melville, born in 1819 on Pearl Street, near the Battery, settled in the Village after his marriage to Elizabeth Shaw and lived there until 1850, when he went to Pittsfield to write *Moby-Dick*. In June 1851 he wrote to his new friend Nathaniel Hawthorne: "In a week or so, I go to New York to bury myself in a third-story room, and work & slave on my 'Whale' while it is driving thro' the Press." That room seems to have been on Dutch Street, near the Hudson River. Nor did Melville forget his Village experiences when, embittered by the failure of *Moby-Dick*, he satirized publishers named "Faint and Asbestos" in *Pierre*. Pierre himself is a would-be writer, and Melville's description of his harried life is one that many a young writer in twentieth-century Greenwich Village could have identified with:

> Now look around in the miserable room, and at that most miserable of all the pursuits of a man, and say if here be the place, and this be the trade, that God intended him for. A rickety chair, two hollow barrels, a plank, paper, pens, and informally black ink, four leprously dingy white walls, no carpet, a cup of water, and a dry biscuit or two. . . . If physical, practical unreason make the savage, which is he? Civilization, Philosophy, Ideal Virtue! behold your victim![4]

Henry James's connection with Washington Square and the Village is legendary. He created the legend in his novel *Washington Square* (1881), but he also wrote memories of childhood there in *A Small Boy and Others* (1913) and gave an extraordinary account of a native's return to New York in *The American Scene* (1907). Born at 21 Washington Place, east of Greene Street, he was often at his grandmother's house, 19 Washington Square. In *Washington Square*, crammed with the irony about "old New York" that had become second nature to the sophisticated James, writing in Europe, he dryly described New York in 1820 as "the small but promising capital which cluttered about the Battery and overlooked the Bay, and of which the uppermost boundary was indicated by the grassy waysides of Canal Street."[5]

The New York James described in *Washington Square* had moved northward from the area around City Hall. The gridiron plan that was to make New York a checkerboard of numbered avenues and streets was so new that James's characters refer to "'The Fifth Avenue,' taking its origin at this point with a spacious and confident air which already marked it for high destinies." But Washington Square itself already possessed the charms that seventy-five years later were to attract not "old New Yorkers," settled and supercilious, like Dr. Sloper, but an army of young bohemians out of everywhere except New York itself. Here is James, looking back:

> I know not whether it is owing to the tenderness of early associations, but this portion of New York appears to many persons the most delectable. It has a kind of established repose which is not of frequent occurrence in other quarters of the long, shrill city; it has a richer, riper, more honorable look than any of the upper ramifications of the great longitudinal thoroughfare—the look of having had something of a social history.[6]

The last great nineteenth-century American writer to have associations with this "established repose" around Washington Square was Mark Twain. He came to live in New York in 1900 when he was the greatest literary celebrity at home and abroad. Because he lived there, 14 West Tenth Street

• • • •

attracted crowds. There are many delightful stories of the crowds following him on Fifth Avenue when he walked uptown to the Century Club. Wearing white both winter and summer, his great mop of white hair (washed every morning with laundry soap) escaping from under his hat, Mark Twain was impossible to overlook on the streets of New York.

And it was on Tenth Street that he spent most of his days in a huge Italian carved bed, dictating to his secretary and future official biographer, Albert Bigelow Paine, the interminable autobiography that would be published—partially—only after his death. "Only dead men tell the truth," Mark Twain explained. The whole of this autobiography has never been published and may never be. Twain was garrulous and repetitive when he dictated, drawing freely on experiences he had already used in print. As he said, "I want to talk without embarrassment and speak with freedom—freedom, comfort, appetite, relish."

Very few of the oncoming "bohemians" (the best of them, like Willa Cather and Marianne Moore, were about as rakish as Calvin Coolidge) were from New York. It was mainstream types from the American hinterland who turned Greenwich Village into a metaphor for "freedom" in every sense—artistic and personal. By the late twenties and early thirties there appeared in the Village the children of recent immigrants—booksellers and publishers like Albert and Charles Boni, Joe Kling, and Eli Wilentz on Eighth Street. But even the New York writers among them—from Henry Roth to the *Partisan Review* group of Philip Rahv, William Phillips, and Delmore Schwartz—were there because they found Italian restaurants on Thompson Street just as exotic as did E. E. Cummings from Cambridge. Adopting a Village life-style was for many a form of protest against one's own family and family traditions.

Essentially, however, the Village in its early twentieth-century days appealed to more conventionally "American" types from Western, church-going, traditionally conservative America. The prototype remains the dashing, romantic, volatile radical journalist John Reed. The son of a Portland, Oregon, law officer, Reed was at Harvard with Walter Lippmann and T. S. Eliot. Unlike them he turned against the American establishment in all its forms—political, social, and moral. Just out of Harvard, he was first influenced by Lincoln Steffens's muckraking of "the shame of the cities" and Ida Tarbell's exposé of the iniquities of John D. Rockefeller and the Standard Oil Company. He soon went beyond the usual "protest" reflexes of the Progressive intellectuals and helped launch *The Masses*, the most famous Greenwich Village magazine of the time.

These were the great and glorious years of rebellion in every sphere, co-inciding with the vigorous opening of the "American Century" under Theodore Roosevelt and the "New Freedom" of Woodrow Wilson. There has never been another time like it. It slowed down with what John Dos Passos

· · · ·

always called "Mr. Wilson's War" and resumed vitality in the 1920s, though without the prewar social idealism. Greenwich Village deserved its early fame. It ushered in the first great literary society in America after Concord. In view of the Village's reputation as "foreign" and "exotic"—*The Masses*'s chief editor Max Eastman called it a "self-conscious entity, an American Bohemia or Gypsy-minded Latin Quarter"—it is ironic that for most of the nineteenth century the Village was known as the "American ward" because of its lack of immigrants.

In the 1890s, however, tenements occupied mostly by Italian immigrants became a feature of the Village. "Little Italy" was spreading, and the streets most famous for their historic houses now saw, as did the Lower East Side, six- and seven-story houses composed of railroad flats. As real estate values fell, young writers, artists, and political rebels found it particularly easy to obtain cheap housing south of the Square. Many of the old brick houses lost their value because of the tenements around them, and were converted into rooming houses.

John Reed, first living at 42 Washington Square South with Harvard classmates, was exhilarated by his new life in New York, proclaiming in a bit of doggerel: "O life is a joy to a broth of a boy / At Forty-two Washington Square."[7]

Lincoln Steffens, who after his wife's death came to live in a room just under Reed's, located the mood of the time and place in Reed himself. Steffens said, "I used to go to bed early and to sleep, but I liked it when Jack, a big, growing, happy being, would slam into my room and wake me up to tell me about the 'most wonderful thing in the world' that he had seen, been, or done that night. Girls, plays, bums, IWWs, strikers—each experience was vivid in him."[8]

The Masses, which the masses notoriously never read, was started by the anarchist Piet Vlag as a vehicle for the growing cooperative movement. It soon passed into the hands of a frolicsome socialist group that had no policy, little money, less consistency, but a great capacity for tomfoolery. It became the principal organ of an existing community of artists and writers living and working together. Of course there were fanatics and hoaxers—"the Swiss innkeepers and Tyrolese bell-ringers of our mountain health resort," as the novelist Floyd Dell described the situation. But the magazine was just the stimulant the Village in its youth needed. Calling itself "a magazine with a sense of humor and no respect for the respectable; frank, arrogant, impertinent, searching for the true causes,"[9] it was like nothing before or since. (*The New Masses*, which succeeded it in the twenties, was a repulsive Communist party organ ferocious in its doctrinaire rigidity. It resembled *The Masses* just as much as Torquemada resembled Saint Francis.) It has been said that *The Masses* was a magazine run like a circus wagon. It believed piously in the class struggle, but though it blew fiercely in its

editorial columns, it also printed poetry of an almost embarrassing flakiness
and illustrations in the style of comic strips. One wit inquired:

> They drew nude women for *The Masses*
> Thick, fat, ungainly lasses—
> How does that help the working classes? [10]

Unlike the usual "radical" magazines that followed it, *The Masses* could
laugh at itself. "Did you know that I am an Anarchist and a Free-Lover?"
one artist asked another in a cartoon. "Oh, indeed!—I thought you were a
Boy Scout!" It contributors were as diverse as Gelett Burgess and Amy Lowell. It has been fondly remembered for decades that what *The Masses* chiefly
reflected was the fun the editors had producing the magazine. "Everybody
was playing," the poet Genevieve Taggard recalled later. "And *The Masses*
editors were playing hardest of all."[11] The novelist Floyd Dell said he found
a convivial "republic" of artists in the Village. In those happy days—so the
survivors into grimmer times liked to remember—the general boast south
of Washington Square was that a happy few worked gaily for the approval of
their peers. These were their friends, not the bourgeoisie uptown. *The
Masses* boasted in its first issue that its only policy was to do as it pleased
and conciliate nobody, "not even its readers."

Nevertheless, a genial socialism was the general idea. John Reed's roman-
ticism and generosity of spirit took him, politically, farther than most. The
articles about the Russian Revolution that became *Ten Days That Shook
The World* were written in an upstairs room at Polly Holladay's new restaurant, at 147 West Fourth Street. Magnetized by the new ideology, Reed
became a founder of the American Communist party and died in Russia of
typhus at thirty-three. He is buried in the Kremlin Wall. So even in death
"Jack" Reed personified the early recklessness of the true Greenwich Villager in those innocent days before "Mr. Wilson's War" shook American
socialism to its foundations.

However eccentric those foundations may have seemed, the "Big Idea"
of the time was to create a new American literature and art. New York was
and remains their center. And it was Greenwich Village that put New York
over at a time when other cities and their staid old magazine editors—Boston was prototypical—could not compete. "Within a block of my
house," John Reed wrote proudly of New York, "was all the adventure in
the world; within a mile was every foreign country."[12]

What a place it was then! What a time! Little magazines were sprouting
everywhere on the tree of dissent. Old magazines were being remodeled,
and even old conservative magazines were finding new uses for themselves.
The "Little Renaissance," as the period has been remembered—the "Joyous
Season" as one literary historian calls it—saw, in addition to *The Masses*,

The New Republic and *The Seven Arts*. In Chicago, Harriet Monroe's *Poetry: A Magazine of Verse* (Ezra Pound, foreign editor) symbolized the beginnings of modern poetry in America. Margaret Anderson's *Little Review* was soon to move from Chicago to New York, as was *The Dial*. In the wonderful optimism of the period *The Dial* announced an editorial policy characterized by the era's experimentalism, skepticism of inherited values, and critical spirit. *The New Republic*, beginning in Chelsea at 419–423 West Twenty-first Street, proclaimed on the cover of its first issue (November 7, 1914) that it was "A Journal of Opinion which seeks to meet the challenge of a new time."

• • • • •

In 1916 the Villagers vacationing in Provincetown at the tip of Cape Cod (including an ex-sailor named Eugene O'Neill) started a summer theater, led by a former Chicagoan, George Cram ("Jig") Cook. To the general amazement, O'Neill, despite his fondness for drink and the evenings he regularly spent at the "Hell Hole," a saloon at the corner of Sixth Avenue and Fourth Street, had a "trunkful" of plays. O'Neill's *Bound East for Cardiff* made an instant impression. Back in New York, Cook opened the Provincetown Playhouse at 139 MacDougal, next door to Polly's, a favorite restaurant that would enjoy several Village incarnations, and that Village institution the Liberal Club.

There was no serious American drama before the Provincetown Players and Eugene O'Neill. His intense, even wearing seriousness came out of a typically American identification of playwriting with his tormented personal history. Writers on the theater brought up on modern European stage classics understandably groan over O'Neill's stilted style and mechanical expositions. But he was irresistible in his drive to put outcasts and oppressed people on the stage, and he had an almost violent eagerness for experimental forms. There has never been anyone else in the American theater remotely like him.

In the 1920s the Village, no longer a seat of political rebellion for American expatriates in their own country, became a kind of institution. It was natural for young writers—especially those who had their "big experience" in France, first in the army and then on the Left Bank—to settle in the Village. This was one way of showing their independence. They were not wedded to the status quo, to the magazines, publishing houses, universities where they earned a living. More than ever writers in Greenwich Village—Willa Cather from Nebraska, E. E. Cummings from Massachusetts, Edmund Wilson from New Jersey, Malcolm Cowley from Pennsylvania, Marianne Moore from Missouri—came from solid American stock. They were definitely not New Yorkers to begin with. Their life on Bank Street

• • • •

(Cather) or Eighth Street (Wilson) or Patchin Place (Cummings) represented the particular fineness and even delicacy of their taste rather than the flaming politics of a Jack Reed.

Who could have been less bohemian than Willa Cather? In 1908 she had lived at 82 Washington Place with her friend Edith Lewis while editing *McClure's Magazine*. In 1913 she returned to the Village to live in a seven-room apartment at 5 Bank Street. She had a French cook, wrote *O Pioneers!* and *The Song of the Lark*, and had D. H. Lawrence in for tea. In 1927 she moved from Bank Street to a hotel on lower Fifth Avenue when her apartment house was torn down to make room for an extension of the IRT subway.

Edmund Wilson, who in the 1930s, having become a radical of sorts, satirized the Village in *This Room, This Gin and These Sandwiches*, went straight from Princeton in 1916 to Eighth Street while working as a reporter on the very conservative *New York Sun*. Back from the army in 1919, he lived at 114 Sixteenth Street and was managing editor of *Vanity Fair*, a magazine crazy about celebrities in literature, art, and films. Like a great many other men in the Village, he was (for a time) infatuated with Edna St. Vincent Millay (from Maine), the most famous glamour girl of the period. No one but Millay could have published "First Fig" in 1920:

> My candle burns at both ends;
> It will not last the night;
> But ah, my foes, and oh, my friends—
> It gives a lovely light! [13]

Wilson was definitely not one of her "foes." Long after all passion was spent, she continued to haunt him in a way that gave more personal resonance to his writing than usual. In 1921 Wilson, as managing editor of *The New Republic*—he was to be more identified with this journal than with any other—moved to 3 Washington Square North. After marrying the actress Mary Blair and producing a baby (not customary in the early Village), he attained a commanding position in American letters with *Axel's Castle* (1931). This remarkably close pioneer study of the great early modernists, from Yeats to Proust and Joyce, stressed their alienation from conventional society. Wilson in the 1930s came to disapprove of such alienation and favored Marxian socialism in *To the Finland Station*, his study of the thinkers whose ideas led up to the Russian Revolution. Eventually he repudiated Marxism.

Malcolm Cowley, who succeeded Wilson as literary editor of *The New Republic*, had a notable gift for representing his every move as typical of a whole "lost" generation. When he lived in the Village, at 16 Dominick Street, it seemed that everybody worth knowing lived in the Village—Hart

Crane, William Slater Brown, Susan and James Light, Kenneth Burke, Allen Tate, and Matthew Josephson. His famous memoir, *Exile's Return*, became the story of "us":

> After college and the war, most of us drifted to Manhattan, to the crooked streets south of Fourteenth, where you could rent a furnished hall-bedroom for two or three dollars weekly or the top floor of a rickety house for 30 dollars a month. . . . We came because living was cheap, because friends of ours had come already . . . because it seemed that New York was the only city where a young writer could be published.[14]

And as a young reviewer for Cowley at *The New Republic* in the 1930s, I was fascinated by the fact that any restaurant he frequented—notably John Squarcialupi's on Perry Street, later on Waverly Place—became another historical place sacred to his generation's sense of itself in American literature.

E. E. Cummings, self-conscious enough in his way, was the prototypical Villager after 1920. Everything about his background and personal bearing was so unlike the bohemia that fascinated him. A product of Harvard and Cambridge in the deepest sense—his father was a minister who taught at Harvard, and Cummings had been a medical volunteer during the war in France—he was really a rigid New England individualist with a passion for making gestures at an establishment he thoroughly believed in. In France he had been imprisoned by the French military for refusing to give lip service to the hatred of all things German (out of this experience came his memoir *The Enormous Room*). In the Village, Cummings typically lived in the most Villagey of "places"—Patchin Place, a most exclusive "alley" off Sixth Avenue.

By habitually writing his name and many of his poems without capitals, e. e. cummings established his style (or his typography) as a personal trademark that became as recognizable as an automobile's. It gave to its very appearance on the page the instant feel of spontaneity, of lyric bitterness against the mob age. It constantly unhorsed all words sacred to our conformism and replaced them with private words and contractions. Such goings-on made for living contrasts within a language actually full of abstractions, but one determinedly coming apart at the seams, impertinent and mock-important. A lifelong addict of the circus, vaudeville, and burlesque, Cummings loved to puncture words so that he could fling their stale rhetoric like straw all over the floor of his circus tent. Nothing pleased him more than to take a pompous stance that instantly collapsed under him, to come out with a profane antirhetoric meant to disconcert the reader.

Actually, this clown and word-rebel was the most sentimental traditionalist. He denounced trade unions as slavery and hated the New Deal even more than did the National Association of Manufacturers. In print, and especially in his most moving poem, "my father moved through dooms of love," he positively worshipped his Cambridge inheritance. Which made for his keynote, the opposition between the idyllic past and the New York world. He would trust nothing beyond Fourteenth Street! The Village was at least an oasis for the self-proclaimed last individualist in America.

Greenwich Village marched right into the Depression, the 1930s, the war, as if nothing had changed since Jack Reed and 1910. For a long time the rents were still low, the bars and familiar hangouts and cheaper restaurants still familiarly rakish. A new generation of surly combative writers was personified most by the gifted James Agee. Just out of Harvard, Agee lived first on Perry Street, then on Bleecker, next kept a studio on Cornelia, and finally ended up on King Street. He could not be wrested from the Village. But Agee earned his living writing reviews for Henry Luce in the Time-Life Building, Rockefeller Center. Which just went to show you, as the leftovers from the 1920s lamented, "what has happened to the Village."

What happened most to the Village in the 1940s was that many of the new arrivals were not from Tennessee like Agee, but from Brooklyn and the Bronx. They tended to be the children of Jewish immigrants from Eastern Europe. This was especially true of the *Partisan Review* circle, headed by the editors Philip Rahv and William Phillips, and its most gifted poet, Delmore Schwartz. There were others—the visionary editor of Blake, Milton Klonsky, and the novelist-philosopher Isaac Rosenfeld from Chicago. Of course many of the new Villagers were non-Jews—Anatole Broyard, Jan Garrigue, William Barrett, and William Gaddis. But it can truly be said that rarely in Jewish history was there so much coupling outside the faith as took place in the Village. And with equal truthfulness it must be said that for many of the Jewish writers, the Village was their way, their occasion, and their excuse for sexual rebellion.

Isaac Rosenfeld made his way from Chicago to Barrow Street to take up a fellowship in philosophy at New York University. Philosophy went by the board as Rosenfeld became so captivated by the freedom of sex in the Village that he went mad for Wilhelm Reich's rites of psychoanalysis. Following Reich's conviction that some of the "orgone" energy at large in the universe could be absorbed by an individual sitting inside a wooden box lined with metal, Rosenfeld, determined to extract more "genitality" from the universe at large, built himself an orgone box in his bedroom.

It was too evidently a homemade, bargain-basement orgone box. Belligerently sitting inside it, daring philistines to laugh, Rosenfeld nevertheless looked lost, as if he were waiting in a telephone booth for a call that was not coming through. In the dashing days of John Reed and Edna St. Vincent Millay, love in the Village had been romantic, fresh, and somehow associated with the necessary renovation of the United States. Now it seemed grim. There were no ideals to the bedroom except more of the same. Rosenfeld died in 1956, age thirty-eight.

Greenwich Village, meaning the West Village, still had its spell for tourists in New York. But the older and more "successful" writers became, the easier they found it to depart from the Village. They said it was out of date and wondered if *they* were. For the real bohemia you had to go now to the East Village, where Allen Ginsberg, Gregory Corso, William Burroughs, and Jack Kerouac typified an abandon and a literary style that spoke not so much for a neighborhood as it did for a family of friends. No one in the *old* Village could have sung out, as Allen Ginsberg did in his famous poem *Howl*: "I saw the best minds of my generation destroyed by madness, starving hysterical naked."[15]

"Best minds" or none, and minus the calculated hysteria and "nakedness," this was the way the old Village, the traditional rebellion, had once thought of itself. So the East Village came to the rescue of the West Village, and a cycle was completed.

• • • • •

NOTES

1. William Sydney Porter, *Selected Stories of O. Henry* (New York: Modern Library, 1963), 137.
2. Ibid., 138.
3. Susan Edmiston and Linda Cirino, *Literary New York* (Boston: Houghton Mifflin Company, 1976), 11.
4. Herman Melville, *Pierre* (New York: Library of America, 1984), 352.
5. Henry James, *Washington Square* (New York: Library of America, 1985), 4.
6. Ibid., 15.
7. Quoted in Edmiston and Cirino, *Literary New York*, 51.
8. Ibid., 51.
9. Alfred Kazin, *On Native Grounds: An Interpretation of American Prose Literature* (1942; reprint, Garden City, N.Y.: Doubleday & Co., 1956), 169.
10. Ibid.
11. Ibid.
12. Ibid., 170.
13. Edna St. Vincent Millay, "First Fig," *The Norton Anthology of Modern Poetry*, edited by Richard Ellman and Frances O'Clair (New York: W. W. Norton and Company, 1973), 2nd ed., 525.
14. Malcolm Cowley, quoted in Edmiston and Cirino, *Literary New York*, 69–70.
15. Allen Ginsberg, "Howl," from *The Norton Anthology of Modern Poetry* (New York: W. W. Norton and Company, 1973), 2nd ed., 1210.

• • • •

THE JAMESIAN HOUSE OF FICTION

Denis Donoghue

The calendar of Henry James's *Washington Square* is not computed with any notable precision. James was precise when he cared to be, but he did not bother about a year or two. We are free to assume that his Austin Sloper was born in 1793, or as near to that year as makes no difference, and that in 1820 he married Miss Catherine Harrington, "one of the pretty girls of the small but promising capital which clustered about the Battery and overlooked the Bay, and of which the uppermost boundary was indicated by the grassy waysides of Canal Street." Their first child, a boy, died at three years of age, and, two years later, Mrs. Sloper gave birth to a girl, Catherine, the heroine of *Washington Square*. A week later Mrs. Sloper died. So let us say that Catherine was born in 1826, and that the events of the novel take place in the years beginning 1843. Father and daughter, accompanied by Mrs. Penniman, the father's widowed sister, are living in Washington Square.

But already we have rushed too far ahead. From his marriage in 1820 to 1835, Dr. Sloper lived "in an edifice of red brick, with granite copings and an enormous fan-light over the door, standing in a street within five minutes' walk of the City Hall, which saw its best days (from the social point of view) about 1820." After that date "the tide of fashion began to set steadily northward, as, indeed, in New York, thanks to the narrow channel in which it flows, it is obliged to do, and the great hum of traffic rolled farther to the right and left of Broadway." When "the murmur of trade had become a mighty uproar," and most of his neighbors' houses had been turned into offices, warehouses, and shipping agencies, "and otherwise applied to the

120. Washington Place in 1892 shows New York University's building and the house where Henry James was born *(at right)* in 1843. *(Museum of the City of New York)*

base uses of commerce," Dr. Sloper determined to look for a quieter home. Since he was wealthy enough to choose, he settled on Washington Square. "The ideal of quiet and of genteel retirement, in 1835," James reports, "was found in Washington Square, where the Doctor built himself a handsome, modern, wide-fronted house, with a big balcony before the drawing-room windows, and a flight of white marble steps ascending to a portal which was also faced with white marble." This house, James continues, "and many of its neighbors, which it exactly resembled, were supposed, forty years ago, to embody the last results of architectural science, and they remain to this day very solid and honorable dwellings."

"This day" was 1881, the year in which *Washington Square* was published. We are encouraged to believe that the Square and its dwellings had changed very little between 1835 and 1881. James's description of the place wanders between past and present tenses, as if the chief pleasure of the wandering were to record an impression that the lapse of forty-six years had made little difference:

> In front of them was the square, containing a considerable quantity of
> inexpensive vegetation, enclosed by a wooden paling, which increased

• • • •

its rural and accessible appearance; and round the corner was the more august precinct of Fifth Avenue, taking its origin at this point with a spacious and confident air which already marked it for high destinies. I do not know whether it is owing to the tenderness of early association, but this portion of New York appears to many persons the most delectable. It has a kind of established repose which is not of frequent occurrence in other quarters of the long, shrill city; it has a riper, richer, more honorable look than any of the upper ramifications of the great longitudinal thoroughfare—the look of having had something of a social history.

In the next sentences, James yields so much to his sense of having lived his first years on and around the Square that he hardly bothers to distinguish himself from his narrator:

> It was here, as you might have been informed on good authority, that you had come into a world which appeared to offer a variety of sources of interest; it was here that your grandmother lived, in venerable solitude, and dispensed a hospitality which commended itself alike to the infant imagination and the infant palate; it was here that you took your first walks abroad, following the nursery-maid with unequal step, and sniffing up the strange odor of the ailanthus trees which at that time formed the principal umbrage of the Square and diffused an aroma that you were not yet critical enough to dislike as it deserved.

The house in Washington Square is the moral center of the book's drama: We are led to believe that it appropriately represents the just but unbending doctor and the unwaveringly mistaken Catherine. The residence of the mischief-making Mrs. Penniman in such a house makes her appear even more definitively silly. It is worth noting that Catherine first meets her lover, Morris Townsend, not in her own house but much farther uptown, at her aunt's house, "in an embryonic street, with a high number—a region where the extension of the city began to assume a theoretic air, where poplars grew beside the pavement (when there was one), and mingled their shade with the steep roofs of the desultory Dutch houses, and where pigs and chickens disported themselves in the gutter." Townsend's interest in Catherine is entirely theoretical: It is a cad's theory, and it assumes that she, a dull if in every particular respect worthy girl, will supply the money and he will supply the brilliance she lacks. In the event she gives him what he shows no sign of wanting, her implacable love, once for all. When her father sets his face, patience, silence, and fortune against the marriage, Townsend gives her up, goes away, and, many years later, returns to find her as set in her woundedness as she has remained set in her affection. At the end of the novel we see her still in the house in Washington Square, choosing not to leave it even to escape the July heat.

· · · ·

The first edition of *Washington Square* has six illustrations by George Du Maurier. They are not bad, or at least not disgraceful, but there should have been a seventh, a view of the house from the outside, with a suggestion of the Square and the abused ailanthus trees. A seventh would have been justified by the scene in chapter 30 in which Dr. Sloper, coming home, sees Catherine at the window, looking out; he stops and, "with an air of exaggerated courtesy," lifts his hat to her. Indeed, an eighth would have been justified, too, this time an indoor scene, in which Townsend is found making free with the doctor's room and lounging in his favorite chair while the doctor and Catherine are on holiday in Europe. It is an indecency, a grossness.

After an absence of more than twenty years, James came back to New York in the summer of 1904, a visit that resulted, if we add many impressions of other places, in the publication in 1907 of *The American Scene*. Mostly what he found distressed him, and he set his memories free so that they might issue in "an artful evasion of the actual." Nearly everything provoked in him an urge to evade it: the height of the buildings, suppressing the spires of his favorite churches, and the air of brashness that ousted the air he recalled of ease and decency. But there were alleviations:

> I count as quite a triumph in this interest an unbroken ease of frequentation of that ancient end of Fifth Avenue to the whole neighborhood of which one's earlier vibrations, a very far-away matter now, were attuned. The precious stretch of space between Washington Square and Fourteenth Street had a value, had even a charm, for the revisiting spirit—a mild and melancholy glamour which I am conscious of the difficulty of "rendering" for new and heedless generations.

The quickened memory in James, "its reference to a pleasanter, easier, hazier past," finds the lower end of Fifth Avenue tolerable, or at least reports that the place "still just escapes being a wholly bad thing":

> What held the fancy in thrall, however, as I say, was the admonition, proceeding from all the facts, that values of this romantic order are at best, anywhere, strangely relative. It was an extraordinary statement on the subject of New York that the space between Fourteenth Street and Washington Square *should* be counted for "tone," figure as the old ivory of an overscored tablet.

But some things could not be evaded; the archway, for instance, incorrigible in its asserted presence, "the lamentable little Arch of Triumph which bestrides these beginnings of Washington Square—lamentable because of its poor and lonely and unsupported and unaffiliated state."

James hoped that the arch would go away if he turned his back on it and set his fancies free among "the felicities of the backward reach." But nothing could console him for the loss of his birth house, once Number 21 Washington Place:

> That was where the pretence that nearly nothing was changed had most to come in; for a high, square, impersonal structure, proclaiming its lack of interest with a crudity all its own, so blocks, at the right moment for its own success, the view of the past, that the effect for me, in Washington Place, was of having been amputated of half my history. The grey and more or less "hallowed" University building—wasn't it somehow, with a desperate bravery, both castellated and gabled?—has vanished from the earth, and vanished with it the two or the adjacent houses, of which the birthplace was one.

There were, indeed, a few consolations left: the Church of the Ascension, with John La Farge's painting "of the theological event from which the church takes its title"; "the divine little City Hall," extant though grudged at one moment to within an inch of its life; the old Waldorf-Astoria; and here and there something charmingly done, "some bid for the ampler permanence," some object, some house, "shining almost absurdly in the light of its merely comparative distinction":

> All but lost in the welter of instances of sham refinement, the shy little case of real refinement detaches itself ridiculously, as being (like the saved City Hall, or like the pleasant old garden-walled house on the north-west corner of Washington Square and Fifth Avenue, of so beneficent an admonition as to show, relatively speaking, for priceless.

We have James's authority, if we need it, for referring to "the house of fiction." He thought of fiction as he thought of houses, and of writing novels as an architect would think of building houses. He thought of his characters as living in houses made significant by their residence in them. He was sensitive, as any serious writer must be, to time, but the poetics of space was even more congenial to him. His novels are spaces filled with their appropriate presences: Think of them, and recall their rooms, gardens, fireplaces, furniture. His theme, in this context: how, among the diverse possibilities, best to be present in the world. His criteria for such presence arise from his sense of possible relations, by analogy with the arch, and call upon four adjectives to release his impatience: because of "its poor and lonely and unsupported and unaffiliated state"—in brief, because of its isolation, its unrelatedness to anything in its setting. Why, in one paragraph of chapter 3 of *Washington Square*, does he use the word *honorable* twice, first in commenting upon Dr. Sloper's house and its neighbors, second in describing the "tone" of Washington Square and its surroundings? In his second

· · · ·

use of the word, he answers our question: The Square and its streets have "the look of having had something of a social history." Uptown had no such look, no such luck.

It is more than merely interesting that James should use a moral word to describe houses, streets, and gardens that, strictly accounted for, do not come into the moral question. The case is simple, though his exemplification of it is not. He presents his characters in an intimate relation to the houses they inhabit. And the reverse is also true. He requires of houses and streets that they stand up to the criteria he brings to bear on people, and acquire the look of having a personal and civic history.

"SOMETHING GLORIOUS"

GREENWICH VILLAGE AND THE THEATER

Brooks McNamara

Blazing our nights with arguments uproarious;
What care we for a dull old world censorious
When each is sure he'll fashion something glorious?

—"The Day in Bohemia,"
JOHN REED

In 1872 James McCabe published a popular guidebook, *Lights and Shadows of New York Life*. McCabe devotes a chapter of his guide to Bleecker Street, "the headquarters of Bohemianism" in the city. Among the colorful residents of the street is an actress who lives unchaperoned on the second floor of an old house. It is an unusual arrangement, but as McCabe points out, "This is Bleecker Street and she may live here according to her own fancy, and 'no questions asked.'" On the floor above the actress "dwells one Betty Mulligan, a pretty little butterfly well known to the lovers of ballet as Mademoiselle Alexandrine." The dancer seems to live quite well, McCabe says, but "people shrug their shoulders and hint that ballet girls have resources unknown to the uninitiated."[1]

The actress and the ballet girl were members of a somewhat raffish theatrical subculture that flourished in Greenwich Village in the years after the Civil War. In their free and easy approach to life and love, the two were clearly ancestors of the theatrical bohemians who would make such a mark in the Village forty years later. But there was an important difference.

Madame Alexandrine and her fellow lodger were connected with the commercial theater of their day, then centered nearby on Broadway and in the Union Square area. The actors, directors, and playwrights who would congregate in Greenwich Village in the years before World War I, however,

• • • •

were firmly committed to an alternative theater, as well as to an alternative life-style. And, more than any other quality, it was this commitment to so-called noncommercial values in entertainment that would come to define performance in the Village during the mid-teens. Perhaps, in a way, these same values have been the principal influence on Greenwich Village theater down to our own time, although the pattern is by no means as clear-cut as it might at first appear.

For the most part the New York theater in the mid-teens was in the hands of conservative uptown producers and theater owners whose only real interest was commodity entertainment. The vast majority of them discouraged innovation, relying on safe and unusually uninspired scripts and traditional production values. New York, as producer Lee Shubert would note at the time, was the "theatrical manufacturing city of the country," and for the most part theater people were content to keep it that way.[2] But there were signs of change below Fourteenth Street. The European idea of an "art theater" or "little theater" devoted to experiments in playwriting and production methods had begun to take hold in many parts of the country, and Greenwich Village was becoming one of its most vital centers.

The prehistory of the idea may be seen in the Paterson Strike Pageant of 1913. The pageant's concept had emerged from Mabel Dodge's famous salon at 23 Fifth Avenue. Masterminded by radical journalist John Reed and designed by scenic artist Robert Edmond Jones, the production represented an extraordinary use of the pageant form. On a two-hundred-foot-long stage at Madison Square Garden, more than a thousand workers from the Paterson silk factories re-created the central events of their ongoing strike before an audience of some fifteen thousand people. The Paterson Strike Pageant—a considerable artistic success and a disastrous financial failure—foreshadowed two principles that were to govern much of Village theater during the teens: innovative form and radical content.

A number of experimental theater groups sprang up in Greenwich Village during the period, most of them without much artistic staying power. The Bruno Players is a case in point. Formed during the winter of 1916, the company was housed on the second floor of a brownstone at Fifth Avenue and Eighth Street, in the Thimble Theatre. The tiny performance space, created by Charles Edison, the son of the famous inventor, was managed by Village poet and editor Guido Bruno. The theater company, Bruno said, was formed to present plays by those staples of the art theater movement, "Strindberg, Tchekoff, Wedekind, Artzibasheff, and Gogol . . . in the simple and sincere way in which these playwrights created their characters."[3] There were a few productions on a miniature platform, without conventional stage lights or scenery. But critics and audiences seem not to have been much interested, and the company sank, apparently without a trace, by the summer of 1916.

· · · ·

Two years earlier, however, a group of Village intellectuals had conceived what would prove to be a far more viable version of the art theater idea. Among the group's members were Jones; Reed; Max Eastman; his wife, Ida Rauh; Philip Moeller; Lawrence Langner; Helen Westley; George Cram ("Jig") Cook; and Susan Glaspell. The story goes that someone asked Jones whether a conventional theater building was necessary to stage plays. He supposedly answered the question by mounting a production of a play by Lord Dunsany in the back room of the Washington Square Book Shop on MacDougal Street, thus initiating the Washington Square Players.

Jones's minimalist production may or may not have led directly to the founding of the group—sources vary on the point—but the unusual event offers a convenient symbol for its unorthodox approach to producing. Every member of the Washington Square Players was to have a voice in play selection and casting; funding would come from subscriptions rather than ticket sales; and the commitment was to the newest European theories of stagecraft and to the noncommercial one-act play, including new American scripts and "the works of well-known European authors which have been ignored by the commercial managers."[4] The group would, as Eastman put it, forget about "the box office and adhere to pure standards of art."[5]

There were theaters available in the Village at this point, especially in the Union Square area, but probably none small and cheap enough for amateurs performing only on weekends. As a result, in 1915, the Washington Square Players imported their production concept uptown to East Fifty-seventh Street and the little Bandbox Theatre, which could be rented cheaply on Friday and Saturday nights.

Now a pattern began that would soon become familiar in the history of Greenwich Village theater. The results of the move uptown were initially gratifying; audiences liked the new, experimental plays and the unusual stagings, and the group was soon performing four times a week. By 1917 the Washington Square Players had moved to a Broadway theater and begun hiring professional actors. A year later the company was defunct, the victim of a complex of difficulties, among them overexpansion and internal strife. Out of its work would come a very important uptown group devoted to so-called noncommercial production, the Theatre Guild. But the aggressive and idealistic amateurism of the original Washington Square Players would gradually fade away in the far-from-idealistic atmosphere of Broadway.

A similar story can be told about the famous Provincetown Players, known for its promotion of the works of Eugene O'Neill. The company had been founded in Provincetown, Massachusetts, during the summer of 1915, by a group of artists and intellectuals. Most of the founders had Village roots, and several in fact, including Reed, Jones, Cook, and Glaspell, had been connected with the Paterson Strike Pageant, the Washington Square Players, or both. During the winter, the group re-formed in the Village, taking space in a brownstone at 139 MacDougal Street, which they converted into a tiny theater with a stage "scarcely large enough to accommodate half a dozen actors."[6]

As in the case of the Washington Square Players, the initial emphasis was on enlightened amateurism. "The gifted amateur," Cook said, "has possibilities the professional has lost."[7] Unlike the Players, however, which promoted both European and American scripts, the Provincetown's mission was the production of American plays by new writers committed to experimentation. Under Cook's leadership the group was emphatically—and most successfully—devoted to the development of a new American repertory.

The Provincetown prospered, moving to a less primitive space at 133 MacDougal and producing actively. But gradually questions arose about production standards, with both members and spectators pressing for greater professionalism. The big change for the Provincetown came in 1920, when its extremely successful production of O'Neill's *The Emperor Jones* moved to Broadway. The ultimate result was confusion and unrest among the members, and Cook declared the 1922–1923 season a kind of sabbatical year. From that point on—although various offshoots of the company were active in the Village and uptown until the end of the twenties—the distinctive spirit of the pioneer bohemians was no longer much in evidence.

For that matter the pioneer spirit had largely disappeared from the whole of Greenwich Village. During the late teens, New York's bohemia had become, in many ways, a kind of parody of what it once was, and by 1918 uptown theater was having a field day with Village poseurs who "leave off frocks / And wear Greek smocks / And study Guido Bruno."[8] But some downtown theater was also beginning to take the Village—and itself—less seriously, and one result was the *Greenwich Village Follies* of 1919.

The annual musical revue had become a staple of Broadway entertainment in the teens as a result of Florenz Ziegfeld's *Follies* and a number of imitations by other producers. Now there was a homegrown Village revue that centered around bohemian life and treated it with a certain light-minded detachment. The *Greenwich Village Follies* was the creation of a talented young director named John Murray Anderson, and it spoofed all the Village conventions, from berets and batiks to free love. The show, which opened at the Greenwich Village Theatre on Sheridan Square, was a smash hit, and—following yet another Village convention—shortly moved to Broadway under the aegis of the most commercial of commercial managers, the Shuberts. The second edition in 1920 followed the same route uptown. By the next year, however, the *Follies* had left the Village forever. During the remainder of the twenties, half a dozen more editions of the show would appear. But increasingly they became standard Broadway revues, distinguished from other, similar productions only by a Village reference point.

· · · ·

121. In 1921, after two smash-hit seasons on Sheridan Square, the *Greenwich Village Follies* moved to the Shubert Theatre and Broadway prices. This shift effectively ended bohemian spoofs mounted in Village theaters, for producers saw little need to bankroll these indigenous revenues when the district's nonconformist culture could so profitably be transplanted to Times Square. *(Museum of the City of New York)*

The reference point was changing, however. By the twenties the received view uptown—and throughout America—was that "anything goes in the Village." Like Harlem, Greenwich Village was now seen by many as a kind of permanent carnival, an exotic entertainment center where the ordinary rules of behavior were suspended. As historian Lewis Erenberg has pointed out, the neighborhood "had increasingly become a tourist area and night-life zone . . . a playground where uptowners could indulge in the wilder forms of sensuality." In part the area's attraction lay in its "overtones of free sexuality." Beyond that, revelers in the Village "could see people apparently uninterested in success, caring little about money, desiring to live the good life without responsibilities."[9] But there was a third important element as well.

One of the songs from the 1919 *Follies*, "I'm the Hostess of a Bum Cabaret," had satirized a development that was antithetical to the freewheeling life of the Village—Prohibition. And the more-than-casual attitude of Villagers toward the "great experiment," of course, only added to the area's attractiveness in the twenties and early thirties. Greenwich Village naturally and inevitably became a center of speakeasy culture. "The Village," as journalist Stuart Walker pointed out in 1933, "true to its reputation as a hellhole, probably was the easiest place in New York to get a drink."[10] The shows in the Village cabarets tended to be informal, sometimes erotic, and usually intellectually untaxing. Earnest old-time Villagers complained about the rising commercialism of entertainment in the area. And for the most part their assessment was right: During Prohibition the neighborhood had become largely a home for tourist-oriented popular entertainment. As a result, for years to come there would be relatively little theater activity in the Village like the pioneering efforts of the teens.

There were exceptions, of course; for example, the Cherry Lane Theatre, on Commerce Street, which served as the home of the now-forgotten New Playwrights group in the post–World War I period. Two especially interesting examples were Eva Le Gallienne's Civic Repertory, which opened in 1926, and the 1933 Theatre Union, both of which took up quarters at the northern edge of the Village in the old Fourteenth Street Theatre, near the corner of Sixth Avenue. Both companies represented unconventional, noncommercial approaches to theater, but in fact neither drew its inspiration directly from the old radical tradition of Village culture. Instead, the Civic Repertory and Theatre Union both selected Greenwich Village as their venue for a combination of practical and ideological reasons.

As Le Gallienne pointed out in her autobiography, the Civic Repertory was founded "to provide the people of New York with a popular-priced classical repertory theatre similar to those that have existed as a matter of course for many years in every large city in Europe." It was a bold idea at the time, and Greenwich Village became almost the inevitable choice for the theater.

· · · ·

But, as Le Gallienne also noted, her choice of the Village was based largely on three essentially negative considerations. "To my indignant surprise," she wrote, "the uptown theatre managers refused to permit regular performances at the popular prices I had decided on—thirty-five cents to $1.50 top. They were afraid of lowering the prestige of their houses. I therefore had to find a place outside their jurisdiction."[11]

Beyond that, the stages of uptown Broadway theaters were generally too small to hold all the scenery necessary for repertory. And finally there was the issue of perceived competition on the part of powerful and often vindictive Broadway managers. "I felt, too," Le Gallienne wrote, with a certain delicacy, "that since our theatre in no way intended to compete with the regular run of Broadway attractions it might be best to remove ourselves completely from that particular arena."[12]

Thus Le Gallienne settled in for what would come to be a historic run of six seasons at the old Fourteenth Street Theatre. The building's next major tenant, Theatre Union, likewise represented a departure from the conventional theater practice of the day. Unlike Le Gallienne's troupe, however, it was fiercely revolutionary in terms of its content. Formed in 1933 as a professional company aimed at providing workers with left-wing theater, it was the creation of a united front organization of liberals, trade unionists, socialists, and communists. The founders chose the Fourteenth Street Theatre as the company's venue because it was cheap and already well known to audiences as a result of the Civic Repertory—and of course because it was within a few blocks of Union Square, the center of labor activism in New York.

Theatre Union's announced mission was to "present plays that deal boldly with the deep-going social conflicts, the economic, emotional and cultural problems that confront the . . . great mass of working people."[13] But as the historian of radical theater Morgan Himmelstein has noted, the plays were "uniformly lugubrious," and the great mass of working people did not turn up in sufficiently large numbers to keep the operation afloat.[14] Starting in 1936 the Federal Theatre Project plays presented uptown began to lure away many of Theatre Union's potential audience members, and by 1937 the company had disappeared.

In 1933 playwright Clifford Odets was giving classes for actors at Theatre Union, while director Harold Clurman was teaching nearby at the New School for Social Research. Previously the locus of most theater training—especially studios offering professional actor training—had been uptown, chiefly in and around the Times Square area. From the thirties onward, however, an increasing amount of training activity began to develop downtown, and a number of important acting studios still have their headquarters in the area.

Perhaps the most interesting Village training program of them all began

• • • •

in January 1940—Erwin Piscator's Dramatic Workshop at the New School for Social Research. The workshop was a two-year course that attempted to bridge the gap between academic education and a professional career. In many ways the program developed by the famous German experimental director was in the same spirit as the work of the Village rebels of the teens. According to the director's widow, Maria Ley Piscator, who participated actively in the Workshop, its three objectives were to create a school that was in fact a theater, "to stimulate the avant-garde movement from which playwrights, designers and actors would emerge," and to create a "tradition—a possible ensemble, which would eventually lead to a repertory theatre."[15]

The school-cum-theater largely lived up to its radical promise. Its productions were, for the most part, genuinely experimental, and its faculty over the years would include such innovative figures in American theater as Lee Strasberg, Mordecai Gorelik, and Stella Adler. But the relationship between the New School and the workshop was a stormy one. Piscator's operation lost money from the outset, and its production activities in the school's auditorium were seen as disruptive by New School faculty and unsafe by the fire marshal. There was perhaps an even more crucial point: Academic officials soon came to believe that the Workshop contained too many "egocentric anti-social individuals."[16]

By 1945 Piscator's Workshop had severed its connection with the New School—a decision presumably met by a sigh of relief all around—and had become an independent entity. Classes and productions now moved uptown to the President Theatre on West Forty-eighth Street, although not long afterward Piscator acquired a second space on Houston Street at the southern edge of the Village. By the end of the forties the Workshop was in total financial disarray, and in 1951 its founder returned to Germany. His wife would continue the school for a short time uptown, but by the early fifties an extraordinary Village-based experiment in theater education was at an end.

There was little or no comparably radical theater activity in Greenwich Village during the forties. To some extent this was a function of the changing neighborhood, many parts of which had become increasingly fashionable and expensive. As a tourist guide would note in 1950: "Greenwich Village is a fascinating place, but it is not Bohemia any more. Some of it is 'arty' and much of it is charming. But it is not the mad and wonderful place it used to be."[17] Perhaps as important, there was little radical theater activity anywhere in America during the decade. In the fifties, however, the Village would once again become a center of theatrical innovation.

Broadway was in trouble by the early fifties. Beginning in the mid-forties, television had begun to capture an increasingly large segment of the traditional theater audience. At the same time costs were rising on Broadway, and the number of operating theaters was decreasing. During the 1949–1950 season the total number of shows reached an all-time low. Producers were desperately attempting to win back spectators with popular scripts and lavish presentations. The upshot was a feeling among many theater people that American playwriting—and indeed the whole of the American theater—was in decline.

A potential answer seemed to lie in a revised theatrical geography—new, modest, often improvised playhouses outside the old Times Square theater district. The search led to the Village, which still contained odd corners of inexpensive real estate, and which, of course, had given birth to experimental theater in America. As a result the Village was to become, if not the only venue for Off-Broadway during the fifties, at least its spiritual center and the place most closely associated with experiment in the minds of theatergoers.

As critic Stuart Little would note, "clusters of small, dusty theatres" soon appeared, forming "three bands across Manhattan at the level of Eighth Street: some theatres in Sheridan Square, more theatres farther east along MacDougal and Bleecker streets, and more still farther east on Second Avenue."[18] The result was a flowering of noncommercial performance in the Village like nothing seen in the area since the teens. The symbolic beginning of Off-Broadway, in fact, is often traced to a 1952 Greenwich Village production of Tennessee Williams's *Summer and Smoke*. A failure uptown, Williams's controversial play found an attentive and enthusiastic audience at the Circle in the Square downtown. Founded in 1951 in a former Village nightclub by Jose Quintero and Theodore Mann, the Circle in the Square would soon become a vital center of the new Off-Broadway approach to the theater.

For the most part, that approach did not involve especially radical production concepts, except in comparison to Broadway. Most of it was essentially "progressive" theater, conceived as an alternative to the commercial fare uptown, with an emphasis on challenging plays, often presented in repertory. Among them were revivals of classic plays by Ibsen, Shaw, Chekhov, and O'Neill and works by the new European "absurdist" writers Ionesco, Beckett, and Genet. Although the plays were produced simply, often on the comparatively unadorned arena and thrust stages then becoming popular, genuinely experimental directorial and scenic ideas would not become common until the next decade, with the growth of a so-called Off-Off-Broadway theater.

The commitment to experiment, however, was already beginning to surface in or near the Village toward the end of the fifties, with hints of a politically, socially, and artistically radical theater yet to come. (The words "or near," as we shall see, would shortly assume a crucial importance.) Several institutions pointed in new directions, in particular Julian Beck and Judith Malina's Living Theatre and Joe Cino's Caffe Cino.

• • • •

Cino's coffeehouse, begun in 1958 on Cornelia Street, was to become, in effect, both the first Off-Off-Broadway playhouse and New York's first gay theater. It was an archetypal bohemian hangout in the great tradition of the early Village, with distinctive Beat Generation overtones. As Albert Poland and Bruce Mailman described it, Caffe Cino was "dark, smoky, cluttered and dirty. The walls were covered with posters, old photographs, crunched foil, glitter stars and hundreds of pieces of assorted memorabilia, which in time became ten and twelve thick. Periodically everything was taken down and the room was painted in an attempt to defeat the roach problem; everything was then put back exactly as it had been. Joe Cino insisted."[19]

Founded initially as a place for poetry readings and art and photography exhibitions, Caffe Cino became an important home away from home for people in the arts. Many of them were gay and lived only a few blocks away in the longtime center of New York's gay community around Christopher Street. And in the sixties the coffeehouse would also become the home of some of the most adventurous and extraordinary new productions to be found in the city. As John Gruen would write in the *Herald Tribune* at the time of Cino's death in 1967, "Caffe Cino presented the outrageous, the blasphemous, the zany, the wildly poetic, the embarrassingly trite, the childish, and frequently, the moving and the beautiful."[20]

Although its character was very different from that of Caffe Cino, much the same could be said about the Living Theatre. Its cofounder, Julian Beck, had been a student in Piscator's Dramatic Workshop. In 1946, with his wife, Judith Malina, Beck had formed a company to present poetic drama in innovative ways. Over the years the two had been associated with the Village, performing for some time at the Cherry Lane Theatre. By 1959 they had settled in a building on Sixth Avenue and Fourteenth Street and had produced Jack Gelber's *The Connection*, a play about addicts that was to make the Living Theatre famous and to lead the Becks, confirmed pacifists and anarchists, into creating extraordinary and, to many, shocking new connections between politics and their art.

The Becks now began to perform for audiences around the world. Although they returned to Fourteenth Street at various points until they were evicted from their theater by IRS agents in 1963 during the run of their antiwar play, *The Brig*, the company had in fact outgrown the Village. "The new mobility, the world appeal were evidence that the little theatre at Fourteenth Street probably was already obsolete for the Becks when it opened only three years before," wrote theater historian Stuart Little. "They had burst the walls of the small theatre and found their audience in moving outward into the world traveling among the people."[21]

In the early sixties other groups with an important commitment to radical form or content, or both, would find homes in Greenwich Village, among them Joseph Chaikin's Open Theatre and Al Carmines's Judson Poets' Theatre, a producing organization housed in the famous old Judson Memorial Church on Washington Square. But in fact the Village was no longer so clearly the center of radical theater activity. In 1972, when Poland and Mailman published an anthology of avant-garde plays called *The Off Off Broadway Book,* they included a map of the Off-Off Broadway theater district. The map included the locations of thirteen important venues that presented or had recently presented avant-garde theater. Only four of them were in Greenwich Village. Of the remaining theaters, one was uptown, one was in SoHo, and seven were in the East Village.

As early as 1953 T. Edward Hambleton and Norris Houghton had looked to the East Village—then simply a part of the Lower East Side—when they chose a location for their Phoenix Theatre, a company that would become an Off-Broadway institution. Hambleton and Houghton chose the vacant Stuyvesant Theatre, a former playhouse and later a movie theater, on Second Avenue, the by-then-defunct Yiddish Rialto. Their choice seemed eccentric to many theater people, who believed that audiences would not come to such a shabby neighborhood. But audiences did come, and, beginning in the fifties, the section of the Lower East Side adjacent to Greenwich Village began to acquire a certain cachet. In fact, it seemed to become, in many ways, what Greenwich Village itself had been half a century before. Rents were undeniably cheap and, depending on one's point of view, the neighborhood possessed a certain tarnished charm.

Artists and avant-garde-oriented galleries began to move into the area, and with them came a new influence on performance based in the art world. To the same area, during the sixties, came a number of the most dynamic Off-Off Broadway producing organizations, among them Theatre Genesis, Ellen Stewart's La Mama ETC., and Joseph Papp's Public Theatre. Although Happenings and Off-Off-Broadway productions would also be seen in the Village, on the West Side, and elsewhere in the city, the spiritual home of such radical performance was the area soon to be known as the East Village. From there it would spread south and west.

By the end of the decade Richard Schechner's Performance Group had taken over a loft space in the rundown warehouse area just to the south of Greenwich Village, below Houston Street. The neighborhood turned out to contain a virtually unnoticed treasure, the nation's greatest surviving concentration of cast-iron architecture, and it would shortly achieve fame as SoHo. Like the East Village, SoHo was pioneered by artists in search of cheap space and a colorful atmosphere. Like the East Village, it would become a kind of crucible for the arts in the seventies.

Greenwich Village itself, meanwhile, had become somewhat staid and middle class and, at the same time, a tourist mecca—and, in any case, far too expensive to serve any longer as a magnet for impoverished avant-garde painters, sculptors, and theater people. Much of the radical creative activity had finally been priced out of Greenwich Village, both in a literal and a symbolic way. But it had remained downtown in more compatible and perhaps more vital satellite neighborhoods where—to return to John Reed's vision of bohemia—each artist could be sure that he or she would "fashion something glorious."

· · · · ·

NOTES

1. James D. McCabe, Jr., *Lights and Shadows of New York Life; or The Sights and Sensations of the Great City* (Philadelphia: National Publishing Company, 1872), 388.
2. Lee Shubert, quoted in Keene Sumner, "Sometimes You Fight Better When You're Driven to the Wall," *American Magazine*, October 1921, 81.
3. *Bruno's Weekly*, February 26, 1916, 503.
4. Program, Washington Square Players, February 19, 1915, quoted in Olive M. Sayler, *Our American Theatre* (New York: Brentano's, 1923), 78.
5. Max Eastman, quoted in Robert K. Sarlos, *Jig Cook and the Provincetown Players* (Amherst: University of Massachusetts Press, 1982), 12.
6. Ibid., 80.
7. George Cram Cook, quoted in Allen Churchill, *The Improper Bohemians* (New York: E. P. Dutton Co., 1959), 86.
8. P. G. Wodehouse and Guy Bolton, *Bring on the Girls!* (New York: Simon & Schuster, 1953), 97.
9. Lewis A. Erenberg, *Steppin' Out: New York Nightlife and the Transformation of American Culture, 1890–1930* (Westport, Conn.: Greenwood Press, 1981), 252–253.
10. Stuart Walker, *The Night Club Era* (New York: Frederick A. Stokes Company, 1933), 286.
11. Eva Le Gallienne, *With a Quiet Heart* (New York: Viking Press, 1953), 18.
12. Ibid., 19–20.
13. Program, *Let Freedom Ring*, February 10, 1936, 8.
14. Morgan V. Himmelstein, *Drama Was a Weapon: The Left-Wing Theatre in New York, 1929–1941* (New Brunswick, N.J.: Rutgers University Press, 1963), 73.
15. Maria Ley Piscator, *The Piscator Experiment* (New York: James H. Heineman, 1967), 103.
16. "Report of the Assistant Financial Secretary, New School for Social Research," quoted in John Willett, *The Theatre of Erwin Piscator: Half a Century of Politics in the Theatre* (London: Eyre Methuen, 1978), 159.
17. Eleanor Early, *New York Holiday* (New York: Rinehart and Co., 1950), 204.
18. Stuart W. Little, *Off-Broadway: The Prophetic Theatre* (New York: Coward, McCann and Geohegan, 1972), 14.
19. Albert Poland and Bruce Mailman, eds., *The Off Off Broadway Book* (Indianapolis: Bobbs-Merrill Co., 1972), xvii.
20. Ibid., xviii.
21. Little, *Off-Broadway*, 209.

· · · ·

AVANT-GARDE ARTISTS OF GREENWICH VILLAGE

Irving Sandler

Few, if any, of the abstract expression-
ists of the 1940s and 1950s and their successors would have owned up to
being Greenwich Village artists. That was because Village artists were
thought of as bohemian "creative-livers" who lived the life of art without
making much art, at least not seriously. But my artist friends were also
bohemians, alienated outsiders contemptuous of middle-class values who
lived in relative poverty. They accepted that to be avant-garde artists in the
United States, they would have to take vows of poverty and live with alienation. In fact, many believed, as Clement Greenberg wrote in 1948, that
alienation was "the condition under which the true reality of our age is
experienced. And the experience of this true reality is indispensable to any
ambitious art . . . the shabby studio on the fifth floor of a cold-water, walk-
up tenement on Hudson Street; the frantic scrambling for money; the two
or three fellow-painters who admire your work; the neurosis of alienation
that makes you such a difficult person to get along with. . . . The alienation
of Bohemia was only an anticipation in nineteenth-century Paris; it is in
New York that it has been completely fulfilled."[1]

The artists made no public show of their poverty. Indeed, as most photographs reveal, they wore tweed or corduroy jackets and knitted ties in
public (and even when they met among themselves) to disassociate them-

. . . .
320

selves from the creative-livers. Their appearance calls to mind Degas's re-mark to the flamboyant Whistler: "You dress as if you had no talent."

Yet, for most of the twentieth century, avant-garde painters and sculptors have made it a point to live in Greenwich Village or within easy walking distance of Washington Square: north as far as Fourteenth Street, south in SoHo, and from the Hudson to the East River. There had to be good reasons to be there, and there were. Until fairly recently cheap rents—although they were also to be found elsewhere—were one reason. A second was the need for a milieu favorable to the creation of art, particularly the need to be with other artists, and in the case of avant-garde artists, to provide mutual support. (As Stuart Davis supposedly commented, it was easy to be Picasso in Paris, but imagine Picasso in Kansas City.) A third reason was the general desire to be in New York, a major art center and after World War II the hub of the international art world. Ambitious artists were drawn to this center because they wanted to establish dialogues with their peers and with enter-prising art professionals: editors and critics who worked for the art magazines published in New York; bright directors and curators who were attracted by the great museums; private dealers who were committed to discovering, exhibiting, and selling the best and most provocative art; and knowledgeable collectors who lived there.

Moreover, large numbers of lively intellectuals and creative individuals in the other arts were to be found in the proximity of the painters and sculptors. They participated in the artists' activities and made up a consid-erable part of their audience. As such they played a critical role. By paying enthusiastic attention, this public made the art count in the world of mod-ernist culture—the world that mattered most to the artists. Such attention bolstered the artists and encouraged them to work with greater intensity. In turn, because of their number and concentration, visual artists provided the primary audience for the avant-garde in the other arts. John Cage once told me that most of the people who came to his concerts were artists of the New York School. I asked him whether they liked his music; he said that he thought not, but they came anyway because he was a kindred spirit and they knew that no one else would. Finally, the Village attracted avant-garde artists because it had a long, distinguished history as a haven in a middle-class society that they for the most part despised and that on the whole rejected them.

* * * * *

The role of the Village as a center for artists generally extended well back into the nineteenth century—to 1857, for example, when the Tenth Street Studio Building was opened. Recognizing that American artists needed comfortable, live-in studios at reasonable rents, James Boorman Johnston commissioned Richard Morris Hunt to design a three-story brick building containing about twenty-five airy studios, whose dimensions—some fifteen by twenty feet, others twenty by thirty feet—were ample by contemporary standards. The list of tenants—a who's who of American art in the second half of the nineteenth century—includes John La Farge (from 1857 until his death in 1910), Winslow Homer (for eight years), Frederic E. Church, William Merritt Chase, Sanford R. Gifford, Martin J. Heade, and Albert Bierstadt.

So many artists in one building made for "a constant coming-and-going of buyers, sight-seers, pupils and arbiters of taste from the press" and for a continual exchange of ideas, some of it more than verbal. Apparently "at least once, Church painted half of one of Martin J. Heade's canvases in the latter's absence." The building included a large exhibition space/salesroom that was used for openings as well. Indeed, artists' receptions became the center of social life. Although they "were the rage [and] no effort was spared to make them gala affairs, . . . the atmosphere was much more like that of an established gentlemen's club."[2]

From 1858 to 1861 the National Academy of Design—many of whose leading members lived and worked at the studio building and whose annual salons were major artistic and social events—was situated at the corner of Tenth Street and Fourth Avenue. Mathew Brady's New Photographic Gallery, a popular attraction at the time, was close by. Chase's studio was a meeting place for the Society of American Artists, which resisted successfully the hegemony of the Academy; the Art Club, whose members included Walter Shirlaw, James Beckwith, Frederick Dielman, and Augustus Saint-Gaudens; and later, the Society of American Painters in Pastel, including La Farge, Twachtman, J. Alden Weir, and Edwin Blashfield.

The story of the world of culture in Lower Manhattan in the early decades of the twentieth century, as Thomas Bender remarked, has been told many times in histories, in fiction, and in film:

> The cultural highlights are familiar: a happy collaboration of "revolutionary" writers and artists at the editorial offices of *The Masses* on Greenwich Avenue; the wide-ranging discussion of politics and culture, from syndicalism (with Bill Haywood) to Freudianism (with A. A. Brill), from Isadora Duncan's modern dances to Harlem jazz, held on Wednesday evenings in Mabel Dodge's living room at 23 Fifth Avenue; the innovative Provincetown Players—Susan Glaspell, George Cram Cook, Eugene O'Neill, and, at one time or another, almost every man or woman of the Village rebellion; Alfred Stieglitz's famous gallery at 291 Fifth Avenue, where Village intellectuals were tutored in modern aesthetics . . . ; the Armory Show (1913), which in a single dramatic moment forced a larger art public out of its comfortable provincial standards and introduced those of international modernism; the Paterson Strike Pageant at Madison Square Garden, organized by John Reed in support of IWW strikers; the founding of new magazines, al-

ways a sign of cultural change—*The Masses, The New Republic*, and *Seven Arts* as well as a group of short-lived but consciously avant-garde and coterie magazines with such names as *Broom, Quill, Glebe, Others, Rouge, Pagan*, and *Rong-Wrong*; meeting places such as the Liberal Club, Polly's restaurant, Albert Boni's bookstore, and, finally, Petitpas, where the painter John Butler Yeats, who had been a correspondent of Whitman and was the father of the great poet of the Irish renaissance, William Butler Yeats, assured the Young Intellectuals that in America, too, "the fiddles are tuning up."[3]

Bender went on to say that what became "most salient about the rebellion is its sense of itself as a youth movement, as the *young* intellectuals" in search of a newer and more vital culture, a modern culture.[4]

This sense of youthfulness would persist among visual artists in Greenwich Village, particularly the abstract expressionists and their successors, in the period after World War II. It was natural for these alienated, radical artists to band together; they needed to discuss art, if only to reassure themselves that their enterprise was not insane; to exhibit their work when no one else would; and to bid for recognition or combat antagonism. They had already developed the habit during the 1930s on the Federal Art Project; at the meetings of the Artists Union, the American Abstract Artists, and the Ten; and in Village bars and restaurants such as the San Remo and the Minetta Tavern on MacDougal Street and the Stewart Cafeteria on Sheridan Square.

During World War II *the* meeting place of avant-garde artists was the Waldorf Cafeteria on Sixth Avenue off Eighth Street. However, they were not comfortable there; when weather permitted they gathered in nearby Washington Square Park. The cafeteria was a cruddy place frequented by bums, delinquents, and cops. Moreover, the management did not want the artists; they were coffee drinkers who preferred to eat where the fare was better and cheaper, like Riker's on Eighth Street near University Place (which was too small to make a good hangout). When the Waldorf management began to harass the artists, they decided to find their own meeting place, and in the late fall of 1949 a group met in sculptor Ibram Lassaw's studio and organized the Club.

What would become the most important avant-garde artists' organization in the 1950s had its precedents first in a series of lectures at the Subjects of the Artist School at 35 East Eighth Street. Founded in 1948 by William Baziotes, David Hare, Robert Motherwell, Mark Rothko, and Clyfford Still (who participated in the initial planning but did not teach), and joined somewhat later by Barnett Newman, the school sought to broaden its students' experience with Friday-evening lectures by advanced artists—sessions open to the public at which many of the artists who subsequently organized the Club spoke or attended.

• • • •

The school closed after only one semester. In fall 1949, at roughly the same time the Club started, Robert Iglehart, Tony Smith, and Hale Woodruff, all professors at the New York University Department of Art Education, took over its loft for the use of their students. They named it Studio 35 and continued the Friday evenings until April 1950. Among those who lectured were Jean Arp, John Cage, Joseph Cornell (who showed his films), Herbert Ferber, Fritz Glarner, Adolph Gottlieb, John Hulsenbeck, Willem de Kooning, Barnett Newman, Ad Reinhardt, Harold Rosenberg, and Mark Rothko.

The Club, located in a rented loft at 39 East Eighth Street, was formed to provide a place where artists could meet their peers to exchange ideas of every sort, including such perpetual topics as tips on good studios and bargains in art materials. Above all was the need to talk about art to sympathetic colleagues. Outworn styles—social realism, regionalism, geometric abstraction, and surrealism—had lost their meanings and new ones had to be conceived. The need to talk was urgent enough to keep "these highly individualistic artists together, their ideas criss-crossing and over-lapping in a conflict that would tear apart any other togetherness," as Philip Pavia put it. "They faced each other with curses mixed with affection, smiling and evil-eyed each week for years." [5]

Most artists who came to be labeled abstract expressionists joined within a few months. The membership, which initially included artists such as Kline, Pavia, Milton Resnick, Jack Tworkov, Lassaw, de Kooning, and Reinhardt, jumped quickly. By 1951 an entry in the minutes reads: "77 members + 11 deadheads." Although at first every member had a key and came when he or she pleased, it soon took on a more public and formal character, first by inviting speakers (prompted by the Studio 35 sessions) and then by presenting panels open to guests—mainly critics, historians, curators, dealers, collectors, and avant-garde allies in the other arts. The programs, which constituted the major activity, were organized by Pavia until the spring of 1955, by John Ferren the following year, and by a committee I headed from 1956 to the end of the Club in the spring of 1962.

The early lectures covered many facets of modern culture. Among the speakers were the philosophers William Barrett, Hannah Arendt, and Heinrich Bluecher; composer Edgard Varèse; social critic Paul Goodman; anthropologist Joseph Campbell; and art critic Thomas Hess. Parties were also held in honor of such artists as Alexander Calder and Dylan Thomas. A selection of events in 1951–1952 indicates the range of artists' interests and aesthetic positions:

> October 12   Peter Blake spoke on "The Collaboration of Art
>   and Architecture."

• • • •

November 9   "An Evening with Max Ernst" was introduced by Robert Motherwell.

November 23 Lionel Abel lectured on "The Modernity of the Modern World."

December 14 Abel lectured again on "Work or Free Work."

December 21 Hubert Kappell spoke on Heidegger.

The publication of Thomas B. Hess's *Abstract Painting* prompted a series of panels on abstract expressionism. The first, on January 18, 1952, was moderated by Harold Rosenberg and included Hess, Baziotes, Guston, Kline, Reinhardt, and Tworkov. One week later Ferren moderated "Abstract Expressionism II," which included Peter Busa, Burgoyne Diller, Perle Fine, Gottlieb, Harry Holtzman, and a paper sent by Elaine de Kooning.

These were some of the other panels in this series on abstract expressionism:

February 20 Mercedes Matter moderated a conversation between Guston, Kline, Willem de Kooning, George McNeil, and Tworkov.

March 7   John Myers moderated a discussion among younger artists including Jane Freilicher, Grace Hartigan, Alfred Leslie, Joan Mitchell, Frank O'Hara, and Larry Rivers.

And the Club's lecture series included these additional events:

March 14   John Cage spoke on "Contemporary Music."

April 11   Nicolas Calas moderated a discussion of "The Image in Poetry and Painting" by Edwin Denby, David Gascoyne, Frank O'Hara, and Ruthven Todd.

May 2   Dr. Frederick Perls spoke on "Creativeness in Art and Neurosis."

May 14   Larry Rivers chaired a discussion of "New Poets" by John Ashbery, Barbara Guest, Frank O'Hara, and James Schuyler.

The variety and richness of the discourse prompted Tworkov to write in his journal for April 26, 1952:

> The enthusiastic clash of ideas that takes place in the Club has one unexpected and, in my mind, salutary effect—it destroys, or at least

• • • •

325

reduces, the aggressiveness of all attitudes. One discovers that rectitude is the door one shuts on an open mind. The Club is a phenomenon—I was at first timid in admitting that I like it. Talking has been suspect. There was the prospect that the Club would be regarded either as bohemian or as a self-aggrandizing clique. But now I'm consciously happy when I'm there. I enjoy the talk, the enthusiasm, the laughter, the dancing after the discussion. . . . I say to myself there are the people I love, that I love to be with. Here I understand everybody, however inarticulate they are. Here I forgive everyone their vices, and I'm learning to admire their virtues. . . . I think that 39 East 8th is an unexcelled university for an artist. Here we learn not only about all the possible ideas in art, but learn what we need to know about philosophy, physics, mathematics, mythology, religion, sociology, magic.[6]

Despite Tworkov's claim it was not always easy to understand everybody at the Club. Members rarely discussed art in formal terms. Instead they tended to talk about the function of art, how and why an artist involved him- or herself with art, and the nature of the artist's moral commitment and existential role. This is understandable: as artists in the vanguard, without models to fall back on, club members constantly experienced both doubt and elation. Discussions among themselves enabled them to share their feelings of anxiety and excitement—a process that not only informed their work but also buoyed their spirits.

Conversation was treated as the verbal counterpart of painting, and artists tried to convey what they really felt in both activities. Self-confession did lead artists to take liberties and to strain both language and logic, but there were compensations. What they had to say they said directly, personally, and passionately, often to the point of brutality. At times this resulted in incoherent and egotistic bombast, but more frequently it led to original, trenchant, and provocative insights.

The Club's verbal style also generated bitter personality conflicts, for as Robert Goldwater remarked: "Since the artist identifies with his work, intention and result were fused, and he who questioned the work, in however humble a fashion, was taken to be doubting the man."[7] On the other hand the artists prized individualism. "We Agree Only to Disagree" was the unwritten motto. Therefore there were no manifestos. No exhibitions of pictures were mounted lest size and placement indicate a hierarchy, and as much as possible, no names of contemporaries were mentioned lest through repetition some be made heroes and, as Goldwater quipped, cause riots.

Despite the bluntness of the discourse at the Club, the panel format made it somewhat self-conscious and inhibited. The place for more informal and private conversation came to be the Cedar Street Tavern on University Place off Eighth Street. Artists began to go there when Club panels got dull or after they were over. Then they started to gather there every night when the Club was not open, arriving late and staying later. During the day the tavern served an entirely different clientele—NYU professors and students and a group of horse-racing enthusiasts.

Unlike the Waldorf Cafeteria, the Cedar catered to artists. But its owners knew better than to make it look "arty" by hanging paintings, driftwood, travel posters, or other emblems of Village bohemia on the walls. That would have attracted the creative-livers; the Madison Avenue types who posed as artists after five o'clock; the chic of all varieties who came slumming; and tourists who came to gape at the way-out characters. Their presence would have driven away the artists. Aside from the absence of television, except during the World Series, there was nothing to distinguish the Cedar from the run of nondescript bars all over America. Artists were attracted by the food, which was fair and inexpensive, and by the fact that credit was extended when one got to know the owners. However, the move to the Cedar also reflected a new affluence, represented by the artists' switch from coffee to alcohol.

In its colorlessness the Cedar was a "no-environment"—de Kooning's term for the contemporary milieu—typified by no nostalgia, romance, or picturesqueness. It may also be, as Harold Rosenberg suggested, that artists could best engage in discovering their own identities in as neutral an environment as possible. Moreover, the very name, or more accurately misname—the Cedar Street Tavern for a bar located on University Place—symbolized, unintentionally of course, its customers' refusal to accept fixed categories. An establishment that could not get its own name straight must be the right place for a group that could never decide on a name for its club.

The idea of mounting an exhibition of the works of club members—like a big salon—was raised but rejected many times because it might indicate a trend or position and curb the Club's open character. However, in the spring of 1951 it was finally decided to have a show, but not under the direct auspices of the Club. A group of charter members, with the help of Leo Castelli, leased an empty floor at 60 East Ninth Street, chose sixty-one artists, and installed their works. Contrary to the expectations of most of the exhibitors, the show attracted a large crowd on opening night and was well attended during the rest of its run. The "Ninth Street Show" generated a sense of exultation, a feeling that something important had been achieved in American art.

As the 1950s progressed, older members began to attend the Club less often, even though many continued to pay dues. In 1956 a younger generation took over and continued the Club until 1962. By organizing panels and allowing an audience, even an invited one, to attend, the Club assumed a semipublic function—a new role that both reflected and contributed to the changing nature of abstract expressionism. During the late forties, shows by Pollock, de Kooning, Still, Rothko, Motherwell, Kline, and others received growing attention. Such critics as Greenberg, Rosenberg, Hess, and Goldwater called public attention to these exhibitions. What had been an underground movement came out into the open. Convinced that the art they were creating was more vital, radical, and original than any being produced elsewhere, the artists themselves began to demand their just due from art officialdom or, to put it more accurately, to denounce discrimination.

In 1948 a meeting called by artists at New York's Museum of Modern Art censured hidebound art critics in general and a statement attacking modernism, published by Boston's Institute of Contemporary Art, in particular. This led to a policy statement issued in 1950 by the Museum of Modern Art, the Whitney Museum of American Art (then on Eighth Street off Fifth Avenue), and the Institute of Contemporary Art, proclaiming "the continuing vitality . . . of modern art"; that is, "art which is aesthetically an innovation."[8] The three museums promised that in the future they would treat advanced art fairly, an attitude that came to be shared by American museums generally.

Avant-garde artists welcomed the statement from the three museums, but they still believed with justification that they were being discriminated against by the art establishment. Thus in 1950, at a three-day meeting at Studio 35, eighteen abstract expressionist painters, supported by ten sculptors, most of whom lived in the Village, decided to protest against a national juried exhibition. The Metropolitan Museum of Art had invited eighteen thousand painters, including several of the dissenting artists, to submit work. The protesters, among whom were Pollock, de Kooning, Gottlieb, Newman, Still, Motherwell, Reinhardt, Hofmann, and Rothko, sent a letter to the president of the museum denouncing the jurors' conservatism and vowing to boycott the show. The letter was hand-delivered to the *New York Times*. Luckily there was no major news, and the *Times* ran the story on the front page the following day. The *New York Herald Tribune* picked it up and published an editorial titled "The Irascible Eighteen," giving the artists a catchy label. The controversy continued in the pages of *Art News*, *Arts Magazine*, and *Time*. Even the *Daily News* ran a three-and-one-half-inch item. Then *Life* covered the story, illustrating it with Nina Leen's now-famous group photograph of the artists. It has become *the* image whereby we envision the artists who achieved the triumph of American painting.

Collaborating with *Life* troubled the artists; after all, they were alienated bohemians and *Life* was the enemy. At a meeting Rothko and Richard Pousette-Dart voiced strong reservations about having anything to do with the magazine: Rothko because it epitomized mass culture, and Pousette-Dart because it represented the establishment. Equally distressing was *Life's*

122. The Irascible Eighteen included *top row, left to right:* Willem de Kooning, Adolph Gottlieb, Ad Reinhardt, and Hedda Sterne; *middle row:* Richard Pousette-Dart, William Baziotes, Jackson Pollock, Clyfford Still, Robert Motherwell, and Bradley Walker Tomlin; and *bottom row:* Theodoros Stamos, Jimmy Ernst, Barnett Newman, James Brooks, and Mark Rothko. *(Nina Leen,* Life *magazine © 1951, Time Warner Inc.)*

long campaign against new art. But other artists argued that if the photograph was "honest," meaning dignified, it would be permissible to pose, and they prevailed.

The Irascibles' letter became significant because it was featured not only in the art magazines but also in the mass media. This indicated that they had become sufficiently well known to warrant such coverage. The three-museum statement and the Irascibles' protest in 1950 exemplified a dramatic change in American taste. It suddenly became intellectually disreputable to dismiss avant-garde art out of hand or ridicule it as a lunatic or infantile aberration. The Irascibles' action had an additional effect: The protesting artists had chosen not to include dozens of other advanced painters, thereby proclaiming their superiority and destroying the sense of camaraderie of the first generation of abstract expressionists.

Among younger artists of the New York School, however, the sense of camaraderie remained strong. In 1956, one year short of its centennial, the Tenth Street Studio Building was demolished. But in that very year, the artists' scene on Tenth Street entered into its most active phase, as if in anticipation of the international recognition of "The New American Painting," a show of abstract expressionist painting organized by the Museum of Modern Art in 1958 and sent to eight European countries. Fifties artists no longer lived in one building but in a low-rent neighborhood centered around East Tenth Street and within walking distance of the Cedar Street Tavern and the Club. Indeed, on this street alone in 1956 were the lofts of twenty-five painters and sculptors, including de Kooning and Guston.

Younger artists who believed that their work merited exhibition but could find no uptown gallery willing to take the risk founded eight galleries, five on Tenth Street between Third and Fourth avenues. The first of the cooperatives was the Tanager. Among its better-known members were Alex Katz, Philip Pearlstein, and Tom Wesselmann. The other major galleries with artists of stature were the Brata, which numbered among its members Al Held, George Sugarman, and Ronald Balden, and the Reuben Gallery. Although the latter was a private gallery, its owners relied heavily on the ideas of the artists they exhibited, most of whom—notably Allan Kaprow, Red Grooms, Claes Oldenburg, and Jim Dine—created environments and Happenings.

Sales were not expected and in fact were rare. But selling did not matter much: what counted was the approval of other artists. The artist-run galleries became centers of communal activities, where artists could always find other artists to talk with and, on joint Friday-night openings of all the galleries, where they could participate in festivities that resembled big block parties.

Around 1960, however, Tenth Street went into a decline. The better artists joined prestigious commercial galleries uptown and appeared less and less often. A new generation of innovative artists found the scene there hostile and avoided it. Contributing most to the decline, however, was the influx of mediocre newcomers who could, and did, show their work with greater ease. This glut of inferior art drove away the audience and discouraged lively and ambitious young artists from exhibiting downtown. To state it bluntly: It was no longer *important* to show on Tenth Street, or to be—or even visit—there. When this occurred, the scene declined.

But downtown New York remained the place where artists lived, worked, and congregated in studios, bars, coffeehouses, and clubs. Indeed, in the late sixties, SoHo (*South of Houston*) became the artists' quarter. When the need arose artists formed their own organizations, such as the Art Workers Coalition, to protest the Vietnam War and social and art world evils. The resident artists attracted large numbers of commercial galleries, among them Leo Castelli, Paula Cooper, Mary Boone, Metro Pictures, Holly Solomon, Ileana Sonnabend, and John Weber.

Nevertheless, even with the new commercial galleries devoted to difficult art, there were still not enough to represent all the new artists who merited shows, many of them working in new media that did not yield salable products. At that moment the National Endowment for the Arts and the New York State Council on the Arts made sizable sums of public money available through grants that could only be awarded to not-for-profit organizations. In response spaces alternative to commercial galleries arose to meet the needs of artists. Those in the Village included 112 Greene, the Kitchen, Artists Space, the Clocktower, the Alternative Museum, and Franklin Furnace. A number of artist-run galleries representing causes or single constituencies also emerged. Combative in a way the fifties cooperatives had not been, these galleries included Bowery, First Street, and Green Mountain, all of which promoted realist art, and A.I.R. and SoHo 20, which promoted feminist art.

Although it was widely hoped that alternative spaces might constitute a new art support network apart from the commercial one, that did not occur. Much as they tried, their administrators did not succeed in selling much art. Commercial dealers followed these shows and invited participating artists to join their stables, and many did. Thus alternative spaces turned out to serve as conduits to private galleries.

Because of the success of commercial galleries in marketing the new art, it occurred to members of a new generation that emerged around 1980, most of them artists, that they could open private galleries in order to exhibit their own work and that of friends in whom they believed. A number took the risk with relatively little investment, transforming hole-in-the-wall storefronts in dilapidated tenements in the East Village into exhibition spaces. A community composed of young artists who were attracted by the low rents had already developed in the community. They became friends, visited each other's studios, exchanged ideas, and partied together. Club 57 on St. Marks Place, conceived of by its denizens as a kind of Club Voltaire, and the Limbo Lounge on Tenth Street, were two of many bars and clubs frequented by these artists.

The East Village community was based not only on geographic proximity and generational and social ties, but also on shared expectations of what new art should be. Although it was very heterogeneous, the art tended to be small in scale because of the size of studios and galleries, and was usually figurative, often alluding to the neighborhood's mean but ethnically diverse street life and its art (graffiti) and/or pop art and mass-media imagery. If the

• • • •

art had any claim to being new, it was because it had appropriated existing imagery, quoting it directly, and because it had muscled into "high" art such "low" art forms as ghetto-spawned spray-can writing, the trashiest of kitsch, and the crudest "bad" painting, thereby exacerbating an abrasive tendency in modern art that went back to the unfinished-looking pictures of Delacroix, Courbet, and Manet.

New commercial galleries in large number could only have arisen at a time when painting and sculpture—works of art as salable objects—were valued. And the art world in the eighties had become, in Edith DeAk's words, more "canvas-happy" than it had been for over a decade; art had become chic again, and sales and prices skyrocketed. This led young artists and their friends to assume as role models rich and fashionable art stars, many of the most celebrated in their early thirties, and their counterparts in the gallery business. And when business required it, the more successful East Village dealers moved into SoHo, most of them in large buildings at Broadway and Prince, causing the rapid decline of the East Village art scene.

In this age of the commodification of art, it may seem that bohemia is dead. And for a commercially successful segment of the art world, larger than ever before in America (but still relatively small), it is. But it may also be that bohemia, still alive, has gone underground. If it has, we will have to wait for it to emerge to find out where it has been hiding. Given the high rents, chances are that it is no longer in Greenwich Village.

• • • • •

NOTES

1. Clement Greenberg, "Art Chronicle: The Situation at the Moment," *Partisan Review* 15:1 (January 1948): 82–83.
2. Mary Sayre Haverstock, "The Tenth Street Studio," *Art in America* (September–October 1966): 50–51.
3. Thomas Bender, *New York Intellect* (New York: Alfred A. Knopf, 1987), 228–229.
4. Ibid.
5. P. G. Pavia, "The Unwanted Title: Abstract Expressionism," *It Is* 5 (Spring 1960): 9.
6. Jack Tworkov, "Four Excerpts from a Journal," *It Is* 4 (Autumn 1959): 12.
7. Robert Goldwater, "Reflections on the New York School," *Quadrum* 8 (1960): 30.
8. James S. Plaut, Frederick S. Wight, René d'Harnoncourt, Alfred H. Barr, Jr., Andrew C. Ritchie, Herman More, and Lloyd Goodrich, "A Statement on Modern Art," by the Institute of Contemporary Art, Boston; the Museum of Modern Art, New York; and the Whitney Museum of American Art, New York, March 1950.

• • • •

"GREENWICH THRILLAGE"
VILLAGE COMMERCE

The Tourist Trade Takes Hold

The modern discovery of the Village as a tourist destination has generally been fixed around 1915, when the neighborhood and its natives burst into bloom as a favorite subject for Sunday magazine spreads. Armed with maps and guidebooks, and versed in the lore that now clung to the district, day-trippers began to spill into its maze of crooked streets. Conveniently accessed by the Fifth Avenue Coach line, Washington Square emerged as the epicenter of this nascent tourist industry. After its connection to the West Side subway system in 1917, Sheridan Square gained the edge as the area's most active tourist hub.

Local realtors and restaurateurs, merchants and moviemakers, bus lines and theater companies capitalized on the notion of nonconformity that distinguished Village culture. Candlelit tearooms, novelty clubs, bizarre boutiques, and counterfeit artist garrets sprouted under their clever cultivation. The onslaught of sightseers into the prewar Village was deplored by most residents. The community's committed radicals abhorred the carnival mood their arrival introduced. But there was also a conspicuous minority of colorful cranks and freethinking freeloaders who were only too willing to collude with the enemy by playing to their presumptions about life, love, and lawlessness in this wittingly mischievous precinct, often for a price.

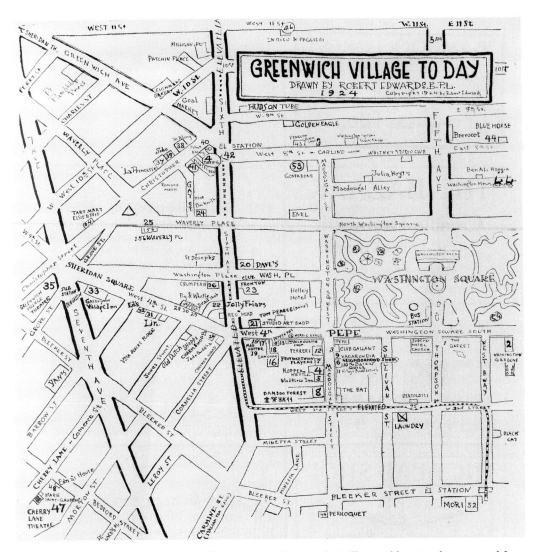

123. *The Quill's* **map of Greenwich Village** A typically nomadic Village publication that operated from a variety of addresses between 1917 and 1928, *The Quill* was a local humor magazine that orbited around Sheridan Square, liberally puffing its arty cafés, tearooms, and novelty shops. (*Museum of the City of New York*)

124. Washington Square Park stanchions—section no. 3 Passengers from uptown riding the Fifth Avenue Coach Company line were discharged near the Square's southern border, the coaches then turning around to head north on a fresh run. Since this debarkation point was where many excursionists first made contact with Greenwich Village, and where coach drivers lingered on their layovers, Washington Square South and its side streets became the testing ground for entrepreneurial efforts to market an assortment of bohemian products and experiences. *(Courtesy of The New-York Historical Society, N.Y.C.)*

125. Nickolas Muray's studio Some members of the Village art colony volunteered their studios for the tourist circuit. On Wednesday evenings Nickolas Muray, the Hungarian-born photographer known for his celebrity portraits, hosted open-invitation parties at his atelier on MacDougal Street. For a price those dropping by were treated to food, drink, and chance encounters with a cross-section of Village theatrical and artistic personalities. Among the evenings' highlights were the fencing demonstrations performed by the host, who twice represented the United States on Olympic fencing teams. *(Nickolas Muray Papers, Archives of American Art, Smithsonian Institution)*

126. Bobby Edwards making ukeleles Edwards, editor of *The Quill*, manufactured "futuristic ukeleles" as a remunerative sideline, using cigar boxes emblazoned with wild, vividly colored designs. According to the inventor, he conceived the prototype as a prop for a production by the Washington Square Players, whose success thereafter propelled the playing of these unusual instruments into a Village fad. *(Courtesy of The New-York Historical Society, N.Y.C.)*

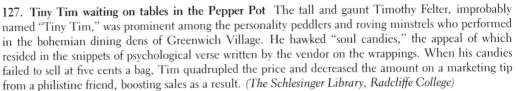

127. Tiny Tim waiting on tables in the Pepper Pot The tall and gaunt Timothy Felter, improbably named "Tiny Tim," was prominent among the personality peddlers and roving minstrels who performed in the bohemian dining dens of Greenwich Village. He hawked "soul candies," the appeal of which resided in the snippets of psychological verse written by the vendor on the wrappings. When his candies failed to sell at five cents a bag, Tim quadrupled the price and decreased the amount on a marketing tip from a philistine friend, boosting sales as a result. *(The Schlesinger Library, Radcliffe College)*

128. Alice Palmer of the Village Store Conveniently located across from the Washington Square bus depot, the Village Store was a basement craft emporium warmed by a cheerful fireplace and a proprietress who served her visitors refreshments and offered them cigarettes from copper bowls. *(The Schlesinger Library, Radcliffe College)*

129. Sonia, the Cigarette Girl In the guise of a bizarrely clad Slavic soothsayer, Ella Breistein/aka Eleanor Brandt operated a popular smoke shop on West Fourth Street during the teens. Under the name "Sonia, the Cigarette Girl," she sold love potions, books on the soul, and hand-rolled art cigarettes. By 1921, however, she began to distance herself from this self-invented persona; writing to one correspondent, she summarized her bohemian career as "meaningless." *(The Schlesinger Library, Radcliffe College)*

The Republic of Washington Square

As the war cast a pall over the mood of the United States, Greenwich Village became the target of a theatrical insurrection. A high-spirited group of bohemians seized the Washington Arch and declared the Village a strife-free zone dedicated to free self-expression rather than issues of class oppression. To the displeasure of many sensible, hardworking citizens, the gambols of these bohemian mutineers quickly took the upper hand in the public's perception of the Village. The picture painted was that of a hotbed of bohemianism; a place of midnight revels and liberated liaisons, where scorning the status quo was a sacred duty. While never stopping the flow of innovative work produced by the Village's best minds and talents, the regime of the Republic of Washington Square often obscured their achievements.

130. *Arch Conspirators* John Sloan's etching memorializes a midwinter incident of 1916 when the artist (*at right*, wearing glasses), in collusion with five other conspirators, staged a mock revolution at the summit of Washington Arch. After a midnight picnic, they festooned the Arch with balloons and announced that Greenwich Village was seceding from the Union and would henceforth be known as the "Free and Independent Republic of Washington Square." (*Kraushaar Galleries, New York City*)

131. Webster Hall on East Eleventh Street In 1913 a run-down community center on East Eleventh Street hosted the first in a long line of masquerade balls that would inflate the image of Greenwich Village as a perpetual party place. Though the balls were initially conceived as fund-raisers for local radical organizations, the original causes they stood to support receded as the merrymaking intensified. At the peak of their popularity around 1918, as many as two balls per week were being held at what Villagers branded "the Devil's Playhouse." *(Museum of the City of New York)*

132. Costume ball at Webster Hall A variety of Village organizations founded in the teens seized upon the costume ball as a fund-raising vehicle. In addition to netting the sponsoring institution a cut of the gate receipts, these galas promised some rowdy fun to all who attended. *(Alexander Alland, Sr., Collection)*

133. *A New Year's Eve Carnival Celebrating the Repeal of Prohibition* Painter John Sloan blamed the passage of the Volstead Act for spoiling the intimacy of Village life. Slummers searching for surreptitious drink filled the district's narrow streets with automobiles and spawned a "nightmare of clubs and commercial entertainment." Webster Hall, long connoting tipsy entertainment, continued to draw merrymakers despite Prohibition and hosted the ball welcoming the repeal of Prohibition. *(Museum of the City of New York)*

The Garret

Those exiting the Fifth Avenue Coach line in Greenwich Village were greeted by a weatherbeaten landmark known by 1915 as the Garret, which beckoned from the southeast corner of Thompson Street and Washington Square. An architectural relic of the past, this rickety old roadhouse had an intriguing pedigree: Lafayette once stayed as a guest there, and a prior resident included the official gravedigger who had serviced the municipal gallows and potter's field located in the area.

The building's reputation as a bohemian art lair was created by flamboyant tenant Guido Bruno, who in 1914 enthroned himself in the ramshackle suite of rooms above the ground-floor ice-cream parlor. Lest prospective patrons overlook his loft, he posted a boldly lettered sign on the exterior proclaiming its identity and mission: "To get it written/to get it spoken/to get it down at any cost/at any hazard/it is for this only/that we are here." The Garret's reputation endured under Grace Godwin, who took over the premises after Bruno's departure. Before the Garret fell victim to the wrecker's ball, it passed into the hands of "Romany Marie" Marchand, the doyenne of cozy Village eateries.

• • • •

134. Bruno's Garret Billed as a "First Aid Station for Struggling Genius," the Garret housed an extensive publishing operation, for Bruno was an astute judge of talent lying outside traditional molds. Among his discoveries were the poets Djuna Barnes, Alfred Kreymborg, and Hart Crane, and the local artists Clara Tice, Coulton Waugh, and Ilonka Karasz. During the heyday of Bruno's reign, the Garret was also rumored to be a front for the seduction of gullible girls and a printshop for smut, untrue allegations that only served to increase traffic. Bruno's publication of Kreymborg's controversial tale about a pragmatic prostitute and her pickup proved his downfall when authorities won a lawsuit that stilled the Garret's presses late in 1916. *(Museum of the City of New York)*

135. *Bruno's Weekly* (*Museum of the City of New York*)

136. Guido Bruno of the Garret Branded by critics as the "Czar of Charlatanism," Guido Bruno was the peerless bohemian poseur and pitchman to emerge on the prewar Village scene. Prone to ostentatious attire and a cryptic foreign accent, Bruno dodged questions about his origins by replying, "I, Bruno, have given birth to myself." His real biography, however, unmasked him as Curt Josef Kisch, a former hospital morgue attendant and happily married family man who commuted to work from Yonkers. Born in a village north of Prague, "Bruno" was by the curious accident of nationality an authentic Bohemian. *(Museum of the City of New York)*

137. The Oasis of Washington Square Remodeled into a cozy if shabby coffee and spaghetti house after the demise of Guido Bruno, Grace's Garret occupied the floor above the "Oasis of Washington Square," an Italian-run soda fountain that advertised a progressive policy of selling cigarettes to women: "No criticism, no hard looks," the management assured its female customers. *(Courtesy of The New-York Historical Society, N.Y.C.)*

138. Grace Godwin serving spaghetti A homey breakfast room by day, at night Grace's Garret was transformed into a lively dinner spot specializing in spaghetti, red wine, and intimacy. *(Courtesy of The New-York Historical Society, N.Y.C.)*

139. MacDougal Alley soirée from act two of *Oh, Lady! Lady!* P. G. Wodehouse and Jerome Kern's musical *Oh, Lady! Lady!* at the Princess Theater promoted the view of Greenwich Village as a center of freewheeling, after-hours entertainment. This scene depicts the predawn party finale on the roof garden of Willoughby Finch's studio in Waverly Mews. Authentic as the scene may have played on Broadway, at least one reviewer complained, "Why locate a scene in Greenwich Village . . . and then have everybody look, dress, act, and talk like a Mineola weekend?" *(Museum of the City of New York)*

140. *The "Movey" Troupe* By the mid-teens, the new motion picture industry, which had passed its infancy just north of the Village in Union Square, started dispatching film crews to Greenwich Village to put its pleasant background scenery and offbeat reputation to use. John Sloan's etching depicts an early movie troupe on location in "Bohemia." (*Kraushaar Galleries, New York City*)

Bohemia as Burlesque

Around 1916 both Broadway and New York's fledgling film industry began to turn commercial eyes on the escapades of the Village counterculture. The corralling of local bohemian gossip and personalities into scripts intended for public consumption was a practice borrowed from the Provincetown Players, the Washington Square Players, and other acting companies with amateur roots in the prewar Village. Missing from this newer genre of slapstick movies and playhouse farces, however, were the elements of self-therapy and group intimacy characteristic of these home-grown productions. What prompted the interest of midtown theater managers and motion picture producers was the bottom line: As the tide of Greenwich Village's notoriety rose, bohemianism added up to good business.

141. Scene from *Toby's Bow* Scripts for the rash of slapstick comedies about Village bohemianism that began to appear on screen after 1915 generally revolved around two main themes: the ingenue who strays into the debauched vortex of bohemia, and the high jinks hatched in Village cafés. *Toby's Bow*, released in 1919, featured a cast of Village "extras" in a scene dramatizing the diversions of a typical Village drinking den. *(The Schlesinger Library, Radcliffe College)*

Atmospheric Eateries

Hungry strollers had two principal options for dining in "bohemian" surroundings in Greenwich Village: tiny tearooms that exuded personality or restaurants serving heartier fare that were tucked into back parlors or submerged in basements. Both types of eating establishments specialized in modestly priced meals dished up in a theatrical atmosphere. Of the forty-five or so tearooms vying for tourist business by 1920, most had whimsical names and featured decor that ranged from the homespun colonial look to the menacingly macabre. Village bistros also cashed in on mood. Accounts of the period describe their vividly discordant color schemes and the bits of odd crockery and native handicrafts decorating them. A picnic spirit generally prevailed, with food frequently served "family style" and patrons encouraged to share their talents with fellow diners, whether through poetry recitals, dream interpretations, or embellishing the premises with artistic graffiti.

• • • •

WHEN LIFE IS VERY STRENUOUS AND SPIRITS ARE WAY DOWN
YOU'D BETTER GO TO POLLYS IN LITTLE GREENWICH TOWN
FOR THERE THE CLANS ARE GATHERED - ITS THERE YOU'LL FIND 'EM ALL
THE ARTISTS AND THE WRITERS RANGED ALONG THE WALL.
MISS POLLY TAKES THE MONEY AND MIKE SAYS HE JUST CAN'T
WAIT ANY FASTER ON THE FOLKS IN POLLY'S RES TAU-RANT.
J.T.B.

GREENWICH VILLAGE — NEW YORK

142. Interior of Polly Holladay's restaurant Owned by anarchist Polly Holladay, formerly of Evanston, Illinois, this cozy canteen was staffed by radicals and catered to bohemian customers with its cheap meals and easy credit. The restaurant also hosted a number of spillover activities for the Liberal Club, including exhibitions of "revolutionary art," dances, and the occasional poker game. *(Museum of the City of New York)*

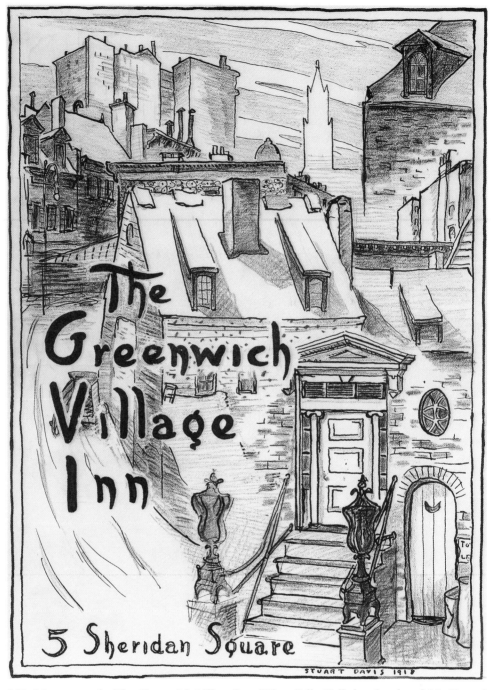

The Greenwich Village Inn

5 Sheridan Square

STUART DAVIS 1918

143. Menu cover for The Greenwich Village Inn When Polly Holladay abandoned MacDougal Street to move her operation to more spacious quarters, she hired Stuart Davis to paint the sign for her new establishment, The Greenwich Village Inn. Advertisements announcing its opening touted the inn as "an unspoiled rendezvous where spontaneous entertainment frequently occurs among a talented and distinguished patronage." *(Collection of Earl Davis)*

144. Edith Unger serving tea in the Mad Hatter By the late teens the area around Sheridan Square had attracted a galaxy of gaily colored tearooms with fey names and an intentionally jumbled decor. The Mad Hatter, which opened in 1916 on West Fourth Street, featured an "Alice in Wonderland" theme chosen by Edith Unger, the well-to-do sculptress who was its proprietor. *(Alexander Alland, Sr., Collection)*

145. The Crumperie, 6½ Sheridan Square Furnished with braided rugs, weatherbeaten antiques, and assorted chipped teacups, the Crumperie was a typically itinerant Village tearoom, shuttling back and forth between a half dozen different addresses. From the outset this particular establishment had discouraged the radical element from lingering over its famous crumpets, gearing its trade instead to an artistic and theatrical clientele, many drawn from the Greenwich Village Theatre nearby. *(Museum of the City of New York)*

• • • •

146. *The Bandit's Cave* John Sloan's engraving bore out the warning conveyed in one Greenwich Village guidebook: "If you stumble and fall in the Village you are sure to land in a restaurant." *(Kraushaar Galleries, New York City)*

147. **Speako de Luxe** Before repeal in 1933, Barney Gallant mounted his most audacious coup—the establishment of the exclusive "Speako de Luxe" in a town house on Washington Square North. A last bastion of patrician New York, this border of the Square had long resisted the onslaught of commerce and tourism before succumbing to Gallant's campaign to serve expensive cocktails to thirsty members of the smart set. *(Museum of the City of New York)*

GREENWICH VILLAGE NIGHTLIFE 1910–1950

Lewis Erenberg

Way down South in Greenwich Village
  Where the spinsters come for thrillage,
Where they speak of 'soul relations,'
  With the sordid Slavic nations,
'Neath the guise of feminism,
  Dodging social ostracism,
They get away with much
  In Washington Square.

—BOBBY EDWARDS, 1920

In her guide to Greenwich Village, Anna Alice Chapin highlighted the growing popular view of Village restaurants and tearooms.[1] Part of the untrammeled bohemianism of the area below Fourteenth Street, the Village's eating places represented the "play spirit" liberated from everyday conventions and inhibitions and dedicated in part to a concept of freer living. Unfortunately Chapin was writing for tourists, and they came in droves, a fact confirmed by Bobby Edwards's poem.[2] By 1920 Village tearooms and restaurants, once the center for an intellectual bohemianism, were seen by New Yorkers in general as symbols of free love and exotic experience in an area removed from midtown

• • • •
357

conventions. Starting around World War I and increasing dramatically in the 1920s, the Village's bohemian associations turned the area into a metropolitan nightlife amusement zone that merchandised the "atmosphere" of rebellion and the Village itself. The commercialization of Village nightlife in turn helped to erase the differences between the area and the rest of New York City. [3]

The linkage between nightlife, Greenwich Village, and unconventional behavior was not accidental. As part of the intellectual, political, and social rebellion against the bourgeois conventions in American society, a number of artists and intellectuals flocked to Greenwich Village during the second decade of this century. They were bent on pursuing a different mode of life than many of them had experienced in the smaller cities and towns of the interior. For them, the Village possessed a European charm, replete with crooked streets, human-scaled buildings, and a foreign flavor that derived from the Italians of the neighborhood. Seeking a way out of genteel conventions and traditional models of success, the bohemians enjoyed living in and among the lower classes. They also enjoyed the anonymity that the furnished rooms of the area provided them.

Much of the social life of the early Villagers was conducted in local public restaurants and tearooms, many of the latter created and frequented by the rebels in search of nonbourgeois forms of behavior. As Caroline Ware described them in *Greenwich Village*, the tearooms were business ventures that also filled social functions. Unlike the cabarets that followed in the 1920s, the tearooms were run by Villagers who identified with the bohemian way of life and the patrons they served. As such, the rooms offered places where the intellectuals and artists of the area could meet to discuss such issues as socialism, anarchism, and feminism as well as the quest for a new style of sexual relations that would combine intellectual and sexual intimacy. [4] Down in gaily decorated semipublic basements, intellectuals, theatrical folk, artists, and writers gathered to discuss politics and art and to pursue their social and sexual lives. Many of these institutions were run by women who saw in the serving of food the chance to combine a traditional woman's function with intellectual and artistic expression. In the early days, then, the tearooms were part of a larger personal, social, and political rebellion.

These meeting grounds were relatively inexpensive and informal, and they featured a Village "atmosphere" that highlighted the departure from the everyday. As such names as the Purple Pup and the Blue Horse (the latter at 6 Christopher Street) denote, garish colors played an important role in the early decor. The gaily painted doorways and interiors suggested heightened experience as opposed to the drab colors associated with puritan interiors. Anna Alice Chapin noted that the patrons of the tearooms adorned themselves in arty shades of magenta and red. Indeed, offbeat smocks and batiks for women not only expressed life, their very simplicity also contributed to the demystification of the female body. Young women also favored bobbed hair and smoked, while young males wore rolled collars and slouch hats or went hatless entirely.

Many of the tearooms emphasized that they were environments quite out of the ordinary. Romany Marie's Rumanian Tavern, for example, offered a hint of a foreign land, while the Pirate's Den on Christopher Street recreated the riggings, fittings, and buccaneer imagery of a pirate's ship. At Toby's Tavern, an upstairs room, the major feature was a coffin topped by a candle, suggesting an offbeat artist's garret. The Mad Hatter (150 West Fourth Street), opened by wealthy sculptress Edith Unger as a pastime in 1915, was a brightly colored basement that appeared Carrollian in its decor. Above the entrance, scrawled backward, were the words "Down the Rabbit Hole." Presumably patrons followed Alice down to a Wonderland quite different than what existed at street level. One commentator noted the presence of a young man with a manuscript and a young girl with a monkey on her shoulder, while other patrons played bridge, engaged in chess games, or just talked.

The evolution of Paula Holladay's restaurant ventures shows us some of the deeper links between the quest for personal experience and political and intellectual life in the early Village. Polly Holladay, along with her brother Louis, migrated from Evanston, Illinois, to the Village. An anarchist, she opened Polly's Restaurant in the basement of the Liberal Club about 1913. Tied to one of the most important political and artistic meeting grounds, her gaily decorated restaurant quickly gained a reputation as a homey place that featured simple food cooked by Polly herself and easy credit for fellow bohemians. Polly was accepted in artistic circles, argued poet Harry Kemp, because "in the creation of her unique little restaurant she had achieved art; she had hit upon her right form of expression."[5] The most fun-loving of the Village artists, intellectuals, and political thinkers ate at Polly's before ascending the stairs for one-act plays, poetry readings, or political and cultural arguments at the Liberal Club. Those who remained behind played poker at a table in the kitchen.

Polly was deeply involved in the political, intellectual, and sexual life of bohemia. One of her waiters, for example, Hippolyte Havel, was her acknowledged lover in a circle that made public its love affairs. Havel was also an anarchist who had lived with Emma Goldman and had contributed articles to *Mother Earth*. While Polly's political and intellectual connections soon made the restaurant a center for intellectuals and writers from across the city, it did not live by food alone. It also offered a place for patrons to indulge in the new ragtime dances sweeping New York. Lawrence Langner, a patent attorney with theatrical interests, recalled that as he clutched his partner in a tight embrace and swayed to the new syncopated rhythms, he felt that he was "doing something for the progress of humanity."[6] The penchant for sexual experimentation, meanwhile, was exercised in informal environments very different from the Broadway cabarets where the new dancing and personal adventure were enshrouded in luxury and status. At Polly's the belief was that challenges to sexual repressions would also undermine capitalist civilization.

For reasons that are not entirely clear, by 1916 Holladay had broken with the Liberal Club and moved her operations to Sheridan Square under the name Greenwich Village Inn. Her new partner was local entrepreneur Barney Gallant. The split may have derived from the equally explosive political or sexual conflicts in which Villagers embroiled themselves. Whatever the cause, Polly remained friendly with the major figures in the Village and drew on her many contacts with celebrities to attract a large tourist business. The Greenwich Village Inn became a Village fixture that lasted into the early 1930s. It was known as a dance place patronized by uptowners and tourists seeking real "bohemian atmosphere" and a chance to see the famous names that Barney Gallant now used as part of a citywide marketing strategy. Village nightlife was about to change from one that combined bohemian and intellectual life to one that fully exploited bohemian imagery.

As "outsiders" began to pursue the new ways of relating between the sexes, they too sought experiences that heightened personal impulse. As a result people from uptown and other boroughs, seeking release from social and sexual constraints, turned to Greenwich Village as a place where they could realize their personal desires. At first they were attracted to the tearooms, which had already proved capable of offering stereotyped settings for Village life. The guidebooks of Chapin and others advanced the exotic and unconventional image of the tearooms, and soon the area was inundated by urbanites and suburbanites seeking to meet "real" artists and bohemians. The fascination with artists apparently living without restraint in their personal lives and seemingly unhampered by the need to work was also advanced by the press, as the tabloids in the early 1920s played up the scandalous goings-on in Village studio parties.

While the tearooms maintained links to their intellectual and artistic past it was the cabarets that most aggressively marketed the personal experiences available in the Village during the early 1920s. Prohibition likewise played an important role in the development of Village nightlife. The end to legal liquor sales forced Broadway cabaret owners to close their doors. Café entrepreneurs sought relatively out-of-the-way parts of the city in which to sell liquor and entertainment. As an Italian neighborhood, the Village had access to a ready supply of homemade red wine, and it quickly became known as a good place to get a drink. As a result many cabarets and speakeasies opened in the Village. Prohibition also helped remove personal impulses from social regulation. Drinking became an act of defying authority, and as such it appealed to the young. Also, enjoying a drink along with a dance and entertainment became an extension of one's personal rights that the society tried to deny. With its bohemian background, the Village was the perfect spot to merchandise the concept of free expression of personal desires on all levels.

The cabarets went farther in commercializing the most exotic aspects of the Village. Unlike the owners of the tearooms, most of the cabaret proprietors were themselves outsiders and knew what other "slummers" wanted. As the Sunshine Alley Inn advertised in the *Greenwich Villager*, it was "Where Cosmopolitan and Bohemian Meet." The cabarets offered outsiders, college students, and tourists places of "real life," sexual meeting grounds, and what Caroline Ware called "conventional unconventionality."

Barney Gallant's Club Gallant on West Third Street exemplified the shift in nightlife. Initially Gallant involved himself with the Greenwich Village Inn. Because of the large influx of visitors, he opened another cabaret, Club Gallant, in 1923. *Variety* called it an "art" cabaret when it debuted and the forerunner of New York's newest fad. Apparently its small stage and sophisticated artistic entertainment earned it that accolade. Future Senator George Murphy and his dance partner performed "clean cut" dances for patrons, who paid a two-dollar cover charge. Unlike the Village Inn, Club Gallant featured velvet carpets and elegant surroundings. Himself a celebrity, Gallant used his contacts with other well-known city figures, such as Mayor Jimmy Walker, newspaperman Heywood Broun, and cartoonist Peter Arno, to attract a metropolitan patronage. In 1926 *Variety* noted that there were many such clubs. The Caravan, the Club Chalet, Peacock Club, Club Arthur, Green Fan, Club Marathon, and fifteen others were high- and medium-priced cafes. Many featured either flappers or B-girls who acted as "hostesses."[7]

In large part Village nightlife catered to people who wanted excitement, novelty, personal exploration, and freedom in leisure but respectability in their everyday lives. As a consequence the Village became an area of fantasy, where uptowners could easily buy an experience, where they could vicariously partake of an imaginary world removed from rational conventions. The nightlife of the 1920s did not seek to challenge the underlying assumptions of American society; it only sought to offer experimentation within its forms.

The split between personal experience and public identities occurred most notably in the cabarets that featured "atmospheric" Village settings, rather than amid Broadway's nudity and glitter. Don Dickerman's Pirate's Den easily evolved from a tearoom into a nightclub. The den expanded even further its fantasy environment of lawless pleasure. Painter N. C. Wyeth and a friend visited the den in 1926, and he described it in a letter to his father. "We entered by a small but heavily bolted oaken door—a pirate,

• • • •

148. Don Dickerman   Owner of three Village "dives," Don Dickerman was by the nature of his trade a public personality. The proprietor kept in character with the themes of his establishments. Guests descending the gangplank to the Pirate's Den on Christopher Street, for example, were greeted by the swashbuckling Pirate King himself. *(The Schlesinger Library, Radcliffe College)*

• • • •

6'6" in great coat, cocked hat, heavily belted, bristling with flintlock pistols and a cutlass at his side, let us in." The fun only began there. "We crept along a narrow hallway dimly lighted by flickering candles in ships' lanterns. At the tunneling end of passage came the sound of a brawl, yells and clashing steel. . . . Through the dim light we could make out the kaleidoscope movement of figures, the flash of metal and an occasional report of a pistol." After submerging themselves in this tunnel, "we entered through this bedlam, so it is that all patrons are received. As we groped our way up twisting stairways, along ships' balconys [*sic*], captains' walks, and such-like paths, we reached a large room stacked with guns, racks of cutlasses and hundreds of pistols. Ropes, tackle of all description, boarding irons, culverines, brass cannon, cages of parrots and monkeys—all lighted with ships' lanterns!"[8]

Other clubs merchandised the unusual in other ways. *The New Yorker* reported that one club was designed as a jail, with the patrons being served inside a cell, by waiters in convict stripes. Meyer Horowitz's Nut Club featured topsy-turvy decorations, slapstick comedians, and a general air of an irrational hurly-burly. At Don Dickerman's County Fair one could ride an old-fashioned bicycle. Horowitz's Village Barn also offered rural imagery, strange colors, and barn dancing to commercial country orchestras. As part of their role in a nightlife catering to the entire metropolis, the Barn and the Nut Club used radio to broadcast their entertainment throughout the city.

Usually located along Third, Fourth, and Christopher streets and Sheridan Square, these cafés offered a full range of heterosexual delights at less-expensive prices than their uptown competitors. Geared more to college students and other young people, Village cabarets were usually more wholesome than the "chorus-girl–sugar-daddy" glitter centers of Broadway and midtown. The cabarets provided young people with places to meet, go on dates, dance, or just be entertained in informal surroundings. The key to the café experience was the floor show, which took place either on a small platform or on the dance floor. Situated amid the diners and drinkers, entertainers performed at eye level, wandering among the tables. Diners, meanwhile, had the option of dancing on the same floor. The intermixing of boundaries between performer and audience in a drinking atmosphere fostered a modicum of audience self-expression.[9]

John Dos Passos captured some of the false exoticism of Village spots in *The Big Money*. His protagonist, Charley Anderson, goes to a Village speakeasy where he meets Bobbie. Dos Passos highlights the anonymous nature of urban life, for Bobbie mistakes Charley for a famous celebrity. On the way to a cabaret, they pass tenements and "crowded little Italian stores." Prohibition is a fact of life: "The girl rang at a basement door." Dos Passos has Bobbie say that she'll pay half: "I believe in sexual equality, don't you?" A basement speakeasy functions as the cabaret. To get in Charley and

Bobbie give the proper password through a peephole to "a sleek-looking young man in a brown suit." They sit at a table next to the dance floor in "the stuffy little cabaret hot from the spotlights and the cigarettesmoke [*sic*] and the crowded dancers." After drinks and a bite to eat, she drags him to the floor: "They danced. The girl rubbed close to him till he could feel her little round breasts through the Bulgarian blouse." After the cabaret ritual that includes drinking, dancing, and smoking, all associated with new kinds of expressive behaviors open to young women, she proceeds to bed him.

By the mid-1920s the heyday of Village nightlife had passed. As *Variety* declared, it had become "the Boobery's Gehenna," a commercialized amusement zone. Real bohemians, meanwhile, withdrew from the tearooms and cabarets to private parties behind closed doors. According to Malcolm Cowley's *Exile's Return*, artists and intellectuals abandoned the Coney Island atmosphere for farms in Connecticut. When midtowners and out-of-towners wanted real life after 1926, they went uptown to Harlem, which appeared totally uninhibited and capable of releasing repressed middle-class whites from all civilized inhibitions. By 1930, in fact, a club like the Black Cat could abandon all pretense of being part of the Village and instead provided segregated black entertainment similar to Harlem's. The commercialization of "the different" had succeeded in undermining much of what was truly unique about the Village.

Yet the Village did not lose all its distinctiveness. In 1925 *Variety* noted that many "joints" in the Village were catering to the "temperamental" element, with as many as twenty cafés, tearooms, and clubs serving homosexuals.[10] As George Chauncey notes elsewhere in this volume, commercialization helped make the Village the center of gay nightlife in the nation. Moreover, homosexuals were attracted to the Village initially as part of the general bohemian and unconventional subculture of the 1910s. The area's cheap furnished rooms offered privacy, relative anonymity, and minimal supervision to all kinds of unmarried people, including gays. Because of small living spaces, residents tended to socialize in the saloons, cheap restaurants, and tearooms that grew up to serve them in the neighborhood. More important, the region's bohemian reputation attracted homosexuals. The search for new forms of sexual expression encouraged greater tolerance of all behavior, while artistic rebellion included acceptance of different modes of dress and self-presentation. The relative openness thus served as a cover for homosexuals who looked and acted "different." Hence, as part of the "free love" and free expression aspects of the Village, homosexuals helped create bohemia just as they were created by it.

According to Chauncey, homosexuals were present at some of the tearooms and institutions of bohemia before World War I and then, after the war, developed their own spots. For example, many gay men and lesbian women took advantage of the balls at Webster Hall, first given by the Liberal

Club and *The Masses*, to take part in open, costumed nightlife events. By the mid-1920s they presented their own balls at Webster Hall. Commercialization also served to attract gay people throughout the entire metropolitan region. Prohibition helped, too, for the Volstead Act drove all saloons and clubs, including gay ones, behind closed doors. As a result gay cafés could continue in operation by paying off the police like those that catered to heterosexuals.

Gay and lesbian entrepreneurs had created a number of speakeasies, tearooms, and cabarets, and they could draw on a wide patronage for support. In this way the development of gay nightlife also emphasized the search for personal freedom outside the eye of community standards and supervision. Supported by citywide patronage, homosexuals developed such clubs and tearooms as the Flower Pot on Christopher Street, the Red Mask on Charles Street, and Trilby's around the corner. Chauncey notes that "personality clubs" opened in the 1920s, led by Paul and Joe's, which featured female impersonators. The Jungle, at Cornelia Street and Sixth Avenue, advertised a party with female impersonators (Countess and Rosebud), a jazz band, and refreshments. Many gay restaurants, speakeasies, and tearooms were found south and west of Washington Square as far as Sixth Avenue and Sheridan Square. There were also numerous lesbian speakeasies and tearooms in and around MacDougal and Washington Square, among them the Howdy Club, and Eve Adams's Black Rabbit. Gay folks also turned Stewart's Cafeteria and Life Cafeteria, at the corner of Christopher and Sheridan streets, into late-night meeting spots. As they became known as "fairy" spots, the clubs and cafeterias attracted other young women and men looking for companionship. Despite commercialization the Village retained some of its distinctiveness as a center for gay nightlife and a haven for gay people throughout the entire New York region.

The fact that many of the neighborhood's inhabitants were well equipped to operate an illegal alcohol industry also contributed to the important role the Village played in nightlife during the 1920s. This was especially true of the speakeasies that dotted the neighborhood. As Irish saloonkeepers retired with the Volstead Act, local Italians took over, purveying their homemade wine in bars, restaurants, cordial shops, and other spots. Because they were illegal enterprises, the speakeasies all had to pay protection, usually to Democratic politicians. Through the entire dry era, nightlifers were pretty sure of getting a drink in the Village, and this only added to its reputation as a fun zone.

By 1930 the Village's reputation as both a heterosexual and homosexual meeting ground was secure. Yet, its heyday had passed. The sightseeing buses and the commercialization of the bohemian image had made the tearooms and clubs less for bohemians and more for visitors seeking their own brand of personal freedom. In the early 1930s, moreover, Village nightspots also suffered from the Depression, which wiped out nightclubs and other forms of amusement nationwide. Still, the Village had much to contribute to the city's entertainment. Indeed, during the late 1930s and 1940s Barney Josephson's Café Society at 2 Sheridan Square established the first politically oriented nightclub in New York City.

Three things made possible the appearance of a leftist-oriented café in the Village. Repeal of Prohibition played a major role in stimulating the revival of all amusements. In the nightclub business it had the effect of encouraging legitimate businessmen, such as Barney Josephson, to enter an industry that was dominated largely by criminals in the 1920s. The growth of the political left in the 1930s created an audience hospitable to a more populist entertainment policy. Finally the Village retained enough of a bohemian and radical political reputation to make it home to nightclubs that challenged mainstream entertainment and politics. As such, the Village played host to a Popular Front nightclub that attempted to reintegrate personal freedoms and social criticism in ways reminiscent of the pre–World War I tearooms.

The major goal of Café Society was the creation of a racially integrated nightclub where black people would be welcomed in the audience as well as on the stage. Barney Josephson first conceived of the idea of an integrated nightclub after a trip to Harlem's Cotton Club in the early 1930s. As a buyer for his family's shoe business in Trenton, New Jersey, he was taken to the Cotton Club, where he was delighted with the black entertainers and musicians but appalled by the segregated audiences and humiliating jungle-and-plantation atmosphere of the "Aristocrat of Harlem." His interest was heightened by his political beliefs, which at a minimum were in accord with the Popular Front alliance against foreign and domestic fascism. As such, he made his club available for benefits for the Abraham Lincoln Brigade, and in general created the first "progressive" entertainment policy in the café business. Café Society soon became a regular spot for radicals and intellectuals dissatisfied with American society.

The club's name was a sarcastic dig at wealthy Upper East Side café society. The club's decor underscored the theme. In exchange for bar and food credits, struggling WPA artists such as Adolf Dehn, Gregor Duncan, Anton Refregier, William Gropper, and Abe Birnbaum painted murals depicting rich wastrels out with their poodles. Moreover, advertisements for the room emphasized that Café Society was "The wrong place for the right people" and suitable for "Celebs, Debs, and Plebs."[11]

The existence of Café Society demonstrates the effects of leftist and New Deal political attitudes in hitherto unrecognized areas of life during the 1930s and 1940s. Josephson and the café were part of a larger circle involved in a struggle to integrate the music and entertainment businesses. Among the financial backers of Café Society, for example, were "King of Swing"

· · · ·

Benny Goodman, who led the first nationally known racially integrated band, and who also gave money to the Abraham Lincoln Brigade; Willard Alexander, a booker for the powerful band agency, MCA, and a fighter for racial integration; and John Hammond, politically committed and wealthy talent scout and promoter, Village resident, and Goodman's brother-in-law. Hammond wanted an integrated place on principle, and as a spot to bring his black friends—including singer Paul Robeson and actor Canada Lee—without embarrassment. The wealthy young rebel became the club's unofficial musical director because of his many contacts in the jazz and blues worlds, and his desire to find regular bookings for the many acts he brought to New York for his "Spirituals to Swing Concerts" in 1938 and 1939.

Under Josephson's leadership Café Society became the first white-owned integrated nightclub in New York City. Blacks were permitted in the audience as well as on the small stage, and they were presented with dignity. No minstrel or jungle decor marred the proceedings. White patrons unable to refrain from racially insulting epithets were encouraged to leave. Josephson also discouraged racial stereotypes among the performers. He prohibited Lena Horne from singing "When It's Sleepy Time Down South," for instance, and fired Carol Channing when she continued to employ racial caricatures in her act. On the positive side Billie Holiday first achieved renown among the white intelligentsia at the café when she agreed to sing Lewis Allen's "Strange Fruit," a moving account of lynchings in the South. The club also featured integrated bands. Teddy Wilson, Edmond Hall, and Frankie Newton led mixed bands there. Finally the club served as a home for certain authentic blues and folk acts that fit the Popular Front interest in the culture of the "people." Boogie-woogie pianists Albert Ammons, Meade Lux Lewis, and Pete Johnson established a craze for boogie-woogie through starring appearances at Café Society.

The club also featured comedians who criticized the status quo. Master of ceremonies Jack Gilford gained a measure of fame for his spoofs of current movies and his generally irreverent attitude, while comedian Zero Mostel, in his guise of Senator Phineas T. Pellagra, lampooned the South's backward attitude toward segregation, poll taxes, and the CIO. In general the entertainment policy marked a departure from the standard nightclub fare of nude girls, bad liquor, gangsters, and a café society free list. The club showed that a nightclub could be a place for social and political satire, intelligent acts intelligently presented, and an intelligent audience. As a result, the café was frequented by an audience of regulars like Budd Schulberg, Lionel Stander, Paul Robeson, Eleanor Roosevelt, Lillian Hellman, S. J. Perelman, and St. Clair McKelway.[12]

Other club owners in the Village followed in the same path, although their politics were less explicit. Max Gordon's Village Vanguard, for example, presented satirical comedy revues, folk and blues singers, and

· · · ·

integrated jazz jams in the late 1930s. Soon after arriving from Portland, Oregon, to attend Columbia University Law School, Max Gordon began running clubs in Greenwich Village, among them the Village Fair, which he managed in 1932. A confirmed Villager, by 1935 he opened his first Vanguard in a Charles Street basement. His friend, electrician Harry Simon, convinced him to decorate with a mural celebrating a workers' demonstration in Union Square. A year later Max moved to another basement on Seventh Avenue, where he remained through the 1980s.

Drawing on local traditions, the Vanguard initially featured poets who declaimed their work to audiences made up of WPA writers, hustlers, college students from the Bronx and Brooklyn, women on the make, moochers, and tourists. From this informal "Village" café style, the Vanguard evolved into an entertainment room with some social purpose. From 1939 to 1941 Gordon presented Judy Holliday, Betty Comden, Adolph Green, and Alvin Hammer—young, ambitious theater hopefuls with political and social concerns. As the Revuers, they spoofed the bloodthirsty New York press and the selling of scrap from the dismantled "El" to Japan, which would come back in the·form of bullets, and the World's Fair. After leaving for a spell the group reappeared at Gordon's midtown Blue Max in 1943.

After the Revuers departed in 1941, Gordon replaced them with Huddie Ledbetter (Leadbelly) and Josh White, two black folk-blues singers. Along with Café Society, the Vanguard became an early leader in the growing folk music scene. As leftist intellectuals sought the "true" American folk culture, they helped support cafés in the early 1940s that presented such entertainment fare. Leadbelly had rural blues roots, while White was more urban, but together they attracted the folk music crowd, including Woody Guthrie, Pete Seeger, Burl Ives, Richard Dyer-Bennet, Millard Lampel, and the Almanac Singers.

Guthrie was so delighted by Gordon's bill that he sent him a ten-page letter rhapsodizing how they would "make real night club history in New York, and . . . give the Negro people a real honest chance to bring their music and singing before the general public." As he saw it the bill would "open up a whole new field for entertainers of all colors, namely just plain, common, everyday American music." By the end of the decade Gordon presented the Weavers before they were blacklisted by HUAC.[13] The Vanguard also contributed to the integration of the music business by presenting integrated jazz jams on Monday nights starting in the early 1940s. Not until the folk craze died off, however, did Gordon concentrate fully on the jazz policy that placed his room at the forefront of black music in the United States.

For Gordon and Josephson, then, the New Deal and the radical politics of the era had a large impact. Under the influence of the Depression they

• • • •

presented socially conscious entertainment, such as blues, folk music, and pointed satire. While the Village Vanguard continued in the forefront of jazz into the 1980s, Café Society was dead by 1950, a victim of the Red Scare. Josephson's brother Leon, an admitted communist, was called before HUAC in 1948. The resultant publicity and the club's radical connections worked against it and the club was forced to close. The government was not kind to Josephson and many of his entertainers and regular patrons. Barney was investigated by the FBI, as were John Hammond and Benny Goodman. The café's publicist, Ivan Black, was blacklisted, and so too were Mostel, Gilford, and Robeson. While the Red Scare brought Café Society to an end, it did not dampen the principle of racial integration, political and topical humor, and the nightclub as a place of mental stimulation. This sense of social commitment carried on in Josephson's Cookery, which he opened in the 1960s with black blues and jazz performers, and in Art D'Lugoff's Village Gate, which opened in 1955.

Hence, over the course of the twentieth century, Village cafés have helped establish this glorious section of the city as a place where, as part of the urban experience, young and old New Yorkers might breathe more freely at night than they would in the more restricted circumstances of their everyday lives. May the nights be ever glorious!

• • • • •

NOTES

1. "In all the typical Greenwich restaurants you will find the same elusive something, the spirit of the picturesque, the untrammelled, the quaint and charming—in short, the different!" Anna Alice Chapin, *Greenwich Village* (New York: Dodd, Mead, and Company, 1917), 209.
2. Bobby Edwards, *Champion Monographs* (April 6, 1920): 27.
3. This chronological scheme owes much to Caroline Ware's pathbreaking *Greenwich Village, 1920–1930: A Comment on American Civilization in the Post-Wars Years* (1935; reprint, New York: Harper and Row, 1965).
4. Ellen Kay Trimberger, "Feminism, Men, and Modern Love: Greenwich Village, 1900–1925," in *Powers of Desire: The Politics of Sexuality*, ed. Ann Snitow, Christine Stansell, and Sharon Thompson (New York: Monthly Review Press, 1983), 131–152, discusses the desire to combine intellectual and sexual companionship.
5. Harry Kemp, *More Miles: An Autobiographical Novel* (New York: Boni and Liveright, 1926), 357–358, as in Robert E. Humphrey, *Children of Fantasy, The First Rebels of Greenwich Village* (New York: John Wiley & Sons, 1978), 26. Jan Seidler Ramirez has been exceptionally kind in sharing with me some of her information on Polly Holladay.

• • • •

6. Lawrence Langner, *The Magic Curtain* (New York: E. P. Dutton, 1951), 68, as in Humphrey, *Children of Fantasy*, 26.
7. *Variety*, January 5, 1923, p. 9.
8. Betsy Janes Wyeth, ed., *The Wyeths: The Letters of N. C. Wyeth, 1901–1945* (Boston: Gambit, 1971), 717–723. The Hollywood film *Dancing Mothers* used the club as an important setting.
9. For a general discussion of cabarets and floor shows, see Lewis A. Erenberg, *Steppin' Out: New York Nightlife and the Transformation of American Culture, 1890–1930* (1981; reprint, Chicago: University of Chicago Press, 1984).
10. *Variety*, May 6, 1925, p. 19.
11. Peter J. Silvester, *A Left Hand Like God* (New York: Da Capo Press, 1989), 145–160, has pictures of the advertisements and the best description of the boogie-woogie craze fostered by the club.
12. The list of regulars as well as background for the club comes from Helen Lawrenson, "Black and White and Red All Over," *New York*, August 21, 1978, 36–41. Lawrenson, the club's first publicity director, claims the club was founded to raise money for the Communist party.
13. The letter is reprinted in Max Gordon, *Live at the Village Vanguard* (New York: St. Martin's Press, 1980), 45–53.

THE TOURIST TRADE TAKES HOLD

Jan Seidler Ramirez

As a member of New York's underpaid fraternity of newspapermen in the late nineteenth century, James L. Ford often patronized the back-street bistros of Greenwich Village. In these cheap, foreign-run eating houses, Ford and his budget-conscious colleagues could savor one another's company while feasting on four-course meals, *vin compris*, for less than fifty cents. The bargain and bonhomie of dining "à la Bohème," however, remained the privileged secret of Ford's literary set all too briefly. In a short story inspired by a MacDougal Street haunt frequented by his journalistic friends, Ford recounted the fate suffered by the "Garibaldi," the fictitious name assigned to the restaurant, once its modest fare and colorful clientele caught the interest of commercial intruders.

Titled "Bohemia Invaded," Ford's sketch describes the events set in motion by the seating of a new guest, one Walter Etchley, at the table occupied by the Garibaldi's resident corps of creative exiles from the workaday world. A poseur adept in the use of "kettledrum art talk," Etchley is invigorated by the restaurant's novel ambience and proceeds to invite his well-heeled acquaintances to experience this unconventional canteen. Like fleas on a dog the Philistines descend to sample its quirky customers and cuisine. Their reign—marked by the demoralizing of the waiters with large tips, the unfamiliar consumption of champagne, and loud prattling about its eccentric habitués—comes to a halt when a clever Garibaldi veteran unleashes the rumor that the "aboriginals" whom Etchley and his cronies presume to be authentic poets and painters are actually financiers and respectable trades-

. . . .
371

men in disguise. The trespassers quickly vacate the premises to pursue a bohemian adventure elsewhere.[1]

The story's 1895 publication date merits comment because it attests to Greenwich Village's popular identity as a bohemian precinct well before *The Masses* magazine–Mabel Dodge–Liberal Club crowd staked its claim to the community around 1912. Locally, of course, this particular New York neighborhood had long been recognized as a "district of difference," a dubious acclaim rooted in the individualistic geography that had distinguished the Village from the orderly grid of mainstream Manhattan. Its reputation as a closet for mavericks and freethinkers took root with the folklore that flowered around Pfaff's basement saloon during its heyday of operation in the 1850s. That identity was further accentuated by demographic and economic changes that stripped the Village of its fashionable residential cachet later in the nineteenth century, permitting the infiltration of a more indeterminate sort of citizen.

Ford's tale is also noteworthy because it chronicles a cyclical pattern of invasion and corruption that has characterized the historical interpretation of Greenwich Village as the hotbed of American bohemianism. The core of this argument, endlessly retold, is that bohemian culture thrives most purely within itself. Once its unique attributes are exposed for study and imitation by those alien to it, bohemia is devitalized. Like a fragile conservatory specimen whose habitat has been subjected to periodic disturbance, the bohemian colony of Greenwich Village has bloomed, withered, and mutated in direct proportion to its encroachment by outsiders. Its fluctuating health over time—a phenomenon already measurable by the turn of the century—prompted a columnist for *Everybody's Magazine* in 1905 to reflect: "There seems to be something intangible about a genuine Bohemia. As soon as the public puts its finger on it and says 'this is the real thing,' it crumbles away."[2]

The notice that Greenwich Village's anomalous enclave of bohemians began to attract from the early-twentieth-century press and magazine trade unquestionably fanned the public curiosity these same writers cited as hazardous to bohemia's survival. More paradoxically, the inhabitants themselves seemed to court this unwelcome attention.

Although deeply felt ideological issues and political commitments engrossed the radical vanguard who settled in Greenwich Village before World War I, many of its rank and file also reserved time to perform the bohemian roles expected of them with considerable flair. By instinct and training, this generation of Village rebels formed an inkpot and paint-box army. "Inglorious Miltons by the score / and Rodins, one to every floor," bantered John Reed of his fellow recruits at 42 Washington Square, the boardinghouse barracks that served as a makeshift alumni club for Reed and other Ivy League intellectuals who gravitated to the neighborhood in this period.[3]

• • • •

A number of personalities on this bohemian front line made an occupation out of self-biography. Through poems and prose, plays and paintings, they broadcast to the outside world the rude delights of their encounter with Greenwich Village as a bohemian refuge. They celebrated its backwater charm, extolled its dirt-cheap amenities, and chronicled the madcap adventures that its tolerant atmosphere allowed. The artists among them commemorated this calendar of activities while documenting the neighborhood's genteel decrepitude. These bulletins from the front did much to fuel interest in the district's rollicking subculture. The sheer quantity of this confessional outpouring, it should be added, indicates that there was nothing reclusive or anonymous about Greenwich Village bohemianism. From the outset its conscripts carried on a running dialogue with the bourgeois press and art public, who, inevitably enough, developed a taste for their insider communiqués.

Hippolyte Havel, a Village anarchist better known as the contentious cook and general factotum of Polly's, a local restaurant catering to the radical fringe, advanced a theory that Greenwich Village was not a place but a concept. "Greenwich Village has no geographical borders," he wrote in an issue of the short-lived fortnightly *Greenwich Village* in 1915. It was, he insisted, a "spiritual zone of mind."[4] Despite the insight of Havel's claim, his map-conversant contemporaries knew the Village as a discrete territorial entity bounded by Fourteenth Street, Houston Street, Fourth Avenue, and the Hudson River. For just as Havel was proposing the geographical inconsequence of Greenwich Village, the neighborhood was gaining national publicity as America's Latin Quarter. Versed in the mythology of bohemianism that now clung to the Village like ivy to a wall, sightseers began to throng the district, eager to explore its maze of crooked streets and ogle its idiosyncratic populace.

The precise inception date of this tourist invasion may be arguable, inasmuch as Greenwich Village as early as 1800 had drawn day-trippers, many wishing to inspect the Newgate Prison, a progressive penal facility at the foot of Christopher Street where inmate uprisings erupted from time to time. However, its popular discovery as a bohemian quarter has generally been fixed around 1915, when the neighborhood and its natives burst into bloom as a favorite subject for Sunday magazine spreads. In the Village, promised correspondents of the widely read periodicals of the day, one could depend on seeing "ladies with short hair and long fingernails, and men with long hair and short bank accounts." Full-page photo features in newspapers like the *Sun* and magazines like *McCall's* and *Vanity Fair* helped to prime visitors for the encounter by picturing some of the neighborhood's notable nonconformists—few of whom seem to have shied from the camera—anchored at their customary moorings. As one Villager quipped of this tourist onslaught: "Snoop, snoop in cellar and coop / the Slummers have

• • • •

373

come to the Square / To see the nuts, who live in huts / and at them rudely stare."[5]

The majority of Village bohemians, valuing their autonomy from the scrambling metropolis that hemmed them in, deplored the disruption posed by these curiosity seekers. Their letters and diaries of the period bristle with indignation at the carnival atmosphere that had permeated the quarter. Many expressed dismay at finding their ideals, pastimes, and hideaways suddenly hawked as commodities to the very materialistic masses they had come to Greenwich Village to avoid. But there was also a conspicuous minority of Villagers—a term applied to the area's colorful bohemian occupants rather than to the numerically predominant immigrant and working-class residents also living there—who were only too willing to collaborate with the "enemy." And they were hardly alone in this activity.

Realtors and restaurateurs, merchants and moviemakers, bus lines and theater companies were all among those who recognized the profit potential lying in the district's spiraling fame as America's Left Bank. Seizing the opportunity to capitalize on its renown as a mischievously picturesque precinct, they proceeded to exploit the notion of nonconformity that had set Village culture apart from the conventions of midtown. The transformation in community mood and outlook resulting from this marketing initiative opened a chapter in the neighborhood's history sometimes tagged "Greenwich Thrillage."

Neither the first nor the last chapter in the saga of the farming of Village bohemianism as a cash crop, this particular episode, which spanned from the middle teens to the late twenties, was singularly inventive in its far-ranging applications. Although not interrupting the flow of innovative work produced by the community's best minds and talents, the frenetic commercialism of this fifteen-year period often obscured their achievements.

The metamorphosis of Greenwich Village into America's capital of unorthodox entertainment coincided with the escalation of World War I abroad. At a fundamental level the diversions manufactured by the Village supplied welcome if ephemeral relief to a country sobered by the prospect of entry into international conflict. Initially Washington Square emerged as the epicenter of this nascent tourist industry. Apart from its renown as the symbolic heart of Greenwich Village, the Square also served as the terminal station for the Fifth Avenue Coach Company, a fact of no small consequence.

The company's distinctive double-decker buses, introduced onto this heavily traveled line in 1907, discharged their uptown passengers at a stop across from the southern border of Washington Square before turning around to head north up Fifth Avenue on a fresh run. Since this exiting point was where shoppers and excursionists made first contact with the Village, and where the coach drivers also lingered on their layovers, entrepreneurs targeted the Square's southern edge as the logical testing ground for pitching an assortment of bohemian products and experiences to the curious public. Evidently the Fifth Avenue Coach Company conspired in the experiment, for by 1918 a regular column called "Bohemian Excursions" had been incorporated into *From a Fifth Avenue Bus*, the complimentary magazine the line distributed to an annual ridership numbering over one million. Presumably for a small fee, the magazine endorsed and gave directions to a selection of Village establishments of bohemian persuasion, including some tearooms it touted as "mad dens of iniquitous vice."[6]

The flagship in this maiden fleet of tourist taps was Bruno's Garret, which beckoned at 58 Washington Square South. It warrants special discussion as a landmark because it anticipated so many of the stageworthy trends that became synonymous with "Greenwich Thrillage."

In full operational swing by May 1915, the Garret was a factory of simultaneous creative enterprise, fulfilling the functions of a lecture hall, art gallery, talent agency, press office, and printing house. In this last role the Garret turned out a succession of small-format publications underwritten by its versatile proprietor, Guido Bruno, most of which bore some version of his name and allusion to the Garret's locale on the masthead.[7]

The Garret conglomerate occupied a suite of rooms above the "Oasis of Washington Square," an Italian soda fountain that advertised a progressive policy of selling cigarettes to women. ("No Criticism, No Hard Looks," the store assured its female customers.) Both businesses were garrisoned in a rickety frame dwelling on the east corner of Thompson Street with a colorful pedigree. Among the former tenants of this old roadhouse had been the official Village gravedigger, Daniel Magie, whose residency dated to the era when the Square had served as a municipal gallows and potter's burial ground.

Although modeled after the Left Bank art lairs immortalized in the nineteenth-century tales of Henri Murger, the setting of Bruno's loft was neither discreet nor difficult to find. To ensure that busloads of prospective patrons wouldn't overlook it, boldly lettered signs were posted on the building's exterior proclaiming the Garret's identity and mission: "To get it written / to get it spoken / to get it down at any cost / at any hazard / it is for this only / that we are here." Bruno's atelier quickly assumed the role of Village orientation center, distributing information that would steer tourists to the neighborhood's bohemian attractions. The local boosterism it incarnated earned Guido Bruno a reputation as "the Mayor of Greenwich Village," a title the contemporary press subsequently bestowed on a string of Village hucksters, thereby erasing its honorific connotations.

Billed by Bruno as a "First Aid Station for Struggling Genius," the Garret also doubled as a clearinghouse for local talent that fell outside traditional promotional molds. Walk-in guests were offered an eclectic menu of poetry readings, lectures, and art exhibits of deliberately offbeat flavor. "The Nude in American Bookplates" and thumbtacked installations of picture post-cards, for example, were typical gallery fare. Though admission to these various entertainments was free, the Garret brimmed with opportunities to subscribe to the literary chapbooks and neighborhood news gazettes that were Bruno's bread and butter. In addition passes were issued to current features at the nearby Thimble Theatre—a satellite venture managed by Bruno in partnership with Charles Edison, the inventor's son—which staged experimental plays and concerts of music by neglected American composers.

During its meteoric existence, which lasted from mid-1914 until November 1916, the Garret surfaced repeatedly as the target of sensationalist gossip. It was rumored to be a front for the seduction of young girls, a venue for obscene art displays, and a printshop for smut. Although at best a shred of truth underlay these allegations, they increased traffic through the Garret and were consequently braved by its owner with a businessman's mettle.

Bruno's performance as majordomo clearly contributed to this controversy. Onlookers recall his ostentatious mode of dress, featuring a pinky ring, brocaded waistcoat, and emerald-green fedora, and his self-important locutions uttered in an indefinable foreign accent. Bruno's arrival in the Village in 1914 was also a matter of mystery. Although he dodged questions about his background with the cryptic reply, "I, Bruno, have given birth to myself," his real biography reveals him to have been a former hospital morgue attendant and happily married family man who commuted to work from Yonkers. "Guido Bruno," it further emerged, was an alias for Curt Josef Kisch.

Critics were quick to excoriate the flamboyant Garret host for this falsity of facade, branding him the "Superb Pretender" and "Czar of Charlatanism." But hindsight shows Guido Bruno to have been an astute talent broker who provided formative opportunities for expression to a number of struggling Village artists and writers—Djuna Barnes, Alfred Kreymborg, and Hart Crane among them. Interestingly, although Curt Kisch aspired to pass as a Greenwich Village native, he was actually born and raised in a village north of Prague. Hence by curious accident of nationality, "Bruno" was a *genuine* Bohemian.

The operations of the Garret were suspended first by a fire that devastated much of the property in 1916 and then by a legal imbroglio that erupted over Bruno's publication of a booklet (about a prostitute and her pickup) that authorities classified as indecent. After the beleaguered Bruno relinquished his premises, the Garret passed into the hands of Grace Godwin, a young single mother who remodeled it into a cozy if shabby tearoom and spaghetti house.

Grace Godwin catered to locals with her tasty, inexpensive *table d'hôte* and good-natured service. But she also enlisted her regulars, as well as her own children, as bait to lure in a more lucrative tourist clientele. Word soon spread that at Grace's Garret one could observe aspiring Village painters scratching graffiti onto the restaurant walls, or rub elbows with impoverished poets and budding Bolsheviks. The philosophically inclined proprietress made a practice of engaging customers in "soul chats" while inveigling them to purchase the painted cigarette cases that her cherubic daughter Nancy peddled from table to table. The drama of dining was the house special at Grace's.

The Garret was the most visible of the prewar Village ventures to package bohemian atmosphere as a profit-making business. Others materialized in short order, in a variety of forms. One important testament to the Village's bustling tourist trade was the surge in guidebooks and maps dedicated to the bohemian history, past and present, of New York's "Latin Quarter." Anna Alice Chapin's *Greenwich Village* (1917) and Egmont Arens's *The Little Book of Greenwich Village* (1918) set the precedent for this genre. Souvenir albums of Village views had also appeared by 1918, two pioneering specimens being Arthur Moss's *Greenwich Village by its Artists* and Bernhardt

149. Grace Godwin in her Garret   Grace Godwin, Bruno's attractive young successor, was a single mother who launched a restaurant venture in the Garret as a means of supporting her four children. *(Courtesy of The New-York Historical Society, N.Y.C.)*

• • • •

Wall's *Greenwich Village: Types, Tenements & Temples*. Wall's etchings, which included sketches of local studio and restaurant interiors, were the offshoot of a career devoted in part to postcard designs. His prolific output had gained him recognition as New York's "Postcard King" in addition to a one-man show at Bruno's Garret in 1916.

Picture postcards evoking the bohemian ambience of Greenwich Village developed as a specialty item of this souvenir trade. Jessie Tarbox Beals, a photojournalist who settled in the Village in 1917, was the source of the most memorable of these images. Recognizing the public's hunger for mementoes of their excursions through bohemia, Beals produced a series of postcard vignettes that encompassed everything from moody nocturnes of Washington Square to whimsical mug shots of the quarter's celebrated cranks. Rhymed captions often accompanied the cards. A shrewd retailer as well as a perceptive photographer, Beals sold her copyrighted pictures through a Sheridan Square gallery and tearoom she managed, where short-cake was dispensed along with postage stamps.

Another facet of the campaign to bolster the Village's identity as a caldron of creative rebellion was the launching of a historic marker program in the early 1920s. Conceived by the newly formed Greenwich Village Historical Society, this scheme was intended to draw public attention to local shrines associated with the cause of defiant genius over the years. The putative homes of Thomas Paine and Edgar Allan Poe, two venerable figures connected with the Village in this context, were so consecrated, as was the famous House of Genius at 61 Washington Square South. Although its past was actually quite recent, this shabby rooming house—run by the matriarchal Katarina Blanchard—won landmark status because of its illustrious roster of bohemian boarders, who had included writers Stephen Crane, Theodore Dreiser, and Frank Norris and poet Alan Seeger.

By the late teens special sightseeing tours of "Manhattan's Montmartre" began to be scheduled. Greeting those who signed on for the adventure was a newly minted force of native guides eager to offer their navigational expertise. Information about guide availability was advertised through handbills and local publications emphasizing Village gossip and services, like *The Quill*, *The Ink-Pot*, and *The Spectator*. Typical of these notices was the one placed by "Mademoiselle de Maupassant" in a September 1917 issue of *The Quill*, in which she consented to "pilot your footsteps through our byways and towpaths" for twenty-five cents an hour per person.

If frequency of mention is an accurate index of popularity, then Adele Kennedy seems to have won nomination as the most proficient Village tour conductor. Her walks inspired numerous compliments, as did her uniform of smudged artist's smock, tam-o'-shanter, and open-toed sandals, weather permitting. Like many of her fellow guides, Kennedy—who evidently moonlighted as a tearoom hostess—deliberately maneuvered her clients into local craft shops and bistros owned by friends.

· · · ·

Select members of the Village art colony were soon volunteering their studios for duty on the tour circuit. Although the extent of the practice was probably greatly exaggerated, reports circulated repeatedly of painters and sculptors who charged visitors admission to peer at their works in progress—usually something in the cubist or futurist vein. Apparently some fulfilled expectations by stationing minimally clad models in their studios and by keeping their couches in a state of provocative disarray.

One of the more bizarre of these atelier installations was the "Soul Light Shrine," the remunerative ruse of a Village junk-shop owner named Merton Clivette, who had once studied painting in Paris. (Clivette was only half of a pair of neighborhood celebrities; his wife, Catherine Parker Clivette, was instrumental in founding the Greenwich Village Historical Society.) For a quarter, visitors could descend into Clivette's pitch-black cellar on West Fourth Street to see an eerie mural executed in a rudimentary form of Day-Glo paint. "Thrilling as is this alleged incandescence of pigment," confessed a reporter for *The Ladies' Home Journal* after inspecting the Shrine, "my own soul was strangely unaffected."[8]

A free—and more legitimate—studio experience could be found at Nickolas Muray's, the Hungarian-born photographer known for his celebrity portraits. On Wednesday evenings Muray hosted open-invitation parties that invariably drew a cross-section of theatrical and artistic personalities to his studio at 129 MacDougal Street. Those dropping by these dimly lit and widely publicized soirées were treated to food, drink, and stimulating conversation. A highlight of his studio mixers were the fencing demonstrations presented by Muray, who twice represented the United States on Olympic fencing teams.

Another invention that tapped into the Village's ripening tourist market was the novelty craft shop specializing in idiosyncratic merchandise and "bohemian" decor. The majority of these emporia of eccentricity were strategically situated near bus depots and main transportation lines, where visitor traffic was thickest.

It is important to qualify this development by first acknowledging the sincere impulse that lay behind much of the handicraft movement anchored in Greenwich Village. Many of the skilled artisans who established shops in the prewar Village approached their work with a high degree of integrity, influenced by the aesthetic ideals and production practices that John Ruskin, William Morris, and other design reformers had advocated. Finely carved wooden toys and studio furniture, intricate hand-tooled embroideries, and vibrant silk batiks were only some of the local products to earn the Village justifiable comparison to an oasis in the desert of American industrialism.

But to a less principled branch of white-collar craftspeople, the temptation to bilk the gullible tourist with money to spend proved irresistible. In tandem with the opening of counterfeit artists' garrets, "oddity cellars" began to mushroom, selling items that were marketed as one-of-a-kind keepsakes indigenous to the bohemian Village. According to period advertisements, a sampling of goods kept in inventory ran the gamut from gypsy beads, batik lampshades, and tin vanity cases to cigar-box ukeleles, "art" cigarettes, and predripped candles socketed in old beer bottles—a ubiquitous Greenwich Village item.

Contemporary descriptions of Village shops dating from 1915 to 1925 suggest the innovative browsing milieu their proprietors created for customers. Many featured boldly painted walls, polychromatic seating furniture, and such exotic appointments as birdcages, incense braziers, and peasant shawls arranged as window shades.

The Village Store, opened by Alice Palmer in 1916 at 60 Washington Square South, is sometimes credited with originating the idea that shopping for unconventional goods should, in itself, be an experience reflective of bohemian values. Conveniently located opposite the bus stop in a basement warmed by a cheerful open hearth, Palmer's mart broke down the traditional barriers between retailer and buyer by abolishing the crass fixture of the sales counter. Visitors (the established jargon of the salesroom was also discarded) were welcomed personally by the owner, who often lounged on a prayer rug in front of the fireplace. Refreshments were served, and complimentary cigarettes were proffered from copper bowls. Although business at the Village Store was transacted with a geniality reminiscent of country trading posts, its bohemian inflection was unmistakable, for the talk prevailing around its hearth was of free love instead of free trade, of Strindberg instead of string beans.

By 1917 a variant on the oddity cellar had appeared in the Village: stores specializing in counterculture couture. The notion driving this merchandising strategy was that if one could dress the part, one might be taken for the person. The Paint-Box Gallery, which occupied an abandoned stable on West Fourth Street, was the model for these bohemian boutiques. Its young owner, Florence Gough, retained the stalls as props on which to drape her line of *outré* attire. An odd lot of preternatural mannequins added a bizarre undercurrent to the shop. Among the competitors that took their cue from the success of the Paint-Box were Linn's Shop, nearby on West Fourth Street; and the aptly named La Frivolité, on West Third. "Over a glass of tea let us discuss blouses becoming to you," summoned another bohemian *modiste*, who managed an establishment called Little Russia on Thompson Street.

All sold clothing that fashion editors dismissed as the wardrobe of frowsy radicals and "overly picturesque persons." Signature articles of apparel, critics observed, included loose-fitting smocks typically dyed in fauvist hues. Popular, too, were hand-embroidered peasant blouses and floppy slouch hats, often covering a bobbed haircut, the coiffure then in vogue with Village women. Painted beads, patterned stockings, and moccasins or sandals were also characteristic accessories. (The latter supposedly exemplified the credo of unfettered expression espoused by bohemians, whose feet, philosophically, couldn't abide the confines of conventional footwear.) Aside from flowing ties, corduroy workshirts, and the occasional beret, bohemian trappings for male Villagers rarely came new off the racks, since the prescribed style for men favored an intentionally threadbare look.

Spokesmen from Ladies' Mile naturally ridiculed the eccentric dress styles emanating from Greenwich Village. But as modern costume history has demonstrated, fashion often percolates from the bottom up. By the twenties even discriminating society matrons could be spotted in bohemian smocks, shawls, and peasant costumes purchased from Bonwit's, striving to achieve what *Vogue* now commended as the "Soulful Artist Look."[9]

With its official connection to the West Side transit system in the fall of 1917, Sheridan Square quickly gained an edge over Washington Square South as the Village's most active tourist hub. As *Vanity Fair* observed in a January 1918 article, "The New Heart of Bohemia," Sheridan Square, remodeled and repeopled, teemed with "artists, decorators, writers of *vers libre*, scene painters, playwrights, bird stick varnishers and smock designers."[10] *The Quill*, a recently launched Village humor magazine, was spurred to locate its operations in the area, and its pages soon abounded with puffs for the arty cafés, gift shops, and tearooms that orbited around the "new" sun of Sheridan Square. Sassy and self-impressed in tone, *The Quill* clearly viewed itself as a major star in this constellation.

By the late teens the culinary capital of bohemia had also shifted to the vicinity of Sheridan Square. Proceeding, like an army, on its stomach, the horde of hungry tourists in Greenwich Village had two principal options for dining cheaply in "authentic" native surroundings: tiny teashops that exuded individual personality or restaurants serving heartier fare, nestled in back parlors or submerged in basements. Fittingly enough eating in the Village often proved to be literally an underground experience. As one contemporary guidebook warned visitors: "If you stumble and fall in the Village you are sure to land in a restaurant."[11]

Both kinds of establishments served modestly priced meals in a theatrical atmosphere. Village tearooms were especially clever in this regard, featuring decorations ranging from the homespun colonial look to the menacingly macabre. The Crumperie on Sheridan Square, furnished with braided rugs and weatherbeaten antiques, epitomized the more conservative teashop mode.

A venture run by Mary Alletta Crump and her aged mother from an annually changing architectural vest pocket in the Sheridan Square neighborhood, the Crumperie took pride in its honor-box system and the grateful poems and drawings that patrons penned in its guest book. The younger

Miss Crump often entertained customers with ukelele concerts and im-promptu spiritual sing-alongs, a repertoire geared to the theatrical clientele the tearoom drew from the newly opened (1917) Greenwich Village Play-house on Sheridan Square. The Crumperie's female management, it should be noted, was standard in Village tearooms of the period. The modest start-up costs—menus were very limited, space requirements were minimal, and rents were commensurately low—slanted the trade toward women. Like social work or teaching, running a teashop was considered an honorable vocation to tide the proprietress over until the right marriage proposal or more profitable employment came her way.

More whimsical in decor and mood was the Mad Hatter on West Fourth Street, over which Edith Unger, a well-to-do sculptress, presided. This base-ment establishment, with its *Alice in Wonderland* motif, is said to have inaugurated the local tearoom trend when it opened late in 1916. After descending "down the Rabbit Hole" to enter it, customers encountered a cozy, candlelit interior with such quizzical wall inscriptions as: "We're all Mad here—I'm Mad, You're Mad, You must be or You wouldn't have come here." The playful drama of the place was perpetuated by Unger's successor, Jimmie Criswell, who traded on her notoriety as a former high school teacher dismissed from service for the flagrant crime of smoking in public, and installed a pet cat named Cocaine on the premises. (Sightseers were also intrigued by the Mad Hatter's celebrity clientele, which on any given night might include the Gish sisters or the chess-playing avant-garde artist Marcel Duchamp.)

Like the Mad Hatter, most Village tearooms catering to tourists had gim-micky names. Some played blatantly to the neighborhood's Latin Quarter allure with catchy titles—La Bohème, the Trilby Waffle Shop, Vagabondia, and the Garret. However, a majority of the forty-five or so tearooms vying for local business by 1920 leaned toward "tinted zoology," a preference re-flected in the nomenclature of such establishments as the Purple Pup, the Black Parrot, the Green Witch, the Blue Mushroom, and the Vermillion Hound. The common denominator among them was their snug sociability, an ambience heightened by such trademark amenities as inglenooks, home cooking, and the mellow glow of candlelight. In the opinion of *The Ink-Pot Magazine*, these intimate tearooms nurtured Village culture by coaxing guests to indulge in extended conversations over "coffee and cake" rather than to "crank up the phonograph or rush madly into a moving-picture melodrama."[12]

Village restaurants also cashed in on mood. Many accounts dating from the period describe their vivid, eye-catching color schemes: street facades washed in Mediterranean hues and interiors painted in apple green, Span-ish yellow, lavender, and, for melodramatic impact, midnight black. Walls functioned as post offices, with broadsides announcing local lectures, costume balls, and political rallies covering them. Bits of odd crockery, bric-a-brac, and native handicrafts were also part of this decorative vernacular. Pictorial stencils often underscored the restaurant's defining theme.

Inside a communal picnic spirit frequently prevailed, with food served "family style" in trenchers on long trestle tables, to which newcomers were invited to pull up a chair. Patrons were expected to share their talents with fellow diners, whether through poetry recitals, dream interpretations, or embellishments of the premises with artistic graffiti. One popular café employed a sculptor to model figures from the wax candle drippings that mounded nightly on its tabletops. Unlike fashionable public eating houses elsewhere in the city, the dress code in these bohemian canteens was kept deliberately casual. A tourist manual of 1921 advised wearing a costume "that might be suitable for going eel-bobbing in a dory on a dark, dank night in summer."[13]

By the mid-to-late teens, a variety of Village restaurants began to advertise their connections to the neighborhood's freethinking underground. Charley Reed's Purple Pup, for example, promoted itself with the interrogatory "Are You Looking for the Real Spirit of Bohemia?" At the higher-profile Greenwich Village Inn near Sheridan Square, diners were promised "an unspoiled rendezvous where spontaneous entertainment frequently occurs among a talented and distinguished patronage." The more solvent of these establishments incorporated dance floors and makeshift galleries, where ragtime music was played and local artwork exhibited.

A favorite Village resort for the uptown dining crowd was the Pepper Pot on West Fourth Street, an amusement center combining a basement bistro with an upstairs dance floor, gaming rooms, and an adjoining novelty shop. The owner, "Doc" Sherlock, a veteran of the fledgling motion picture industry, also permitted customers to tour his top-floor studio quarters.

Other forms of floor show featured at these lively cafés were the performances of itinerant minstrels and "personality" peddlers. Cruising the same paths trodden by tourists, they sang doggerel ballads and hawked curiosity items like "soul candy" and art cigarettes from one restaurant to the next. The posturings of some of the more clever of these entrepreneurs, such as "Tiny Tim" Felter, known as the Candy Man, have become part of the legendary bedrock of "Greenwich Thrillage."

The escalating theatricalism of Village life after 1915 also attracted a new breed of resident: the self-invented "character" or poseur who exploited the district's publicity as an incubator of eccentricity by acting accordingly, usually for a price. The impulse to flaunt individuality through outlandish attire, attitudes, and antics crossed a wide grain within the community. Baroness Elsa von Freytag-Loringhoven, who appeared in the Village during the war years, personified this trend. Reportedly the baroness (whose maiden name was Ploetz) had separated from her husband, a wealthy

• • • •

German businessman, to pursue a career as a cubist painter and Dadaist poet. She is known to have contributed poems to *The Little Review* and to have posed as a model for such artists as Robert Henri, George Bellows, and William Glackens. But her true avocation seems to have been that of bohemian priestess. Contemporary accounts of her activities in the Village confirm that the baroness made a cult out of freedom of dress and behavior, a passion that periodically compelled her to shave her head, paint her face with strangely colored powders, and wear an inverted coal scuttle as a hat. As recent biographies of Freytag-Loringhoven disclose, these were among her more restrained peculiarities.

A number of old-time Village personalities also modified their public posture to run with this dramatic current. "Romany Marie" Marchand, a popular restaurant hostess and former acolyte of the anarchist Emma Goldman, was said to have acquired a more pronounced Romanian accent and gypsy air as tourist traffic increased in her tavern. Wearing large hoop earrings and jangling beads, she took to reading tea leaves and telling fortunes, talents that enthralled her clientele. Her ripening Romanianism caused her to exchange verbal blows with Bobby Edwards, himself no stranger to affectation. By day, Edwards dabbled in portrait photography and held the editorial chair at *The Quill*. By night he roamed the Village in the guise of a troubadour, singing for his supper on a homemade ukelele. According to Maxwell Bodenheim's summary of the exchange, Marchand initiated the tiff by accusing Edwards of buying his ukeleles from a factory supplier in Hoboken. He retaliated by asserting that her bohemian wardrobe was a sham. Marie protested, reminding him that her Romanian father had been the respected chief of a "proud, roving gypsy tribe." Edwards ended the debate by replying: "I've heard Delancey Street called a lot of things but this is the first time I've heard it called Romania."[14]

In addition to its crop of idiosyncratic residents, the Village of the teens aggressively harvested another tourist product, packaged as "snappy" sin. By 1915 Greenwich Village was generally recognized as the place where thrill seekers came on Saturday night to atone (in advance) for their Sunday virtue. Freud and free love had made their public debut in the Village slightly earlier, and as a result the neighborhood surfaced as a special destination for those hoping to liberate their libidos.

Webster Hall, a run-down community center on East Eleventh Street, emerged as the wellspring of Village ribaldry. In 1913 the hall was the scene of the first in a long line of masquerade balls that increased the naughty connotations of Greenwich Village. Patterned after the bacchanals staged in the art-student quarter of Paris, these costume spectacles were conceived initially as fund-raisers for local radical organizations with chronic cash-flow needs. But as the merrymaking at these functions intensified, the causes they originally stood to support receded in importance.

• • • •

From the start Webster Hall's dances had drawn outsiders who were intrigued by their provocative billing as "Pagan Romps" and "Art Model Frolicks." The element of disguise, which afforded anonymity to anyone who might revel to excess, undoubtedly proved an attraction as well. Although costumes were required for admission, they grew skimpier as publicity about the balls spread, a fact that brought even more oglers and exhibitionists to Webster Hall. Djuna Barnes, an observer at many Webster Hall dances, summarized the masculine uniform fad as panpipes, leopardskin, and Hindu-colored greasepaint.[15] At the peak of their popularity around the time of the 1918 Armistice, as many as two balls per week were being held at what Villagers termed "the Devil's Playhouse." The quantity and notoriety of these functions helped to inflate the neighborhood's image as a perpetual party place.

The advent of the Eighteenth Amendment, outlawing the consumption of intoxicants, in 1919 also heightened the Village's rowdy profile. Overnight, or so it seemed, Greenwich Village gained fame as the easiest place in New York to buy bootleg. In the quarter's predominantly Italian sections, gutters oozed purple with grape pulp as the market for homemade wine suddenly ballooned. Speakeasies proliferated, and attendance soared in certain neighborhood tearooms, where rumor had it that the house brew came laced with more than honey. Barney Gallant, the affable manager of the Greenwich Village Inn, acquired immediate folk-hero status through his distinction as the first New Yorker to be arrested for violating the new Volstead Act. Marches for repeal were mounted by Villagers around Washington Square. Even Jimmy Walker, the city's debonair mayor, who lived in the Village on St. Luke's Place, made no secret of his thirst or his sympathy with the cause of noncompliance.

Although the Volstead Act dealt a lethal blow to some of the Village's older saloons and underfinanced teashops, its enforcement was arrantly lax due to the payoff system that was instituted to protect those watering holes that could afford it. Indeed, Prohibition actually contributed to the vigor of another drinking and dining venture equated with the Village during its bohemian boom season. Categorized as the novelty nightclub, this entertainment institution (surveyed in Lewis Erenberg's essay in this volume) appealed to "thrillage hounds," or so the native argot described them, with crazy theme decorations and cleverly titled refreshments that were theoretically nonalcoholic.

The first cabaret of this type, the Toby Club, had been in operation as early as 1910 at the corner of Charles and West Fourth streets. Its gimmicks included artificial cobwebs encrusted with fake spiders and tables constructed as coffins. Buoyed by the upsurge in nocturnal amusements offered by the Village as a whole, these clubs reached their zenith of popularity in the twenties, through such ingeniously appointed and staffed establishments

• • • •

as the Pirate's Den, the Nut Club, the Wig-Wam, and the Village Barn. As their names suggest, themes had started to drift away from instantly identifiable bohemianism, perhaps because this hook was losing its bait of originality.

These "mild whoopee parlors," as residents referred to them, appealed primarily to the college-age carouser rather than to the serious adult sin seeker. But for those who knew the access code, the Village certainly offered its share of more decadent attractions. Prostitution and drugs were fixtures of the Village underworld; and, while theirs was not a conspicuous presence, the neighborhood sheltered a demimonde of "dainty fairies and stern women," as one contemporary euphemism termed gays. By the early twenties the Village had developed a network of restaurants, rooming houses, baths, and so-called personality clubs to service lesbian and homosexual couples. (The neighborhood's evolution as a harbor for gay culture is reviewed by George Chauncey in this volume.)

The innumerable attractions of bohemia, from the benign to the bawdy, loomed as a topic of vicarious interest to a national readership by the late teens. The uproarious affairs of America's Left Bank offered a feast to journalists, who exploited the sensational aspects of Village customs and culture at the expense of any serious underpinnings left in the district's nonconformist canon. With increasing regularity the period press fed its readers a spicy diet of bulletins about the excesses and aberrations of Village life. And when time showed the scandal of these activities to be tamer than originally reported, the press shifted gears to make Greenwich Village the butt of cheap jokes instead.

Village-based magazines like *The Quill* and *The Ink-Pot* professed great irritation with this slanderous publicity and defended the integrity of their community by slinging arrows back at specific editors and staff writers. A frequent target was Irvin S. Cobb, the humor columnist for the *Saturday Evening Post,* an especially unrelenting satirist of bohemia. But in point of fact, some of the silliest and most lurid revelations about Greenwich Village to appear in print carried pen names that are traceable to Village writers.

Little time elapsed before the new motion picture industry, which had passed its infancy just north of the Village in Union Square, entered the act and began taking advantage of bohemia's box-office potential. By the mid-teens, New York movie producers were dispatching companies to the Village to put to use its pleasant background scenery and offbeat reputation. *Woman, Woman,* filmed on MacDougal Street in 1917, and the slapstick comedy *A Little Journey to Greenwich Village* (1918), reportedly shot in an outdoor studio on Greenwich Avenue, were two resulting products.

Early movie plots often spoofed the Village café. *Within the Cup* (1918), for example, featured a Greenwich Village character named Tea-Cup Ann

• • • •

who dispensed fortunes in a grotto tearoom. The action of *The Dangerous Moment* (1921) unfolds in a Village snuggery dubbed the Black Beetle; another film of 1921, *Smiling All the Way*, is set in an apocryphal restaurant called the Purple Guinea Pig. Other scripts, such as those for *The Trap* and *The Forbidden Path* (both released in 1918), pivoted around the theme of the ingenue who strays into the debauched vortex of bohemia. The cameo appearances of local personalities in these Village films invariably drew loud applause.

The bohemian Village emerged simultaneously as a bankable subject for commercial theater. The corralling of Greenwich Village gossip and settings into plays that were aimed at the paying public was a notion borrowed from the popular stage productions of both the Provincetown and Washington Square players, two of the many acting companies with amateur origins in the prewar Village. Missing from these newer bohemian parodies, however, was the element of self-therapy that had guided these locally authored, modestly staged shows. What prompted commercial production interest was the pragmatic realization that as the tide of Greenwich Village's notoriety rose, "bohemianism" added up to good business.

Although judged a critical flop, one of the first shows to test the commercial viability of this assumption was the 1919 production of *Hobohemia* at the recently opened Greenwich Village Theatre on Sheridan Square. This three-act farce, adapted from a Sinclair Lewis story originally published in the *Saturday Evening Post* in April 1917, poked fun at Freudianism, feminism, cubism, anarchism, and several other "isms" held sacred by the Village vanguard.

That same year the Greenwich Village Theatre also housed the premiere of the *Greenwich Village Follies*, a native musical revue directed by John Murray Anderson and produced by a company promoting itself as "The Bohemians." As one could divine from the shows' packaging, librettos were liberally sprinkled with allusions to Village people, causes, and customs. Sets were often evocative of local scenery and places as well. The 1920 edition, for instance, featured numbers in which the cast sang and danced the roles of popular Village dining dens, with solos performed by "The Purple Pup" and "The Pirate's Den Girl" and a chorus by "The Mad Hatters."

Significantly, after two successful seasons on Sheridan Square, the *Follies* left the Village in location although not in name. Under the new management of the formidable Shubert brothers, the company headed north to perform its burlesque of bohemia before uptown and out-of-town audiences at Broadway prices. This shift in venue signaled the demise of locally mounted bohemian farces, for commercial producers saw little need to support such home-grown stage efforts when Greenwich Village's amusing nonconformist culture could be so profitably transplanted to Times Square. A string of comedies quoting from the lore of "Greenwich Thrillage" played on Broadway thereafter until the late 1920s, when public interest in them tapered off.

•••••

The extensive machinery that had been mobilized to market Greenwich Village bohemianism during the teens ultimately lost its powers of persuasion. Among the complex causes of this failure was the vulnerable nature of Village economics. Because it was settled as a colonial residential outpost rather than as a vital port, marketplace, or manufacturing center, Greenwich Village historically had a limited revenue base on which to draw. Although the Village was fringed by light industries and a waterfront that had infused some steady profits into the community, its economy was challenged in 1916 with the passage of new zoning regulations that restricted future commercial development from intruding into its residential core. Necessity being the mother of invention, local entrepreneurs and tradespeople turned inward instead to mine the unique attributes of the neighborhood's Latin Quarter reputation. But the monetary vein that Village bohemianism represented was only of limited depth. Inevitably it became depleted, and the joke grew stale.

Various other factors emerged to undermine the profitable returns the district's counterculture had come to represent. As early as 1914 a committee of Village property owners, merchants, social workers, and realtors had embarked on a campaign to combat the scruffy image the local bohemian populace had created for the community. One offshoot of this effort was the formulation of a local "re-colonialization movement." The elegant charm of the neighborhood's Georgian architecture was stressed, and its proud past celebrated through lavish Old Home Week pageants, antiquarian exhibits, and other testimonials to its pre-bohemian history.

Under the banner of the Greenwich Village Improvement Society and the Greenwich Village Rebuilding Corporation, this alliance of residents and businesses also rallied to arrest the district's physical deterioration. Although an immediate goal was to improve neighborhood streetlighting, pavements, and playgrounds, their ultimate purpose was to reinstate higher-income-level families and young professionals in the Village to stimulate its economy. Shrewd realtors began to amass their holdings of dilapidated housing. For profit, they proceeded to rehabilitate these run-down residences into stylish apartments and studios, an objective accomplished with little else than the addition of modern plumbing and several coats of fresh paint.

Vincent Pepe, the Croesus of Village landlords, stood at the helm of

••••

many of these remodeling projects. Pepe, who converted blocks of tumble-down tenements into desirable residential enclaves, including the notorious tangle of back streets known as the Minettas, proved especially clever at promoting the Village as a quaint but accessible urban address. The restoring touch he bestowed on his vast real estate realm led to a sharp inflation in rent-scales throughout the Village.

By the late teens, local newspapers teemed with editorials protesting the neighborhood's gentrification and the displacement of tenants who couldn't pay for quarters upgraded with window boxes and refrigerators. Nestled on those same pages, however, were the ads of "Village home-finders" and interior decorators licensed to locate and outfit ultrafashionable bohemian flats. Noting the neighborhood's diminishing affordability to its bohemian inhabitants, one contemporary observer lamented, "Artistically inclined shirt merchants, and atmosphere crazy shoe manufacturers are the welcome lessees to our Greenwich Village real estate shark." [16]

Another cloud rising over the horizon of the bohemian tourist trade by the late teens was the conspicuous flight of a number of prominent radicals from the Village. Unable or unwilling to absorb the escalating costs of residing in this once-reasonable section of the city, and increasingly dismayed by the "vulgarians and Rotarians" encamped in their midst, many bohemian luminaries quit the Village rather than conform to these distasteful changes. Some moved uptown, but many departed New York altogether, scattering to destinations as remote as Moscow and New Mexico.

Others from the old guard defected to respectability: "After much tom-catrimony / They succumb to matrimony / Then it's Harlem flatrimony," went a Village jingle of the early twenties. Former warriors in the battle against materialism began to succumb to its bourgeois comforts. Guido Bruno, to cite only one notable case, left the Village for Pelham Manor in the 1920s, moving into a comfortable suburban home with a two-car garage. Some seemed to simply weary of their bohemian pose and routines. "I am getting more formal and conventional in my attitudes and manners," admitted Ella Breistein, also known as Eleanor Brandt but best known to tourists as "Sonia, the Cigarette Girl." In the guise of a bobbed-haired Slavic soothsayer, she had managed a popular smoke shop on West Eighth Street during the teens. By 1921, however, the disenchanted Sonia summed up her career as a bohemian persona to a young admirer as "meaningless." [17]

Accompanying the alienation felt by many individuals who had participated in the invention of Greenwich Village's bohemian personality over the first quarter of the twentieth century were a series of public works projects aimed at modernizing the district. The extension of Sixth and Seventh avenues south through the heart of the Village, subway excavations, and the ruthless widening of certain local streets to allow for increased through traffic were among the reforms engineered to facilitate the flow of day-trippers

• • • •

and other outsiders into the area. By the late twenties the Village's former isolation was a memory. Like Wall Street or the Upper West Side, bohemia had been reduced to a convenient stop on the city's transit system.

The outcropping of luxury high-rises that appeared at the northern perimeter of Washington Square beginning in 1927 was another omen of bohemia's dissolution. The replacement of what developers derided as "rattle trap shacks" with new apartment towers would bring Greenwich Village "a more circumspect type of resident," as a period guidebook correctly predicted. Although the Stock Market Crash of 1929 would brake the momentum of this construction, the heart of the bohemian Village already had been damaged. What remained of its genuine counterculture, whose survival depended on cheap subsistence, was driven, if not into exile, then at least into hibernation.

Greenwich Thrillage ultimately died of its own commercial success. The popularity of its unorthodox rites and deviant attractions had upset the equation on which true bohemian communities are premised: the bohemians' rejection of bourgeois values, and the bourgeoisie's disdain for bohemian habits. This chapter in the neighborhood's history came to an end, reflected Malcolm Cowley, who had witnessed the transformation of New York's Left Bank into the Land of Babbittry, because "women smoked cigarettes on the streets of the Bronx and drank gin cocktails in Omaha. . . . because American business and the whole of middle-class America had been going Greenwich Village."[18]

• • • • •

NOTES

1. James L. Ford, "Bohemia Invaded," in *Bohemia Invaded and Other Stories* (New York: Frederick A. Stoke & Co., 1895), 1–19.

2. George B. Mallon, "The Hunt for Bohemia," in *Everybody's Magazine* 12 (February 1905): 197.

3. John Reed, *The Day in Bohemia: or, Life Among the Artists* (New York: privately printed, 1913).

4. Hippolyte Havel, "The Spirit of the Village," *Greenwich Village, A Fortnightly* (January 20, 1915): 1.

5. Millia Davenport, *The Quill* 3: 3 (August 1918): 9.

6. Tom Springer, "Rounding the Square—Bohemian Excursions," *From a Fifth Avenue Bus* (February 7, 1918).

7. For an interesting biography of Guido Bruno, see Arnold I. Kisch, *The Romantic Ghost of Greenwich Village: Guido Bruno in His Garret* (Frankfurt: Peter Lang Publishers, 1976).

8. Corrine Lowe, *The Ladies' Home Journal*, March 1920, 28.

9. See, for example, the fashion spread photographed by Edward Steichen titled "Wrong-Right" in *Vogue*, June 1, 1927, 88–89.

10. "The New Heart of Bohemia—Sheridan Square," *Vanity Fair*, January 1918, unpaged.

11. George S. Chappell, *The Restaurants of New York* (New York: Greenberg Publishers, 1925), 59.

12. "Greenwich Village—Its Spirit and Significance," *Ink-Pot Magazine*, October 1916, unpaged.

13. Helen W. Henderson, *A Loiterer in New York: Discoveries Made by a Rambler Through Obvious Yet Unsung Highways and Byways* (New York: George H. Doran Co., 1921), 180.

14. Maxwell Bodenheim, *My Life and Loves in Greenwich Village* (New York: Bridgehead Books, 1954), 12–13.

15. Djuna Barnes, "How the Villagers Amuse Themselves," in *New York Morning Telegraph Sunday Magazine*, November 26, 1916.

16. "The Lost Greenwich Village," *Bruno's Review of Two Worlds* (July 1921): 212.

17. "Sonia" to Flora Bond Cotterill, letter dated September 19, 1921, Manuscript Collection, Museum of the City of New York.

18. Malcolm Cowley, *Exile's Return: A Literary Saga of the 1920s* (New York: Viking Press, 1951), 65.

• • • •

NOTES ON CONTRIBUTORS

DANIEL AARON is professor emeritus of English and American Literature at Harvard University. His *Cincinnati, Queen City of the West, 1819–1858* was published in 1992.

PAUL R. BAKER is professor of history and former director of the Program in American Civilization, Faculty of Arts and Science, New York University. He is author of *Richard Morris Hunt* and *Stanny: The Gilded Life of Stanford White*.

RICK BEARD (coeditor) was from 1986 to 1992 associate director of the Museum of the City of New York, where he served as project director for such exhibitions as *Within Bohemia's Borders: Greenwich Village, 1830–1930* and *Broadway! 125 Years of Musical Theater*, conceived and directed *Democracy's Poet: A Walt Whitman Festival*, and edited *On Being Homeless: Historical Perspectives*. He is currently executive director of the Atlanta Historical Society.

THOMAS BENDER is University Professor of the Humanities and professor of history, Faculty of Arts and Science, New York University. He is the author of *New York Intellect* and, most recently, *Intellect and Public Life*.

CAROL RUTH BERKIN is professor of history, Baruch College and the Graduate Center, City University of New York. She is currently completing a history of American colonial women entitled *The American Eve: Women in Colonial Society*.

LESLIE COHEN BERLOWITZ (coeditor) is vice president for Institutional Advancement at New York University and a founding director of the University's Humanities Council and Faculty Resource Network. Mrs. Berlowitz is coeditor of *American in Theory* with Denis Donoghue and Louis Menand.

CHRISTINE BOYER teaches at the School of Architecture at Princeton University and the School of Architecture at Cooper Union. Her publications include *Dreaming the Rational City: Myth of American City Planning 1890–1945*; *Manhattan Manners Architecture and Style 1850–1900*; and *The City of Collective Memory: Its Historical Imagery and Architectural Entertainments* (forthcoming).

MINDY CANTOR received a National Endowment for the Humanities grant for *Around the Square: 1830–1890*, a series of events and a book published in 1982 by New York University. She was also curator of "Henry James's Washington Square" at the New York Public Library.

GEORGE CHAUNCEY is assistant professor of history at the University of Chicago and coeditor of *Hidden From History: Reclaiming The Gay and Lesbian Past*. This article is based on his forthcoming book *Gay New York: Urban Culture and the Making of a Gay Male World, 1890–1970*.

• • • •

BLANCHE WIESEN COOK is the author of *Crystal Eastman on Women & Revolution*, *The Declassified Eisenhower*, and *Eleanor Roosevelt*, a two-volume biography. A journalist and historian, she is professor of History at John Jay College and The Graduate Center, City University of New York.

DENIS DONOGHUE is Henry James Professor of English and American Letters, Faculty of Arts and Science, New York University. Among other volumes, he has written *We Irish*, *Reading America*, *England*, *Their England*, and *Warrenpoint*. Among his most recent works are *Being Modern Together* and *The Pure Good of Theory*.

LEWIS ERENBERG is professor of history at Loyola University of Chicago and the author of *Steppin' Out: New York City Nightlife* and *The Transformation of American Culture 1890–1930*. He has written numerous articles on nightlife and popular entertainment and is currently working on a history of swing bands and popular music.

LESLIE FISHBEIN, an associate professor of American studies at Rutgers, The State University of New Jersey, is the author of *Rebels in Bohemia: The Radicals of THE MASSES, 1911–1917* and the historical introduction to Rebecca Zurier's *Art for THE MASSES: A Radical Magazine and Its Graphics*. She has published widely on Greenwich Village and served as script consultant for *Within Bohemia's Borders: Greenwich Village, 1830–1930*.

THELMA WILLS FOOTE is assistant professor of history, University of California, Irvine. She is author of the forthcoming book, *Black and White Manhattan: Race Relations and Collective Identity in Colonial Society, 1626–1783*.

JOAN H. GEISMAR is an urban archeologist working in the New York metropolitan area. Her many projects have included sites in Upper and Lower Manhattan as well as the other four boroughs and New Jersey. Dr. Geismar has lectured and published widely and taught at Marymount College and Columbia University.

JOSEPHINE GATTUSO HENDIN is professor of English, New York University. She is author of *The Right Thing to Do* and *Vulnerable People: A View of American Fiction Since 1945*.

ALFRED KAZIN is author of *A Walker in the City*, *Starting Out in the Thirties*, *New York Jew*, and *Our New York* (with David Finn).

SARAH BRADFORD LANDAU is associate professor of fine arts, New York University, and vice chair of the New York City Landmarks Preservation Commission. Her most recent publications include contributions to *The Experimental Tradition: Essays on Competitions in Architecture* and *Changing Places: Remaking Institutional Buildings*. She is currently working on a book about the development of the New York skyscraper for Yale University Press.

• • • •

BROOKS MCNAMARA is professor of performance studies in the Tisch School of the Arts, New York University, and the founding director of the Shubert Archive, a collection of materials on the history of Broadway theater.

BARRY MILES has been both an observer and a participant in the life and times of Allen Ginsberg. He was cofounder of *International Times*, Europe's first counter-culture newspaper, and has written and edited numerous works on the writers of the Beat Generation, including the annotated edition of Ginsberg's *Howl* and *Ginsberg: A Biography*.

JAN SEIDLER RAMIREZ is the curator of paintings and sculpture and assistant director for collections at the Museum of the City of New York. She conceived and curated the Museum's exhibition "Within Bohemia's Borders: Greenwich Village, 1830–1930" (October 1990–June 1991). She has written numerous articles and exhibition catalogs on American material culture and art and is currently at work on a biography of the nineteenth-century American sculptor and poet William Wetmore Story.

IRVING SANDLER, professor of art history at State University of New York at Purchase, is author of *The Triumph of American Painting: A History of Abstract Expressionism, The New York School: Painters and Sculptors of the 1950s,* and *American Art of the 1960s.* He is a contributing editor to *Art in America,* an editorial board member and former president of the American Section of the International Art Critics Association, and a former board member of the College Art Association.

BAYRD STILL, who died in November 1992, was professor emeritus of history, New York University. Chair of the History Department from 1955 to 1970, acting dean in the College of Arts and Sciences from 1958 to 1960, and acting dean in the Graduate School of Arts and Sciences in 1971, he also served as director of the NYU Archives from 1974 to 1989. Professor Still was the author of numerous books, including *Essays in the History of New York City.*

DANIEL J. WALKOWITZ, professor of history and director of Metropolitan Studies at New York University, is author of *Worker City, Company Town: Iron and Cotton Worker Protest in Troy and Cohoes, New York, 1855–1884* and coeditor of *Workers in the Industrial Revolution: Recent Studies of Labor in the United States and Europe* and *Working-Class American: Essays in Labor, Community and Society.*

INDEX

· · · ·